Expert Systems in the Micro-electronic Age

EDITED BY DONALD MICHIE

FOR EDINBURGH
UNIVERSITY
PRESS

22 George Square, Edinburgh
ISBN 0 85224 381 2
Printed in Great Britain by
Redwood Burn Limited
Trowbridge, Wiltshire

EXPERT SYSTEMS
IN THE MICRO-
ELECTRONIC
AGE

CONTENTS

RULE-BASED SYSTEMS

THEMES AND CASE STUDIES OF KNOWLEDGE ENGINEERING

Edward A. Feigenbaum

INTRODUCTION – AN EXAMPLE

This paper will examine emerging themes of knowledge engineering, illustrate them with case studies drawn from the work of the Stanford Heuristic Programming Project, and discuss general issues of knowledge engineering art and practice.

Let me begin with an example new to our workbench: a system called PUFF, the early fruit of a collaboration between our project and a group at the Pacific Medical Center (PMC) in San Francisco.*

A physician refers a patient to PMC's pulmonary function testing lab for diagnosis of possible pulmonary function disorder. For one of the tests, the patient inhales and exhales a few times in a tube connected to an instrument/computer combination. The instrument acquires data on flow rates and volumes, the so-called flow-volume loop of the patient's lungs and airways. The computer measures certain parameters of the curve and presents them to the diagnostician (physician or PUFF) for interpretation. The diagnosis is made along these lines: normal or diseased; restricted lung disease or obstructive airways disease or a combination of both; the severity; the likely disease type(s) (e.g., emphysema, bronchitis, etc.); and other factors important for diagnosis.

PUFF is given not only the measured data but also certain items of information from the patient record, e.g., sex, age, number of pack-years of cigarette smoking. The task of the PUFF system is to infer a diagnosis and print it out in English in the normal medical summary form of the interpretation expected by the referring physician.

Everything PUFF knows about pulmonary function diagnosis is contained in (currently) 55 rules of the IF . . . THEN . . . form. No textbook of medicine currently records these rules. They constitute the partly-public, partly-private knowledge of an expert pulmonary physiologist at PMC, and were extracted and polished by project engineers working intensively with the expert over a period of time. Here is an example of a PUFF rule (the unexplained acronyms refer to various data measurements):

Rule 31
IF:
1) The severity of obstructive airways disease of the patient is greater than or equal to mild, and
2) the degree of diffusion defect of the patient is greater than or equal to mild, and
3) The tlc (body box) observed/predicted of the patient is greater than or equal to 110, and

*Dr. J. Osborn, Dr. R. Fallat, John Kunz, Diane McClung.

4) The observed-predicted difference in rv/tlc of the patient is greater than or equal to 10
THEN:
1) There is strongly suggestive evidence (.9) that the subtype of obstructive airways disease is emphysema, and
2) It is definite (1.0) that 'OAD, Diffusion Defect, elevated TLC, and elevated RV together indicate emphysema,' is one of the findings.

One hundred cases, carefully chosen to span the variety of disease states with sufficient exemplary information for each, were used to extract the 55 rules. As the knowledge emerged, it was represented in rule form, added to the system and tested by running additional cases. The expert was sometimes surprised, sometimes frustrated, by the occasional gaps and inconsistencies in the knowledge, and the incorrect diagnoses that were logical consequences of the existing rule set. The interplay between knowledge engineer and expert gradually expanded the set of rules to remove most of these problems.

As cumulation of techniques in the art demands and allows, a new tool was not invented when an old one would do. The knowledge engineers pulled out of their toolkit a version of the MYCIN system (to be discussed later), with the rules about infectious diseases removed, and used it as the inference engine for the PUFF diagnoses. Thus PUFF, like MYCIN, is a relatively simple backward-chaining inference system. It seeks a valid line-of-reasoning based on its rules and rooted in the instrument and patient data. With a little more work at fitting some existing tools together, PUFF will be able to explain this line-of-reasoning, just as MYCIN does.

As it is, PUFF only prints out the final interpretation, of which the following is an example:

PATIENT DATA
The degree of dyspnea: MODERATELY-SEVERE
The severity of coughing: MILD
Sputum production: MODERATELY-SEVERE
The number of pack-years of smoking: 48
referral diagnosis: BRONCHITIS
IVC/IVC-predicted: 80
RV/RV-predicted: 191
FVC/FVC-predicted: 87
TLC(body box) observed/predicted: 127
Predicted FEV1/FVC: 83
TLC(DLCO)observed/predicted: 83
FEV1/FVC ratio: 50
RV/TLC observed/predicted: 21
MMF/MMF-predicted: 19
the DLCO/DLCO-predicted: 48
The slope (F50_obs-F25_obs)/FVC_obs: 19

DEGREE OF OBSTRUCTIVE AIRWAYS DISEASE:
OAD degree by SLOPE: (MODERATELY-SEVERE 700)
OAD degree by MMF: (SEVERE 900)
OAD degree by FEV1: (MODERATELY-SEVERE 700)
FINAL OAD DEGREE: (MODERATELY-SEVERE 910) (SEVERE 900)
No conflict. Final degree:
(MODERATELY-SEVERE 910)

INTERPRETATION:
Obstruction is indicated by curvature of the flow-volume loop.
Forced Vital Capacity is normal and peak flow rates are reduced, suggesting airway obstruction.
Flow rate from 25-75 of expired volume is reduced, indicating severe airway obstruction.
OAD, Diffusion Defect, elevated TLC, and elevated RV together indicate emphysema.
OAD, Diffusion Defect, and elevated RV indicate emphysema.
Change in expired flow rates following bronchodilation shows that there is reversibility of airway obstruction.
The presence of a productive cough is an indication that the OAD is of the bronchitic type.
Elevated lung volumes indicate overinflation.
Air trapping is indicated by the elevated difference between observed and predicted RV/TLC ratios.
Improvement in airway resistance indicates some reversibility of airway obstruction.
Airway obstruction is consistent with the patient's smoking history.
The airway obstruction accounts for the patient's dyspnea.
Although bronchodilators were not useful in this one case, prolonged use may prove to be beneficial to the patient.
The reduced diffusion capacity indicates airway obstruction of the mixed bronchitic and emphysematous types.
Low diffusing capacity indicates loss of alveolar capillary surface.
Obstructive Airways Disease of mixed types

150 cases not studied during the knowledge acquisition process were used for a test and validation of the rule set. PUFF inferred a diagnosis for each. PUFF-produced and expert-produced interpretations were coded for statistical analysis to discover the degree of agreement. Over various types of disease states, and for two conditions of match between human and computer diagnoses ('same degree of severity' and 'within one degree of severity'), agreement ranged between approximately 90 percent and 100 percent.

The PUFF story is just beginning and will be told perhaps at a later NCC. The surprising punchline to my synopsis is that the current state of the PUFF system as described above was achieved in less than 50 hours of interaction with the expert and less than 10 man-weeks of effort by the knowledge engineers. We have learned much in the past decade of the art of engineering knowledge-based intelligent agents!

In the remainder of this essay, I would like to discuss the route that one research group, the Stanford Heuristic Programming Project, has taken, illustrating progress with case studies, and discussing themes of the work.

ARTIFICIAL INTELLIGENCE & KNOWLEDGE ENGINEERING

The dichotomy that was used to classify the collected papers in the volume *Computers and Thought* still characterizes well the motivations and research efforts of the AI community. First, there are some who work toward the construction of intelligent artifacts, or seek to uncover principles, methods, and techniques useful in such construction. Second, there are those who view artificial intelligence as (to use Newell's phrase) 'theoretical psychology,' seeking explicit and valid information processing models of human thought.

For purposes of this essay, I wish to focus on the motivations of the first group, these days by far the larger of the two. I label these motivations 'the intelligent agent viewpoint' and here is my understanding of that viewpoint:

'The potential uses of computers by people to accomplish tasks can be "one-dimensionalized" into a spectrum representing the nature of instruction that must be given the computer to do its job. Call it the WHAT-to-HOW spectrum. At one extreme of the spectrum, the user supplies his intelligence to instruct the machine with precision exactly HOW to do his job, step-by-step. Progress in Computer Science can be seen as steps away from the extreme "HOW" point on the spectrum: the familiar panoply of assembly languages, subroutine libraries, compilers, extensible languages, etc. At the other extreme of the spectrum is the user with his real problem (WHAT he wishes the computer, as his instrument, to do for him). He aspires to communicate WHAT he wants done in a language that is comfortable to him (perhaps English); via communication modes that are convenient for him (including perhaps, speech or pictures); with some generality, some vagueness, imprecision, even error; without having to lay out in detail all necessary subgoals for adequate performance – with reasonable assurance that he is addressing an intelligent agent that is using knowledge of his world to understand his intent, to fill in his vagueness, to make specific his abstractions, to correct his errors, to discover appropriate subgoals, and ultimately to translate WHAT he really wants done into processing steps that define HOW it shall be done by a real computer. The research activity aimed at creating computer programs that act as "intelligent agents" near the WHAT end of the WHAT-to-HOW spectrum can be viewed as the long-range goal of AI research.' (Feigenbaum, 1974)

Our young science is still more art than science. Art: 'the principles or methods governing any craft or branch of learning.' Art: 'skilled workmanship, execution, or agency.' These the dictionary teaches us. Knuth tells us that the endeavour of computer programming is an art, in just these ways. The art of constructing intelligent agents is both part of and an extension of the programming art. It is the art of building complex computer programs that represent and reason with knowledge of the world. Our art therefore lives in symbiosis with the other worldly arts, whose practitioners – experts of their art – hold the knowledge we need to construct intelligent agents. In most 'crafts or branches of learning' what we call 'expertise' is the essence of the art. And for the domains of knowledge that we touch with our art, it is the 'rules of expertise' or the rules of 'good judgment' of the expert practitioners of that domain that we seek to transfer to our programs.

Lessons of the Past

Two insights from previous work are pertinent to this essay.

The first concerns the quest for generality and power of the inference engine used in the performance of intelligent acts (what Minsky and Papert [see Goldstein and Papert, 1977] have labeled 'the power strategy'). We must hypothesize from our experience to date that the problem-solving power exhibited in an intelligent agent's performance is primarily a consequence of the specialist's knowledge employed by the agent, and only very secondarily related to the generality and power of the inference method employed. Our agents must be knowledge-rich, even if they are methods-poor. In 1970, reporting the first major summary-of-results of the DENDRAL program (to be discussed later), we addressed this issue as follows:

'. . . general problem-solvers are too weak to be used as the basis for building high-performance systems. The behaviour of the best general problem-solvers we know, human problem-solvers, is observed to be weak and shallow, except in the areas in which the human problem-solver is a specialist. And it is observed that the transfer of expertise between specialty areas is slight. A chess master is unlikely to be an expert algebraist or an expert mass spectrum analyst, etc. In this view, the expert is the specialist, with a specialist's knowledge of his area and a specialist's methods and heuristics.' (Feigenbaum, Buchanan and Lederberg, 1971, p. 187)

Subsequent evidence from our laboratory and all others has only confirmed this belief.

AI researchers have dramatically shifted their view on generality and power in the past decade. In 1967, the canonical question about the DENDRAL program was: 'It sounds like good chemistry, but what does it have to do with AI?' In 1977, Goldstein and Papert write of a paradigm shift in AI:

'Today there has been a shift in paradigm. The fundamental problem of understanding intelligence is not the identification of a few powerful techniques, but rather the question of how to represent large amounts of knowledge in a fashion that permits their effective use and interaction.' (Goldstein and Papert, 1977).

The second insight from past work concerns the nature of the knowledge that an expert brings to the performance of a task. Experience has shown us that this knowledge is largely heuristic knowledge, experiential, uncertain – mostly 'good guesses' and 'good practice,' in lieu of facts and rigor. Experience has also taught us that much of this knowledge is private to the expert, not because he is unwilling to share publicly how he performs, but because he is unable. He knows more than he is aware of knowing. [Why else is the Ph.D. or the Internship a guild-like apprenticeship to a presumed 'master of the craft?' What the masters really know is not written in the textbooks of the masters.] But we have learned also that this private knowledge can be uncovered by the careful, painstaking analysis of a second party, or sometimes by the expert himself, operating in the context of a large number of highly specific performance problems. Finally, we have learned that expertise is multi-faceted, that the expert brings to bear many and varied sources of knowledge in performance. The approach to capturing his expertise must proceed on many fronts simultaneously.

The Knowledge Engineer

The knowledge engineer is that second party just discussed. She works intensively with an expert to acquire domain-specific knowledge and organize it for use by a program. Simultaneously she is matching the tools of the AI workbench to the task at hand – program organizations, methods of symbolic inference, techniques for the structuring of symbolic information, and the like. If the tool fits, or nearly fits, she uses it. If not, necessity mothers AI invention, and a new tool gets created. She builds the early versions of the intelligent agent, guided always by her intent that the program eventually achieve expert levels of performance in the task. She refines or reconceptualizes the system as the increasing amount of acquired knowledge causes the AI tool to 'break' or slow down intolerably. She also refines the human interface to the intelligent agent with several aims: to make the system appear 'comfortable' to the human user in his linguistic transactions with it: to make the system's inference processes understandable to the user; and to make the assistance controllable by the user when, in the context of a real problem, he has an insight that previously was not elicited and therefore not incorporated.

In the next section, I wish to explore (in summary form) some case studies of the knowledge engineer's art.

CASES FROM THE KNOWLEDGE ENGINEER'S WORKSHOP

I will draw material for this section from the work of my group at Stanford. Much exciting work in knowledge engineering is going on elsewhere. Since my intent is not to survey literature but to illustrate themes, at the risk of appearing parochial I have used as case studies the work I know best.

My collaborators (Professors Lederberg and Buchanan) and I began a series of projects, initially the development of the DENDRAL program, in 1965. We had dual motives: first, to study scientific problem solving and discovery, particularly the processes scientists do use or should use in inferring hypotheses and theories from empirical evidence; and second, to conduct this study in such a way that our experimental programs would one day be of use to working scientists, providing intelligent assistance on important and difficult problems. By 1970, we and our co-workers had gained enough experience that we felt comfortable in laying out a program of research encompassing work on theory formation, knowledge utilization, knowledge acquisition, explanation, and knowledge engineering techniques. Although there were some surprises along the way, the general lines of the research are proceeding as envisioned.

THEMES

As a road map to these case studies, it is useful to keep in mind certain major themes:

Generation-and-test. Omnipresent in our experience is the 'classical' generation-and-test framework that has been the hallmark of AI programs for two decades. This is not a consequence of a doctrinaire attitude on our part about heuristic search, but rather of the usefulness and sufficiency of the concept.

Situation⇒Action Rules. We have chosen to represent the knowledge of experts in this form. Making no doctrinaire claims for the universal applicability of this representation, we nonetheless point to the demonstrated utility of the rule-based representation. From this representation flow rather directly many of the characteristics of our programs: for example, ease of modification of the knowledge, ease of explanation. The essence of our approach is that a rule must capture a 'chunk' of domain knowledge that is meaningful, in and of itself, to the domain specialist. Thus our rules bear only a historical relationship to the production rules used by Newell and Simon (1972) which we view as 'machine-language programming' of a recognize⇒act machine.

The Domain-Specific Knowledge. It plays a critical role in organizing and constraining search. The theme is that in the knowledge is the power. The interesting action arises from the knowledge base, not the inference engine. We use knowledge in rule form (discussed above), in the form of inferentially-rich models based on theory, and in the form of tableaus of symbolic data and relationships (i.e., frame-like structures). System processes are made to conform to natural and convenient representations of the domain-specific knowledge.

Flexibility to modify the knowledge base. If the so-called 'grain size' of the knowledge representation is chosen properly (i.e., small enough to be comprehensible but large enough to be meaningful to the domain specialist), then the rule-based approach allows great flexibility for adding, removing, or changing knowledge in the system.

Line-of-reasoning. A central organizing principle in the design of knowledge-based intelligent agents is the maintenance of a line-of-reasoning that is comprehensible to the domain specialist. This principle is, of course, not a logical necessity, but seems to us to be an engineering principle of major importance.

Multiple Sources of Knowledge. The formation and maintenance (support) of the line-of-reasoning usually require the integration of many disparate sources of knowledge. The representational and inferential problems in achieving a smooth and effective integration are formidable engineering problems.

Explanation. The ability to explain the line-of-reasoning in a language convenient to the user is necessary for application and for system development (e.g., for debugging and for extending the knowledge base). Once again, this is an engineering principle, but very important. What constitutes 'an explanation' is not a simple concept, and considerable thought needs to be given, in each case, to the structure of explanations.

CASE STUDIES

In this section I will try to illustrate these themes with various case studies.

DENDRAL: Inferring Chemical Structures

Historical Note. Begun in 1965, this collaborative project with the Stanford Mass Spectrometry Laboratory has become one of the longest-lived continuous efforts in the history of AI (a fact that in no small way has contributed to its success). The basic framework of generation-and-test and rule-based representation has proved rugged and extendable. For us the DENDRAL system has been a fountain of ideas, many of which have found their way, highly metamorphosed, into our other projects. For example, our long-standing commitment to rule-based representations arose out of our (successful) attempt to head off the imminent ossification of DENDRAL caused by the rapid accumulation of new knowledge in the system around 1967.

Task. To enumerate plausible structures (atom-bond graphs) for organic molecules, given two kinds of information: analytic instrument data from a mass spectrometer and a nuclear magnetic resonance spectrometer; and user-supplied constraints on the answers, derived from any other source of knowledge (instrumental or contextual) available to the user.

Representations. Chemical structures are represented as node-link graphs of atoms (nodes) and bonds (links). Constraints on search are represented as subgraphs (atomic configurations) to be denied or preferred. The empirical theory of mass spectrometry is represented by a set of rules of the general form:

Situation: Particular atomic configuration (subgraph)

↓ Probability, P, of occurring

Action: Fragmentation of the particular configuration (Breaking links)

Rules of this form are natural and expressive to mass spectrometrists.

Sketch of method. DENDRAL's inference procedure is a heuristic search that takes place in three stages, without feedback: plan-generate-test.

'Generate' (a program called CONGEN) is a generation process for plausible structures. Its foundation is a combinatorial algorithm (with mathematically proven properties of completeness and non-redundant generation) that can produce all the topologically legal candidate structures. Constraints supplied by the user or by the 'Plan' process prune and steer the generation to produce the plausible set (i.e., those satisfying the constraints) and not the enormous legal set.

'Test' refines the evaluation of plausibility, discarding less worthy candidates and rank-ordering the remainder for examination by the user. 'Test' first produces a 'predicted' set of instrument data for each plausible candidate, using the rules described. It then evaluates the worth of each candidate by comparing its predicted data with the actual input data. The evaluation is based on heuristic criteria of goodness-of-fit. Thus, 'test' selects the 'best' explanations of the data.

'Plan' produces direct (i.e. not chained) inference about likely substructure in the molecule from patterns in the data that are indicative of the presence of the substructure. (Patterns in the data trigger the left-hand-sides of substructure rules). Though composed of many atoms whose interconnections are given, the substructure can be manipulated as atom-like by 'generate'. Aggregating many units entering into a combinatorial process into fewer higher-level units reduces the size of the combinatorial search space. 'Plan' sets up the search space so as to be relevant to the input data. 'Generate' is the inference tactician; 'Plan' is the inference strategist. There is a separate 'Plan' package for each type of instrument data, but each passes substructures (subgraphs) to 'Generate'. Thus, there is a uniform interface between 'Plan' and 'Generate'. User-supplied constraints enter this interface, directly or from user-assist packages, in the form of substructures.

Sources of knowledge. The various sources of knowledge used by the DENDRAL system are:

Valences (legal connections of atoms); stable and unstable configuration of atoms; rules for mass spectrometry fragmentations; rules for NMR shifts; experts' rules for planning and evaluation; user-supplied constraints (contextual).

Results. DENDRAL's structure elucidation abilities are, paradoxically, both very general and very narrow. In general, DENDRAL handles all molecules, cyclic and tree-like. In pure structure elucidation under constraints (without instrument data), CONGEN is unrivaled by human performance. In structure elucidation with instrument data, DENDRAL's performance rivals expert human performance only for a small number of molecular families for which the program has been given specialist's knowledge, namely the families of interest to our chemist collaborators. I will spare this computer science audience the list of names of these families. Within these areas of knowledge-intensive specialization, DENDRAL's performance is usually not only much faster but also more accurate than expert human performance.

The statement just made summarizes thousands of runs of DENDRAL on problems of interest to our experts, their colleagues, and their students. The results obtained, along with the knowledge that had to be given to DENDRAL to obtain them, are published in major journals of chemistry. To date, 25 papers have been published there, under a series title 'Applications of Artificial Intelligence for Chemical Inference: ⟨specific subject⟩' (see for example, the Buchanan, Smith, et al., 1976, reference).

The DENDRAL system is in everyday use by Stanford chemists, their collaborators at other universities and collaborating or otherwise interested chemists in industry. Users outside Stanford access the system over commercial computer/communications network. The problems they are solving are often difficult and novel. The British government is currently supporting work at Edinburgh aimed at transferring DENDRAL to industrial user communities in the UK.

Discussion. Representation and extensibility. The representation chosen for the molecules, constraints, and rules of instrument data interpretation is sufficiently close to that used by chemists in thinking about structure elucidation that the knowledge base has been extended smoothly and easily, mostly by chemists themselves in recent years. Only one major reprogramming effort took place in the last 9 years – when a new generator was created to deal with cyclic structures.

Representation and the Integration of multiple sources of knowledge. The generally difficult problem of integrating various sources of knowledge has been made easy in DENDRAL by careful engineering of the representations of objects, constraints, and rules. We insisted on a common language of compatibility of the representations with each other and with the inference processes: the language of molecular structure expressed as graphs. This leads to a straightforward procedure for adding a new source of knowledge, say, for example, the knowledge associated with a new type of instrument data. The procedure is this: write rules that describe the effect of the physical processes of the instrument on molecules using the situation⇒action form with molecular graphs on both sides; any special inference process using these rules must pass its results to the generator only (!) in the common graph language.

It is widely believed in AI that the use of many diverse sources of knowledge in problem solving and data interpretation has a strong effect on quality of performance. How strong is, of course, domain-dependent, but the impact of bringing just one additional source of knowledge to bear on a problem can be startling. In one difficult (but not unusually difficult) mass spectrum analysis problem,* the program using its mass spectrometry knowledge alone would have generated an impossibly large set of plausible candidates (over 1.25 million!). Our engineering response to this was to add another source of data and knowledge, proton NMR. The addition on a simple interpretive theory of this NMR data, from which the program could infer a few additional constraints, reduced the set of plausible candidates to one, the right structure! This was not an isolated result but showed up dozens of times in subsequent analyses.

DENDRAL and data. DENDRAL's robust models (topological, chemical, instrumental) permit a strategy of finding solutions by generating hypothetical 'correct answers' and choosing among these with critical tests. This strategy is opposite to that of piecing together the implications of each data point to form a hypothesis. We call DENDRAL's strategy largely model-driven, and the other data-driven. The consequences of having enough knowledge to do model-driven analysis is a large reduction in the amount of data that must be examined since data is being used mostly for verification of possible answers. In a typical DENDRAL

* The analysis of an acyclic amine with formula $C_{20}H_{45}N$.

mass spectrum analysis, usually no more than about 25 data points out of a typical total of 250 points are processed. This important point about data reduction and focus-of-attention has been discussed before by Gregory (1968) and by the vision and speech research groups, but is not widely understood.

Conclusion. DENDRAL was an early herald of AI's shift to the knowledge-based paradigm. It demonstrated the point of the primacy of domain-specific knowledge in achieving expert levels of performance. It development brought to the surface important problems of knowledge representation, acquisition, and use. It showed that, by and large, the AI tools of the first decade were sufficient to cope with the demands of a complex scientific problem-solving task, or were readily extended to handle unforeseen difficulties. It demonstrated that AI's conceptual and programming tools were capable of producing programs of applications interest, albeit in narrow specialities. Such a demonstration of competence and sufficiency was important for the credibility of the AI field at a critical juncture in its history.

META-DENDRAL: inferring rules of mass spectrometry

Historical note. The META-DENDRAL program is a case study in automatic acquisition of domain knowledge. It arose out of our DENDRAL work for two reasons: first, a decision that with DENDRAL we had a sufficiently firm foundation on which to pursue our long-standing interest in processes of scientific theory formation; second, by a recognition that the acquisition of domain knowledge was the bottleneck problem in the building of applications-oriented intelligent agents.

Task. META-DENDRAL's job is to infer rules of fragmentation of molecules in a mass spectrometer for possible later use by the DENDRAL performance program. The inference is to be made from actual spectra recorded from known molecular structures. The output of the system is the set of fragmentation rules discovered, summary of the evidence supporting each rule, and a summary of contra-indicating evidence. User-supplied constraints can also be input to force the form of rules along desired lines.

Representations. The rules are, of course, of the same form as used by DENDRAL that was described earlier.

Sketch of method. META-DENDRAL, like DENDRAL, uses the generation-and-test framework. The process is organized in three stages: Reinterpret the data and summarize evidence (INTSUM); generate plausible candidates for rules (RULEGEN); test and refine the set of plausible rules (RULEMOD).

INTSUM: gives every data point in every spectrum an interpretation as a possible (highly specific) fragmentation. It then summarizes statistically the 'weight of evidence' for fragmentations and for atomic configurations that cause these fragmentations. Thus, the job of INTSUM is to translate data to DENDRAL subgraphs and bond-breaks, and to summarize the evidence accordingly.

RULEGEN: conducts a heuristic search of the space of all rules that are legal under the DENDRAL rule syntax and the user-supplied constraints. It searches for plausible rules, i.e., those for which positive evidence exists. A search path is pruned when there is no evidence for rules of the class just generated. The search tree begins with the (single) most general rule (loosely put, 'anything' fragments from 'anything') and proceeds level-by-level toward more detailed specifications of the 'anything.' The heuristic stopping criterion measures whether a rule being generated has become too specific, in particular whether it is applicable to too few molecules of the input set. Similarly there is a criterion for deciding whether an emerging rule is too general. Thus, the output of RULEGEN is a set of candidate rules for which there is positive evidence.

RULEMOD: tests the candidate rule set using more complex criteria, including the presence of negative evidence. It removes redundancies in the candidate rule set; merges rules that are supported by the same evidence. tries further specialization of candidates to remove negative evidence; and tries further generalization that preserves positive evidence.

Results. META-DENDRAL produces rule sets that rival in quality those produced by our collaborating experts. In some tests, META-DENDRAL re-created rule sets that we had previously acquired from our experts during the DENDRAL project. In a more stringent test involving members of a family of complex ringed molecules for which the mass spectral theory had not been completely worked out by chemists, META-DENDRAL discovered rule sets for each subfamily. The rules were judged by experts to be excellent and a paper describing them was recently published in a major chemical journal (Buchanan, Smith, et al., 1976)

In a test of the generality of the approach, a version of the META-DENDRAL program is currently being applied to the discovery of rules for the analysis of nuclear magnetic resonance data.

MYCIN and TEIRESIAS: Medical diagnosis

Historical note. MYCIN originated in the Ph.D thesis of E. Shortliffe (now Shortliffe, M.D. as well), in collaboration with the Infectious Disease group at the Stanford Medical School (Shortliffe, 1976). TEIRESIAS, the Ph.D. thesis work of R. Davis, arose from issues and problems indicated by the MYCIN project but generalized by Davis beyond the bounds of medical diagnosis applications (Davis, 1976). Other MYCIN-related theses are in progress.

Tasks. The MYCIN performance task is diagnosis of blood infections and meningitis infections and the recommendation of drug treatment. MYCIN conducts a consultation (in English) with a physician-user about a patient case, constructing lines-of-reasoning leading to the diagnosis and treatment plan.

The TEIRESIAS knowledge acquisition task can be described as follows:

In the context of a particular consultation, confront the expert with a diagnosis with which he does not agree. Lead him systematically back through the line-of-reasoning that produced the diagnosis to the point at which he indicates the analysis went awry. Interact with the expert to modify offending rules or to acquire new rules. Rerun the consultation to test the solution and gain the expert's concurrence.

Representations. MYCIN's rules are of the form:

IF ⟨conjunctive clauses⟩ THEN ⟨implication⟩

Here is an example of a MYCIN rule for blood infections:

Rule 85
IF:
1) The site of the culture is blood, and
2) The gram stain of the organism is gramneg, and
3) The morphology of the organism is rod, and
4) The patient is a compromised host
THEN:
There is suggestive evidence (.6) that the identity of the organism is pseudomonas aeruginosa

TEIRESIAS allows the representation of MYCIN-like rules governing the use of other rules, i.e., rule-based strategies. An example follows.

METARULE 2
IF:
1) the patient is a compromised host, and
2) there are rules which mention in their premise pseudomonas
3) there are rules which mention in their premise klebsiellas
THEN:
There is suggestive evidence (.4) that the former should be done before the latter.

Sketch of method. MYCIN employs a generation-and-test procedure of a familiar sort. The generation of steps in the line-of-reasoning is accomplished by backward chaining of the rules. An IF-side clause is either immediately true or false as determined by patient or test data entered by the physician in the consultation); or is to be decided by subgoaling. Thus, 'test' is interleaved with 'generation' and serves to prune out incorrect lines-of-reasoning.

Each rule supplied by an expert has associated with it a 'degree of certainty' representing the expert's confidence in the validity of the rule (a number from 1 to 10). MYCIN uses a particular ad-hoc but simple model of inexact reasoning to cumulate the degrees of certainty of the rules used in an inference chain (Shortliffe and Buchanan, 1975).

It follows that there may be a number of 'somewhat true' lines-of-reasoning – some indicating one diagnosis, some indicating another. All (above a threshold) are used by the system as sources of knowledge indicating plausible lines-of-reasoning.

TEIRESIAS' rule acquisition process is based on a record of MYCIN's search. Rule acquisition is guided by a set of rule models that dictate the form and indicate the likely content of new rules. Rule models are not given in advance, but are inferred from the knowledge base of existing rules.

Language of interaction. The language used looks like it might be English but is actually the dialect 'Doctor-ese' used by members of the tribe of healing arts practitioners. Reasonably simple language processing methods suffice. When ambiguities of interpretation are encountered, they are fed back to the user for decisions about meaning.

Example diagnosis and treatment plan. The following is an example of a diagnosis reported by MYCIN to one of its users following a consultation. An example consultation will not be shown, but one can be found in Shortliffe's book (Shortliffe, 1976).

My therapy recommendations will be designed to treat for organisms that are either very likely or, although less likely, would have a significant effect on therapy selection if they were present. It is important to cover for the following probable infection(s) and associated organism(s):

INFECTION-1 is CYSTITIS
⟨Item 1⟩ PSEUDOMONAS-CEPACIA [ORGANISM-5]
⟨Item 2⟩ CITROBACTER-DIVERSUS [ORGANISM-4]
⟨Item 3⟩ E.COLI [ORGANISM-3]

INFECTION-2 is UPPER-RESPIRATORY-INFECTION
⟨Item 4⟩ LISTERIA [ORGANISM-2]

INFECTION-3 is BACTEREMIA
⟨Item 5⟩ ENTEROCOCCUS [ORGANISM-1]

[REC-1] My preferred therapy recommendation is as follows:
In order to cover for Items ⟨1 2 3 4 5⟩:
Give the following in combination:
1) KANAMYCIN
Dose: 750 mg (7.5 mg/kg) q12h IM (or IV)
for 28 days
Comments: Modify dose in renal failure
2) PENICILLIN
Dose: 2,500,000 units (25,000 units/kg)
q4h IV for 28 days

Results. No clinical evaluation of MYCIN is currently being done. In a preliminary evaluation, done outside of the clinical setting, a panel of expert judges was asked to rate MYCIN's performance along a number of dimensions (e.g., infecting organism identification, organism significance). In 90 percent of the cases submitted to the judges, a majority of the judges said that the program's decisions were the-same-as or as-good-as the decisions they would have made.

Explanation. MYCIN can expose its line of reasoning by offering explanations of various kinds. 'Why' and 'How' questions can be asked by the user during the consultation. 'Why' is the user's way of inquiring, 'Why do you want to know that?' 'How' is his way of asking, 'How did you conclude that . . . ?' In a post-consultation, he can similarly inquire about the reasons why certain other conclusions were ruled out. Examples of the MYCIN-TEIRESIAS explanation capabilities follow:

MYCIN: Is the patient's illness with ORGANISM-1 a hospital-acquired infection?
USER: WHY
TEIRESIAS: (i.e., WHY is it important to determine whether or not the infection with ORGANISM-1 was acquired while the patient was hospitalized?)
[1.0] This will aid in determining the category of ORGANISM-1.
It has already been established that
[1.1] the gram stain of ORGANISM-1 is gramneg, and
[1.2] the morphology of ORGANISM-1 is rod, and
[1.3] the aerobicity of ORGANISM-1 is facultative
Therefore, if
[1.4] the infection with ORGANISM-1 was not acquired while the patient was hospitalized
then
there is strongly suggestive evidence (.8) that the category of ORGANISM-1 is enterobacteriaceae
Also: there is weakly suggestive evidence (.1) that the identity of ORGANISM-1 is pseudomonas-aeruginosa
[RULE 37]
USER: HOW 1.3
TEIRESIAS: [i.e. HOW was it established that the aerobicity of ORGANISM-1 is facultative?]
The following were used:
[3.1] RULE 27 indicated there is strongly suggestive evidence (.8) that the aerobicity of ORGANISM-1 is facultative
[3.2] RULE 27 indicated there is weakly suggestive evidence (.2) that the aerobicity of ORGANISM-1 is anaerobic
Since this gave a cumulative CF of (.8) for facultative, and (.2) for anaerobic, it has been established that the aerobicity of ORGANISM-1 is facultative.
USER: WHY DIDN'T YOU CONSIDER STREPTOCOCCUS AS A POSSIBILITY FOR ORGANISM-1?
TEIRESIAS: The following rule could have been used to determine that the identity of ORGANISM-1 was streptococcus: RULE 33
But clause 2 ('the morphology of the organism is coccus') was already known to be false for ORGANISM-1, so the rule was never tried

Discussion. A few short comments aimed at knowledge engineering are in order.

English is the language most natural and comfortable for our experts and users, and was therefore the language chosen for interactive consultation, explanation, and external representation of the rules (the internal format is INTERLISP). This situation is not peculiar to doctors; in most areas of application of intelligent agents I believe that English (i.e., natural language) will be the language of choice.

Programming an English language processor and front-end to such systems is not a scary enterprise because:

(a) the domain is specialized, so that possible interpretations are constrained.

(b) specialist-talk is replete with standard jargon and stereotyped ways of expressing knowledge and queries – just right for text templates, simple grammars and other simple processing schemes.

(c) the ambiguity of interpretation resulting from simple schemes can be dealt with easily by feeding back interpretations for confirmation. If this is done with a pleasant 'I didn't quite understand you . . . ' tone, it is not irritating to the user.

English may be exactly the wrong language for representation and interaction in some domains. It would be awkward, to say the least, to represent DENDRAL's chemical structures and knowledge of mass spectrometry in English, or to interact about these with a user.

Simple explanation schemes have been a part of the AI scene for a number of years and are not hard to implement. Really good models of what explanation is as a transaction between user and agent, with programs to implement these models, will be the subject (I predict) of much future research in AI.

Without the explanation capability, I assert, user acceptance of MYCIN would have been nil, and there would have been a greatly diminished effectiveness and contribution of our experts.

MYCIN was the first of our programs that forced us to deal with what we had always understood: that experts' knowledge is uncertain and that our inference engines had to be made to reason with this uncertainty. It is less important that the inexact reasoning scheme be formal, rigorous, and uniform than it is for the scheme to be natural to and easily understandable by the experts and users.

All of these points can be summarized by saying that MYCIN and its TEIRESIAS adjunct are experiments in the design of a see-through system, whose representations and processes are almost transparently clear to the domain specialist. 'Almost' here is equivalent to 'with a few minutes of introductory description.' The various pieces of MYCIN – the backward chaining, the English transactions, the explanations, etc. – are each simple in concept and realization. But there are great virtues to simplicity in system design; and viewed as a total intelligent agent system, MYCIN/TEIRESIAS is one of the best engineered.

SU/X: signal understanding

Historical note. SU/X is a system design that was tested in an application whose details are classified. Because of this, the ensuing discussion will appear considerably less concrete and tangible than the preceding case studies. This system design was done by H.P.Nii and me, and was strongly influenced by the CMU Hearsay II system design (Lesser and Erman, 1977).

Task. SU/X's task is the formation and continual updating, over long periods of time, of hypotheses about the identity, location, and velocity of objects in a physical space. The output desired is a display of the 'current best hypotheses' with full explanation of the support for each. There are two types of input data: the primary signal (to be understood); and auxiliary symbolic data (to supply context for the understanding). The primary signals are spectra, represented as descriptions of the spectral lines. The various spectra cover the physical space with some spatial overlap.

Representations. The rules given by the expert about objects, their behaviour, and the interpretation of signal data from them are all represented in the situation ⇒action form. The 'situations' constitute invoking conditions and the 'actions' are processes that modify the current hypotheses, post unresolved issues, recompute evaluations, etc. The expert's knowledge of how to do analysis in the task is also represented in rule form. These strategy rules replace the normal executive program.

The situation-hypothesis is represented as a node-link graph, tree-like in that it has distinct 'levels,' each representing a degree of abstraction (or aggregation) that is natural to the expert in his understanding of the domain. A node represents an hypothesis; a link to that node represents support for that hypothesis (as in HEARSAY II, 'support from above' or 'support from below'). 'Lower' levels are concerned with the specifics of the signal data. 'Higher' levels represent symbolic abstractions.

Sketch of method. The situation-hypothesis is formed incrementally. As the situation unfolds over time, the triggering of rules modifies or discards existing hypotheses, adds new ones, or changes support values. The situation-hypothesis is a common work-space ('blackboard,' in HEARSAY jargon) for all the rules.

In general, the incremental steps toward a more complete and refined situation-hypothesis can be viewed as a sequence of local generate-and-test activities. Some of the rules are plausible move generators, generating either nodes or links. Other rules are evaluators, testing and modifying node descriptions.

In typical operation, new data is submitted for processing (say, N time-units of new data). This initiates a flurry of rule-triggerings and consequently rule-actions (called 'events'). Some events are direct consequences of data; other events arise in a cascade-like fashion from the triggering of rules. Auxiliary symbolic data also cause events, usually affecting the higher levels of the hypothesis. As a consequence, support-from-above for the lower level processes is made available; and expectations of possible lower level events can be formed. Eventually all the relevant rules have their say and the system becomes quiescent, thereby triggering the input of new data to reenergize the inference activity.

The system uses the simplifying strategy of maintaining only one 'best' situation-hypothesis at any moment, modifying it incrementally as required by the changing data. This approach is made feasible by several characteristics of the domain. First, there is the strong continuity over time of objects and their behaviours (specifically, they do not change radically over time, or behave radically differently over short periods). Second, a single problem (identity, location and velocity of a particular set of objects) persists over numerous data gathering periods. (Compare this to speech understanding in which each sentence is spoken just once, and each presents a new and different problem.) Finally, the system's hypothesis is typically 'almost right,' in part because it gets numerous opportunities to refine the solution (i.e., the numerous data gathering periods), and in part because the availability of many knowledge sources tends to over-determine the solution. As a result of all of these, the current best hypothesis changes only slowly with time, and hence keeping only the current best is a feasible approach.

Of interest are the time-based events. These rule-like expressions, created by certain rules, trigger upon the passage of specified amounts of time. They implement various 'wait-and-see' strategies of analysis that are useful in the domain.

Results. In the test application, using signal data generated by a simulation program because real data was not available, the program achieved expert levels of performance over a span of test problems. Some problems were difficult because there was very little primary signal to support inference. Others were difficult because too much signal induced a plethora of alternatives with much ambiguity.

A modified SU/X design is currently being used as the basis for an application to the interpretation of x-ray crystallographic data, the CRYSALIS program mentioned later.

Discussion. The role of the auxiliary symbolic sources of data is of critical importance. They supply a symbolic model of the existing situation that is used to generate expectations of events to be observed in the data stream. This allows flow of inferences from higher levels of abstraction to lower. Such a process, so familiar to AI researchers, apparently is almost unrecognized among signal processing engineers. In the application task, the expectation-driven analysis is essential in controlling the combinatorial processing explosion at the lower levels, exactly the explosion that forces the traditional signal processing engineers to seek out the largest possible number-cruncher for their work.

The design of appropriate explanations for the user takes an interesting twist in SU/X. The situation/hypothesis unfolds piecemeal over time, but the 'appropriate' explanation for the user is one that focuses on individual objects over time. Thus the appropriate explanation must be synthesized from a history of all the events that led up to the current hypothesis. Contrast this with the MYCIN-TEIRESIAS reporting of rule invocations in the construction of a reasoning chain.

Since its knowledge base and its auxiliary symbolic data give it a model-of-the-situation that strongly constrains interpretation of the primary data stream. SU/X is relatively unperturbed by errorful or missing data. These data conditions merely cause fluctuations in the credibility of individual hypotheses and/or the creation of the 'wait-and-see' events. SU/X can be (but has not yet been) used to control sensors. Since its rules specify what types and values of evidence are necessary to establish support, and since it is constantly processing a complete hypothesis structure, it can request 'critical readings' from the sensors. In general, this allows an efficient use of limited sensor bandwith and data acquisition processing capability.

Other Case Studies

Space does not allow more than just a brief sketch of other interesting projects that have been completed or are in progress.

AM: mathematical discovery. AM is a knowledge-based system that conjectures interesting concepts in elementary mathematics. It is a discoverer of interesting theorems to prove, not a theorem-proving program. It was conceived and executed by D.Lenat for his PhD thesis.

AM's knowledge is basically of two types: rules that suggest possibly interesting new concepts from previously conjectured concepts; and rules that evaluate the mathematical 'interestingness' of a conjecture. These rules attempt to capture the expertise of the professional mathematician at the task of mathematical discovery. Though Lenat is not a professional mathematician, he was able successfully to serve as his own expert in the building of this program.

AM conducts a heuristic search through the space of concepts creatable from its rules. Its basic framework is generation-and-test. The generation is plausible move generation, as indicated by the rules for formation of new concepts. The test is the evaluation of 'interestingness.' Of particular note is the method of test-by-example that lends the flavor of scientific hypothesis testing to the enterprise of mathematical discovery.

Initialized with concepts of elementary set theory, it conjectured concepts in elementary number theory, such as 'add,' 'multiply' (by four distinct paths!), 'primes,' the unique factorization theorem, and a concept similar to primes but previously not much studied called 'maximally divisible numbers.'

MOLGEN: planning experiments in molecular genetics. MOLGEN, a collaboration with the Stanford Genetics Department, is work in progress. MOLGEN's task is to provide intelligent advice to a molecular geneticist on the planning of experiments involving the manipulation of DNA. The geneticist has various kinds of laboratory techniques available for changing DNA material (cuts, joins, insertions, deletions, and so on); techniques for determining the biological consequences of the changes; various instruments for measuring effects; various chemical methods for inducing , facilitating, or inhibiting changes; and many other tools.

Some MOLGEN programs under development will offer planning assistance in organizing and sequencing such tools to accomplish an experimental goal. Other MOLGEN programs will check user-provided experiment plans for feasibility; and its knowledge base will be a repository for the rapidly expanding knowledge of this speciality, available by interrogation.

In MOLGEN the problem of integration of many diverse sources of knowledge is central since the essence of the experiment planning process is the successful merging of biological, genetic, chemical, topological, and instrument knowledge. In MOLGEN the problem of representing processes is also brought into focus since the expert's knowledge of experimental strategies – proto-plans – must also be represented and put to use.

One MOLGEN program (Stefik, 1978) solves a type of analysis problem that is often difficult for laboratory scientists to solve. DNA structures can be fragmented by chemicals called restriction enzymes. These enzymes cut DNA at specific recognition sites. The fragmentation may be complete or partial. One or more enzymes may be used. The fragmented segments of the DNA are collected and sorted out by segment length using a technique called gel electrophoresis. The analytical problem is similar to that faced by DENDRAL: given an observed fragmentation pattern, hypothesize the best structural explanation of the data. More precisely, the problem is to map the enzyme recognition sites of a DNA structure from complete or partial 'digests'.

The program uses the model-driven approach that is similar to DENDRAL's and is discussed earlier. The method is generate-and-test. A generator is initiated that is capable of generating all the site-segment maps in an exhaustive, irredundant fashion. Various pruning rules are used to remove whole classes of conceivable candidates in light of the data. Some of the pruning rules are empirical and judgmental. Others are formal and mathematically based.

The program solves simpler problems of this type of analysis better than laboratory scientists. The harder problems, however, yield only to the broader biological knowledge known by the scientists and not yet available to the program's reasoning processes. In a recent test case, a problem whose solution space contained approximately 150,000,000 site-fragment 'maps' was solved in 27 seconds of PDP-10 time using the INTERLISP programming system.

Interestingly, the computer scientist's formal understanding of the nature of the problem, his formal representation of the knowledge used for pruning out inappropriate candidates, and the computational power available to him enabled him to suggest a few new experiment designs to his geneticist collaborators that were not previously in their repertoire.

CRYSALIS: inferring protein structure from electron density maps. CRYSALIS, too, is work in progress. Its task is to hypothesize the structure of a protein from a map of electron density that is derived from x-ray crystallographic data. The map is three-dimensional, and the contour information is crude and highly ambiguous. Interpretation is guided and supported by auxiliary information, of which the amino acid sequence of the protein's backbone is the most important. Density map interpretation is a protein chemist's art. As always, capturing this art in heuristic rules and putting it to use with an inference engine is the project's goal.

The inference engine for CRYSALIS is a modification of the SU/X system design described above. The hypothesis formation process must deal with many levels of possibly useful aggregation and abstraction. For example, the map itself can be viewed as consisting of 'peaks,' or 'peaks and valleys,' or 'skeleton.' The protein model has 'atoms,' 'amide planes,' 'amino acid sidechains,' and even massive substructures such as 'helices.' Protein molecules are so complex that a systemic generation-and-test strategy like DENDRAL's is not feasible. Incremental piecing together of the hypothesis using region-growing methods is necessary.

The CRYSALIS design (alias SU/P) is described in a recent paper by Nii and Feigenbaum (1977).

SUMMARY OF CASE STUDIES

Some of the themes presented earlier need no recapitulation, but I wish to revisit three here: generation-and-test; situation ⇒ action rules; and explanations.

Generation and test

Aircraft come in a wide variety of sizes, shapes, and functional designs and they are applied in very many ways. But almost all that fly do so because of the unifying physical principle of lift by airflow; the others are described by exception. If there is such a unifying principle for intelligent programs and human intelligence it is generation-and-test. No wonder that this has been so thoroughly studied in AI research!

In the case studies, generation is manifested in a variety of forms and processing schemes. There are legal move generators defined formally by a generating algorithm (DENDRAL's graph generating algorithm); or by a logical rule of inference (MYCIN's backward chaining). When legal move generation is not possible or not efficient, there are plausible move generators (as in SU/X and AM). Sometimes generation is interleaved with testing (as in MYCIN, SU/X, and AM). In one case, all generation precedes testing (DENDRAL). One case (META-DENDRAL) is mixed, with some testing taking place during generation, some after.

Test also shows great variety. There are simple tests (MYCIN: 'Is the organism aerobic?'; SU/X: 'Has a spectral line appeared at position P?') Some tests are complex heuristic evaluations (AM: 'Is the new concept 'interesting?'; MOLGEN: 'Will the reaction actually take place?') Sometimes a complex test can involve feedback to modify the object being tested (as in META-DENDRAL).

The evidence from our case studies supports the assertion by Newell and Simon that generation-and-test is a law of our science (Newell and Simon, 1976).

Situation ⇒ Action Rules

Situation ⇒ action rules are used to represent experts' knowledge in all of the case studies. Always the situation part indicates the specific conditions under which the rule is relevant. The action part can be simple (MYCIN: conclude presence of particular organism; DENDRAL: conclude break of particular bond). Or it can be quite complex (MOLGEN: an experimental procedure). The overriding consideration in making design choices is that the rule form chosen be able to represent clearly and directly what the expert wishes to express about the domain. As illustrated, this may necessitate a wide variation in rule syntax and semantics.

From a study of all the projects, a regularity emerges. A salient feature of the Situation⇒Action rule technique for representing experts' knowledge is the modularity of the knowledge base, with the concomitant flexibility to add or change the knowledge easily as the experts' understanding of the domain changes. Here too one must be pragmatic, not doctrinaire. A technique such as this cannot represent modularity of knowledge if that modularity does not exist in the domain. The virtue of this technique is that it serves as a framework for discovering what modularity exists in the domain. Discovery may feed back to cause reformulation of the knowledge toward greater modularity.

Finally, our case studies have shown that strategy knowledge can be captured in rule form. In TEIRESIAS, the metarules capture knowledge of how to deploy domain knowledge; in SU/X, the strategy rules represent the experts' knowledge of 'how to analyze' in the domain.

Explanation

Most of the programs, and all of the more recent ones, make available an explanation capability for the user, be he end-user or system developer. Our focus on end-users in applications domains has forced attention to human engineering issues, in particular making the need for the explanation capability imperative.

The Intelligent Agent viewpoint seems to us to demand that the agent be able to explain its activity; else the question arises of who is in control of the agent's activity. The issue is not academic or philosophical. It is an engineering issue that has arisen in medical and military applications of intelligent agents, and will govern future acceptance of AI work in application areas. And on the philosophical level one might even argue that there is a moral imperative to provide accurate explanations to end-users whose intuitions about our systems are almost nil.

Finally, the explanation capability is needed as part of the concerted attack on the knowledge acquisition problem. Explanation of the reasoning process is central to the interactive transfer of expertise to the knowledge base, and it is our most powerful tool for the debugging of the knowledge base.

ACKNOWLEDGMENT

The work reported herein has received long-term support from the Defense Advanced Research Projects Agency (DAHC 15-73-C-0435). The National Institutes of Health (5R24-RR00612, RR-00785) has supported DENDRAL, META-DENDRAL, and the SUMEX-AIM computer facility on which we compute. The National Science Foundation (MCS 76-11649, DCR 74-23461) has supported research on CRYSALIS and MOLGEN. The Bureau of Health Sciences Research and Evaluation (HS-10544) has supported research on MYCIN. I am grateful to these agencies for their continuing support of our work.

I wish to express my deep admiration and thanks to the faculty, staff and students of the Heuristic Programming Project, and to our collaborators in the various worldly arts, for the creativity and dedication that has made our work exciting and fruitful.

This paper also appears, in essentially the present form, in the *Proceedings of the National Computer Conference* 1978.

REFERENCES

Feigenbaum, E.A. 'Artificial Intelligence Research: What is it? What has it achieved? Where is it going?,' invited paper, *Symposium on Artificial Intelligence,* Canberra, Australia, 1974.

Feigenbaum, E.A. and J. Feldman, *Computers and Thought,* New York, McGraw-Hill, 1963.

Goldstein, I. and S. Papert, 'Artificial Intelligence, Language, and the Study of Knowledge,' *Cognitive Science,* Vol. 1, No. 1, 1977.

Gregory, R., 'On How so Little Information Controls so Much Behavior,' Bionics Research Report No. 1, Machine Intelligence Department, University of Edinburgh, 1968.

Lesser, V.R. and L.D. Erman, 'A Retrospective View of the HEARSAY-II Architecture,' *Proceedings of the Fifth International Artificial Intelligence-1977,* Massachusetts Institute of Technology, Cambridge, Massachusetts, August 22-25, 1977, Vol. I.

Newell, A. and H.A. Simon, *Human Problem Solving,* Prentice-Hall, 1972.

Newell, A. and H.A. Simon, 'Computer Science as Empirical Inquiry: Symbols and Search,' *Com ACM,* 19, 3, March, 1976.

DENDRAL and META-DENDRAL

Feigenbaum, E.A., B.G. Buchanan, and J. Lederberg, 'On Generality and Problem Solving: a Case Study Using the DENDRAL Program,' *Machine Intelligence 6*, Edinburgh University Press, 1971.

Buchanan, B.G., A.M. Duffield, and A.V. Robertson, 'An Application of Artificial Intelligence to the Interpretation of Mass Spectra,' *Mass Spectrometry Techniques and Applications*, G.W.A. Milne, Ed., John Wiley & Sons, Inc., p. 121, 1971.

Michie, D. and B.G. Buchanan, 'Current Status of the Heuristic DENDRAL Program for Applying Artificial Intelligence to the Interpretation of Mass Spectra,' *Computers for Spectroscopy*, R.A.G. Carrington, ed., London: Adam Hilger, 1974.

Buchanan, B.G., 'Scientific Theory Formation by Computer,' Nato Advanced Study Institutes Series, Series E: Applied Science, 14:515, Noordhoff-Leyden, 1976.

Buchanan, B.G., D.H. Smith, W.C. White, R.J. Gritter, E.A. Feigenbaum, J. Lederberg, and C. Djerassi, 'Applications of Artificial Intelligence for Chemical Inference XXII. Automatic Rule Formation in Mass Spectrometry by Means of the Meta-DENDRAL Program,' *Journal of the ACS*, 98:6168, 1976.

MYCIN

Shortliffe, E. *Computer-based Medical Consultations: MYCIN*, New York, Elsevier, 1976.

Davis, R., B.G. Buchanan, and E.H. Shortliffe, 'Production Rules as a Representation for a Knowledge-Based Consultation Program,' *Artificial Intelligence*, 8, 1, February, 1977.

Shortliffe, E.H. and B.G. Buchanan, 'A Model of Inexact Reasoning in Medicine,' *Mathematical Biosciences*, 23:351, 1975.

TEIRESIAS

Davis, R., 'Applications of Meta Level Knowledge to the Construction, Maintenance and Use of Large Knowledge Bases,' Memo HPP-76-7, Stanford Computer Science Department, Stanford, CA, 1976.

Davis, R., 'Interactive Transfer of Expertise I: Acquisition of New Inference Rules,' *Proceedings of the Fifth International Joint Conference on Artificial Intelligence-1977.* Massachusetts Institute of Technology, Cambridge, Massachusetts, August 22-25, 1977.

Davis, R. and B.G. Buchanan, 'Meta-Level Knowledge: Overview and Applications,' *Proceedings of the Fifth International Joint Conference on Artificial Intelligence-1977.* Massachusetts Institute of Technology, Cambridge, Massachusetts, August 22-25, 1977.

SU/X

Nii, H.P. and E.A. Feigenbaum, 'Rule Based Understanding of Signals,' *Proceedings of the Conference on Pattern-Directed Inference Systems*, 1978 (forthcoming), also Memo HPP-77-7, Stanford Computer Science Department, Stanford, CA, 1977.

AM

Lenat, D., 'AM: An Artificial Intelligence Approach to Discovery in Mathematics as Heuristic Search,' Memo HPP-76-8, Stanford Computer Science Department, Stanford, CA. 1976.

MOLGEN

Martin, N., P. Friedland, J. King, and M. Stefik, 'Knowledge Base Management for Experiment Planning in Molecular Genetics,' *Proceedings of the Fifth International Joint Conference on Artificial Intelligence-1977.* Massachusetts Institute of Technology, Cambridge, Massachusetts, August 22-25, 1977.

Stefik, M., 'Inferring DNA Structures from Segmentation Data,' *Artificial Intelligence*, 1978 (in press).

CRYSALIS

Engelmore, R. and H.P. Nii, 'A Knowledge-Based System for the Interpretation of Protein X-Ray Crystallographic Data,' Memo HPP-77-2, Department of Computer Science, Stanford, CA, 1977.

USER-ORIENTED SYSTEMS FOR CAPTURING EXPERTISE: A RULE-BASED APPROACH

D. A. Waterman

ABSTRACT
User-oriented systems for capturing expertise are discussed and illustrated within the context of RITA and ROSIE, two rule-based systems developed for building intelligent interfaces and modeling expert knowledge. RITA, the Rule-directed Interactive Transaction Agent system is operational and is currently being applied to interface and modeling problems. ROSIE, the Rule-Oriented System for Implementing Expertise, is now under development.

I. INTRODUCTION

The use of a rule-based formalism for development of experimental systems, particularly those connected with knowledge engineering, has proven quite beneficial (Waterman & Hayes-Roth, 1978). A rule-based system is defined as one that consists of a collection of antecedent-consequent rules, a data base and an executive (Hayes-Roth, Waterman, & Lenat, 1978). The rules are conditional statements that describe how to modify the data base when certain patterns are recognized in the data. The executive is tasked with the jobs of pattern matching, monitoring data base changes, deciding which rule should be executed next, and actually carrying out the execution.

The term "knowledge engineering" has been used to describe the process of building expert systems, i.e., programs that embody domain-specific knowledge from an expert and apply it to produce useful inferences for the user (Feigenbaum, 1977). Systems of this sort have been built to analyze molecular structure (Feigenbaum, Buchanan, & Lederberg, 1971), formulate rules of mass spectrometry (Buchanan & Mitchell, 1978), advise physicians regarding antimicrobial therapy (Shortliffe, 1976), and aid geologists in evaluating mineral sites (Duda, et al., 1978), to mention only a few. In some sense all programs try to behave expertly in their attempt to perform some well-defined set of tasks. However, the programs under consideration here are more highly constrained. They require an expert's knowledge to guide their inference processes, they utilize AI principles and tools to formulate and solve the problem, they tend to be applied to fuzzy, ill-defined, or very complex problem domains, and they are usually specialists rather than general-purpose problem solvers.

Two important applications of expert systems are user agents and model building. A user agent (Waterman, 1978b, 1978c; Waterman, et al., 1979) is a type of intelligent interface, usually a small program that sits between the user and the computer facilities he wishes to access. It has many of the characteristics of an intelligent assistant – it performs routine and periodic services for the user or passes messages back and forth between the user and the system he is accessing, modifying them to make them more intelligible to either the user or the system. The net effect is that of a friendly, comprehensible system for the user to access.

A second important application of expert systems is model building. Here the knowledge an expert possesses is embodied in the program, often in the form of decision rules or pattern-directed modules (Waterman, 1978a). The result is often a large, complex program that is used as a tool to infer a recommended course of action.

This paper describes two user-oriented programming systems for creating rule-based expert programs. Section II contains a description of RITA, a system designed for building user agents. Section III describes ROSIE, a system for building large models embodying expertise. ROSIE is currently in the process of being designed and implemented. The conclusions are presented in section IV.

II. RITA – BUILDING USER AGENTS

The RITA system (Anderson, et al., 1977) is a software package that provides the user with a language for defining agents (RITA programs) to serve as interfaces to external data systems. RITA has been designed to be simple, usable and versatile. Simplicity comes from the rule-based formalism adopted for RITA language statements. An agent is defined as a collection of rules of the form "IF premises THEN actions." These rules operate on a simple data structure composed of data elements that are object-attribute-value triples. These restrictions on language statements and data permit the following simple control scheme. The first (highest priority) rule whose premises are true relative to the data base is "fired" by having its actions executed. A rule has a higher priority than another if it was defined or loaded into the data base first. Once a rule is fired the process repeats and all rules are again matched against the data to find the first true one.

The RITA system is human-engineered, i.e., designed to be usable by non-computer specialists and programmers alike with minimal training or instruction. RITA's English-like syntax tends to be self-documenting, facilitating understanding and modifying agents created by other users. In addition, RITA contains an explanation facility that permits a user to query the agent after a deduction has been made to determine what rules were involved in reaching the inferred conclusion.

To achieve versatility RITA has means for interacting with the "outside world" and for building models. Special language primitives allow the user to interact with external computer systems and even initiate and monitor several external jobs in parallel. Powerful pattern-matching routines are available for use during these interactions. Furthermore, a special type of rule called a "goal" is available for performing what is known as "backward chaining" types of deductions (Waterman & Hayes-Roth, 1978). These tend to be useful for heuristic modeling tasks (Waterman and Jenkins, 1977). Goals are used to "prove" a conjecture, effectively answering a question through deductive inference. The process works as follows. Goal actions are checked to find one that could make the conjecture true. When such a goal is found its conditions are examined: if they are true the rule is fired; if not the process continues recursively in an attempt to show that each condition of the rule is true.

Both rules and goals may be used together in a single RITA agent as illustrated by Fig. 1, a RITA agent that deduces ARPANET addresses. The agent of Fig. 1 will now be used to illustrate rule processing in RITA. When the agent is executed, rule 1 is tested and found to be true, since the net-address of Tom Jones is known while his status is not. Rule 1 fires, sending "Tom Jones SU-AI" to the user. Since the rules are tested in order from top to bottom after each firing, rule 1 is again tested but fails. Rule 2 is then tested and found to be true for Sue Myers. It fires, activating the DEDUCE action. DEDUCE accesses the goals to see if any could determine the net-address of a person. Only goal 2 qualifies, so its premises are checked to see if they are true and the goal can be fired. The first and third premises are true but not the second, i.e., existence of a group whose net-address is known. At this point instead of giving up the system automatically attempts to deduce the net-address of the group. It succeeds, using goal 1 and thus can fire goal 2, setting the net-address of Sue Myers to SU-AI. Control now returns to the rules and rule 1 is again checked and fires sending "Sue Myers SU-AI" to the user and setting the status of Sue Myers to "located". Now neither rule is true so processing halts.

RITA has been found useful in many applications ranging from the construction of user agents to the development of heuristic models. It is used to handle routine network and systems interfacing tasks at Rand, and has been applied at NOSC to the development of a user agent of approximately 1000 rules that serves as the NWSS Man-Machine Interface System, an operational interface to a complex military information system.

In the heuristic modeling areas RITA has been used as NOSC to develop the TECA system for performing computer-assisted interactive military situation analysis focusing on threat assessment. At Rand, RITA is currently being used in an ongoing project for studying distributed intelligence architectures (Wesson, et al., 1979). The RITA rules represent heuristics for correlating, understanding and distributing information between nodes in distributed intelligence networks. RITA is also being used at Rand to develop TATR, a rule-based system for tactical planning.

Although RITA has been quite successful as a system for developing small user agents, its use in large modeling tasks has pointed out weaknesses for applications typically thought of as knowledge engineering. These include limitations on processing power, efficiency, data representation and the expressive power of the rules. The processing power limitation derives from the minicomputer environment in which RITA operates and could be alleviated by transfer to a larger machine. The efficiency, data representation and language construct limitations are more difficult problems that are intimately related. RITA is inefficient because when new data is created no special mechanism links rules to data that could satisfy their premises. Thus all rules must be

```
OBJECT person <1>:
   name            IS          "Tom Jones",
   net-address     IS          "SU-AI";

OBJECT person <2>:
   name            IS          "Sue Myers";

OBJECT group <1>:
   name            IS          "Stanford AI Lab",
   type            IS          "ARPANET users",
   members         IS          ("Tom Jones", "Sue Myers", "Bill Wood");

RULE 1:
      IF: THERE IS a person WHOSE net-address IS KNOWN
                   AND WHOSE status IS NOT KNOWN
   THEN: SEND the name OF the person TO the user
         & SEND the net-address OF the person to the user
         & SET the status OF the person TO "located";

RULE 2:
      IF: THERE IS a person WHOSE net-address IS NOT KNOWN
   THEN: DEDUCE the net-address OF the person;

GOAL 1:
      IF: THERE IS a group
                   WHOSE type is "ARPANET users"
                   AND WHOSE net-address IS NOT KNOWN
         & THERE IS a person WHOSE net-address IS KNOWN
         & the name OF the person IS IN the members of the group
   THEN: SET the net-address OF the group TO the net-address
                   OF the person;

GOAL 2:
      IF: THERE IS a person WHOSE net-address IS NOT KNOWN
         & THERE IS a group WHOSE net-address IS KNOWN
         & the name OF the person IS IN the members OF the group
   THEN: SET the net-address OF the person TO the net-address
                   OF the group;
```

FIGURE 1. An Example of a User Agent That Deduces Net-Addresses of Individuals

tested against all the data until a match is found. Also, the data structure and rules can't be partitioned into subcomponents to be dealt with piecemeal when appropriate. Thus all the data objects and all rules are always active and require processing even if only a handful are relevant. Finally, there is no natural way to represent hierarchical structures, especially those that make use of inheritance of attributes.

A rule-oriented system for implementing expertise (ROSIE) is now being developed at Rand that builds on the RITA formalism while attempting to eliminate its weaknesses (Waterman, et al., 1979). This system is discussed in detail in the next section.

III. ROSIE – MODEL BUILDING

ROSIE is a tool that will enable model builders to apply expert knowledge to the analysis of problems and the evaluation of solutions in complex domains, especially domains for which useful analytic models are unavailable. It is in the initial stage of design and development at Rand, so the description that follows represents our current rather than final view of ROSIE.

The ROSIE design exploits and integrates many current ideas in artificial intelligence research. It uses a rule-based language similar to RITA and MYCIN (Anderson & Gillogly, 1976; Waterman, 1976; Shortliffe, 1976). Control in ROSIE models is data directed (Hayes-Roth, Waterman, & Lenat, 1978) that is, actions are specified by sets of rules having the basic form: "IF <conditions> THEN <actions>." The actions are executed when data matching the conditions appear in the model's data base. ROSIE uses both existence-driven rule invocation as in RITA and event-driven rule-invocation as in PLANNER and ARS (Hewitt, 1971, 1972; Stallman & Sussman, 1976). The idea of a hierarchical data structure capable of supporting abstraction and inheritance comes from work on units and frames (Minsky, 1975; Martin, et al., 1977; Lenat, 1976, 1977; Lenat & Harris, 1978; Winograd, 1975; Bobrow & Winograd, 1977; Charniak, 1975; Havens, 1978). Many of the ideas related to the use of rules as data and the inclusion of elaborate user support features were inspired by INTERLISP (Teitelman, 1974).

The main requirements on the ROSIE design are efficient and effective handling of large rule and data sets for realistic modeling, the creation of a "friendly" user environment that facilitates both system building and use, and a system flexibility and modifiability that allows exploration of implementation alternatives. These requirements will now be discussed in turn.

Large Rule/Data Sets

Decisionmaking in complex application areas requires processing large amounts of information. To help address efficiency issues in ROSIE we will use the idea of recognition nets to spread up the rule matching (Hayes-Roth &Mostow, 1975). However, a more fundamental approach must be taken if we hope to solve this difficult problem. As a first step we have modularized the rules and elements so individual modules can be accessed and executed independently.

This provides a means for maintaining only the currently active and perhaps relevant modules in core at any one time. The mechanism for achieving modularity relies on the concepts of partitioning, activation, and abstraction. The user partitions his rules and data into separate sets based on his expectations regarding their interdependencies. Rule and data sets are activated, i.e., permitted to interact to cause rules to fire, only when deemed relevant by the user or the ROSIE monitor.

The user is able to handle many different kinds of rules at different levels of generality through abstraction, i.e., organizing the elements so that the "INSTANCE OF" relations between very general and very specific elements are made explicit. General rules apply to categories of data types called concepts. We have used data abstraction in order to make it easy to write rules that apply to all instances of general concepts. This works by allowing elements that represent low level or very specific concepts (e.g., an ARPANET user) to inherit attributes specified by higher level or more general concepts (e.g., a person) of which they are instances. Thus a rule that checks to see if "ARPANET User" has some attribute x, will be satisfied if either the proper value of the attribute is associated with "ARPANET user" or is associated with a more general instance of it such as "computer user."

Similarly, aggregation is used to permit the user to access collections of elements using simple rules. Here the "MEMBER OF" relation between aggregated elements and their constituent parts is made explicit. Questions about being a member of something are answered by finding the closure of all sets and subsets that are members of the element in question.

Finally, we will achieve added efficiency by permitting the rules to fire in response to events or changes in the data base. This use of an event-driven monitor also simplifies the rules, permitting the user to create rule sets that act as large collections of demons acting independently of one another. In addition, we envisage permitting the user to formulate different control rules, which we call monitor programs, that would be specially adapted to the efficient use of large sets of rules or searches of large data bases.

User Environment

To achieve a friendly user environment ROSIE has been designed around a simple, English-like rule syntax and a support package that facilitates the use of the system. The rule syntax of ROSIE is quite similar to RITA, however, most of the awkwardness of RITA programming is gone. For example, rule semantics have been expanded to facilitate interaction through a data set and to support the abstraction and aggregation hierarchy mechanism. An event-driven monitor is available to allow expressions to be tested for their becoming true. This permits the user to notice when things are changing and simplifies implementing alerts or other kinds of change-detecting processes.

The two main types of rules are IF–THEN and WHEN–THEN rules. The IF–THEN rule is analogous to the standard RITA rule. It is existence-driven; it fires repeatedly as long as the conditions are true, even if the matching value of the element has not been changed. The actions are executed once during each monitor cycle; repeated rule firings require repeated cycles.

Example:

IF the type OF the person IS "ARPANET user"
AND the location OF the person IS "Stanford AI Lab"
THEN SET the net-address OF the person TO "SU–AI";

After the THEN actions have been performed and the conditions are no longer true, rule firing is terminated.

The WHEN–THEN rule, on the other hand, fires exactly once for each knowledge element that matches its conditions. The only way it can fire again on the same element is when the matching value of the element has been changed. This is an example of an event-driven or demon-like rule.

Example:

WHEN THERE IS a person WHOSE net-address IS KNOWN
THEN PUT the name OF the person INTO the net-users-list
AND SEND the name OF the person TO the USER;

In the above example all people whose net-addresses become known are added to the net-users-list. When the net-address is changed the person's name is sent to the user. Because the rule fires only on knowledge base changes and only once for each data element no special mechanism is needed to keep the rule from being invoked continuously for the same knowledge elements.

One of the distinctive strengths of RITA, when compared to other existing production-rule programming systems, is the simplicity and power of its facilities for interaction with the external world. ROSIE will have these facilities plus additional ones for driving graphic and alphanumeric display systems from the user's model.

System Modifiability

It is important to make the system modifiable by the user to reflect his growing insight and expertise. Thus the monitor programs, the code controlling the way the rules make contact with the data base, are themselves formulated as rule-based programs. Two or three alternative rule-based monitors will be made available, although the sophisticated user will have the option of modifying or rewriting them himself. In this way we make almost all of the facilities of the system accessible to the user. Not only have we carried over the idea from LISP that "data equals program," but also the idea that the system facilities themselves are written in the same formalism as the applications. Thus increasing the user's expertise in the applications program simultaneously increases his expertise in the overall system.

We envision a support package for ROSIE that includes many useful features based on the notion that rules are simply another type of data element to be accessed and manipulated by rules. This includes rule-based editing facilities that may be extended or modified by the user, an explanation facility that traces the operation of the system at various levels, and the use of "certainty factors" to facilitate reasoning in the presence of uncertainty.

IV. CONCLUSIONS

Computer systems that incorporate human judgemental expertise offer certain advantages to the user community. They make the expertise widely sharable, helping to relieve the demand for highly trained and experienced personnel. Furthermore, a single system may incorporate the expertise of many contributors, resulting in a net improvement in the overall performance of the system.

Our experience with the design, implementation and application of RITA to interface and modeling problems has demonstrated the usefulness and flexibility of a rule-based approach to modeling human expertise. The key features of RITA – a rule-based formalism, English-like syntax, and powerful real-world interface have proven to be viable and effective for knowledge engineering. These features have been carried over into the design of ROSIE and combined with new features, lacking in RITA, such as partitioning, activation and abstraction to facilitate the efficient and effective handling of large rule and data sets, and rule-based monitors to permit experimentation with various control schemes that could lead to permanent modification of the control structure. We believe this design will prove to be a useful first step in the development of a powerful tool for knowledge engineering.

REFERENCES

Anderson, R.H., Gallegos, M., Gillogly, J.J., Greenberg, R.B., and Villanueva, R. RITA reference manual. R-1808-ARPA, The Rand Corporation, Santa Monica, California, 1977.

Anderson, R.H., and Gillogly, J.J. Rand intelligent terminal agent (RITA): Design philosophy, R-1809-ARPA, The Rand Corporation, Santa Monica, California, 1976.

Bobrow, D.G., and Winograd, T. An overview of KRL, A knowledge representation language. Cognitive Science, 1977, i, 3-46.

Buchanan, B.G., and Mitchell, T. Model directed learning by production rules. In D.A. Waterman and F. Hayes-Roth (Eds.), Pattern-directed inference systems. New York: Academic Press, 1978.

Charniak, E. Organization and inference in a frame-like system of common knowledge. Proc. TINLAP, Cambridge, Massachusetts, June 1975, 46-55.

Duda, R.O., Hart, P.E., Nilsson, N.J., and Sutherland, G. Semantic network representations in rule-based inference systems. In D.A. Waterman and F. Hayes-Roth (Eds.), Pattern-directed inference systems. New York: Academic Press, 1978.

Feigenbaum, E.A. The art of artificial intelligence: I. Themes and case studies of knowledge engineering. Proceedings of the 5th International Joint Conference on Artificial Intelligence, Cambridge, Massachusetts, 1977, 1014-1029.

Feigenbaum, E.A., Buchanan, B.G., and Lederberg, J. On generality and problem solving: A case study using the DENDRAL program. In B. Meltzer and D. Michie (Eds.), Machine intelligence, Vol. 6. New York: American Elsevier, 1971, 165-190.

Havens, W.S. A computational model for frame systems. Ph.D. Thesis, Department of Computer Science, USC, Vancouver, B.C., 1978.

Hayes-Roth, F., and Mostow, D.J. An automatically compilable recognition network for structured patterns. Proceedings of the 4th International Joint Conference on Artificial Intelligence, Tbilisi, USSR, 1975, 246-251.

Hayes-Roth, F., Waterman, D.A., and Lenat, D. Principles of pattern-directed inference systems. In D.A. Waterman and F. Hayes-Roth (Eds.), Pattern-directed inference systems. New York: Academic Press, 1978.

Hewitt, C. Procedural embedding of knowledge in PLANNER. Proceedings of the 2nd International Joint Conference on Artificial Intelligence, London, 1971, 167-184.

Hewitt, C. Description and theoretical analysis (using schemata) of PLANNER: A language for proving theorems and manipulating models in robots. TR-258, MIT AI Laboratory, Cambridge, Massachusetts, 1972.

Lenat, D. AM: An artificial intelligence approach to discovery in mathematics as heuristic search. Stanford University, Artificial Intelligence Laboratory, Memo AIM-286, 1976.

Lenat, D. Automated theory formation in mathematics. Proceedings of the 5th International Joint Conference on artificial Intelligence, Cambridge, Massachusetts, 1977, 833-842.

Lenat, D., and Harris, G. Designing a rule system that searches for scientific discoveries. In D.A. Waterman and F. Hayes-Roth (Eds.), Pattern-directed inference systems. New York: Academic Press, 1978.

Martin, N., Friedland, P., King, J.A., and Stefik, M. Knowledge base management for experiment planning in molecular genetics. Proceedings of the 5th International Joint Conference on Artificial Intelligence, Cambridge, Massachusetts, 1977, 822-887.

Minsky, M. A framework for representing knowledge. In P.H. Winston (Ed.), The psychology of computer vision. New York: McGraw-Hill, 1975.

Shortliffe, E.H. Computer-based medical consultations: MYCIN. New York: American Elsevier, 1976.

Stallman, R., and Sussman, G.J. Forward reasoning and dependency-directed backtracking in a system for computer-aided circuit analysis. Memo 380, MIT AI Laboratory, Cambridge, Massachusetts, 1976.

Teitelman, W. Interlisp reference manual. Xerox Palo Alto Research Center, Palo Alto, California, 1974.

Waterman, D.A. An introduction to production systems. P-5751, The Rand Corporation, Santa Monica, California, 1976.

Waterman, D.A. Rule-directed interactive transaction agents: An approach to knowledge acquisition. R-2171-ARPA, The Rand Corporation, Santa Monica, California, 1978. (a).

Waterman, D.A. Exemplary programming in RITA. In D.A. Waterman and F. Hayes-Roth (Eds.), Pattern-directed inference systems. New York: Academic Press, 1978. (b).

Waterman, D.A. A rule-based approach to knowledge acquisition for man-machine interface programs. International Journal of Man-Machine Studies, 1978, 10, 693-711. (c)

Waterman, D.A., Anderson, R.H., Hayes-Roth, F., Klahr, P., Martins, G., and Rosenschein, S. J. Design of a rule-oriented system for implementing expertise. Rand Note N-1158-ARPA, The Rand Corporation, Santa Monica, California, 1979.

Waterman, D.A., and Hayes-Roth, F. An overview of pattern-directed inference systems. In D.A. Waterman and F. Hayes-Roth (Eds.), Pattern-directed inference systems. New York: Academic Press, 1978.

Waterman, D.A., and Jenkins, B. Heuristic modeling using rule-based computer systems. P-5811, The Rand Corporation, SantaMonica, California, 1977.

Wesson, R., Sunshine, C., Stasz, C., Hayes-Roth, F., and Burge, J. A network simulation for distributed simulation assessment. Rand report (in progress), June, 1979.

Winograd, T. Frame representations and the declarative/procedural controversy. In D.G. Bobrow and A. Collins (eds.), Representation and understanding. New York: Academic Press, 1975.

PRODUCTION SYSTEMS FOR MODELLING HUMAN COGNITION

Richard M.Young

During the past few years, since the pioneering work of Newell & Simon (1972), Production Systems (PSs) have been used more and more widely as a medium for expressing models of human cognition. They are now becoming increasingly accepted as a powerful and general approach to theoretical issues in cognitive psychology (e.g. Hunt & Poltrock, 1974; Anderson, 1976). In this paper I will try to illustrate this trend and examine what properties of PSs are responsible for it. But it may be helpful, particularly in the context of the other contributions to this Summer School, to begin by drawing a distinction.

PRODUCTION SYSTEMS: POWER OR PSYCHOLOGICAL VERACITY?

We can distinguish two main categories of tasks to which PSs are applied. Firstly there are the "intellectual", highly rational, strategy-laden tasks such as mathematics, puzzle solving, or planning, including of course such "expert" intellectual tasks as chemical analysis or mineral prospecting. These high-level tasks constitute the home territory (and historical origin) of AI. They provide areas where the computer program and the human subject can throw light on each other because, on the one hand, to get a computer to do the task is difficult enough that the programmer turns eagerly to observation of the human problem-solver for any inspiration that can provide, and on the other, psychologists have so little idea of even how to talk about how these activities are done that the AI program provides, by default and by the argument of *sufficiency* (see Newell & Simon, 1972), a starting point for a theory of the psychological processes involved.

By contrast with these high-level tasks, experimental psychologists usually study "intermediate level cognition" (cf. Becker, 1973) in people: memory tasks, sentence comprehension, simple reasoning, and so on. For many (though not all) of these tasks there is no difficulty in programming the computer to "do it". The challenge lies in writing a program whose behaviour matches the fine data of human performance. (A loose way of saying this is that the challenge is to get the computer to do the task "in the same way as" the human – but that way of speaking leads to deep metaphysical problems.)

These different kinds of tasks differ in the requirements they make of the PS architecture. The more complex, high level tasks need all the computational devices the programmer can supply: Hence the sophistication and complexity of the expert systems. But for the simpler tasks what matters is not the *power* of the PS architecture, but the extent to which it captures – or lends itself to PSs which capture – the invariants of human cognition. For this reason the PSs I will be describing have, by comparison with almost all the rule-based expert systems being presented here, a very simple structure. For example, they typically have the properties:

a) Of being *single-level*. The PS consists of one, possibly vast, collection of rules with no imposed extrinsic structure. It is not divided into sub-PSs, and there is no way that a rule can "call" part (or the whole) of the PS recursively.
b) Of being *condition-driven* (antecedent-driven, lefthand-side-driven). A rule is applicable if its conditions are satisfied. There is no question of examining the consequent (righthand side) of the rule to see if it is "desirable", in a result-driven (goal-driven) manner.
c) Of having only *simple pattern-matching* capabilities. Usually just a simple syntactic match between pattern and data, with substitution of variables, is allowed. There may be no facility, for example, for evaluating complex predicates as part of the pattern-matching, still less for firing further rules in order to complete the testing of a single rule's conditions.
d) Of employing *syntactic conflict resolution*. When more than one rule in the PS is applicable, "conflict resolution" is the term applied to the process of selecting one (or more) of them as the one(s) to fire. This process is specified as part of the PS architecture, on a fixed, syntactic basis, and is therefore essentially knowledge-free. There is no facility for consulting other rules to help in the selection.

The effect of these restrictions is that the PS can be thought of as operating in a linear sequence of *recognise-act cycles.* At the start of each cycle the applicable rules are found; conflict resolution is applied to choose which one(s) to fire; the right-hand side(s) is/are obeyed; and the cycle repeats. It will be seen that, compared to the more elaborate structures of the expert systems, these restrictions lead to a loss of computational power. But I want to argue that for psychological modelling this is a merit rather than a disadvantage. I will return to this point at the end of the paper.

CHOICE OF ARCHITECTURE

This contrast with AI-style expert systems should not be taken as implying that all psychologists using PSs have agreed to adopt the same conventions. Far from it! Different researchers do tend to share the general framework just described, but within this there are wide variations. The PSG interpreter, for example (Newell, 1973a), is fully deterministic, fires just a single rule on each cycle, handles conflict resolution by a fixed priority ordering of the rules, and represents all long term knowledge in the form of rules. In the ACT interpreter on the other hand (Anderson, 1976), rule selection is partly probabilistic, several rules can fire at a time, there is an elaborate mechanism for detemining which rules are candidates for firing, and an important role is played by long term knowledge represented in a semantic network through which "energy" diffuses by a process of spreading activation.

While it would be nice if everyone could agree on a common architecture, it is important to understand why these variations occur. Partly they are due to differences in the aims and interests of the different researchers. For Newell, the emphasis is primarily upon the flow of control (Newell, 1973b). The tasks modelled with PSG tend to be closed, formal, and largely knowledge-free.

Anderson's main focus is on accounting for the effects of the richness of interconnections in the knowledge base on the speed of retrievals from it. He is essentially uninterested in questions of the flow of control. He guides the PS by the assignment and testing of global variables, and exploits the control possibilities of PSs so little that the behaviour of his PSs is almost independent of the data and can be diagrammed by paths through a simple finite-state network.

These differing emphases go some way towards explaining the contrasting styles of the resulting PSs, but the more fundamental point is that the variation arises because PSs, as a medium for modelling, are not neutral. The architecture chosen actually carries some of the content of the theory being propounded (we say it is *theory-laden*, a point we will return to later). So different researchers need to explore different architectures to see which most closely matches their theories, and to pick the one which best meets their needs. This is totally acceptable, provided that when presenting his PS model the researcher states clearly which aspects of it are to be taken as having theoretical, psychological significance, and which not.

In a survey such as this there is no need to commit ourselves to any one preferred architecture, but for the sake of definiteness I will where necessary assume the properties of the OPS2 interpreter (Forgy & McDermott, 1977), whose structure and conflict resolution are interesting for psychological modelling.

KEY PROPERTIES OF PRODUCTION SYSTEMS

In their excellent review, Davis & King (1977) list various properties of PSs which are crucial for their use in AI programs, including such features as their modularity, the constrained format of the rules, their data-drivenness, and the openness of control. Their discussion is mostly applicable here, but we also need to emphasise a further factor. This is that the gross features of the architecture – the division between long term storage (production memory and possibly semantic networks) and dynamic, short term storage (data base or working memory), the recognise-act cycle, and some aspects of conflict resolution – correspond to aspects of the human cognitive system. This in itself has no great theoretical significance, but it does suggest that PSs offer an appropriate framework within which to specify a more detailed theory. It means, for example, that PSs offer the possibility of modelling explicitly the contents and role of short term memory during task performance in a way which would be obscured by an ordinary programming language allowing sequential flow of control and local data contexts. The nature of the basic recognise-act cycle offers the potential for vast lefthand side parallelism, with each rule being regarded as a little "demon" constantly on the watch for its evoking conditions. This is consonant with a view of the human cognitive system such as that shown in Figure 1, in which long term information – knowledge in the broadest sense – is invoked by (and by supposition, invoked only by) the dynamic contents of the working memory. Such a view is, so far as I know, shared by all of the work in psychology using PSs.

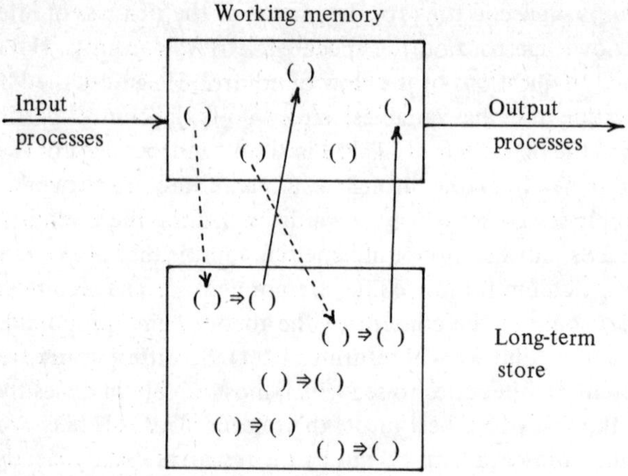

Figure 1. View of the cognitive system

PSYCHOLOGICAL PHENOMENA IN PRODUCTION SYSTEM MODELS

I would like to illustrate how the properties of PSs are exploited in psychological models by considering a few examples, all but one of them very briefly.

1. *Stimulus-dependence and -independence*

Human cognitive behaviour varies in the extent to which it is under the control of, or independent of, information in the immediate external task environment. Near one extreme is a heavily perceptual-motor kind of task, such as using an interactive display-based text-editor, which requires a continual interchange of information with the environment. Near the other extreme is a mental arithmetic task, such as multiplying together two three-figure numbers in the head. Here, once given the numbers, cognitive activity proceeds independent of external input for possibly several minutes.

Because of its data-driven character, a PS is well able to represent behaviours at any point on the scale from data-dependence to -independence. (This is in contrast to ordinary sequential flow programming languages which are strongly biased towards a style of program exhibiting low degrees of data dependence.) This property is well illustrated in a study by Simon (1975) who analysed four different strategies for the well known Tower-of-Hanoi problem. The strategies all generate the "same behaviour", but they differ widely in the extent to which the successive actions are derived from the momentary features of the physical problem configuration. In one of the strategies the next move is generated afresh on each round by an examination of the arrangement of the discs. Whereas in one of the others, successive moves are generated by a purely internal process, and the task can be carried out with the eyes closed. The various strategies differ correspondingly in the demands they make on internal cognitive resources such as working memory. Simon exploits the properties of PSs to exhibit these differences, while at the same time showing how slight are the essential differences among the underlying programs implementing those strategies.

2. *Knowledge-based cognition*

The kinds of human activity closest to the spirit of the AI expert systems are those cases in which the choice between a number of different possible ways of proceeding is made on the basis of a vast store of task-specific knowledge accumulated by the subject over a period of years. A program written by Saito (1978) shows how naturally this kind of behaviour can be captured by a PS. Saito is concerned with explicating one aspect of the impressive calculational skills of A.C. Aitken.

Aitken, who was for some time Professor of Mathematics at Edinburgh University, as well as being an accomplished mathematician had the ability to perform prodigious feats of mental calculation. Unusually for a mental prodigy, he was also quite articulate about the procedures he used in his mental arithmetic, a fact which enabled Hunter (e.g. 1962) to write a number of papers describing his capabilities and techniques. One of Aitken's specialities, for example, is to calculate the decimal value of the reciprocals of two- or three-digit numbers, such as $1/752 = .001329787234 \ldots$. One of his techniques depends on the fact that for numbers of the form $(d \times 10^n) \pm 1$, where d is a digit or at least a small number, there exists a simple method of division well suited to the constraints of mental calculation. Furthermore, it turns out that most of the prime numbers less than a thousand have multiples of this special form. Aitken possesses a vast repertoire of these numerical relationships, and utilises them in choosing an appropriate plan for computing a given reciprocal.

Saito (1978) represents this knowledge as a PS, and shows that its behaviour closely corresponds to Aitken's protocol, and to the grouping of the digits in his spoken answer. Saito's program demonstrates effectively how the procedure chosen to invert a particular number depends crucially upon the pattern of arithemetical facts which Aitken knows about it.

3. *Additivity and cognitive development*

The modularity and independence of production rules leads to their potential for displaying *additivity*, i.e. the possibility of enlarging the PS simply by adding to it one or more further rules. This property in turn suggests that PSs may be highly suitable for modelling the phenomena of human cognitive development, since it should be possible to represent a child's growing ability as a gradually expanding PS.

I took just this approach in some work I did a few years ago (Young, 1974, 1976). I studied 4 to 6 year olds tackling the Piagetian problem of length seriation, in which they are presented with a jumbled heap of wooden blocks and asked to arrange them in order of size. Piaget divides the children's ability into three stages, each characterised by a different way of doing (or failing to do) the task, and claims that the child's ability undergoes a "restructuring" between successive stages. I showed that, in terms of the programs generating the behaviour, the methods used at different ages are closely related. Beginning with a simple PS which was unable to seriate, adding rules one or two at a time yielded a sequence of PSs which displayed many of the developmental phenomena noted by Piaget. This leads to an account of the development of the child's skill as a gradual, cumulative acquisition of production rules and reveals the continuity underlying the striking (and often discontinuous) changes in his overt performance. Developmental research using PSs in a similar way has been done by Baylor & Gascon (1974) and Klahr & Wallace (1976).

More recently, in some research done in collaboration with Tim O'Shea (O'Shea & Young, 1978; Young & O'Shea, 1979) we have been able to show that children's ability to perform paper-and-pencil subtraction can be represented as a PS, and that once this is done their common errors (e.g. Brown & Burton, 1978) can be accounted for by the omission of particular rules from the PS. This again suggests an analysis of learning as the cumulative acquisition of production rules.

4. *Adaptiveness of cognitive skill*

The same research has led towards a picture of cognitive skill which tries to account for the adaptiveness and flexibility inherent in human behaviour (Young, 1978). The analysis is inspired by the characteristics of PSs, but makes use of themin a substantive way as well. The central argument is that instead of regarding skills as being organised into subroutine-like modules which implement an algorithm-like strategy, the skill is composed of a mixture of bits and pieces (each corresponding to a single rule or a small group of closely related rules) which may be quite redundant and untidy, and will typically support a number of different, possibly partial techniques. The organisation is inherently adaptive, in that the actual method – or more usually, mixture of methods – exhibited on a particular occasion will be responsive to the actual materials and circumstances of the task

5. *Flexibility of control*

In my final example, I would like to go into a little more depth, and try and convey some feel for how a PS used as a psychological model functions as a whole, and the sort of insight it yields into the cognitive processes at work.

The openness of PSs – the fact that on each cycle any one of the rules can fire if its conditions are satisfied – enables PSs to capture the flexibility of control that is so typical of human behaviour (and is so hard to capture in a non-data-driven computer program). This is illustrated by some as yet unpublished research being done by John Fox at the University of Sheffield. Fox is investigating the cognitive processes of hospital physicians performing a differential diagnosis of patients suffering from dyspepsia. He finds that he can distinguish three distinct components of the doctor's skill (see Figure 2). First, he finds that the doctor's actions are often made on a pattern-recognition-like basis, in which a particular question to ask (or tentative diagnosis) is suggested by a particular configuration of symptoms. This aspect of the doctor's ability can be represented as a collection of rules of the form:

Symptom A present & Symptom B present & . . . Symptom C absent
  ⇒ Ask Question Q

or

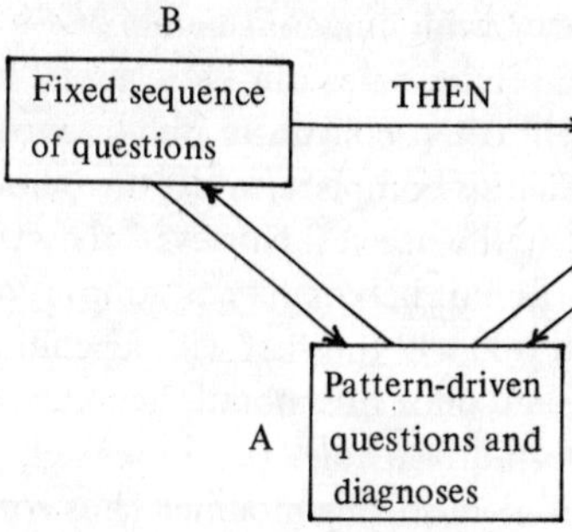

Figure 2. Components of diagnosis skill

Symptom A present & Symptom B present & . . . & Symptom C absent
⇒ Diagnosis D

These rules are shown as module A in Figure 2. Note that this technique contrasts both with a *Bayesian* method in which the weight of accumulating statistical evidence gradually elevates the probability of some disease above those of its alternatives, and also with an *hypothesis-testing* method in which evidence for or against a particular diagnosis is actively pursued.

However, early in the diagnostic process none of these rules will be applicable since not enough information is available about the patient, who "presents" just with information about age and sex, and of course the dyspepsia. Thus the doctor has no alternative but to begin asking questions of the patient, in the hope that some significant pattern will emerge. Equally, in the absence of evidence to the contrary, there are no grounds for asking these questions differently on one occasion than on another, and so each doctor tends to ask his question – or at least the first few – in a routine order. This part of the skill is represented by the rules in module B of Figure 2.

These two modules cooperate to generate behaviour in the following way. Initially, the doctor begins asking questions in a standard order, gradually accumulating information about the presence and absence of the various signs and symptoms. At some point a subset of this information may be sufficient to trigger one of the rules in the pattern-driven module, perhaps leading to the asking of a contingent question, the answer to which may well trigger another of the pattern-driven rules. If this chain of rule firings leads to a diagnosis, well and good. If not, then initiative reverts to module B, and the doctor resumes his list of questions where he left off. The result is that although the production rules themselves are fixed, the actual path through them is heavily data-dependent and the order of questions will vary widely from case to case.

It is quite possible for the system just described to fail, i.e. for the doctor to reach the end of his list of questions without a diagnosis being reached. In this case he continues in a different manner, using a problem-solving strategy in which he actively (and presumably consciously) considers what diseases are still consistent with the evidence so far and chooses further questions to discriminate between them. This aspect is shown as module C in Figure 2.

From one point of view, these problem-solving rules can be regarded as a self-contained technique. Although they will often constitute only a partial strategy, in some cases they may be sufficiently complete to do the whole diagnosis job, in problem-solving mode, all by themselves! However, they will never normally get a chance to do so. They do not behave like a "subroutine", and should not be thought of as one. Which rule will fire first will depend on what information has been gathered so far, and once this module generates a new piece of information, one of the pattern-driven rules (in A) is likely to fire and "snatch control away from" the problem-solving module. Thus control is given to the module only in a series of "lightning strikes", and which rule fires first each time is data-dependent and is essentially unpredictable from examination of the module alone.

This analysis yields a description of diagnosis ability which lays out explicitly the kinds of knowledge used to guide the behaviour. The doctor's activity is seen to be driven by three sources of crystallised knowledge of very different kinds: by a list of useful questions, by a familiarity with different patterns of symptoms and the diseases they are associated with, and by a method for (heuristically) reasoning about the case. But the actual behaviour these modules generate is much richer and more varied than this three-fold division might imply. Control jumps backwards and forwards between them as new information comes to light, according to which rule conditions become satisfied. The relationship between the modules is of course in some ways analogous to that between co-routines, but with the crucial difference that the modules are independent, knowing nothing of each other's existence, and that the flow of control is determined by the data and not by explicit acts of transfer. The organisation is, in fact, a miniature example of the AI paradigm of a "community of co-operating experts", and shows how such a scheme may be realised in a psychologically valid way.

To avoid misunderstandings, two points about this example may need clarification. First, there is the sense in which the PS is "divided into modules". I should stress that the division is a purely functional one, imposed by us, outsiders looking at and discussing the PS. It is not at all a structural division, and does not exist within the PS itself. The PS interpreter sees just a single, undifferentiated collection of rules. Second, it should be realised that I am not offering the PS as an example of a clever, expert AI program. The point of the example is not to show how smart the program is, but to illustrate how the properties of PSs enable us to build a psychological model which captures the main features of the doctor's skill.

REMARKS ON PRODUCTION SYSTEMS AS A LANGUAGE FOR COGNITIVE MODELLING

One thing which may not be evident from the summaries given above but certainly would be from a reading of the original reports, is that the different authors' PSs differ greatly in style and notation. One of Newell's (1973a) PSG rules for the Sternberg scanning task simply doesn't *look* like one of Simon's (1975) rules for moving discs or one of Anderson's (1976) ACT rules for deciding whether the hippie touched the debutante. More confusingly, the authors implicitly take different positions on the much-vexed question of the scientific status of the models: Are PSs a theory of human cognition, or are they ("just") a notation for expressing such theories? There is no way we can hope to resolve that question here, but it may help to clarify the issue if we point out that different investigators use PSs in different ways, for different purposes, and with different relationships between the structure and the content of their models. Any division is arbitrary, but it may be helpful to distinguish three levels in the degree to which the details of the PS architecture are intended to have psychological content.

(a) Firstly, with the least commitment in the architecture, is what one might call the *language level*. Here, PSs are used because of their suitability as a language for expressing certain kinds of computations. The *content* of the PS may express a psychological theory, but the notation is chosen on grounds of its computational convenience (a criterion shared with the use of PSs in expert AI programs).

An excellent example of this kind of usage is provided by Ohlsson's (1977) discussion of the research on three-term series problems (such as: "Adam is taller than Bob; Carl is shorter than Bob; who is tallest?"). None of the research he surveys originally used PSs, but he finds it an ideal medium in which to re-cast the different theories, to see whether rival ones really do differ in their predictions, to expose their hidden assumptions, and to test whether the conclusions drawn by their proponents actually follow.

(b) Secondly one can find a number of studies which operate at what one might call the *rule level*. At this level there is a commitment to the psychological reality of rules, i.e. to the idea that the cognitive "program" is structured as a PS, and also perhaps to some aspects of the conflict resolution. But this commitment does not necessarily extend to the details of the architecture adopted. My own work is cast at this level, as too is Simon's (1975) analysis of strategies for Tower-of-Hanoi. Simon, for example, allows the condition side of his rules to include "perceptual predicates", i.e. predicates which test directly whether or not some property holds true in the current state of the environment. This is justified, since Simon is focussing on the relationships between the various strategies, not on the processes of perception. If one were interested in the latter, one would have to spell out the steps in more explicit detail (cf. Newell, 1972).

(c) Lastly there is the *immediate processor level*, at which the PS architecture is itself intended as a theory of the structure of human cognitive processes. The allowable actions on the righthand side of the rules, for example, are taken to be the "elementary information processes" (Newell & Simon, 1972) of the cognitive system. Newell's work (e.g. 1973a) has usually been intended to be understood at this level, and more recently (Newell, 1979) he has carried much farther this idea of specifying the "architecture" of the human processing system.

Whatever level a particular PS model is cast at, it has in common with other PS work that the notation used for presenting the model is not neutral, but is to some extent *theory-laden*, and is actually carrying some of the content of what is being asserted. (This contrasts with normal practice, where with simulation programs written in FORTRAN or LISP the choice of programming language is assumed *not* to have theoretical significance.) Even at the modest, intermediate *rule level*, aspects of the architecture such as details of the conflict resolution scheme may have considerable psychological import. For example, in OPS2-like interpreters (and many others), conflict resolution is strongly determined by *recency*. In other words, items which have just recently been added to the working memory are more effective at getting rules to fire than are older items. This feature is mainly responsible for capturing the focus-of-attention and continuity characteristic of human problem solving, but also, paradoxically perhaps, its distractibility. It is largely the principle of recency, by its mediation of these complementary tendencies which is responsible for the lifelike behaviour of Fox's PS for medical diagnosis.

To return briefly to a point mentioned early in the paper, what makes PSs attractive as a medium for psychological theorising is not their potential *power* but, on the contrary, the fact that they can be constrained by the specification of the architecture to reflect the proposed structure of the human cognitive processing system. The ideal would be a PS architecture so tightly – but appropriately – constrained that the only programs possible to write for it would be guaranteed to be ones it was possible for the human system to employ. We would then have reached the point where the "open", unmanageable task of furnishing valid accounts of human performance on cognitive tasks had been replaced by the "closed", manageable one of programming the PS.

ACKNOWLEDGEMENT

I would like to thank John Fox for many hours of discussion concerning production systems and their relation to psychology. Both I and this paper have benefited.

REFERENCES

Anderson, J.R. (1976) *Language, Memory and Thought*. Erlbaum.

Baylor, G.W. & Gascon, J. (1974) An information processing theory of the development of weight seriation in children. *Cognitive Psychology, 6*, 1-40.

Becker, J.D. (1973) A model for the encoding of experiential information. In Schank, R. & Colby, K. (eds) *Computer Models of Thought and Language*.

Brown, J.S. & Burton, R.R. (1978) Diagnostic models for procedural bugs in basic mathematical skills. *Cognitive Science, 2,* 155-192.

Davis, R. & King, J. (1977) An overview of production systems. In Elcock, E.W. & Michie, D. (eds) *Machine Intelligence 8: Machine Representations of Knowledge*. Ellis Horwood.

Forgy, C. & McDermott, J. (1977) OPS, a domain-independent production system language. *Proceedings of 5th I.J.C.A.I.,* 933-939.

Hunt, E.B. & Poltrock, S.E. (1974) The mechanics of thought. In Kantowitz, B.H. (ed) *Human Information Processing: Tutorials in Performance and Cognition*. Erlbaum, 277-350.

Hunter, I.M.L. (1962) An exceptional talent for calculative thinking. *British Journal of Psychology, 53*, 243-258.

Klahr, D. & Wallace, J.G. (1976) *Cognitive Development: An Information-Processing View*. Erlbaum.

Newell, A. (1972) A theoretical exploration of mechanisms for coding the stimulus. In Melton, A.W. & Martin, E. (eds) *Coding Processes in Human Memory*. Winston.

Newell, A. (1973a) Production systems: models of control structures. In Chase, W.G. (ed) *Visual Information Processing*. Academic Press, 463-526.

Newell, A. (1973b) You can't play 20 questions with nature and win: Projective comments on the papers of this symposium. In Chase, W.G. (ed) *Visual Information Processing*. Academic Press, 283-308.

Newell, A. (1979) HARPY, production systems and human cognition. In Cole, R. (ed) *Perception and Production of Fluent Speech*. Erlbaum, in press.

Newell, A. & Simon, H.A. (1972) *Human Problem Solving*. Prentice-Hall.

Ohlsson, S. (1977) Production system reconstruction of theories for the solving of three-term series problems. Umea Psychological Reports No.133, University of Umea, Sweden.

O'Shea, T. & Young, R.M. (1978) A production rule account of errors in children's subtraction. *Proceedings of 3rd AISB Conference*, 229-237.

Saito, Y. (1978) Production system approach to mental calculation potency. Unpublished M.Sc. dissertation, Essex University.

Simon, H.A. (1975) The functional equivalence of problem solving skills. *Cognitive Psychology*, 7, 268-288.

Young, R.M. (1974) Production systems as models of cognitive development. *Proceedings of 1st AISB Conference*, 284-295.

Young, R.M. (1976) *Seriation by Children: An Artificial Intelligence Analysis of a Piagetian Task*. Birkhauser.

Young, R.M. (1978) Strategies and the structure of a cognitive skill. In Underwood, G. (ed) *Strategies of Information Processing*. Academic Press, 357-401.

Young, R.M. & O'Shea, T. (1979) Errors in children's subtraction: A production rule account. In preparation.

SPECIAL-PURPOSE PROBLEM-SOLVERS

EXPERT PROBLEM SOLVERS

Mike Brady

[Opening remarks from the Chair at the start of the session.]

A central issue in AI applications, both in computer-based consultation and in robotics and in the framing of a theory of problem solving concerns the way in which generality and specificity can simultaneously be achieved. Human problem solving is as much characterised by its enormous range as by the huge amounts of detailed specific knowledge that can be effectively mobilised for a particular domain. To this end, AI has developed a set of ideas, such as predicate calculus, frame representations, and production systems, about the ways in which knowledge can be uniformly represented.

Within any such framework one faces a number of invariant difficulties, and the papers comprising this section of the proceedings address some of them. First, and perhaps foremost, is the possibility of combinatorial explosion. Put quite simply, extending the knowledge base of a program not only gives it the potential to solve previously unsolvable problems (or at least to solve them more directly), but increases the choice of solution steps available to the solver and can cause it effectively to grind to a halt.

There are a number of ways to counteract this difficulty. Firstly, one attempts to impose structure on the knowledge base, to enable the solver to operate within a relatively narrowly specified context. Thus Bundy *et al.* employ schemas, Carhart relies upon superatoms, and Bratko and Niblett structure long move sequences in their investigation of end-game plays.

A second approach is to make explicit the knowledge one has about the way in which domain specific knowledge can best be used; so-called metaknowledge. The uniformity of knowledge representation really begins to pay off here, as one can turn the full power of the problem solver onto the metaknowledge in exactly the same way as one applies it to the base knowledge. Bundy has a good discussion of this approach, and Bratko and Niblett discuss "advice" and explicit knowledge about plans.

Thirdly, one attempts to exploit the redundancy which seems ever present and crucial for human problem solving and perception. There are several ways in which this might be achieved, but mostly they amount to the exploitation of constraints. Often one can make explicit a number of conditions, none of which uniquely specify a solution, but whose simultaneous satisfaction is unique. This is central to Carhart's account, and is also used by the natural language component of Bundy's system.

While these are possibly the most important issues raised in the three papers in this section, there are also other notable points. Carhart's work clearly illustrates the difficulties involved in designing a usable man-machine interface, while the work of Bratko and Niblett demonstrates once again just how much knowledge is involved in so apparently specialised and esoteric a topic as rook-king vs knight-king end-games in which the black knight is paralysed.

SOLVING MECHANICS PROBLEMS USING META-LEVEL INFERENCE

Alan Bundy, Lawrence Byrd, George Luger, Chris Mellish & Martha Palmer

In this paper we shall describe a program (MECHO), written in Prolog [14], which solves a wide range of mechanics problems from statements in both predicate calculus and English. MECHO uses the technique of meta-level inference to control search in natural language understanding, common sense inference, model formation and algebraic manipulation. We argue that this is a powerful technique for controlling search while retaining the modularity of a declarative knowledge representation.

Keywords: Natural Language, Mathematical Reasoning, Search Control, Meta-level Inference, Predicate Calculus, Mechanics.

This work was supported by SRC grant number B/RG 94493 and an SRC research studentship for Chris Mellish. This paper was also delivered as an invited talk to the 6th IJCAI held in Tokyo in August 1979.

1. INTRODUCTION

The work described in this paper addresses the question of how it is possible to get a formal representation of a problem from an English statement, and how it is then possible to use this representation in order to solve the problem. Our purpose in studying natural language understanding in conjunction with problem solving is to bring together the constraints of what formal representation can actually be obtained with the question of what knowledge is required in order to solve a wide range of problems in a semantically rich domain. We believe that these issues cannot be sensibly tackled in isolation. In practical terms we have had the benefits of an increased awareness of common problems in both areas and a realisation that some of our techniques are applicable to both the control of inference and the control of parsing.

Early work on solving mathematical problems stated in natural language was done by Bobrow (STUDENT – [1]) and Charniak (CARPS – [5]). However, the rudimentary parsing and simple semantic structures used by Bobrow and Charniak are inadequate for any but the easiest problems. Our intention has been to build on advances in natural language processing (eg [18]) in order to study parsing and problem solving in a domain which requires sophisticated knowledge about the world. The domain we have been working in is that of mechanics problems, which deal with idealised objects such as smooth planes, light inextensible strings, frictionless pulleys etc. The idealised nature of this domain made it feasible to consider building an expert inferential system which would be able to cope with a wide range of problems. To date, our program has tackled problems in the areas of: pulley problems, statics problems, motion on smooth complex paths and motion under constant acceleration. Our intention is to continue expanding this in order to force generality into our solutions. In recent years a lot of similar work has been in progress on Physics-type domains such as ours. (eg [13], [7], [15], [11]). We have been concerned to adopt methods developed by these workers into MECHO, and to solve mechanics problems tackled by them.

2. DESCRIPTION OF THE PROGRAM

The block diagram (fig 1) gives a very general overview of the structure of the MECHO program. Each block represents a closely related collection of Prolog clauses (procedures), the arrows between blocks indicate invocation/communication links. (For practical reasons MECHO is split into three separate modules, but this is irrelevant to the overall structure). The accompanying diagram (fig 2) tries to capture the changes in representation and the various types of knowledge required during the execution of the program. The following discussion will elaborate on these.

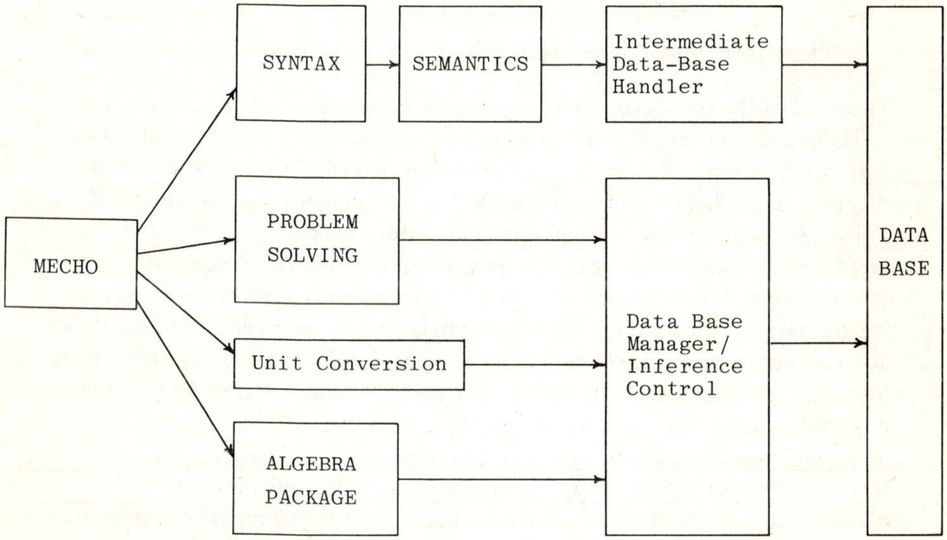

Figure 1. Program block structure

Input to the program is in the form of English text. An example taken from the area of pulley problems would be:

> 'Two particles of mass b and c are connected by a light string passing over a smooth pulley. Find the acceleration of the particle of mass b.' (Taken from [10].) (1)

The purpose of the natural language module is to produce a set of predicate calculus assertions which will enable the problem solver to solve the problem. This objective of producing a symbolic representation of the 'meaning' of the problem statement has been used by us as a vehicle for exploring syntax-semantics interaction. The syntactic parser calls semantic routines as soon as possible in order to interpret fragments of text and quickly reject inappropriate syntactic choices.

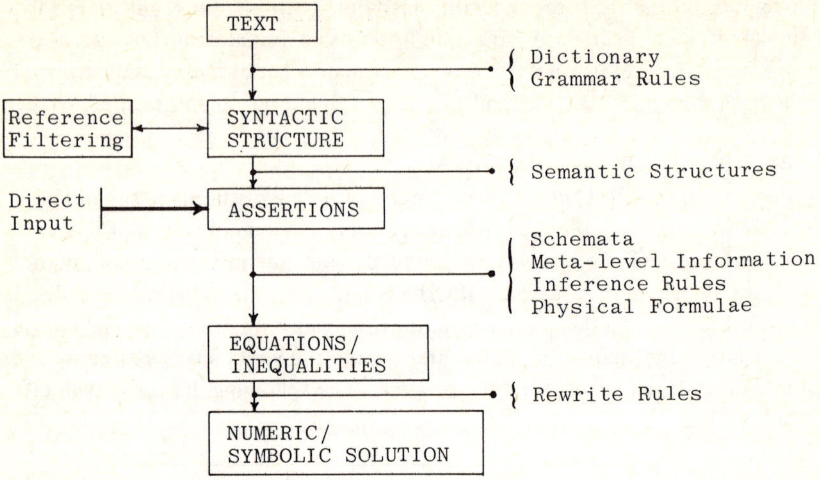

Figure 2. Representation structures

The work of the syntax routines divides into clause syntax and phrase syntax.

The purpose of syntactic analysis at the clause level is to establish clause boundaries and, within each clause, to prepare the ground for the semantic analysis of the main verb. Clause analysis thus involves identifying the start of new phrases, assigning syntactic roles to the phrases and performing phrase analysis to interpret the internal structure of the phrases. The internal phrase analysis typically returns simply a referent (and some typing information) to the higher levels. This means that preliminary reference evaluation is carried out locally, with the information conveyed by a phrase being captured in assertions produced as 'side effects' by semantic routines called during the analysis. These semantic routines are responsible for interpreting what it means for a given object to have a certain property, and indeed for checking whether or not it can have the property. Domain-specific information concerning typing, idealisation and object-property possibilities is used to answer these questions. Failure of the semantics indicates that the parse is invalid. The following (simple) example shows the kind of meta-level structures used in this process.*

meaning (light, Object, mass (Object, zero)).

type_constraint (light, physobj).

The meaning predicate states that the meaning of applying the property light to an object, is that the object has a mass of zero. type_constraint asserts that being a physical object is a necessary condition to having the property light.

* The notation used here, and in following examples, follows the Prolog convention that names starting with an upper-case letter are logical variables which are purely local to the structure (Prolog clause). Atoms, which are in lower case, and compound terms all stand for themselves. Rules are of the form 'P ← Q & R', meaning 'if Q and R then P'. Most examples have undergone slight cosmetic alteration.

It is interesting to note that the declarative assertions which give the meaning of a phrase can be specified independently of how they will be used. Meta-level information concerning the state of the analysis is used to determine whether they are used to add new information or to test necessary constraints on previous information. (This is basically the 'given'/'new' distinction discussed in [8]).

One of the aspects of natural language understanding that has interested us especially is the way in which criteria of semantic well-formedness can be used to resolve cases of ambiguity in reference evaluation. Our program incorporates a full deductive mechanism, as opposed to semantic markers, to capture the global semantic constraints that arise during the interpretation. Reference evaluation proceeds continuously during the combined syntactic and semantic analysis with semantic information being used to filter sets of possible candidates for referents. The method used to achieve this in a general way is basically that of Waltz filtering [16]. As can be seen, the referent returned by the phrase syntax is likely to be incompletely specified and for this reason all interaction between the semantics and the data-base is handled by an intermediate data-base handler which implements the inference system and reference filtering system over these referents.

The syntactic structure built by the clause syntax specifies a main verb, and positions such as 'logical subject' and 'logical object' are filled by referents. (We do not construct a complete parse tree as such). From this structure a set of assertions is generated by invoking semantic routines. The semantic analysis of the verb maps the main verb onto a base verb and establishes a mapping between the syntactic roles of the clause and the deep roles associated with the base verb. As a result the referents are fitted into conceptual slots in a way similar to conventional 'caseframe' analysis. The base verb then specifies the assertions (in terms of the referents) which follow from this mapping. Base verbs differ from case frames in that while they attempt to generalise collections of related verbs, they are not defined in terms of universal primitive roles or slots.

Given a satisfactory parse of a sentence, which produces a set of consistent assertions and disambiguates the referents, we are then able to produce a set of assertions (by instantiating out the referents) about the objects in the problem. These are supplied to the problem solving module. As an example, the assertions produced for the above problem statement (1) would be:

```
isa(period, period 1)
isa(particle,p1)
isa(particle,p2)
isa(string,s1)
isa(pulley,pull)
end(s1,end1,right)
end(s1,end2,left)
midpt(s1,midpt1)
fixed_contact(end1,p1,period1)
fixed_contact(end2,p2,period1)
fixed_contact(midpt1,pull,period1)
```

```
mass(p1,mass1,period1)
mass(p1,mass2,period1)
mass(s1,zero,period1)
coeff(pull,zero)
accel(p1,a1,270,period1)
accel(p2,a2,90,period1)
measure(mass1,b)
measure(mass2,c)
sought(a1)
given(mass1)
given(mass2)                                          (2)
```

In addition the following schema is cued:

```
cue pullsys_stan(sys1,pull,s1,p1,p2,period1)
```

The cueing of schemata is necessary to provide extra information, defaults etc. which are not given explicitly but are 'house rules' in this domain (e.g. that the pulley in a pulley system has negligible weight). We cue schemata, fairly simplistically, by recognising key words and certain object configurations. For example the following structure asserts that a pulley-system schema can be cued if objects can be found which satisfy the ideal-type constraints and have certain relationships between each other.

```
sysinfo( pullsys,
      [Pull,Str,P1,P2],
      [pulley,string,solid,solid],
      [ supports(Pull,Str),
        attached(Str,P1),
        attached(Str,P2)
      ]).
```

The effect of this cue would be to invoke a schema such as:

```
schema( pullsys,
      [Pull,Str,P1,P2], Time,
      [ constaccel(P1,Time),
        constaccel(P2,Time),
        cue stringsys(Str,[Lpart,Rpart]),
        (tension(Lpart,T1,Time)
              <- coeff(Pull,zero) &
                 tension(Rpart,T,Time) )
      ],
      [ coeff(Pull,zero),
        mass(Pull,zero,Time) ]).
```

This schema asserts that in a standard pulley problem the objects undergo constant acceleration, the tension in both parts of the string are equal if there is no friction (only one rule shown), and that the friction and mass of the pulley default to zero if not otherwise given. (This example has been somewhat simplified).

The predicate calculus notation can be used to input problems directly to the problem solver – and in fact research on the problem solver has resulted in it being able to tackle a wider range of problems than the natural language module can currently handle. The representational principles behind these assertions view the objects of Newtonian Mechanics in terms of simple zero and one dimensional objects (points and lines) which are typed and have properties and relations defined over them. For example particles, pulleys, spatial points, moments of time are all types of POINT while rods, strings, paths (trajectories), and periods of time are types of LINE. Physical quantities, such as length, velocity, force etc., form the other main branch of our type hierarchy (see [4]).

The work of the Problem Solver divides into types of task. There is the overall strategic task of deciding what to do, how to solve the problem by producing equations which solve for unknown quantities (including intermediate unknowns introduced during the solution). On the other hand there is the tactical task of combining the input assertions with general facts and inference rules in order to prove required goals. We shall discuss each of these in turn.

Our overall strategy is a general goal directed algorithm for equation extraction developed from a study by David Marples of student engineers [12]. For instance, suppose a1, the acceleration of particle p1, is the (only) sought unknown. (Here we continue the example started above (1) (2)). Resolution of forces about p1 will be chosen to solve for a1 and this produces the equation:

$$-\text{mass1.g} + \text{tension1} = \text{mass1.a1} \tag{3}$$

All possible force contributions on p1 are examined and since p1 is attached to the end of the string this results in the string being considered. tension1 was formerly unknown but the function properties of the predicate 'tension' enable it to be created (see later) to allow the equation to be formed. We have to introduce tension1 as an unknown because it is not possible to solve for a1 without doing so. The next step is to solve for tension1 which is a force and involves the string s1. Again resolution of forces is selected – p1, pull, p2 being objects on the string that are possible candidates for resolving about. p1 has been previously used and only p2 can be used without introducing unknowns. The result is the equation:

$$\text{mass2.g} - \text{tension1} = \text{mass2.a1} \tag{4}$$

These two equations can be solved to produce a solution for a1.

The input assertions provide meta-level information about whether certain quantities are sought or given. The Marples Algorithm works by traversing the list of sought unknowns in a fixed order: the (quantity) type of each unknown being used to provide a shortlist of formulae that could solve for it, and the definition of the quantity (ie the assertion which introduced it) being used to find the physical objects, times and angles involved. Notice that there is a distinction made between 'formulae', which are composed of variables over quantities (eg

'F = M * A'), and 'equations' which are instantiations of formulae (eg (3) and (4) above). In the Marples algorithm we are reasoning about the properties of formulae in order to successfully produce appropriate equations.

Before the application of a formula to produce an equation, there is a stage of qualitative analysis where general facts about the problem are used to decide applicability. Our interest here is in exploring the selective use of meta-level reasoning to guide the equation extraction process. As well as deciding applicability we have to prepare a situation within which to apply a formula. This may involve, for example, collecting together all the objects connected to a particle if we wish to resolve forces about it. General independence criteria (eg 'You can't resolve forces about the same object in linearly dependent directions') are also used to eliminate redundant equations.

The following are (simplified) examples of the meta-level structures used during the above examples:

```
kind(a1,accel,
        relaccel(p1,earth,a1,270,period1)).

relates(accel,
        [resolve,constaccel–N,relaccel]).

prepare(resolve,relaccel(P,earth,A,Dir,Time),
                situation(P,Set,Dir,Time))
     ←isa(particle,P) &
        findall(X, sameplace(X,P,Time), Set).

isform(resolve,situation(Obj,Set,Dir,Time),
               F = M * A )
     ←mass(Obj, M ,Time) &
       accel(Obj,A,Dir,Time) &
       sumforces(Obj,Set,Dir,Time, F).
```

The kind predicate asserts that a1 is a quantity of type accel defined in the given relaccel assertion. relates states that all the formulae whose names are given in the list, contain variables of type accel and therefore can be used to solve acceleration. prepare gives the criteria for constructing the situation within which to resolve forces, and the isform predicate defines the equation by defining the meaning of its component variables.

The equation extraction algorithm is two pass in that it first tries to produce a solution which does not introduce new unknowns before allowing the introduction of extra (intermediate) unknowns which are added to the unknowns list and have to be eventually solved for. Notice that the quantities manipulated are purely symbolic; they can be introduced by the creation mechanism (see later) without their values being known at this stage (e.g. when the first equation (3) was formed in the above example, the quantity tension1 was introduced without the program knowing, or trying to find, its actual value). As can be seen, it is the Marples algorithm which will eventually produce an equation which solves for tension1.

The data-base stores all the facts supplied by the English statement, but to bridge the gap between the explicit information derived from the problem statement and that needed to solve the problem the program requires a general knowledge of mechanics which is formalised in a set of inference rules. An example of such (object-level) inference rules would be:

```
relaccel(P1,P2,zero,Dir,Period)
        constrelvel(P1,P2,Period).

constrelvel(P1,P2,Period)
        fixed_contact(P1,P2,Period).
```

The first rule says that the relative acceleration between two points of reference is zero if there is a constant relative velocity between them (over a certain period), and the second rule says that two points of reference have a constant relative velocity if they are in contact (again, over a certain period). The inference rules are a set of Horn clauses which have been hand ordered and contain certain typing information to guide selection. The search strategy is depth first, with pruning of semantically meaningless goals, and while this could be improved upon, current performance has not yet necessitated such a step.

An important part of our work has been the investigation of search control mechanisms which will enable effective use of this wealth of implicit knowledge. All requests to retrieve assertions from the data-base, either directly or via inference, are handled by the inference control module. This module uses information from the request along with meta-information and inference rules in an attempt to satisfy the goal. The first step involves normalisation of the goal to remove syntactic sugar or to express it in terms of a smaller set of underlying predicates. This is performed with a one pass rewrite rule set. The resulting goal is then classified according to the instantiation state of its component arguments and the possibility of using function properties and certain other mathematical properties of the predicate (such as reflexivity, symmetry and transitivity). This information is used to select appropriate proving strategies. (A basic strategy of 'unit preference' will always first check the data-base directly).

Our two most important strategies are the use of function properties to prune search and the use of equivalence class type mechanisms to direct it. The representation treats what would normally be considered functions as predicates with extra control information. Being a function means that certain arguments are uniquely determined by certain other arguments. For example, in the predicate 'tension (String,T,Time)' the actual tension T is determined once the String and the Time have been given.

These function properties can be used to prevent useless inference if another (different) value of a function argument is already known (uniqueness property); to create new entities to satisfy a goal if all attempts at inference have failed (existence property); and to automatically eliminate backtracking by disregarding choices made during inference (uniqueness again). Examples of the meta-level structures used by the program in performing the above are:

```
rewrite( accel(P,A,Dir,Time),
         relaccel(P,earth,A,Dir,Time),
         strategy(dbinf) ).

meta( relaccel, 5,
      [P1,P2,A,Dir,Time],
      [pt_of_ref,pt_of_ref,accel,angle,time],
      function( [P1,P2,Time] => [A,Dir] ) )
```

The rewrite rule tells us that any accel predicate can be rewritten to a relaccel predicate with the earth as the other point of reference, and that the standard inference strategy is then applicable. The meta predicate specifies the argument types and the function properties of the predicate relaccel.

The second major strategy, which provides an alternative to using the inference rules, is a general similarity class mechanism based on equivalence class ideas. Predicates which are (pseudo-) equivalence relations and would normally produce self-resolving inference rules are defined in terms of this mechanism. A tree is used to represent similarity class membership and the goal (such as 'being in the same place') is proved by establishing equivalence of roots. This can be seen as an alternative (and less explosive) axiomatisation of these predicates. Our extension over traditional uses of this method has been to allow labelled arcs and calculation during the tree traversal. Thus predicates like 'vector separation' and 'relative velocity' which have pseudo-equivalence properties can also use this strategy. Here is an example of a structure used in these cases:

```
rewrite( sameplace(P,Q,Time),
         [ sameclass(P,Q,touch(Time)),
           merge(P,Q,touch(Time))      ],
         strategy(simclass)      ).
```

This states that the predicate sameplace should use the general sameclass mechanism on the particular tree touch(Time). Also specified is an updating mechanism for adding new sameplace assertions; in this case it would involve merging two separate trees.

These general strategies can be applied to a wide range of predicates and often capture important facts about the domain (eg the fact that an object cannot be in two places at once is a fact about the function properties of 'at(Object,Place, Time)'). The explicit control of new object creation coupled with the goal directed backward reasoning method of the Marples algorithm results in a create/consider -by-need type of behaviour. Restrictions, such as 'don't create' or 'don't infer', can be added to the request for a goal to be proved and this enables the Marples algorithm to be selective over its use of the Inference Control in accordance with its needs at the time.

For some mechanics problems a process of prediction is required to answer questions like 'Will the particle reach the top of the slope if it starts with velocity V ?'. Each question about the motion of a particle on a complex slope unpacks into a series of questions about the behaviour on simple parts of the slope. Some of these can be answered immediately on the basis of the qualitative shape of the slope, but others involve the solution of inequalities containing unknown quantities. These unknowns are declared as sought and the equation extraction algorithm is called to solve for them. The prediction system is special purpose and built around problems similar to those tackled by De Kleer, i.e. motion problems.

Since the equations produced by the equation extraction algorithm are in terms of symbolic quantities, there is a stage of Unit Conversion where the actual values are substituted and a final unit system is selected – conversion factors being added where appropriate. (Some problems involve a combination of all sorts of different units – feet, yards, miles ......). The two equations produced above ((3) & (4)) are very simple in that no particular units are involved. The only step will be the substitution of b and c for mass1 and mass2 respectively giving:

$$-b.g + tension1 = b.a1 \qquad (5)$$

$$c.g - tension1 = c.a1 \qquad (6)$$

The set of simultaneous equations and/or inequalities produced by the problem solving module is passed to the algebra module (PRESS) which will solve them to produce a final answer to the problem. Let us look at how PRESS produces a solution for a1 given (5) and (6). The two equations are solved by isolating tension1 in the second equation (which was intended to solve for tension1), and then using the result as a substitution into the first equation. This final result can then be simplified with a1 being isolated on the left hand side to give the final answer:

$$a1 = g.(c-b) / (c+b) \qquad (7)$$

The extension of equation solving techniques to inequalities (there are interesting connections) has enabled us to solve the inequalities produced by the prediction problems, but in addition we have found that the information required to justify the use of certain rewrite rules is often of the form ' only if $X > 0$ ' etc. Solving and proving inequalities is therefore of direct use within the system.

However, PRESS was not developed purely as a service program for MECHO. It was intended as a vehicle to explore ideas about controlling search in mathematical reasoning using meta-level descriptions and strategies [3]. Rather than using exhaustive application over a large set of rewrite rules, it uses the meta-level strategies of isolation, collection and attraction to carefully control application of several different sets of rewrite rules. This selectivity has many advantages: principled methods for guiding search cut down useless work, identical rules may be used in different ways (eg left to right or right to left) in different circumstances without causing problems, and theoretical requirements such as proof of termination of the rewrite rules are made much easier.

When PRESS is used as an equation and inequality solver (ie as a module of MECHO), it classifies the equations (inequalities) to be solved so as to generate guidance information. An exciting area of research that we would like to expand on is that of designing inclusion and ordering criteria to classify algebraic identities which are produced by a theorem power. This would enable the system to automatically learn new rules. The use of meta-level reasoning to place new rules into a framework where they will be selectively and correctly applied overcomes many of the obvious 'explosion' and 'looping' problems that would occur with haphazard additions to a large rewrite rule set.

3. DISCUSSION

Throughout the above discussion of the MECHO program we have constantly emphasised the importance of 'meta-information' in controlling search. This has been applied in the rejection of semantically meaningless parses, the control of inference, the extraction of equations and the guiding of algebraic manipulation.

The theme that has emerged from our work is the benefit to be gained from axiomatizing the meta-level of the domain under investigation and performing inference at this level, producing object level proofs as a side effect. This is the methodology investigated by Pat Hayes in the GOLUX project [9], except that we have developed our meta-level representation for a particular domain rather than adopting general purpose representations based on resolution theorem proving systems.

In [2] we showed how GPS could be viewed in this way. At the object-level the search space can be viewed as an operator/state OR tree in which the states are nodes and the operators are arcs between them. At the meta-level the search space can be viewed as a method/goal AND/OR tree in which the goals are nodes and the methods are arcs between them. A simple depth-first search at the meta-level then induces a highly complex, middle-out search at the object-level.

In order to make clear the distinction we are drawing between meta-level and object-level representations in MECHO, we shall list examples of the descriptions used at each level. When defining a notation it is usual to define the constants, variables, function symbols and predicate symbols of the language; and then to show how terms and formulae can be formed by composing them together with the logical connectives. We shall follow this type of outline in an informal fashion. (To avoid confusion with earlier terminology we shall use the words 'assertion' and 'rule' to replace 'formula').

At the object-level we have the following kinds of primitive:

constants p1, end1, mass2, a1, right, 90, 270, lbs, feet, etc.

variables P1, Str, Period, Accel, F, M, etc.

function symbols +, *, cos, etc.

predicate symbols accel, relaccel, mass, fixed_contact, etc.

These are formed into terms such as 'M * A' and assertions such as 'F = M * A', 'accel(p1,a1,270,period1)' etc. Finally, logical connectives are used to form these assertions into inference rules like:

relaccel(P1,P2,zero,Dir,Period)
    ←constrelvel(P1,P2,Period).

The only function symbols at the object-level are for straight forward arithmetic and trigonometric functions. This is because we have recorded function properties by making meta-level assertions about object-level predicates.

At the meta-level all these object-level descriptions are meta-constants along with additional meta-constants for schema names, formula names, object types, strategy types etc. As examples of meta-level primitives we have:

constants (Any object level description). physobj, pullsys, resolve, particle, line, length, dbinf etc.

variables Type, Eqn, Goal, Strategy, Expr1, etc. (see below)

function symbols Constructors for lists, sets, bags, etc.

predicate symbols meaning, sysinfo, schema, kind, relates, isform, rewrite, meta etc.

Again these can be formed into meta-terms and meta-assertions and we gave several examples during the program description. What we shall now examine are the meta-rules which are formed from these assertions. (These use the same logical connectives as the object-level rules). We shall take simplified examples from each of the four main areas of our work.

The first example is a rule used by the Natural Language module, which specifies the conditions for a property to be correctly applied to a particular entity.

```
attribute(Property,Entity,State)
  ← type_constraint(Property,Type) &
    isa(Type,Entity) &
    meaning(Property,Entity,Assertion) &
    consistent(Assertion,State).
```

This rule states that a particular Property can be attributed to an Entity in a given State (of the parse), if the Entity satisfies the type_constraint of the Property, and if the meaning of the attribution is consistent with all the other assertions in the current State. (If, for example, the Assertion was 'mass(s1,zero)' then this would involve checking that no other mass was known for s1. It is here that we see one of the key connections with our work on Problem Solving, since this is precisely a matter of 'function properties'!).

The following is an example taken from the Marples Algorithm, and it defines the requirements for an equation to solve for a particular quantity.

```
solves_for(Q,Eqn)
  ← kind(Q,Type,Defn) &
    relates(Type,F_list) &
    select(Formula,F_list) &
    prepare(Formula,Defn,Situation) &
    isform(Formula,Situation,Eqn).
```

This rule states that Eqn solves for Q if Q has type Type and Formula is a formula that relates Type quantities to other quantities, and if Situation is the situation within which to apply the Formula given the Defn of Q, and if Eqn is the instantiation of the formula in the given Situation. It can be seen that this rule is a direct axiomatisation of our earlier description of how the Marples algorithm extracts equations. (The select goal would specify the qualitative guidance and apply the independence criteria (given extra arguments)).

In a similar way we give the following example of rules which describe how the Inference Control uses function properties.

```
is_satisfied(Goal)
    ← rewrite(Goal,Newgoal,Strategy) &
      decompose(Newgoal,Pred,Args) &
      meta(Pred,N,Args,Types,Func_info) &
      method(Strategy,Func_info,Newgoal).

method( strategy(dbinf),
        function(Fargs => Vals), Newgoal)
    ← all_bound(Fargs) &
      use_function_properties(Newgoal).
```

The first rule states that Goal is satisfied if it rewrites to Newgoal whose predicate symbol has certain Func_ info, and if a method is used based on the Strategy and this Func_info. (Certain arguments to meta have been ignored). The second rule states that the normal inference method will prove Newgoal given its function properties if all the function arguments, Fargs, are bound, and if object-level inferencing is performed using function property pruning.

As a final example we take a rule concerned with algebraic equation solving. This rule is interesting in that while PRESS does not currently use it, it could be derived from rules PRESS does have. Automating this procedure would be an interesting area for study.

```
solve(U,Expr1,Ans)
    ← occ(U,Expr1,2) &
      collect(U,Expr1,Expr2) &
      isolate(U,Expr2,Ans).
```

This rule states that Ans is an equation which solves for U given Expr1 if Expr1 contains two occurrences of U, if Expr2 is an equation derived from Expr1 in which these two occurrences have been collected together, and if Ans is an equation derived from Expr2 in which U has been isolated on the left-hand side.

All the above rules can be seen as classifying object-level descriptions and using this information in deciding what to do. However the effects are very different in the different areas. In the natural language processing meta-level rules monitor object-level assertions, rejecting semantically unacceptable consequences of a parse. In equation extraction the effect is to select equations using a means/ends analysis technique. In Inference Control the result is use of the most effective axiomatisation for the goal in hand, and in Algebraic manipulation multiple rewrite rules are selectively brought to bear on expressions. Thus relatively simple meta-level search strategies can induce a wide variety of complex object-level behaviours.

These meta-inference techniques were strongly suggested by our use of the programming language Prolog. The fact that Prolog procedures are also predicate calculus clauses and the fact that predicate calculus has a clear semantics, encourages the user to attach meanings to his procedures and these meanings are usually meta-theoretic. However, Prolog as a programming language only offers a single level of 'syntactic' structures (atoms, compound terms etc.), and a lack of care can lead to a blurring of theoretical distinctions. During the development of MECHO, a lack of emphasis (realisation?) of these distinctions resulted in a mixing of object and meta levels (for example, the use of Prolog variables to represent variables at both levels, the mixing of object and meta level assertions in rules such as isform). We plan to remove these aberrations.

Weyrauch's work on the FOL system (See [17]), is of importance in relation to this need for an adequate theoretical formalism. The distinction between the object-level and the meta-level is fundamental within his system, and his use of 'reflection principles' is designed to capture the relation between these levels. We feel that his work is of direct value to workers in the field of expert systems, such as ourselves.

The principle of utilising 'knowledge about knowledge' is becoming increasingly important in practical AI programs. Davis and Buchanan [6] classified four different kinds of meta-level knowledge used by their TEIRESIAS system. They represent knowledge about objects and the data-structure used to describe them in schemata and describe the argument type characteristics of their functions in templates. Their program can classify and build models of the inference rules it uses and meta-rules are used to guide the choice of inference rules to be used and the order of using them. In MECHO, the Natural Language and Inference Control modules both use information like that stored in TEIRESIAS templates. MECHO meta-level inference rules are similar in spirit to TEIRESIAS meta-rules except that the MECHO rules are more general purpose and they generate a variety of different search strategies in different contexts.

4. CONCLUSION

In this paper we discussed MECHO, a program for solving mechanics problems. We have shown how the technique of using and controlling knowledge about the domain by inference at the meta-level, can be applied to a range of different areas. Many workers in the field (e.g. [9], [6], [17]), have argued that controlling search by using meta-level inference is superior to built-in, smart search strategies because the search information is more modular and transparant. The argument is for systems to make explicit the full knowledge involved in their behaviour, which in turn aids the modification of their data and strategies, thus improving their robustness and generality. This leads the way to systems which could automatically modify their strategies and explain their control decisions.

We conclude that meta-level inference can be used to build sophisticated and flexible strategies, which provide powerful techniques for controlling the use of knowledge, while retaining the clarity and modularity of a declarative knowledge representation.

5. REFERENCES

1. Bobrow, D. *Natural Language input for a computer solving system*. PhD thesis, MIT, 1964.
2. Bundy, A. 'Computational models for problem solving' *Learning and Problem Solving (part 3)*, The Open Univ. Press, 1978. Units 26-27 of the Open University Cognitive Psychology Course D303.
3. Bundy, A. & Welham, R. *Using Meta-level descriptions for selective application of multiple rewrite rules in algebraic manipulation.* Forthcoming working paper, Dept. of Artificial Intelligence, Edinburgh, 1979.
4. Bundy, A., Byrd, L., Luger, G., Mellish, C., Milne, R. and Palmer, M. *Mecho: A program to solve Mechanics problems*. Working Paper No. 50, Dept. of Artificial Intelligence, Edinburgh, 1979.
5. Charniak, E. *Computer solution of calculus word problems*, pages 303-316. IJCAI, 1969.
6. Davis, R. & Buchanan, B.G. *Meta-level knowledge: overview and applications,* pages 920-927. IJCAI, 1977.
7. De Kleer, J. *Qualitative and quantitative knowledge in classical mechanics.* Technical Report AI-TR-352, MIT AI Lab, 1975.
8. Haviland, S.E. & Clark, H.H., What's new? Acquiring new information as a process in comprehension. *Journal of Verbal Learning and Verbal Behaviour* 13:512-521, 1974.
9. Hayes, P. *Computation and deduction*. Czech. Academy of Sciences, 1973.
10. Humphrey, D. *Intermediate Mechanics, Dynamics*. Longman, Green & Co., London, 1957.
11. Larkin, J. *Problem solving in Physics*. Technical Report, Group in Science and Mathematics Education, Berkeley, California, 1977.
12. Marples, D. *Argument and technique in the solution of problems in Mechanics and Electricity*. Technical Report CUED/C-Educ/TRI, Dept. of Engineering, Cambridge, England, 1974.
13. Novak, G. *Computer understanding of Physics problems stated in Natural Language*. Technical Report TR NL30, Dept. Computer Science, Univ. of Texas, Austin, 1976.
14. Pereira, L.M., Pereira, F.C.N. and Warren, D.H.D. *User's guide to DEC-system-10 PROLOG*. Technical Report, DAI, 1978.
15. Stallman, R.M. & Sussman, G.J. *Forward reasoning and dependency-directed backtracking in a system for computer-aided circuit analysis*. Technical Report No. 380, MIT AI Lab, 1976.
16. Waltz, D. *Generating semantic descriptions from drawings of scenes with shadows.* Technical Report MAC AI-TR-271, MIT AI Lab, 1972.
17. Weyhrauch, R.W. *Prolegomena to a theory of mechanized formal reasoning.* RWW Informal Note 8, Stanford University, 1979.
18. Winograd, T. *Understanding Natural Language*, Edinburgh University Press, 1972.

CONGEN: AN EXPERT SYSTEM AIDING THE STRUCTURAL CHEMIST

Raymond E. Carhart

ABSTRACT

CONGEN (for CONstrained GENerator) is a complex symbol-manipulation program for the construction of chemical structures. Its input consists of a molecular formula (i.e., a list of atoms to be used as building blocks) together with restrictions ('constraints') on the possible interconnections among the atoms. Using a variety of sophisticated graph-theoretic algorithms, CONGEN finds all possible ways of assembling the atoms into molecular structures which satisfy the specified constraints.

In an interactive session with CONGEN, the chemist supplies the molecular formula together with structural information, in the form of required and forbidden substructures, which he has inferred from physical measurements (e.g., spectra, chemical reactivity) on a compound whose structure is not known. The result of a CONGEN session, presented as a set of easily interpreted structural drawings, is an exhaustive list of candidate structures which are consistent with his analysis. This result may serve one of three purposes: It may verify the chemist's intuition about the identity of the compound by guaranteeing that no plausible alternatives have been overlooked; it may suggest reasonable alternatives to a particular structure the chemist had in mind; or it may suggest to the chemist some further experiment which would help to discriminate among the remaining possibilities.

Aside from a description of CONGEN and some examples of its contributions to structure analysis, our discussion will focus upon two issues which are important in any application of expert systems. One relates to the amount of human engineering needed to overcome the psychological barriers to the use of complex computer programs. This issue encompasses the design not only of a smooth and helpful user-interface, but also of basic algorithms to reformulate the user's input. There are often several alternative ways of expressing a problem to a complex expert system, and what seems to the user to be a perfectly logical statement of the problem may be far from optimum from the program's standpoint. The other issue involves the choice between different representations of the 'expert knowledge' contained in the system: What parts of the knowledge should be 'hand coded' into the system as highly efficient, special-purpose algorithms, and what parts should be left in a more flexible, external form?

BASIC CONGEN CONCEPTS

The CONGEN program (CONstrained structure GENerator) is designed to aid the structural chemist in arriving at a set of possible structures ('candidates') for an unknown compound based upon the chemist's analysis of spectroscopic and chemical data. It is assumed that through this analysis the chemist has determined the molecular formula and has drawn a number of conclusions about the presence or absence of substructural features in the unknown molecule. The assistance provided by CONGEN is to discover all ways of combining the atoms of the molecular formula into complete chemical structures which are consistent with these conclusions. We refer to these conclusions as *constraints* because within the program they serve to restrict, or constrain, the generator to produce (usually) only a tiny fraction of the vast number of structural isomers which could possibly be built from the atoms of the molecular formula.

Constraints are of two general types, for which we use the terms *required* and *forbidden*. Required constraints are features which are believed to be present in the unknown structure, and which thus are required to be present in the generated candidates. For example, the data may indicate the presence of certain well-characterized functional groupings such as amides or phenyl rings, or a sequence of spin-decoupling NMR experiments may have allowed the chemist to 'map out' the detailed structure of one or more portions of the unknown. Forbidden constraints are features whose presence can be ruled out on the basis of either the data or general considerations of chemical stability. For example, spectra obtained from the unknown may lack certain characteristic features which would have been present if certain functional groups such as ketones or cyclopropyl rings occurred in the molecule. Also, CONGEN does not have a built-in sense of chemical stability, and will produce highly strained ring systems and other unstable groupings such as cyclobutadienes and peroxides unless these possibilities are expressly ruled out. It may seem that the number of these unstable substructures could be enormous, but for any given CONGEN problem, it is usually necessary to specify only a few which might arise when all other constraints are satisfied.

Of course, there must be some way for the chemist to communicate to the program the constraints which are applicable to his particular problem. Standard chemical nomenclature provides a means of expressing some features, but it is usually not precise enough or unambiguous enough to allow the chemist to express especially complex or subtle pieces of structural information. Thus, while a 'library' is provided of terms describing common functional groups, it is necessary also to provide a more general method of defining terms to be used in a particular CONGEN problem. The EDITSTRUC subprogram supplies this extended language, in which the chemist can build substructures of arbitrary complexity and associate with them names of his own choosing. In EDITSTRUC, commands are available to construct rings and chains of atoms, to join them together in any chosen fashion, to define bond multiplicities and to associate properties with atoms such as atom name, number of hydrogen atoms and aromaticity. The library of terms is simply a file of commonly used EDITSTRUC structures, with chemically meaningful names like METHYL and HYDROXYL.

In order to communicate his problem to CONGEN, the chemist in principle needs only a means of defining the molecular formula, a means of defining terms not contained in the library and a means of specifying which substructures are required constraints and which are forbidden constraints. However, because of the way in which CONGEN approaches the structure generation problem, there are some additional and somewhat artificial concepts which need to be learned if the user is to make efficient use of the program. The central new concept is that of a *superatom*, which is a polyatomic fragment (*e.g.,* a benzene ring) which is used as a 'building block' in much the same way as are atoms. The advantage of using superatoms for structure generation is easily understood; if a given substructure is known to be present, it is much more efficient to use that substructure as a building block, incorporating it *a priori* into the structures, rather than to generate using only the molecular formula, constantly testing the resulting structures for the presence of the desired substructure. Superatoms are conceptually quite close to required constraints, with the exception that superatoms are not allowed to overlap one another while required constraints may overlap arbitrarily. For example, Naphthalene cannot be built from two benzene-ring superatoms, but it would survive a test requiring the presence of two benzene-ring substructures. Part of the current DENDRAL research is devoted to exploring ways of removing this distinction between superatoms and required constraints without giving up the efficiencies provided by the superatom concept.

A further artificiality is introduced by the specific way in which CONGEN deals with superatoms. The structure-generation algorithm is not capable of dealing directly with these polyatomic fragments, but can only construct structures out of single 'atoms' of specified valences. What actually happens, then, is that the superatoms are initially 'collapsed' and considered to be just single atoms, with 'atom names' supplied by the user and with 'valences' equal to the sum of all the available bonding sites in the fragment. For example, suppose the chemist has used EDITSTRUC to define the term R6 to be a cyclohexane ring with twelve valences left 'free' to bond to other atoms. If R6 is then specified as a superatom, CONGEN will initially take R6 to be a single atom of valence twelve. If the molecular formula were C 8 H 16 in this case, there would also be two carbons and 16 hydrogens to be combined with R6. Only two structures,

```
C–R6–C          R6–C–C
  1               2
```

1 and 2, would result from this generation. (Note that the hydrogen atoms are 'suppressed' in these drawing; the number of hydrogens on an atom is inferred from its valence together with the number of neighbours shown in the drawing.) Now, structure 2 represents only one molecule, ethylcyclohexane, because there is only one way to place an ethyl group on the six-membered ring. However, 1 really represents four structural isomers because the methyl groups may be attached around the ring to give 1, 1–, 1,2–, 1,3– or 1,4–dimethylcyclohexane. Before the structure generation problem is finished, of course, the superatoms must be re-expanded, and there is a special process called *imbedding* to accomplish this. The imbedder accepts structures such as 1 and 2 and determines all unique ways in which this re-expansion can take place. In this simple example, we have used only one superatom, but the typical CONGEN problem has several.

Structures which contain unimbedded superatoms are called *intermediate structures,* as opposed to *final structures* in which all superatoms have been expanded.

It would be possible for CONGEN to carry out these imbeddings automatically so that the user was never aware that a separate procedure was being invoked. But intermediate structures usually contain a great deal of chemically meaningful information, and it is usually possible to phrase constraints which can be applied to these structures even before the imbeddings are done. Suppose, for example, that the chemist has defined one term BZ to represent a benzene ring and another term KET to represent a ketone (C = O) functionality, and has specified these to be superatoms. If he also has information, say from a UV spectrum, telling him whether or not the ketone is conjugated with the benzene ring, he may be able to say something about the presence or absence of the 'substructure' BZ-KET in intermediate structures. For this example, as for most CONGEN problems, it is very useful to give the user access to the intermediate structures and to allow him control over imbedding process (*i.e.,* the decision of which superatoms are to be imbedded at which points in the session). In this way, the user is given many opportunities during the session to examine, and perhaps further constrain, the generation problem. But with this greater flexibility comes an increased responsibility to consider carefully the precise phrasing of constraints, keeping in mind that when CONGEN applies these constraints to intermediate structures, it 'thinks' the superatoms are just ordinary atoms with odd names and peculiar valences. For example, in the BZ-KET case above, the user might wish to specify that the ketone is in fact conjugated with the benzene ring. The temptation is to phrase this constraint as the required substructure $C' - C = 0$ (where C' here represents an aromatic carbon atom). Although this is the appropriate phrasing of the constraint for final structures, it will not accomplish the desired effect for the intermediate structures in which C' is 'hidden' within BZ and C = 0 is 'hidden' within KET. The appropriate phrasing is to require the presence of the two-atom substructure BZ-KET in the intermediate structures. Thus, when applied to intermediate structures, constraints must usually be translated to account for the fact that many details of the structures are hidden within the superatoms, and will not be directly accessible until the superatoms are imbedded.

There are two somewhat unexpected features of intermediate structures which deserve special mention. First, a multiple bond which appears in such a structure does not necessarily represent a 'real' multiple bond. Consider, for example, the superatom R6 (mentioned above – a cyclohexane ring with twelve free valences) in a generation problem for which the molecular formula is C 8 H 14. One possible intermediate structure is 3, in which the 'double bond' C = R6 appears.

```
C=R6-C
```

3

This should be interpreted as meaning that there are two bonds from that carbon to atoms within R6, but that the two bonds may or may not be 'split apart' into two single bonds. If given structure 3, the imbedder would produce twelve final structures some of which would contain multiple bonds (for example, 4 and 5) and some of which would not (for example, 6 and 7).

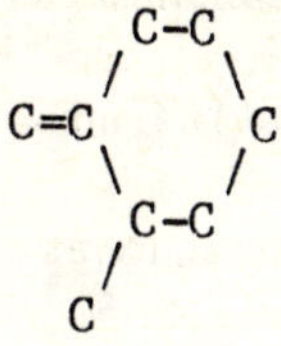
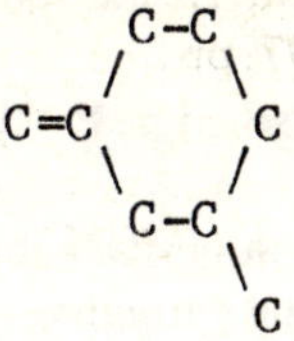
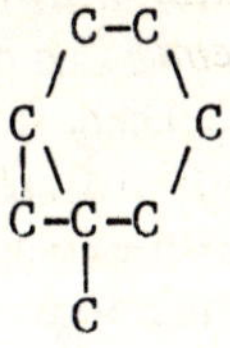
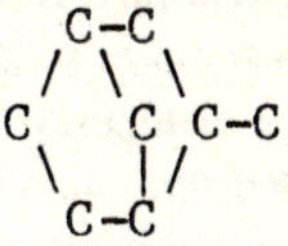

4 5 6 7

If the chemist knew that there were no double bonds in his unknown, he might think that 3 should be eliminated as an intermediate structure, but clearly it should not be. The appropriate time for testing for multiple bonds is during (or after) the imbedding of R6 in this case.

A second feature of intermediate structures is even more unusual: there may be bonds which connect a superatom with itself. These self-bonds are called *internal bonds* or *loops* and have no counterpart in final structures. An internal bond in a superatom is interpreted as a bond which directly interconnects two free valences within the superatom. For example, the intermediate structure 8,

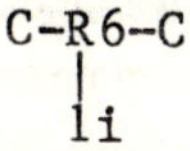

8

in which the symbol 'li' stands for 'one internal bond', is one which would be produced by the generator from the molecular formula C 8 H 14 and the superatom R6. This structure is interpreted to mean that there are two methyl groups attached to R6 and that in addition there is a bond connecting two of the free valences within R6. The imbedder recognizes these loops, and part of its task is to find all unique ways of forming such interconnections while imbedding the superatom. Among the structures produced by the imbedder from structure 8 would be structures 9-11.

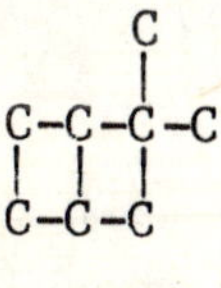
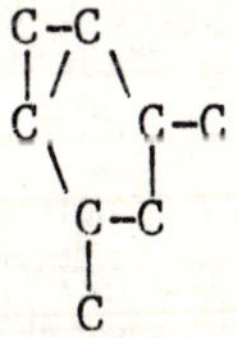
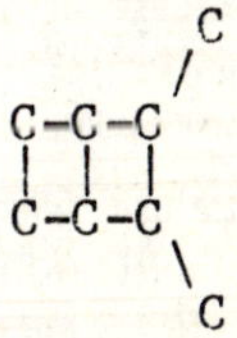

9 10 11

In some cases the chemist has information which restricts the possible distributions of loops, and there is a special type of constraint for expressing restrictions of this kind.

To the chemist who is interested in experimenting with the CONGEN program, the concepts outlined above must be well understood. The interested reader who wishes to get a better understanding of the concepts and see their application to sample problems is referred to the following publications:

1) R.E. Carhart, D.H. Smith, H. Brown and C. Djerassi, *Journal of the American Chemical Society*, vol. 97, pp 5755-5762 (1975).

2) C.J. Cheer, D.H. Smith, C. Djerassi, B. Tursch, J.C. Braekman and D. Daloze, *Tetrahedron*, vol. 32, pp 1807-1810 (1976).

These publications deal with an older version of CONGEN but the concepts and procedures are quite similar to those of the current version.

SAMPLE CONGEN SESSION

The following is an annotated typescript of a CONGEN session which parallels the structure elucidation problem described by Cheer, *et. al* (C.J. Cheer, D.H. Smith, C. Djerassi, B. Tursch, J.C. Braekman and D. Daloze, *Tetrahedron*, vol. 32, pp 1807-1810 [1976] of [+] –Palustrol. Much of the typescript consists of messages printed by the program for the user's information, and only a small fraction is typed by the user himself. To help distinguish the latter from the former, the user's input has been underlined. At the end of each line of information provided by the user, he has also typed a carriage-return which is not explicitly represented but which is needed before the program begins its interpretation of the typed instructions on that line. Annotations are offset from the left margin and are written primarily in lower case type.

First, the user starts CONGEN. The program types # indicating its readiness to accept commands. The user types ? to see a summary of his options.

```
@CONGEN
#?
GENERATE IMBED PRUNE DRAW DEFINE FIX SHOW
FORGET SEARCH SAVE RESTORE EXIT SURVEY STEREO
```

A CONGEN session typically begins with a definition of the molecular formula. Here, the user types ? to see an explanation of what input is expected.

```
#DEFINE
DEFINITION TYPE:?
ATOM SUBSTRUCTURE AROMATICS MOLFORM TERMTYPE
DEFINITION TYPE:MOLFORM
MOLECULAR FORMULA:?
A LIST OF ATOM NAMES AND QUANTITIES (ONES MAY BE OMITTED), SEPARATED
BY BLANKS OR COMMAS (E.G., C 4 H 5 BR)
MOLECULAR FORMULA:C 15 H 26 O
MOLECULAR FORMULA DEFINED
```

Now the user wishes to define the substructures which will be needed later on, starting with a substructure called (arbitrarily) A which will be a superatom, one of the inferred substructures of the unknown compound. Note that the user anticipates the prompt 'DEFINITION TYPE:' and includes the response 'SUBSTRUCTURE' as part of the DEFINE command. Seeing that the information has already been supplied, CONGEN does not type out that prompt. All commands can be extended in this way, e.g., DEFINE SUBSTRUCTURE A will obviate any additional prompts. Unambiguous short forms of keywords such as DEFINE also work, e.g., DE S A.

```
#DEFINE SUBSTRUCTURE
NAME:?
A NAME (OTHER THAN X OR H) WHICH HAS
NOT PREVIOUSLY BEEN DEFINED
NAME:A
(NEW SUBSTRUCTURE)
```

The > prompt indicates that the structure editor EDITSTRUC is ready to accept commands. After looking at the options, the user begins by building a ring of three carbon atoms, drawing it in numbered form, placing a one-carbon branch onto atom 1 and drawing again. Extensions and short forms work here also, e.g., RING 3, DRAW N.

```
>?
CHAIN  RING   BRANCH LINK   JOIN   BORD
ATNAME HRANGE FREEV  TAG    LNODE
UNJOIN ERASE  SHOW   DRAW   DONE   HALT
>RING
RING SIZE:?
AN INTEGER GREATER THAN ZERO
RING SIZE:3
>DRAW
TYPE OF DRAWING:?
NUMBERED ATNAMED
TYPE OF DRAWING:NUMBERED

SUBSTRUCTURE A:

2-3
 \|
  1

>BRANCH
FROM ATOM:1
LENGTH OF BRANCH:1
>DRAW NUMBERED

SUBSTRUCTURE A:

4-1-3
   \|
    2
```

The user is now familiar with the BRANCH command and 'types ahead' the responses to its prompts. In the second BRANCH command below, he supplies two sets of responses to these prompts on the same line. EDITSTRUC will interpret 'BRANCH 2 1 3 1' as two separate commands, 'BRANCH 2 1' followed by 'BRANCH 3 1'. All EDITSTRUC commands may be given multiple sets of responses in this fashion.

```
>BRANCH 1 1
>BRANCH 2 1 3 1
>DRAW NUMBERED

SUBSTRUCTURE A:

4     7
 \   /
  1-3
 / \|
5   2
     \
      6
```

The HRANGE command is used to associate with each atom the appropriate number of hydrogens. In this case, the number is known precisely for each atom, but in general any range consistent with the valences of the atom may be used.

```
>HRANGE
ATOM:4
MINIMUM NUMBER OF H'S:3
MAXIMUM NUMBER OF H'S:3
>HRANGE 5 3 3 6 1 1 7 2 2 2 1 1 3 1 1 1 0 0
>DRAW ATNAMED

SUBSTRUCTURE A:(HRANGES NOT INDICATED)

C     C
 \   /
  C-C
 / \|
C   C
     \
      C
```

The drawings do not show HRANGE values, but the SHOW command presents all information about the structure in tabular form.

```
>SHOW
SUBSTRUCTURE A
ATOM# TYPE NEIGHBORS      HRANGE
  1     C      5  4  3  2  0-0
  2     C      6  3  1     1-1
  3     C      7  1  2     1-1
  4     C      1           3-3
  5     C      1           3-3
  6     C      2           1-1
  7     C      3           2-2
```

Note that two valences on atom 6, and one on atom 7, have been left 'free'; the sum of all neighbors (including hydrogen atoms) is less than the valence on each of these atoms. Because A is not a complete structure, but only a piece of a structure, such free valences are needed by CONGEN to identify the sites in the substructure which are available for forming additional bonds to other parts of completed structures. The HRANGE on each of these atoms has been specified with the maximum number of hydrogens equal to the minimum number, so none of the free valences in A will be allowed to bond to hydrogen. There is an alternative and sometimes simpler way of specifying free valences using the FREEV command. Instead of the above HRANGE commands, the user could have used the command 'FREEV 6 2 7 1' and the substructure would have had the same meaning. However, there are several rules (see the definition of substructure HEP, below) concerning the interpretation definition of substructure FREEV which need to be kept in mind. HRANGE is the simpler and more general command, though it is sometimes more cumbersome than FREEV.

Satisfied that the substructure is accurately defined, the user leaves EDITSTRUC with the DONE command. Following this, he defines other terms B, ETH, CH3, CH2 and CH, all of which will be used as superatoms.

```
>DONE
A DEFINED
#DEFINE SUBSTRUCTURE B
(NEW SUBSTRUCTURE)
>CHAIN
CHAIN LENGTH:2
>ATNAME
ATOM:1
ATOM NAME:O
>HRANGE 1 1 1 2 0 0
>DRAW ATNAMED

SUBSTRUCTURE B:(HRANGES NOT INDICATED)

O-C
```

```
>SHOW
SUBSTRUCTURE B
ATOM# TYPE NEIGHBORS HRANGE
  1     O     2        1-1
  2     C     1        0-0
>DONE
B DEFINED
#DEFINE SUBSTRUCTURE ETH
(NEW SUBSTRUCTURE)
>CHAIN 2
>HRANGE 1 3 3 2 1 1
>DONE
ETH DEFINED
```

The user also wants to specify methyl, methylene and methine groups as super-atoms. Suspecting that these common groups are contained in the general library (GENLIB), he SHOWs the contents of that library. Note that there are many synonymous entries (e.g., ETHYL, ET and C2H5) in the library. Seeing the desired terms CH, CH2 and CH3 he retrieves their definitions with SEARCH. The effect is exactly the same as if he had DEFINEd these substructures.

```
#SHOW LIBRARY GENLIB
THAT LIBRARY CONTAINS THE FOLLOWING SUBSTRUCTURES:
METHYL ME MET CH3 ETHYL ET C2H5 PROPYL PRO PR ISOPROPYL I-PROPYL IPR C1
C2 CH2 C3 CH C4 PRIMARYC SECONDARYC TERTIARYC QUATERNARYC HO OH HYDROXY
HYDROXYL SH THIO THIOL NH2 N1 PRIMARYN NH N2 SECONDARYN N3 TERTIARYN
PRIMARYOH SECONDARYOH TERTIARYOH KET KETO CO ALD PHENYL BENZYL PH
PRIMARYCH3 SECONDARYCH3 TERTIARYCH3 METHYLENE METHINE C=C DB H2C=C CH2=C
CH2=CH CH=CH
#SEARCH GENLIB CH CH2 CH3
CH, CH2 AND CH3 DEFINED
```

The user now defines substructure MET, which will be used as a forbidden substructure during the structure generation. Notice the way the user 'steps through' the prompts of the ATNAME command when specifying the 'polyname' (CH2 B ETH).

```
#DEFINE SUBSTRUCTURE MET
(NEW SUBSTRUCTURE)
>CHAIN 2
>ATNAME 1
ATOM NAME:?
AN ATOM NAME, OR A LEFT PARENTHESIS TO BEGIN A POLYNAME
ATOM NAME:(
(POLY)ATOM NAME:CH2
(POLY)ATOM NAME:B
(POLY)ATOM NAME:EHT
(POLY)ATOM NAME:?
AN ATOM NAME, OR A RIGHT PARENTHESIS OR CARRIAGE RETURN
TO INDICATE THAT THE POLYNAME IS COMPLETE
(POLY)ATOM NAME:)
>SHOW
SUBSTRUCTURE MET
ATOM# TYPE NEIGHBORS POLYNAME
  1   POLY    2          (CH2 B EHT)
  2     C     1
```

Seeing that he has made an error (by typing EHT instead of ETH), the user erases the name and specifies it again. This time, he is familiar with the ATNAME prompts and supplies all the information as the single 'name' (CH2 B ETH).

```
>ERASE
WHAT TO ERASE:?
ATNAME HRANGE FREEV TAG LNODE ATOM
WHAT TO ERASE:ATNAME
WHICH ATOM?:1
>ATNAME 1 (CH2 B ETH) 2 CH3
>SHOW
SUBSTRUCTURE MET
ATOM# TYPE NEIGHBORS POLYNAME
```

```
  1  POLY   2        (CH2 B ETH)
  2  CH3    1
>DONE
MET DEFINED
```

All terms needed for structure generation are now defined, and the user issues the GENERATE command. CONGEN first requests information about superatoms, then requests constraints.

```
#GENERATE
SUPERATOM:A
RANGE OF OCCURRENCES:1
I WAS EXPECTING A WORD
RANGE OF OCCURRENCES:?
PLEASE GIVE ME A RANGE IN ONE OF THE FOLLOWING FORMS:
AT LEAST X      EXACTLY X      RANGE X TO Y
WHERE X AND Y ARE POSITIVE INTEGERS (LESS THAN 100) WHICH YOU SUPPLY
THE WORDS 'AT' AND 'TO' ARE OPTIONAL
RANGE OF OCCURRENCES:AT LEAST 1
```

The response 'AT LEAST n' here will cause Congen to include n superatoms of the specified type in the intermediate structure, but will not prohibit the construction of additional substructures of that type. For example, if CH3 is used as a superatom and there are three hydrogens and one carbon available during generation, the 'AT LEAST n' option would allow the construction of structures in which these atoms were combined into an additional methyl group (note, however, that any extra methyl groups produced in this way would appear in the intermediate structures as primary carbon atoms –C, not as superatoms –CH3). The 'EXACTLY n' option is similar, but prohibits such extra copies from being constructed. The 'Range m TO n' option causes the program to use m superatoms of the specified type, and to test that at most (n-m) additional copies of that superatom are built from other atoms during generation (not frequently used). The choice among 'AT LEAST', 'EXACTLY' and 'RANGE' depends on the precision with which the number of a given substructure can be determined from the available data. Unless there is specific information which places an upper limit on this number, the 'AT LEAST n' option should be used. In the user's responses below, the comma is used for readability and is interpreted as a space.

```
SUPERATOM:B, EXACTLY 1
SUPERATOM:CH3, EXACTLY 1
SUPERATOM:CH2, EXACTLY 3
SUPERATOM:CH, EXACTLY 1
SUPERATOM:ETH, AT LEAST 1
SUPERATOM:
```

When he has specified all of his superatoms, the user types just a carriage return to the 'SUPERATOM:' prompt, telling CONGEN that there are no more. The program reports the collapsed formula (i.e., the formula which the intermediate structures will have) and then requests the constraints.

```
'COLLAPSED' FORMULA IS A 1 B 1 CH3 1 CH2 3 CH 1 ETH 1
CONSTRAINT:?
FIRST, I NEED TO KNOW THE CONSTRAINT TYPE, ONE OF THE FOLLOWING:
SUBSTRUCTURE PROTON RING LOOP
CONSTRAINT:SUBSTRUCTURE
SUBSTRUCTURE NAME:MET
RANGE OF OCCURRENCES:?
PLEASE GIVE ME A RANGE IN ONE OF THE FOLLOWING FORMS:
NONE     AT LEAST X     AT MOST X     EXACTLY X     RANGE X TO Y
WHERE X AND Y ARE POSITIVE INTEGERS (LESS THAN 100) WHICH YOU SUPPLY
THE WORDS 'AT' AND 'TO' ARE OPTIONAL
RANGE OF OCCURRENCES:NONE
```

Note that there are several ways of specifying the quantity here. The options have their usual English meanings; 'NONE' means that the feature is to be completely avoided, 'RANGE m TO n' means that every intermediate structure is to contain not less than m nor more than n occurrences of the feature, and the other options have the obvious meanings.

```
CONSTRAINT:RING
RING SIZE:2
RANGE OF OCCURRENCES:NONE
CONSTRAINT:RING 3, EXACTLY 1
```

The RING constraints are expressed in terms of final structures, not intermediate structures. CONGEN does the constraint translation internally to find the correct expression of these constraints when applied to intermediate structures. One of our goals is to extend this automatic constraint translation to the SUBSTRUCTURE constraints, but at present that remains an unsolved problem. Note that the 'ring size' 2 is a generic way of referring to multiple bonds; each multiple bond in a final structure counts as one 'two-membered ring' regardless of its multiplicity.

```
CONSTRAINT:LOOP
SUPERATOM:A
RANGE OF OCCURRENCES:NONE
```

The LOOP constraint allows the user to restrict the number of internal bonds which CONGEN allocates to each superatom (these are represented as 'loops' – bonds which interconnect a superatom with itself – in intermediate structures, hence the name LOOP). In this case it is possible to interconnect atoms 6 and 7 of superatom A with an internal bond (see above), but the user does not want to consider those possibilities.

```
CONSTRAINT:
```

Again, a simple carriage return typed at this point informs CONGEN that there are no further constraints. The structure generation commences at this point, and the program prints one dot ('.') each time it has built an additional structure. Approximately every two minutes (if the structure generation takes that long) CONGEN will issue a report of the number of structures obtained so far, and a rough (!) estimate of the percentage completion of the problem.

```
..................................................................
..................................................................
...............................
177 STRUCTURES WERE GENERATED
```

The user now draws some of the structures to see if he has overlooked some important constraints. Some of the drawings are presented in an unusually large format to prevent crowding of the three-character atom names. The drawing portion of the program is limited to three characters at most for each atom – any superatom names longer than this will appear truncated to the first three characters.

```
#DRAW
TYPE OF DRAWING:?
NUMBERED ATNAMED
TYPE OF DRAWING:ATNAMED
ITEMS TO BE DRAWN:?
PLEASE TYPE ONE OR MORE ENTRIES IN ANY OF THE FOLLOWING FORMS:
    THE NAME OF A DEFINED SUBSTRUCTURE
OR: AN INTEGER N, INDICATING THE NTH STRUCTURE IN YOUR CURRENT LIST
OR: A PAIR OF INTEGERS IN PARENTHESES, E.G. (1 10); (M N) INDICATES A
    RANGE OF THE MTH THROUGH THE NTH STRUCTURES IN YOUR CURRENT LIST
OR: A # FOLLOWED BY AN INTEGER (E.G. #3) INDICATING THE STRUCTURE WHICH
    IS 'ATTACHED' TO THE INDEX N (THIS INDEX IS PRINTED IN DRAWINGS)
OR: A PAIR (#M #N) INDICATING A THE RANGE OF STRUCTURES ASSOCIATED WITH
    INDICES M THROUGH N
ITEMS TO BE DRAWN:(2 4) 7

#2:

              CH2---CH----CH2
              /     /      |
             /     /       |
            /     /        |
           /     /         |
CH3----A-----B            CH2
              \            /
               \          /
                \        /
                 \      /
                   ETH

#3:

              CH2----A----CH2
              /     /      |
             /     /       |
            /     /        |
           /     /         |
CH3---CH-----B            CH2
              \            /
               \          /
                \        /
                 \      /
                   ETH

#4:
     C
 B=A-H
 |   2\  C
ETH   CH-H
 \C C/   3
  H-H
  2 2

#7:

CH2----A-===-B
 |            \
 |             \
 |              \
 |               \
ETH              CH----CH3
  \              /
   \            /
    \          /
     \        /
      CH2---CH2
```

At this point the user chooses to imbed the methyl, methylene and methine superatoms. These are especially simple imbeddings, one-for-one substitutions of atoms C for superatoms CH3, CH2 and CH, and the overall number of structures does not change. Because no new chemical features will be introduced during these imbeddings, it is not necessary for the user to specify any constraints. As CONGEN begins to consider each starting structure, it prints a '#' mark, and for each new structure produced, it prints a '.' mark.

```
#IMBED
SUPERATOM:CH3
NUMBER TO BE IMBEDDED:1
SUPERATOM:CH2
NUMBER TO BE IMBEDDED:3
SUPERATOM:CH
NUMBER TO BE IMBEDDED:1
SUPERATOM:
THE 'EXPANDED' FORMULA IS C 5 A 1 B 1 ETH 1 H 10
CONSTRAINT:
#.#.#.#.#.#.#.#.#.#.#.#.#.#.#.#.#.#.#.#.#.#.#.#.#.#.#.#.#.#.#.#.#.#.#.#.
#.#.#.#.#.#.#.#.#.#.#.#.#.#.#.#.#.#.#.#.#.#.#.#.#.#.#.#.#.#.#.#.#.#.#.#.
#.#.#.#.#.#.#.#.#.#.#.#.#.#.#.#.#.#.#.#.#.#.#.#.#.#.#.#.#.#.#.#.#.#.#.#.
#.#.#.#.#.#.#.#.#.#.#.#.#.#.#.#.#.#.#.#.#.#.#.#.#.#.#.#.#.#.#.#.#.#.#.#.
#.#.#.#.#.#.#.#.#.#.#.#.#.#.#.#.#.#.#.#.#.#.#.#.#.#.#.#.#.#.#.#.#.
TRANSFERRING STRUCTURES TO FILE...
177 STRUCTURES WERE OBTAINED
```

Now ETH and B will be imbedded. Again, the result is a one-for-one substitution of substructures for superatoms, because each superatom has only one atom to which bonds may be formed. Again, no constraints are needed. The number of structures decreases during this imbedding because some previously unrecognized duplication (e.g., structures 4 and 7 in the above drawings) is perceived once all CH, CH3 and ETH superatoms have been imbedded. The program indicates these duplicates by printing a 'D' mark rather than a '.' mark for each redundant structure, then discarding the duplicate rather than including it in the list of structures.

```
#IMBED
SUPERATOM:ETH
NUMBER TO BE IMBEDDED:1
SUPERATOM:B
NUMBER TO BE IMBEDDED:1
SUPERATOM:
THE 'EXPANDED' FORMULA IS O 1 C 8 A 1 H 15
CONSTRAINT:
#.#.#.#.#.#.#D#.#.#D#D#.#.#.#.#.#.#.#.#.#D#.#.#D#D#.#.#.#.#.#.#.#.#D#.#.
#.#D#D#D#D#.#.#.#.#.#.#D#D#.#.#.#.#D#D#D#.#D#D#.#.#.#.#.#.#.#D#.#.#.#.#.
#.#.#D#D#.#.#.#D#.#D#.#.#D#D#D#.#.#D#D#.#.#.#.#.#D#.#.#D#.#.#.#.#.#.#.#.
#.#.#D#.#.#.#.#.#D#.#D#.#.#D#D#D#.#D#.#D#.#.#.#.#D#.#.#.#.#D#.#.#.#.#.#.
#.#.#D#D#.#.#.#D#.#D#.#D#D#.#.#.#D#D#D#.#.#.#.#.#.#D#.#.#.#D#D#.#D
TRANSFERRING STRUCTURES TO FILE...
124 STRUCTURES WERE OBTAINED
```

Finally, A is imbedded. This is a more complex imbedding because there are several (up to three) ways of permuting the attachments to the 'atom' A among the free valences in the substructure A. Also, this imbedding may introduce new double bonds or three-membered rings. For example, in structure #4 in the drawings above the 'double bond' B=A can be expanded during the imbedding of A to form either a double bond or a five-membered ring. Because of this, it is necessary to specify the ring-size constraints once again.

```
#IMBED
SUPERATOM:A
NUMBER TO BE IMBEDDED:1
SUPERATOM:
THE 'EXPANDED' FORMULA IS O 1 C 15 H 26
CONSTRAINT:RING 2, NONE
CONSTRAINT:RING 3, EXACTLY 1
CONSTRAINT:
#.#...#...#.#.#.#...#.#...#.#.#...#.#..#.#..#.#.#..#..#.#..#.#...#...#.#
.#...#..#...#...#..#..#...#.#.#..#.#...#...#.#.#...#...#..#.#...#...#.
#...#...#..#...#...#...#..#..#..#..#...#...#...#...#...#..#...#...#..#
.#...#...#..#...#...#.#.#...#...#...#...#...#...#...#...#...#...#...#.#.
#.#..#.#.#.#...#.#...#.#...#...#...#...#..#...#...#.#...#..#..#..#...#..
.#...#...#.#...#.#...#...#..#..#..#.
TRANSFERRING STRUCTURES TO FILE...
272 STRUCTURES WERE OBTAINED
#DRAW ATNAMED (1 3)
```

```
#1:
C     O     C-C
 \    |    /   \
  C--C--C       C
 /    |    \   /|
C     |     \ / |
 \    |      C--C-C
  C--C          |
      \         C
       C

#2:
C     O  C        C
 \    |  |       /
  C--C--C--C-C
  |   |     |/ \
  C  C      C   C
   \ |\    /
    \| C-C
     C

#3:
                C
               /
      C    C--C
     / \  /   |
    C   C     |
    |   |     C
    |   |     |\
    C---C--C-C-C-C
   /    |     |
  C     O     C
```

These are now final structures (i.e., no superatoms remain to be imbedded). Additional information about the environment of the cyclopropyl ring became available, allowing the definition of the following substructure, arbitrarily called HEP, which is required to be present.

```
#DEFINE SUBSTRUCTURE HEP
(NEW SUBSTRUCTURE)
>RING 3
>BRANCH 1 1 1 1 2 1 3 3
>DRAW NUMBERED

SUBSTRUCTURE HEP:

  4
  |
5-1-3-7-8-9
  |/
  2
  |
  6
```

It can be cumbersome to use the HRANGE command to identify free valences in large substructures because one needs to specify the range for every atom. The FREEV command offers an alternative and often simpler route. When FREEV is used, there are several assumptions about HRANGE which are made implicitly by the program. First, any atom which does NOT bear one of these special free valences is assumed to be 'saturated' with hydrogen atoms, so that no additional bonds to that atom may be formed. Secondly, a special free valence is assumed to bond only to non-hydrogen atoms (i.e., an atom bearing special free valences is implicitly given an HRANGE with the minimum number equal to the maximum number) unless this assumption is explicitly overridden by a separate HRANGE associated with the corresponding atom. Atoms with 'polynames' or the name X (a special symbol meaning 'any atom') cannot be given special free valences with FREEV, and no implicit assumptions are ever made about the HRANGE on such atoms. The FREEV command below accomplishes the same effect as would the longer command:

HRANGE 1 0 0 2 1 1 3 1 1 4 3 3 5 3 3 6 2 2 7 1 1 8 1 1 9 3 3

```
>FREEV 6 1 7 1 8 1
>DRAW ATNAMED

SUBSTRUCTURE HEP:

              C
       \      |
        C--C-C-C
       /    \|
    -C       C
     |        \
     C         C
                \
```

Note that the special free valences inserted by FREEV are drawn as single bonds with one end left 'open'.

```
>DONE
HEP DEFINED
#PRUNE
CONSTRAINT:SUBSTRUCTURE HEP, AT LEAST 1
CONSTRAINT:
*******************.*.**.**.*.******************************...****...**
****************..*.*..***.*.**..*****.....*.****************.*.*..****..
..*..*.*....*.*....*******........******.*....********..*.******.*..***.
*.***..**.****....*..***************.*..*...****......***
88 STRUCTURES SURVIVED PRUNING
```

At this point, the user has dramatically reduced the number of structural possibilities, but there are still too many to consider individually by manual inspection. The SAVE command allows him to record on file all of his structures and all other information he has given the program during this session. The file name he chooses here will identify this particular file so that he can restore it at a later date.

```
#SAVE
FILE NAME:?
A WORD OF THE FORM XXXXXX.YYY WHERE XXXXXX IS A 'NAME' OF
FROM ONE TO SIX LETTERS AND/OR DIGITS AND WHERE YYY IS AN
OPTIONAL 'EXTENSION' OF FROM ONE TO THREE LETTERS AND/OR DIGITS.
THE '.' MAY BE OMITTED IF THE EXTENSION IS OMITTED
FILE NAME:CASE1.SV
SAVED ON CASE1.SV
```

Since the user has just saved his session, he does not need to save it again at this point.

```
#EXIT
DO YOU WANT TO SAVE YOUR SESSION ON FILE?:NO

EXIT.
^C
@
```

At a later time, the user returns with more structural information in the form of the required substructure PEN defined below. Also, he previously had forgotten to test for the presence of exactly two ETH substructures after imbedding ETH, CH and CH3. He restores the saved session, defines PEN and PRUNEs with both PEN and ETH.

This session demonstrates highly abbreviated input as it might be typed by a very experienced user. Short forms are used for the keywords, and in many places the semicolon (;) is used to terminate variable-length responses (e.g., input following an EDITSTRUC command or the responses to the SUPERATOM: prompts following GENERATE). This allows the user greater flexibility in 'typing ahead' his information.

```
@CONGEN
#RESTORE CASE1.SV
CASE1.SV RESTORED
#DE S PEN
(NEW SUBSTRUCTURE)
```

For example, the following command is equivalent to the several lines:

CHAIN 4
BRANCH 2 1 2 1
ATNAME 1 O
DRAW NUMBERED

```
>C 4;B 2 1 2 1;A 1 O;D N
I TAKE B TO MEAN BRANCH
I TAKE D TO MEAN DRAW

SUBSTRUCTURE PEN:
NON-C ATOMS: 1->O

  5
  |
1-2-3-4
  |
  6

>F 3 1 5 1 6 2;D A
I TAKE D TO MEAN DRAW

SUBSTRUCTURE PEN:

        O
        |    /
  -C--C--C
        |    \
        |
        C
       / \
      C

>DONE
PEN DEFINED
```

The following two commands are interpreted respectively as

'PRUNE SUBSTRUCTURE PEN AT LEAST 1;' and

'PRUNE SUBSTRUCTURE ETH EXACTLY TWO;'

with the semicolon terminating the list of constraints in each case.

```
#P S PEN L 1;
.*...*...*****************************************************.*.....***
*.*..****....*..
22 STRUCTURES SURVIVED PRUNING
#P S ETH E 2;
..........*.......*...
20 STRUCTURES SURVIVED PRUNING
#SA CASE1.SV2
SAVED ON CASE1.SV2
```

Having saved these twenty structures for future reference, the user now decides to see which of the structures satisfy the isoprene rule. Though he has no hard evidence to indicate that the unknown is an isoprenoid structure, he has the structures on file and can now experiment a bit. The use of the '?' below shows him the available libraries and the SEARCH command enables him to restore the appropriate substructure. One of the four surviving structures (#209 below) is in fact the correct structure for the unknown.

```
#S L ?
I TAKE S TO MEAN SHOW
GENLIB ISOLIB BMTERP BSTERP TSTERP SURVLIB MYLIB
LIBRARY TO BE SHOWN:I
THAT LIBRARY CONTAINS THE FOLLOWING SUBSTRUCTURES:
2-HT 2-IRR 3-HT-HT 3-IRR 4-HT-HT-HT 4-IRR
#SE I 3-HT-HT
3-HT-HT DEFINED
#P S 3-HT-HT L 1;
*.*.***.***.*********
4 STRUCTURES SURVIVED PRUNING
#D A(1 4)
I TAKE D TO MEAN DRAW
```

#25:

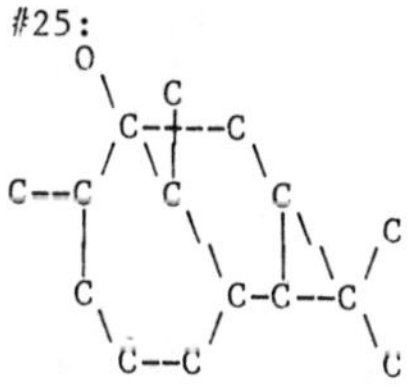

#30:

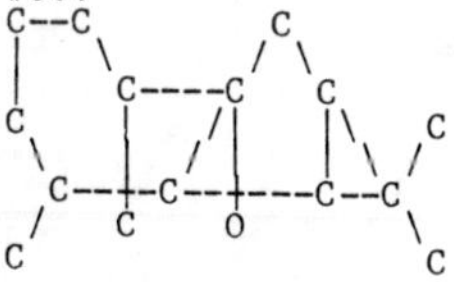

#209:

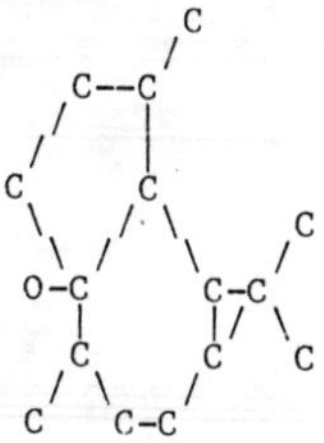

#223:

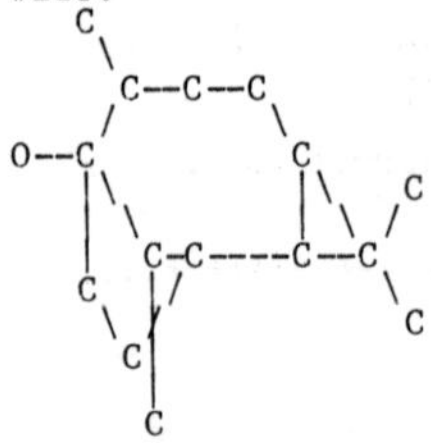

Now,during the GENERATE of the previous session, the user had limited the number of ‘loops’ on superatom A to NONE because those structural possibilities seemed most likely to him. But for thoroughness, he now considers those structures in which A has one loop. (It cannot have two or more loops because it has only three free valences.) Note that with the abbreviated inputs, the user is able to carry out the entire case with just five lines of typed input. The single resulting structure can be ruled out on the basis of NMR evidence because some coupling should have been seen between the methylene and methine protons attached to carbons neighboring the three-membered ring.

```
#G A L 1 B E 1 CH3 E 1 CH2 E 3 CH E 1 ETH L 1;S MET N R 2 N R 3 E 1 L A L 1;
'COLLAPSED' FORMULA IS A 1 B 1 CH3 1 CH2 3 CH 1 ETH 1
.................................
33 STRUCTURES WERE GENERATED
#I CH3 1 CH2 3 CH 1;;
THE 'EXPANDED' FORMULA IS C 5 A 1 B 1 ETH 1 H 10
#.#.#.#.#.#.#.#.#.#.#.#.#.#.#.#.#.#.#.#.#.#.#.#.#.#.#.#.#.#.#.#.#.
TRANSFERRING STRUCTURES TO FILE...
33 STRUCTURES WERE OBTAINED
#I ETH 1 B 1;;
THE 'EXPANDED' FORMULA IS O 1 C 8 A 1 H 15
#.#.#.#D#.#.#.#D#D#.#.#D#.#.#.#.#D#.#D#D#D#D#.#D#.#.#.#D#D#.#.#D#D
TRANSFERRING STRUCTURES TO FILE...
19 STRUCTURES WERE OBTAINED
#I A 1; R 2 N R 3 E 1;
THE 'EXPANDED' FORMULA IS O 1 C 15 H 26
#.#.#.#.#.#.#.#.#.#.#.#.#.#.#.#.#.#.#.
TRANSFERRING STRUCTURES TO FILE...
19 STRUCTURES WERE OBTAINED
#P S HEP L 1 S PEN L 1;
*******************.
1 STRUCTURE SURVIVED PRUNING
#D A 1
I TAKE D TO MEAN DRAW
```

#19:

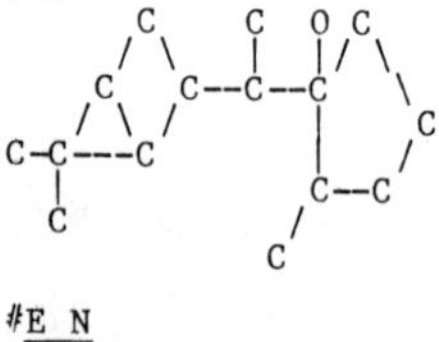

```
#E N

EXIT.
^C
@
```

(end of sample session)

CONJECTURES AND REFUTATIONS IN A FRAMEWORK FOR CHESS ENDGAME KNOWLEDGE

Ivan Bratko and Tim Niblett

ABSTRACT

We present a schema for representing chess endgame knowledge. The knowledge represented within the schema is used to analyse chess positions in an 'hypothesis formation, hypothesis verification' fashion. The proposed schema is investigated by its application to the endgame of King and Rook vs King and Knight and to a pawn ending. We present a number of worked examples, partially programmed using techniques of the AL1 system.

INTRODUCTION

Two approaches to chess programming have been competing for many years: (a) a brute force search using little chess-specific knowledge, with very sophisticated and efficient search techniques, against (b) a knowledge based approach using small, intelligent and knowledge-rich searches.

While programs of type (a) have dominated computer chess tournaments, proponents of approach (b) have been looking for more powerful programming tools and methods for representing expert knowledge in chess. We believe that both approaches will be needed before a program plays at grandmaster level, but are concerned here with issues of knowledge representation and transmission.

Programs of Berliner (1974), Pitrat (1977), and Wilkins (1979) are examples of similar research. The last two of these use plans to guide search, and the behaviour of Pitrat's program on some of his sample problems is particularly impressive. All three programs are intended to find forced combinations in the middlegame, and so are specialised to positions rich in tactical possibilities. In our research however we are interested in chess endgames, in which long-range plans play a particularly important role. Tan's work (1977) deals with the same problem of chess programming. Contrary to popular belief simple endgames such as KRKN can be taxing even for masters (Kopec and Niblett 1979).

DESIDERATA FOR AN ADVICE SYSTEM

In our previous experiments we used the AL1 system (Advice Language 1; Michie 1976, Bratko and Michie 1979) for representing chess endgame knowledge. The suggestions for a chess advice-system in this paper are motivated by the recognition that AL1, or its extension AL2 (Bratko and Michie 1978; AL2 has been partially implemented as AL 1.5, Mozetic 1979) is an insufficient vehicle in itself with which to describe strategies for more complex endgames such as the rook's side of KRKN. It seems unlikely that either AL1 or AL2 can exhibit correct strategies whilst preserving properties we consider essential for an Advice System. We mention some of these properties below.

The system should have a knowledge base that is easy for the user-expert to increment without his considering interactions between various pieces of knowledge.

Experience with AL1 has shown that to play endgames (such as KRKN) correctly often requires the consideration of long move sequences. We believe a desirable way to do this whilst avoiding the 'combinatorial explosion' is to consider plans and counter-plans, a method of 'conjectures and refutations'. These plans should not just be at the level of single moves. For example it may be possible to refute a plan by proving that one of its necessary preconditions cannot be achieved.

AL1 was designed to facilitate formal proof of the correctness of strategies. In our experience empirical testing of such programs often fails to reveal that strategies are incorrect. Therefore we wish in any development of the language to retain the ability to prove correctness formally. To this end the 'Advice structure' must be as simple and elegant as possible, and plans must be constructed with the aim of being able to prove their correctness or incorrectness.

We believe a fundamental concept of AL1, the forcing tree (originally due to Huberman 1968), to be very valuable, not least as an aid to formal correctness proof. Therefore forcing trees should be retained in the present framework. However we envisage search trees as consisting not only of positions and moves, but also of position *sets* and move *sets*. This increases both search efficiency and conceptual clarity, by contracting the problem space.

The system must choose plans or moves which are intelligible to the human user. We believe this to be a fundamental requirement for an interactive chess 'expert system'.

Below we present a partial specification and analysis of an Advice System which we believe can satisfy the above requirements. The discussion is based on positions from the KRKN ending where the black knight is paralysed. We try to find plans for White whereby he can capture the black knight. This problem has been chosen because it combines simplicity of ideas with the need for long-range plans.

SKETCH FOR AN ADVICE SYSTEM

The system deals with two major classes of objects: hypotheses and methods. *Hypotheses* are conjectures about properties of our problem environment. Some of these hypotheses will prove to be true. The system aims to establish the truth of a hypothesis, e.g. of the form: White can win by making move M, which is part of some plan P. To investigate the truth value of hypotheses we use *Methods*. Given a hypothesis (which may be a combination of other hypotheses) a method can be considered as a black box to do one of four things:

(a) Establish that the hypothesis is true.
(b) Establish that the hypothesis is false.
(c) Establish that the hypothesis is true or false if
 some other hypothesis (or hypotheses) is (are) true or false.
(d) Establish that it is unable to produce a conclusion.

Methods are triggered by currently known facts about the current board position, and by other already generated hypotheses. Thus methods act as a set of production rules.

The system considers hypotheses and investigates their truth by applying methods until it can prove or disprove its major hypothesis, or until it finds that its knowledge base (hypotheses and methods) is unable to discover a solution.

We envisage the advice system as consisting of the following modules:

(a) *Control Structure*. This decides how to use the knowledge in the knowledge base; resolve conflicts, allocate resources to investigating particular hypotheses etc.

(b) *Knowledge Base*. This consists of methods, hypothesis schemata and facts about the current position. Results from the application of methods are passes back to the knowledge base.

DEFINITIONS

This section contains definitions of some of our primitive concepts, hypotheses and methods for positions where the black knight is paralysed in the KRKN ending.

We use the following notation: P or pos stands for a legal position in the KRKN space with either White to move (WTM) or Black to move (BTM). Rook's side is always White. We drop P or 'pos' unless context demands it. We use ⟨ . . . ⟩ to enclose plans. We sometimes denote pieces by W, B, R, N as abbreviations for WK, BK, WR and BN. We write WBG for White better-goal (in either White-to-move or Black-to-move position), and BBG, WHG, BHG, WMC, BMC for Black better-goal, White holding-goal, Black holding-goal, White move-constraints, Black move-constraints respectively. Throughout the paper we use X and Y to represent the two sides. Thus X can be either White or Black, and Y is always 'not X'.

DEF *Piece-of-advice*

A *piece-of-advice* for side X is a four-tuple (b_X, h_X, mc_X, mc_Y) where b_X and h_X are predicates on positions and mc_X and mc_Y are predicates on moves. b_X, h_X, mc_X and mc_Y are called *better-goal, holding-goal, move-constraints* for side X, and *move-constraints* for side Y respectively.

Remark: The quadruple (b_X, h_X, mc_X, mc_Y) we also write in the following way:

XBG: b_X (X better-goal)
XHG: h_X (X holding-goal)
XMC: mc_X (X move-constraints)
YMC: mc_Y (Y move-constraints)

DEF *Forcing-tree*

Given a position pos and a piece-of-advice A = (b_X, h_X, mc_X, mc_Y), a *forcing-tree* for A in pos is a subtree T of the game tree rooted in pos such that:

(1) for every node q in T: $h_X(q)$;

(2) for every nonterminal node q in T: not $b_X(q)$;

(3) for every terminal node q in T: $b_X(q)$ or q is a Y-to-move position from there is no legal move that satisfies mc_y;

(4) there is exactly one move in T from every X-to-move nonterminal node in T; that move must satisfy mc_X;

(5) all legal moves from any nonterminal Y-to-move position in T that satisfy mc_y are in T.

Remark: The concept of forcing-tree was introduced by Huberman (1968). The definition of a forcing-tree in this paper differs from the one used in the AL1 system.

DEF *Satisfiable*

A piece-of-advice A is *satisfiable* in a position pos if there exists a forcing-tree for A in pos. We write: s(A,pos)

DEF $S_N(P)$,$S_W(P)$,$S_R(P)$,$S_B(P)$ are sets of squares attacked by the BN,WK,WR and BK respectively. The piece does not necessarily have a legal move to any of these squares.

DEF Rsafe(P) ⇔ S(A,P) where A is advice:

WHG: not(Rdead)

BMC: depth(move) less or equal 2 ply

Remark Throughout the paper we use White and Black instead of Us and Them as in AL1. The root of a forcing tree can be either a WTM or BTM position. Thus the side to move in the root-node is not necessarily the one to which the advice belongs, in contrast to previous usage where the forcing-tree was always rooted in UTM positions.

DEF *Nsafe*

Nsafe(P) ⇔ S(A,P) where A is:

BHG: not(Ndead) and not (Black-mated).

WMC: depth(move) less or equal 2

DEF *Nparalysis*

Nparalysis(P) ⇔ $S_N \subseteq S_W \cup S_R$ and $S_N \cap S_B \subseteq S_W \cap S_R$ and Rsafe(P)

DEF *Rdivides*

Rdivides (s_1,s_2) iff rook divides squares s_1 and s_2 either vertically or horizontally.

DEF *Path*

(Piece)path(p) ⇔ $p = \langle s_1, \ldots, s_n \rangle$ and (piece) dist $(s_i,s_{i+1}) = 1$ for $i = 1, \ldots, n-1$

DEF *Length*

length(p) = n ⇔ $p = \langle s_1, \ldots, s_n \rangle$ for some $s_1, \ldots, s_n$

DEF *King macromove*

$K\ S_1\ S_2(d) = \{p$: kingpath(p) and length(p) = d and $p = \langle s_o, \ldots s_d = b \rangle$ where $a \in S_1$ and $b \in S_2\}$

Remark: If S_1 and/or S_2 consist of only one square we use the notation $K\ s_1\ s_2(d)$ meaning $K\ \{s_1\}\ \{s_2\}\ (d)$.

DEF *Notation for plans*

Plan : : = ⟨ M, h, b ⟩ | ⟨ plan (;plan) * ⟩ | ⟨plan, h, b⟩ where h and b are holding goals and better goals respectively. If there are no better goals we use the notation ⟨ M, h ⟩. Expansion rule is:

⟨⟨plan, h, b⟩, h′, b′ ⟩ = ⟨ plan, h and h′, b or b′ ⟩

We use the following abbreviations and default settings:

(1) ⟨ M, nil, nil ⟩ is equivalent to ⟨ M, true, false ⟩;

(2) ⟨ M, -, - ⟩ is equivalent to ⟨ M, h, b ⟩ for some holding-goals h and better-goal b;

(3) ⟨ M ⟩, where M is a macromove, denotes the plan ⟨ M, true, final state of M ⟩.

DEF *Plan succeeds*

X plan P = ⟨ M,h,b ⟩ *succeeds* in a position pos iff s(A,pos) where A is a piece-of-advice:

XBG: b

XHG: h

XMC: M

YMC: anymove

DEF *Plan pseudosucceeds*

X plan P = ⟨ M,h,b ⟩ *pseudosucceeds* in a position pos iff s(A,pos) where A is:

XBG: b

XHG: h

XMC: M

YMC: dummymove ('dummymove' means a 'passing move', not legal by rules of chess)

DEF *P_y refutes P_x*

Let X plan be $P_x = \langle mc_x, h_x, b_x \rangle$ and Y plan be $Py = \langle mc_y, h_y, b_y \rangle$; then plan P_y *refutes* plan P_x in a position pos iff not s(A,pos) where A is a piece-of-advice

$(b_x$ or not $(h_y), h_x, mc_x, mc_y)$

Remark: Note that the goal b_y is irrelevant to whether P_y refutes P_x or not. It is possible that P_y does refute P_x and that at the same time P_y does not succeed.

DEF *Refutation-tree*

Let X plan be $P_x = \langle mc_x, h_x, b_x \rangle$ and Y plan be $P_y = \langle mc_y, h_y, b_y \rangle$; then a

tree T is a *refutation-tree* for refuting plan P_x by plan P_y in a position pos iff T is a forcing-tree which satisfies a piece-of-advice A where A is:
YBG: not(h_x)
YHG: not (b_x) or not (h_x)
YMC: mc_y
XMC: mc_x

DEF *Refutable*

A plan P is *refutable* by a method M iff M generates an hypothesis H: 'P1 refutes P' and H is true.

DEF *Pseudolegal*

For an X macromove M and a position pos we write *pseudolegal*(M,pos) iff s(A,pos) where A is:
XBG: final state of M
XHG: true
XMC: M
YMC: dummymove

DEF *Completeness*

Given an hypothesis
H: 'P succeeds'
a refutation method is *complete* if it has the following form:
H: 'P succeeds' →
H_i: 'P is refutable by method M_i' | i = 1, . . . , n
H_1 or . . . or H_n ⇔ not (H)

KNOWLEDGE BASE

In this section we present an example knowledge-base whose scope is limited to the KRKN ending, in particular to handle the positions in which the knight is paralysed.

The knowledge base consists of a set of *methods* that have a form of production rules. Some of the methods are called *lemmas*, just to indicate that by them we implement theorems about chess world. In the form there is no difference between methods and lemmas.

We basically use the following notation to represent methods:
H → action to generate H1, H2, . . . , Hn
f(H,H1, . . . , Hn)

Here H is an input hypothesis, or fact, contained in our current knowledge about the particular chess position we are analysing. H acts as a precondition (left-hand side of the production rule) which triggers the method. H1, . . . , Hn are hypotheses generated by the action. f(H1, . . . , Hn) is a logical statement which defines the logical connection among these hypotheses.

In the text we assign names to hypotheses. For example
H3: 'Plan P succeeds'

means that the hypothesis 'Plan P succeeds' can be referenced via the name H3.

Some hypotheses are concerned with the success of *plans*. These consist of sequences of macromoves with holding goals and better goals. All tree searching is done by applying pieces of *advice* (in the sense of AL2) to positions. Within this paper we have made extensive use of the following four facts, as a guide to the correct modification of plans.

(1) If $M_y \Rightarrow M'_y$ then $s((b,h,M_x,M'_y),p) \Rightarrow s((b,h,M_x,M_y),p)$
(2) If $M'_x \Rightarrow M_x$ then $s((b,h,M'_x,M_y),p) \Rightarrow s((b,h,M_x,M_y),p)$
(3) If $b' \Rightarrow b$ then $s((b',h,M_x,M_y),p) \Rightarrow s((b,h,M_x,M_y),p)$
(4) If $h' \Rightarrow h$ then $s((b,h',M_x,M_y),p) \Rightarrow s((b,h,M_x,M_y),p)$

Method NP (Nparalysis)

Nparalysis → H: '⟨ -,-,Nwon ⟩ succeeds'

Method WINN1 (Win N by K macromove)

Nparalysis and H: '⟨ -,-,Nwon ⟩ succeeds' →
H1: '⟨⟨ KXN, Nparalysis, nil ⟩, - , Nwon ⟩ succeeds'
H1 ⇒ H

Method WINN2 (Win N by R macromove)

Nparalysis and H: '⟨ - , -, Nwon ⟩ succeeds' →
H1: '⟨⟨ RXN, Nparalysis, nil ⟩ , - , Nwon ⟩ succeeds'
H1 ⇒ H

Method WINN3 (Win N by K macromove followed by method 2)
We give here the idea behind this method only informally: given same precondition as for method WINN1, hypothesise that N can be won by the following plan: W macromove so as to control N-attainable squares that were so far controlled by the R. Then, as R is released, proceed by applying method WINN2.

Method SPLIT (Split plan and refute its parts: (a) try to refute macromove by method RM, (b) try to refute holding goal by method RH)

H: '⟨ M,h,b ⟩ succeeds' →
H1: '⟨ M,h,b ⟩ refutable by RM'
H2. '⟨ M,h,b ⟩ refutable by RH'
H1 or H2 ⇒ not H

Lemma LRH (Refute plan by refuting holding goal)

H: 'P refutable by RH' and P has *nil* holding goal → H is false

Method RM (Refute WK macromove by BK macromove, BN macromove, or BK *and* BN moves)

H: '⟨ W S1 S2 ($\leqslant \ell$), - , - ⟩ refutable by RM' →
Let P be ⟨ W S1 S2 ($\leqslant \ell$), - , - ⟩

H1: 'P refutable by RM1'
H2: 'P refutable by RM2'
H3: 'P refutable by RM3'
H1 or H2 or H3 $\Leftrightarrow$ H

Method RM1 (Refute K macromove by K macromove)
H: '⟨ XK S1 S2 ($\leqslant \ell$), h, b ⟩ refutable by RM1' $\rightarrow$
H1: '⟨ YK b S ($\leqslant \ell$) ⟩ refutes ⟨ XK S1 S2 ($\leqslant \ell$), h, b ⟩'
H2: 'pseudosucceeds(XK S1 S2 ($\leqslant \ell$), h, b)'
H1 $\Rightarrow$ H
not(H1) and H2 $\Rightarrow$ not(H)

Method RM2 (Refute K macromove by N macromove)
H: '⟨ W S1 S2 ($\leqslant \ell$), h, b ⟩ refutable by RM2' $\rightarrow$
H1: '⟨ N N-square S ($\leqslant \ell$) ⟩ refutes ⟨ W S1 S2 ($\leqslant \ell$), h, b ⟩'
H1 $\Rightarrow$ H
not(H1) and pseudosucceeds (W S1 S2 ($\leqslant \ell$), h, b) $\Rightarrow$ not(H)

Method RM3 (Refute K macromove by K *and* N moves)
H: '⟨ W S1 S2 ($\leqslant \ell$), h, b ⟩ refutable by RM3' $\rightarrow$
H1: '⟨ 'N *and* B moves' ⟩ refutes ⟨ W S1 S2 ($\leqslant \ell$), h, b ⟩'
H1 $\Rightarrow$ H

Method RM1A (Refute K macromove M by K macromove to a certain square in M)
H: '⟨ YK b S ($\leqslant \ell$) ⟩ refutes ⟨ XK a z ($\leqslant \ell$), h, b ⟩ $\rightarrow$
H1: '⟨ YK b y ($\leqslant \ell$) ⟩ refutes ⟨ XK a z ($\leqslant \ell$), h, b ⟩
where y is defined by:
(1) y $\in$ M and
(2) d(a,y) = d(b,y) or d(a,y) = 1 + d(b,y) and
(3) y is the square which maximises d(b,y) over
all squares satisfying (1) and (2).
H1 $\Rightarrow$ H

Lemma LRM1B (Refutability of WK macromove by BK macromove)
H: '⟨ B b S (-) ⟩ refutes ⟨ W a z ($\leqslant \ell$) ⟩' $\rightarrow$
H1: 'pseudolegal(W a z ($\leqslant \ell$))'
H2: 'd(z,b) $\leqslant \ell$ or BTM and d(z,b) $\leqslant \ell + 1$
H and H1 $\Rightarrow$ H2

Lemma LRM1W (Refutability of BK macromove by WK macromove)
H: '⟨ W a S (-) ⟩ refutes ⟨ B b y ($\leqslant \ell$) ⟩' $\rightarrow$
H1: pseudolegal(B b y ($\leqslant \ell$))
H2: 'd(a,y) $\leqslant \ell$ or WTM and d(a,y) $\leqslant \ell + 1$ Rdivides(b,y)'
H and H1 $\Rightarrow$ H2

Lemma LRM2 (Refutability by method RM2)
H: '⟨ M, Nparalysis ⟩ refutable by RM2' → H is false

Lemma LRM3 (Refutability by method RM3)
H: '⟨ M, Nparalysis ⟩ refutable by RM3' → H is false

Method RH (Refute plan by destroying holding goal)
H: '⟨ M, h ⟩ refutable by RH' →
H1: '⟨ M, h ⟩ refutable by RH1'
H2: '⟨ M, h ⟩ refutable by RH2'
H3: '⟨ M, h ⟩ refutable by RH3'
H1 or H2 or H3 ⇔ H

Comment: RH is a complete refutation method.

Lemma LRH1 (Refutability by method RH1)
H: '⟨ W S1 S2 ($\leqslant \ell$), Nparalysis, -⟩ refutable by method RH1' →
H1: '$d(B,R) > \ell$ and $d(B,S_N) > \ell - 1$'
H2: 'pseudosucceeds(W S1 S2 ($\leqslant \ell$), Nparalysis, -)'
H1 and H2 → not H

Remark: In an actual implementation H1 should be verified before H2 is generated.

Lemma LRH2 (Refutability of plan by method RH2)
Same as LRM2 with 'RM2' replaced by 'RH2'.

Lemma LRH3 (Refutability of plan by method RH3)
Same as LRM3 with 'RM3' replaced by 'RH3'.

Lemma LPW ('Piece win-able')
H: '⟨ M, Piece-paralysis, Piece-won ⟩ succeeds' →
H1: '⟨ M, Piece-paralysis ⟩ refutable by RM'
H2: '⟨ M, Piece-paralysis ⟩ refutable by RH'
not(H1) and not(H2) and (Piece-square is target square of M)
→ H

Method PLANS (Plan succeeds)
H: 'X plan ⟨ M, h, b ⟩ succeeds' →
H1: 's(A,pos)' where pos is the current position and A is:
XBG: b
XHG: h
XMC: M
YMC: anymove
H1 ⇔ H

Method PRP (Plan refutes plan)

H: 'Y plan ⟨ M_y, h_y, b_y ⟩ refutes X plan ⟨ M_x, h_x, b_x ⟩ in position pos' →

H1: 'not s(A,pos)' where A is:

XBG: b_x or not(h_y)

XHG: h_x

XMC: M_x

YMC: M_y

H1 ⇔ H

Method PLANPS (Plan 'pseudosucceeds')

H: 'pseudosucceeds(M,h,b)' →

H1: 's(A,pos)' where pos is the initial position of M,
X is the side that executes plan ⟨ M,h,b ⟩,
and A is the following piece-of-advice:

XBG: b

XHG: h

XMC: M

YMC: dummymove

H1 ⇔ H

Method MACROPL (Test if a given macromove is pseudolegal)

H: 'pseudolegal(M)' →

H1: 's(A,pos)' where pos is the initial position of M,
X is the side that executes M, and A is the following piece-of-advice:

XBG: final state of M

XHG: nil

XMC: M

YMC: dummymove

H1 ⇔ H

Method INST1 (instantiate length)

H: '⟨ Piece a b (-), h, b ⟩ succeeds' →

H1: '⟨ Piece a b (Piecedist(a,b)), h, b ⟩ succeeds'

H1 ⇒ H

Method INST2 (instantiate length to a larger value)

H: '⟨ Piece a b (-), h, b ⟩ succeeds' and

H1: '⟨ Piece a b ($\leqslant \ell$), h, b ⟩ succeeds' and

H2: 'H1 is false' →

H3: '⟨ Piece a b ($\leqslant \ell + 1$), h, b ⟩ succeeds'

H3 ⇒ H

Method METRICS

This method is triggered by relational expressions about distances among pieces on the board. It establishes the truth or falsehood of the input distance relations. An example of METRICS application is:

H: 'd(W,N) < d(B,N)' →

H is true if dist. between WK and BN is less than dist. between BK and BN, otherwise H is false.

Method SEARCH

H: 's(A,pos)' →

Do the game-tree search to find whether a piece-of-advice A is satisfiable in position pos. If yes then return a corresponding forcing-tree as a by-product.

Method KILLER ('killer' heuristic)

H1: 'X plan Px succeeds' and

H2: 'Y plan Py refutes Px' and

T is a forcing-tree which guarantees not(H2) →

H3: 'X plan Px *ordered by* T succeeds'

H3 ⇔ H1

DEFINITION (plan *ordered by* a tree)

A plan P is *ordered by* a forcing-tree T thus:

given a position p and several alternatives moves from p contained in plan P then

(a) if p is in T and so is a move from p then that move is chosen first from the list of alternatives in P;

(b) if p is a terminal node in T, or p is not in T, then the corresponding moves in the 'best-matching' variations are chosen first.

The criterion of 'best-matching' is illustrated by figure 1.

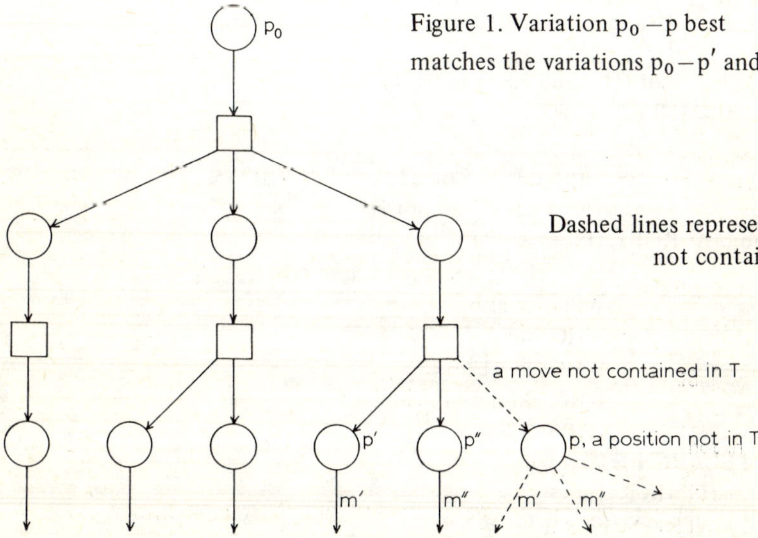

Figure 1. Variation $p_0 - p$ best matches the variations $p_0 - p'$ and $p_0 - p''$.

Dashed lines represent moves not contained in T.

EXAMPLE 1

Consider position in figure 2.

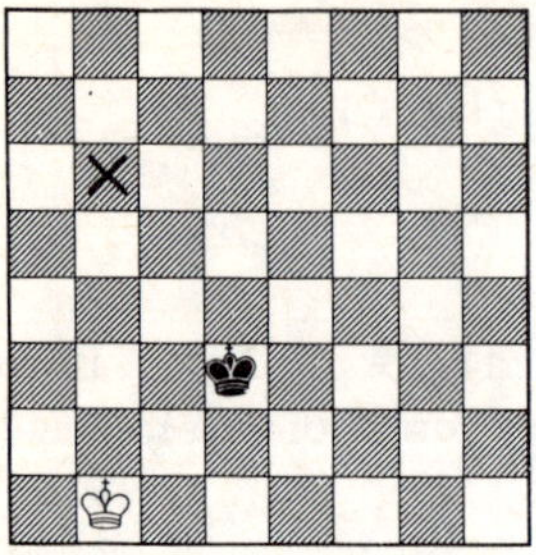

Figure 2. White to move

H1: ⟨ W b1 b6 (5) ⟩ succeeds.

Let P stand for ⟨ W b1 b6 (5) ⟩.

By Method SPLIT H1 : P succeeds →
  H2: P refutable by RM
  H3: P refutable by RH
  H2 or H3 ⇒ not H1

By Lemma LRH H3 is false

By Method RM H2 →
  H4: P refutable by RM1
  H5: P refutable by RM2
  H6: P refutable by RM3
  H4 or H5 or H6 ⇔ H2

By Method RM1 H4 →
  H7: ⟨ B d3 S (⩽ 5) ⟩ refutes P
  H8: pseudolegal(P)
  H7 ⇒ H4
  not (H7) and H8 ⇒ not(H4)

By Lemma LRM1B H7 →
  H8
  H9: d(b6,d3) ⩽ 5 or BTM and d(b6,d3) ⩽ 5 + 1
  not H9 ⇒ not H7 or not H8

By Method MACROFL H8 →
  H10: s(A1, position) where A1 is;
  WBG: W at b6
  WHG: nil
  WMC: W b1 b6 (5)
  BMC: dummy-move
  H10 ⇔ H8

By Method SEARCH H10 is true

Since H10 ⇔ H8, H8 is true

By Method METRICS H9 is true

Thus since H9 is true we do not know the truth value of H7
By METHOD RM1A H7 →
H11: ⟨ B d3 a4 (⩽5) ⟩ refutes P
H11 ⇒ H7
By Method PRP H11 →
H12: s(A2, position) where A2 is;
WBG: W at b6
WHG: nil
WMC: W b1 b6 (5)
BMC: B d3 a4 (5)
H12 ⇔ H11
By Method SEARCH H12 is true
By H12 ⇔ H11 and H11 ⇒ H7, H7 is true
By H7 ⇒ H4 and H4 or H5 or H6 ⇔ H2, H2 is true
By H2 or H3 ⇒ not H1, H1 is false

EXAMPLE 2
Consider position in figure 3.

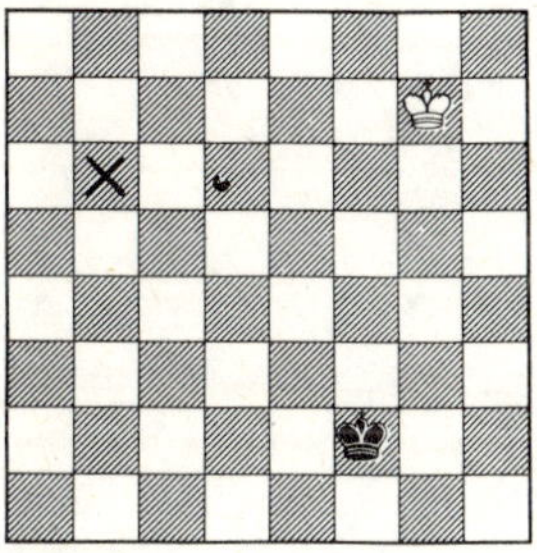

Figure 3. White to move

H1: ⟨ W g7 b6 (5) > succeeds
Let P stand for ⟨ W g7 b6 (5) ⟩.
By Method SPLIT H1 →
H2: P refutable by RM
H3: P refutable by RH
H2 or H3 ⇒ H1
Lemma LRH H3 is false
Method RM1 H4: ⟨ B g2 8 (⩽5) ⟩ refutes P
H5: pseudolegal(P)
H4 ⇒ H2
not H4 and H5 ⇒ not H2
Lemma LRM1B H4 →
H5
H6: d(b6,f2) ⩽ 5
H4 and H5 ⇒ H6

Method METRICS H6 is true

Method RM1A H4 →

H7: ⟨ B f2 b6 (⩽ 5) ⟩ refutes P

H7 ⇒ H4

Method PRP H7 →

H8: not s(A1, position) where A1 is;

WBG: W at b6

WHG: nil

WMC: W s7 b6 (5)

BMC: B f2 b6 (⩽ 5)

H8 ⇔ H7

Method SEARCH H8 is false (as side effect produces a forcing-tree FT1 for A1)

H8 is false

Method KILLER H1 and H8 is false →

H9: 'P ordered by FT1 succeeds'

H9 ⇔ H1

Method PLANS H9 → H10: 's(A2,position)' where A2 is

WBG: W at b6

WHG: nil

WMC: Wg7 b6 (5) ordered by FT1

BMC: B f2 S (⩽ 5)

H10 ⇔ H9

Method SEARCH H10 is true

H9 is true

H1 is true

EXAMPLE 3

Consider position in figure 4.

Figure 4. White to move

Method NP Nparalysis →

H1: ⟨ -, -, Nwon ⟩ succeeds

Method WINN1 Nparalysis and H1 →

H2: ⟨⟨ K × N, Nparalysis ⟩, -, Nwon ⟩ succeeds

H2 ⇒ H1

Plan ⟨⟨ K × N, Nparalysis, - ⟩, -, Nwon ⟩ expands to
⟨ K × N, Nparalysis, Nwon ⟩
Method INST1 H2 →
H3: ⟨ W b4 a8 (4), Nparalysis, Nwon ⟩ succeeds
H3 ⇒ H2
Let M be W b4 a8 (4) and P be ⟨ M, Nparalysis, Nwon ⟩
Method SPLIT H3 →
H4: P refutable by RM
H5: P refutable by RH
H4 or H3 ⇒ not H3
Method RM H4 →
H6: P refutable by RM1
H7: P refutable by RM2
H8: P refutable by RM3
H6 or H7 or H8 ⇔ H4
Method RM1 H6 →
H9: ⟨ B h1 S (⩽ 4) ⟩ refutes ⟨ M ⟩
H9 ⇒ H6
not H9 and pseudolegal (M) ⇒ not H6
Lemma RM1B H9 →
H10: pseudolegal(M)
H11: d(a8,h1) ⩽ 3 and WTM and d(a8,h1) ⩽ 4
H9 and H10 ⇒ H11
Method MACROPL H10 →
H12: s(A,position) where A is;
WBG: W at a8
WMC: W b4 a8 (4)
BMC: dummymove
H10 ⇔ H12
Method SEARCH H12 is true
So H10 is true
Method METRICS H11 is false
By H9 and H10 ⇔ H11, H9 is false
Following the implications, H4 is false
Method RM H5 →
H13: P refutable by RH1
H14: P refutable by RH2
H15: P refutable by RH3
H13 or H14 or H15 ⇔ H5
Lemma RM1B H13 →
H16: d(h1,c6) > 4 and d(h1,{c7,b6}) > 3
H17: pseudosucceeds(M)
H16 and H17 ⇒ not H13
Method METRICS H16 is true

Method PS H17 →

H18: s(A1,position) where A1 is;
WBG: W at a8
WHG: Nparalysis
WMC: W b4 a8 (4)
BMC: dummymove
H18 ⇔ H17

Method SEARCH H18 is true
Following implications, H5 is false
Lemma LPW (a8 is target of M) and H4 is false and H3 is false ⇒ H3 is true
So H1 is true

EXAMPLE 4

Our final example is more complex than the previous ones. We have omitted much of the detail to avoid repetition.

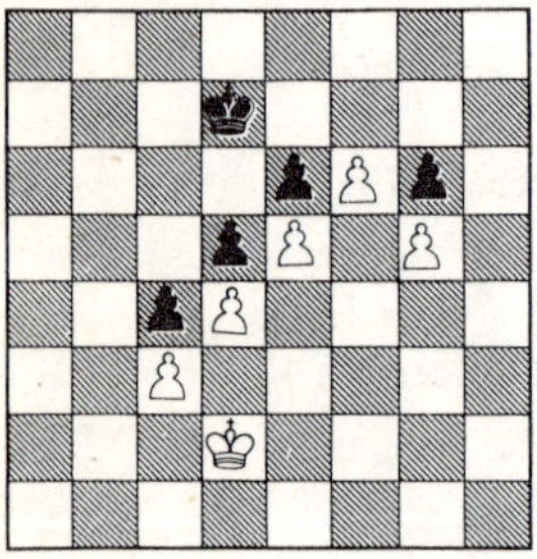

Figure 5. White to move. How does White win?

We use the work of Tan (1977) to analyse the position, finding motifs which can be used to fire methods and generate plans. The position is given because it has been used by Berliner (1974) and Wilkins (1978) to exemplify endgame positions where brute force search has to do a lot of work (at least 17 ply) to find a solution which is simple for the chessmaster.

The ADD is used to generate plans. The most straightforward plan for White is to advance the f-pawn to f8. This plan fails. The next plan is to capture the base pawn of BG1 on e6, this being a threat of length 7 in the ADD. For the rest of this example we consider plans to capture the e6 pawn.

The initial hypothesis (H_O) is that the plan ⟨ W × P(e6),nil,Pwon ⟩ succeeds. Applying methods INST1, SPLIT, RM, and RM1 as in example 3 we form the hypothesis (H_1) that ⟨ B d7 S (⩽ 7) ⟩ refutes ⟨ W d2 e6 (⩽ 7), nil,Pwon ⟩. Method SEARCH produces a piece of advice A, where A is:

WBG: K on e6
WHG: nil
WMC: W d2 e6 (⩽ 7)
BMC: B d7 S (⩽ 7) where S = { d8,e8,f8,g8,h8,h7,f7 }

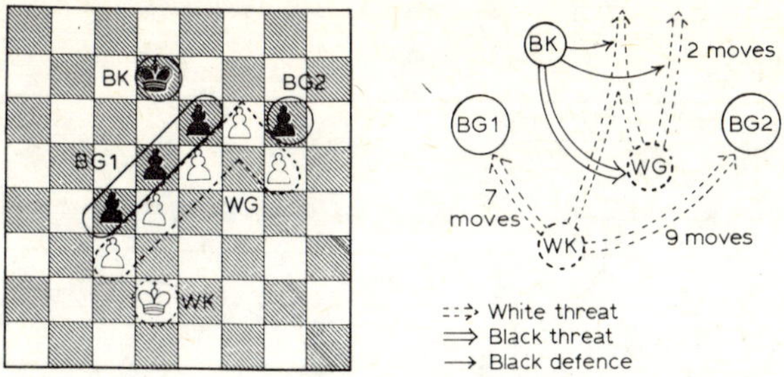

Figure 6. The attack-defence diagram (ADD), after Tan 1977.
In the position shown, Black has two pawn groups (BG1 and BG2) and White has one (WG). The black king is confined to the squares d7, d8, e8, f7, f8, g8, h7, h8, otherwise the f6-pawn queens.

The search uses square sets instead of individual squares. We define for some macromove M = Piece S_1 S_2 (1), M(i), i = 0, . . . , 1, where M(i) = { all squares on the ith move of some path in M} . The search tree uses these square sets and the associated move sets. Branching occurs in this tree only when two move sets conflict. For example, if we have two king macromoves M and M′ for White and Black respectively, with M(3) = {a6, b6, c6} and M′(3) = {d7,e7} then conflict arises between c6 and d7 (they are one king-move apart). We must therefore consider two cases for the move set M(i) → M(4), one where Black is on e7, the other where Black is on d7. .

Let M = W d2 e6 (⩽ 7) and M′ = B d7 S (⩽ 7), then the search tells us that White cannot move from M(5) (c5) to M(6) (d6) with Black at d7 ∈ M′ (5). The advice A is unsatisfiable, and SEARCH returns a refutation tree for A.

A causal method takes the refutation tree returned by A and suggests a new hypothesis (H_2) that if White can reach M(6) from M(5) from the position with Black on d7 but with Black to move then the plan ⟨ W d2 e6 (8),nil,Pwon ⟩ will succeed. In effect this says that if White can lose a tempo to reach the same position with Black on d7 he may be able to continue. This plan also fails, the refutation tree is shown in diagram 7.

Applying the causal method again produces, H_3 : ⟨ W d2 e6 (9),nil,Pwon ⟩ succeeds and this hypothesis is true, a forcing tree exists for the appropriate piece of advice.

Thus using this simple causal method, together with square sets and their associated move sets, we can find and prove correct plans which enable White to win. For pawn endings we consider that some form of high-level description, such as Tan's ADD, can be used to find motifs and generate hypotheses.

DISCUSSION

Our examples were worked out with pencil and paper. But we have partially programmed our solutions both using the AL1.5 package (Mozetic 1979) written in FORTRAN, and in PROLOG.

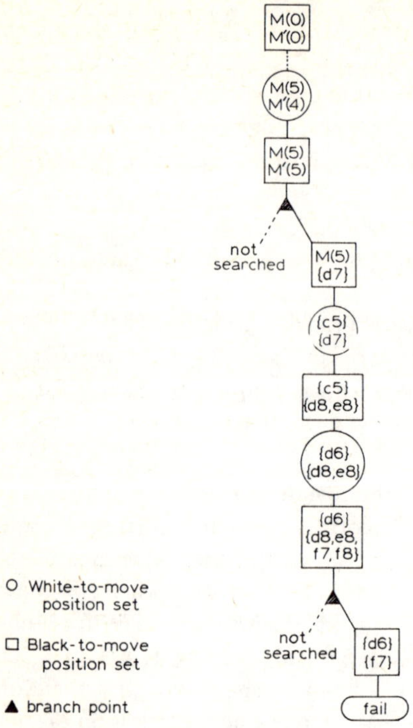

Figure 7. The refutation tree

AL1.5 is a FORTRAN implementation of AL1 on a PDP-11 with some additional features, among these being:

(1) One piece of advice may be called from another. This permits recursive calls of pieces of advice.
(2) The user can specify the outcome of search if no legal move is available satisfying both move constraints and holding goals.
(3) Semi-static search is available where moves are considered for one side only.
(4) Move constraints are applicable at any depth in the search tree (in AL1 they are applicable at ply 1 only).

It proved surprisingly easy to program macromoves as move constraints, and the number of nodes searched for solutions up to 17 ply deep was small, in the order of hundreds of nodes. The average branching factor was well under 1.5.

Forcing trees, move constraints and a few simple methods were programmed in PROLOG on a DEC-10 to assess PROLOG's practicality as an implementation language. Compiled code seems as fast as the POP-2 implementation of AL1. We consider PROLOG to be a suitable implementation for the system. An example of PROLOG code is given in the appendix.

ACKNOWLEDGEMENTS

We would like to thank Professor Donald Michie for his help and encouragement. This work was made possible by a grant from the British Council in support of an academic link between the Edinburgh Machine Intelligence Research Unit and the Josef Stefan Institute, Ljubljana, Yugoslavia. One of us (Tim Niblett) was supported by a Science Research Council research studentship.

REFERENCES

Berliner, H. (1974) Chess as problem solving: the development of a tactics analyzer. Ph.D. Thesis, Carnegie-Mellon University.

Bratko, I. & Michie, D. (1978) AL2 design specification. Working paper, Edinburgh: Machine Intelligence Research Unit, University of Edinburgh.

Bratko, I. & Michie, D. (1979) A representation for pattern-knowledge in chess end-games, in *Advances in Computer Chess 2* (ed M.R.B.Clarke) Edinburgh: University Press (in press).

Kopec, D. & Niblett, T. (1979) How hard is the play of the King-Rook-King-Knight ending? in *Advances in Computer Chess 2* (ed M.R.B.Clarke) Edinburgh: University Press (in press).

Michie, D. (1976) An advice-taking system for computer chess. *Computer Bulletin 10* (ser.2) 12-14.

Mozetic, I. (1979) Advice Language and the AL1.5 system. Work report and manual, Ljubljana: J.Stefan Institute.

Pitrat, J. (1977) A chess combinations program which uses plans. *Artificial Intelligence 8*, 275-321.

Tan, S. (1977) Describing pawn structures, in *Advances in Computer Chess 1* (ed M.R.B.Clarke) Edinburgh: University Press.

Wilkins, D. (1979) Using plans in chess. Stanford: Artificial Intelligence Laboratory.

APPENDIX

PROLOG CODE FOR SATISFIABILITY OF ADVICE

The following PROLOG clauses define what it means for a piece of advice to be satisfiable in a given position. 'srec' is a recursive version of 's', which takes an extra argument, the depth of the forcing tree.

```
s(Advice,Position) :-
      Depth is 0,
      srec(Advice,Position,Depth).

srec(Advice,white:Position,Depth) :-
      sum(Depth,1,Depth_plus_1),
      legal(white:Position,Successor),
      move_constraints(Advice,Successor,Depth_plus_1),
      holding_goal(Advice,Successor,Depth_plus_1),
      (better_goal(Advice,Sucessor,Depth_plus_1);
       not(srec(Advice,Successor,Depth_plus_1))).

srec(Advice,black:Position,Depth) :-
      sum(Depth,1,Depth_plus_1),
      legal(black:Position,Successor),
      move_constraints(Advice, Successor,Depth_plus_1),
      (not(holding_goal(Advice,Successor,Depth_plus_1));
       (not(better_goal(Advice,Successor,Depth_plus_1)),
        not(srec(Advice,Successor,Depth_plus_1)))).
```

Note: This is a limited form of forcing tree generator, capable of coping with examples 1 to 3.

KNOWLEDGE-HANDLING FORMALISMS

THE LOGICAL BASIS OF PROGRAMMING BY ASSERTION AND QUERY

J.A.Robinson

Kowalski has described a style of programming (which he has called 'logic programming') in which the program is simply a collection P of *assertions*, stored inside the 'logic machine'. Thus primed with P as its 'knowledge', the machine is ready to respond to *queries.* A query is simply a sentence Q, written in the same language as is used to write the assertions. Given such a Q and P, the machine attempts to *deduce* Q from P by a series of logical steps called *resolutions.* There may be no such series, in which case the machine may (a) terminate its attempt to find one and report that all the possibilities have been explored to no avail, or (b) continue to investigate what is in fact an infinite variety of possibilities, until the computation is arbitrarily terminated by the user.

On the other hand there may in fact be one or more such deductions of Q from P. In this case, the machine will find them all if allowed to run for sufficient time and if their totality is finite. If (as can happen: an example will be given later) there are infinitely many essentially different deductions of Q from P, the machine will generate as many of them as the user can afford to let it.

It is not the deductions themselves which are the useful output of the logic machine, but rather certain information associated with these deductions.

For example, if P happened to consist of the assertions

for all X, if X is human then X is fallible
Socrates is human
Aristotle is human
Socrates is Athenian

then the query

there are Z, Z is Athenian and Z is fallible?

would generate the output:

Z = Socrates

while the query:

there are Z, Z is fallible?

would generate the output:

Z = Socrates
Z = Aristotle.

The first query elicits one output, the second query, two outputs; or if one prefers a uniform type of response, each query returns a list of 'solutions' but the list is longer for some queries than for others. Indeed, the list may be empty: the query

Aristotle is Athenian?

would generate no solution, in accord with the fact that the sentence 'Aristotle is Athenian' cannot be deduced from the given assertions. (This is of course not the same thing as saying that 'Aristotle is *not* Athenian' *can* be deduced from the given assertions. Inability to prove Q is very different from ability to prove not-Q).

Far more complex problems than this can be handled by the logic machine. P can consist of hundreds or thousands of assertions, and an assertion can be very much 'larger' than those in our example.

Assertions have, in general, the form

for all $X_1, \ldots, X_k$, if A_1 and ... and A_m then B

in which there may occur arbitrarily many *variables* $X_1, \ldots, X_k$, and arbitrarily many *conditions* $A_1, \ldots, A_m$. The *conclusion* B must always be present, but both k and m may be 0. If $m > 0$ the assertion is *conditional*; if m=0 it is *unconditional.* Each of the X_i must occur at least once in the 'body': if A_1 and ... and A_m then B. Queries have, in general, the form:

there are $X_1, \ldots, X_k$, A_1 and ... and A_m

It is possible here too that k=0, or m=0, or both. In the case that m=0, k must also be 0, since the variables $X_1 \ldots X_k$ are required to occur at least once each in the 'body' A_1 and ... and A_m.

In the above schemata for assertions and queries, the components $A_1, \ldots, A_m$ and B are all simple sentences of the same syntactic structure. They are *predications* of the form

$t_1 \ldots t_n$ is R

in which R is a *predicate symbol* and $t_1, \ldots, t_n$ are *individual expressions.* A predication is often written

$R(t_1 \ldots t_n)$

or even

$(R\ t_1 \ldots t_n)$

but this is an unimportant detail of 'syntactic sugar'. The individual expressions which are the immediate constituents of predications are either *variables*, or *names* (e.g. Socrates, Aristotle, 348) or else *constructions* of the form:

the F of $t_1 \ldots t_n$

in which F is an *operation symbol* and $t_1 \ldots t_n$ are individual expressions: for example,

the sum of 3, 5;
the cons of A, (the cons of B, nil).

A construction is often written

$F(t_1 \ldots t_n)$

or

$(F\ t_1 \ldots t_n)$.

The important thing to note about constructions is that they are *recursively* defined: constructions can be nested within constructions *ad libitum*, as in

(cons (plus (times (quotient 5 X) (cos (plus A Y))) 4) nil).

It is in this recursive structuring of individual expressions – considered as data-objects – that much of the power of the logic machine seems to reside. It permits the formulation of assertions whose collective effect is to specify elegant descriptions of recursive procedures for creating and manipulating such data-structures as lists, trees and formulas.

Table 1. Keith Clark's Treesort Assertions

```
(sorted L M) ← (convert L T)
               (flatten T M)
(convert L T) ← (push nulltree L T)
(push T nullist T) ←
(push T (conslist X L) T′) ← (insert T X U)
                             (push U L T′)
(insert nulltree X (constree X nulltree)) ←
(insert (constree L X R) Y (constree L X R′)) ← (less X Y )
                                                (insert R Y R′)
(insert (constree L X R) Y (constree L′ X R)) ← (less Y X)
                                                (insert L X L′)
(insert (constree L X R) X (constree L X R′)) ← (insert R X R′)
(flatten nulltree nullist) ←
(flatten (constree L X R) Y) ← (flatten L Z)
                               (flatten R U)
                               (append Z (conslist X U) Y)
(append nullist L L) ←
(append (conslist X L) M (conslist X N)) ← (append L M N)
(less 0 1) ←; (less 0 2) ←; . . . ;
(less 1 2) ←; (less 1 3) ←; . . . ;
```

Assertions shown in brief notation:

'$B \leftarrow A_1 \ldots A_n$' = 'for all $X_1 \ldots X_k$, if A_1 and . . . and A_n then B'

Similarly, queries are written briefly as in:

'$\leftarrow A_1 \ldots A_n$' = 'there are $X_1 \ldots X_k$, A_1 and . . . and A_n'

For example the collection of assertions shown in Table 1 defines the procedures for sorting lists of numbers by the 'treesort' technique of building, given a list L of numbers, a binary tree with the numbers in L labelling its nodes. The tree is arranged in such a way that it *ordered* in the sense that either (a) it is the null tree or (b) its *left* subtree and *right* subtree are ordered, and contain only numbers which are respectively *less than,* and *greater than or equal to,* the number at its root. A tree T having been constructed from L in this way, the desired list M is obtained by 'flattening' T. In order to express this collection of ideas it is necessary to characterize several relations among data-objects:

- (sorted L M) is intended to mean that the list M is the result of sorting the the list L;
- (convert L T) is intended to mean that the list L produces the ordered binary tree T;
- (push T L T′) is intended to mean that the ordered binary tree T′ is pro duced by inserting, one at a time, the numbers on list L into the ordered binary tree T;

- (insert T x T′) is intended to mean that the ordered binary tree T′ results from inserting the number X into the ordered binary tree T;
- (flatten T L) is intended to mean that the list of numbers L results from flattening the ordered binary tree T;
- (append L M N) is intended to mean that the list N results from concatenating the list L with the list M;
- (less X Y) is intended to mean that the number X is less than the number Y;
- nullist, nulltree are intended as (representations of) the null list and the null ordered binary tree, respectively;
- the individual expression (conslist α β) is intended as the (representation of the) list whose head is (represented by) the individual expression α and whose tail is (represented by) the individual expression β;
- the individual expression (constree λ ν ρ) is intended as the (representation of the) ordered binary tree whose left subtree, root, and right subtree are (represented by) the individual expressions λ, ν and ρ.

The logic machine, when furnished with the collection of assertions in Table 1, will for example respond to the query:

← (sorted (conslist 3 (conslist 2 (conslist 1 nullist))) X) ?

with the solution:

X= (conslist 1 (conslist 2 (conslist 3 nullist))).

It can easily be arranged to display the individual expression (conslist a_1 (conslist . . . (conslist a_n nullist) . . .)) as, say:

[a_1 . . . a_n]

and nullist as : [ ].

The internal logical mechanism uses the *unification* algorithm to construct *environments,* which are sets

$\langle\xi_1\ \tau_1\rangle \ldots \langle\xi_r\ \tau_r\rangle$

of *variable-bindings* $\langle\xi\ \tau\rangle$ in which ξ is a variable and τ is an individual expression. The variables $\xi_1, \ldots, \xi_r$ are all distinct from one another.

The logical machine's innermost cycle consists of processing a *query/environment* pair, say, the pair

$\langle \leftarrow BC_1 \ldots C_m, \theta\rangle$

by extracting from the knowledge-base all those assertions, say,

$$B_1 \leftarrow A_{11} \ldots A_{1q_1}$$
$$\vdots$$
$$B_p \leftarrow A_{p1} \ldots A_{pq_p}$$

for which the unification algorithm, given B, B_j and θ as input, will *succeed* with output environment θ_j. The query/environment pair $\langle \leftarrow B\ C_1 \ldots C_m, \theta\rangle$, considered as a *state* of the logical machine, is thus found to have p *successor* states:

$\langle \leftarrow A_{j1} \ldots A_{jq_j}\ C_1 \ldots C_m,\ \theta_j\rangle$, j=1, . . . , p

For some j, it is possible that q_j= 0, i.e. that the corresponding assertion is unconditional. In that case the corresponding successor state is just

$\langle \leftarrow C_1 \ldots C_m, \theta_j \rangle$

It is also possible that p= 0; in that case the state $\langle \leftarrow B\ C_1 \ldots C_m, \theta \rangle$ is an *unsuccessful terminal state,* or *failure.*

A query/environment pair $\langle \leftarrow, \theta \rangle$, whose query part is the empty query, is a *successful terminal state.* The logical machine, on encountering such a state in its basic cycle, simply *outputs* θ in a suitably edited form, this being a solution to the original query.

The original query Q is used to initialize the process by constructing the state ⟨Q, {}⟩ with Q as its query part and the empty environment {} as its environment part.

The machine then begins its cycles with the *set of states*

{⟨Q {}⟩}

as its 'control', In general, the cycle consists of selecting a state S from the control C, and

(a) discarding S if *S is a failure*;

(b) outputting θ if *S is a success* with environment part θ, and then discarding S;

(c) discarding S, but adding to C all the p successor states of S, otherwise;

thus modifying the control C for the beginning of the next cycle.

If the control C is found to be empty, the entire computation evoked by the query Q is complete and the logic machine halts.

What, then, is the unification algorithm, around which this entire process revolves? It is a procedure which, when supplied with expressions A and B, and an environment 0, as *input*, will succeed if, and only if, there is an extension σ of 0 in which A and B both reduce to some common expression C (or are 'unified').

Intuitively, an expression A reduces to an expression C in an environment μ if we can use the variable-bindings ⟨ ξ τ ⟩ in μ as 'rewrite rules' to produce C from A by a series of rewrite-operations. For example, the expression:

(f X Y)

reduces to the expression:

(f (g a) (h b (g a)))

in the environment:

{⟨ X (g Z) ⟩
⟨ Y (h W X) ⟩
⟨ W b ⟩
⟨ Z a ⟩}

As far as the unification algorithm is concerned, an expression is either a *constant* (i.e. a predicate symbol, function symbol, or name), or a *variable*, or a *list of expressions* (in which case it is either *empty* or else has a *head*, which is an expression, and a *tail*, which is a list of expressions). The head and tail of a non-empty list L are denoted respectively by: hL, tL.

We say that a variable ξ is *defined* in an environment θ if θ contains a binding ⟨ ξ τ ⟩ of ξ, and in this case we say that τ is the immediate associate of ξ and write τ = imm (ξ θ). More generally we define *the ultimate associate of A in θ* (Written: ult (A θ)) for any expression A and environment θ, by:

ult (A θ) = *if* (A is a variable defined in θ)
then ult (imm (A θ) θ)
else A

Finally, we introduce the fictitious environment 'impossible', which is returned as the result of the unification algorithm in cases where no unifying environment exists.

With the aid of these ideas we can now define the function unify which computes the 'most general unifier' of two expressions A and B in an environment θ:

unify (A B θ) = *if* (θ is 'impossible')
then 'impossible'
else equate (ult (A θ) ult (B θ) θ),

where:

equate (A B θ) =
if A = B *then* θ
else if (A is a variable) *then* θ ∪ {⟨A B⟩}
else if (B is a variable) *then* θ ∪ {⟨B A⟩}
else if (A and B are non-empty lists) *then* unify (hA hB unify (tA tB θ))
else 'impossible'

(This version of the unification algorithm is due to my colleague F.L.Morris.)

The expression to which A reduces in an environment θ is computed by:

reduce (A θ) =
if (A is a constant) *then* A
else if (A is a variable not defined in θ) *then* A
else if (A is a variable defined in θ) *then* reduce (ult (A θ) θ)
else if (A is the empty list) *then* A
else if cons (reduce (hA θ) reduce (tA θ))

where by cons (α β) is meant the non-empty list whose head is α and whose tail is β.

[It might be noted that for some (finite) A and θ the expression reduce (A θ) is infinite. For example, if A is the variable X and θ is {⟨X (f X)⟩} then reduce (A θ) is the infinite list whose head is f and whose tail is itself:

reduce (X {⟨X (f X)⟩}) = (f (f (f . . .)))

This is a very interesting and useful phenomenon whose exploitation is under investigation but which cannot be further discussed here.]

Each of the query/environment pairs which are the states of the logic machine's control set can be intuitively understood as representing the query (expression) to which the query-part of the state reduces in the environment-part. For example the state:

⟨←(human Z),{⟨ Z Aristotle ⟩}⟩

represents the query:

←(human Aristotle).

If we plot the successive contents of the control set as the nodes of a tree, with the successors of a state being made its immediate descendants in the tree, we see that the *branches* of the tree correspond to linear sequences of query/environment pairs which either terminate (in which case with either a failure or a success) or else run on indefinitely. These sequences are essentially the various *deductions* which the logical machine is exploring in order to deduce the original query from the assertions in the knowledge base.

The control set need never become empty. For example, given the assertions

(number 0)←
(number (s X))← (number X)

the query

←(number N)?

would cause the logic machine to grow the tree:

⟨← (number N) {} ⟩
↓ ↘
⟨←, {⟨N 0⟩}⟩ ⟨← (number X) {⟨N (s X)⟩}⟩
↙ ↘
⟨←, {⟨N (s X)⟩, ⟨X 0⟩}⟩ ⟨← (number X′) {⟨N (s X)⟩, ⟨X (s X′)⟩}⟩
↙ ↓
⋮

The control set is the 'fringe' of the growing 'control tree'. There is no intrinsic logical reason why the control tree should be grown in one way rather than another – the selection of the state to be expanded next' is logically arbitrary. However, in practice (as e.g. in the Prolog system) the control set may well be implemented as a *list* (either implicitly or explicitly) whose *head* is always selected for processing and to whose '*head end*' the list of its successors is appended. Such a regime corresponds to 'depth-first' development of the control tree: this can of course in some cases lead to 'infinite runaways' which leave states deep in the list forever unprocessed.

The step from a state ⟨Q θ⟩ to a successor ⟨Q′ θ′⟩ corresponds to an *inference.* The inference's content is that the 'sequent'

$P \Rightarrow \langle Q\ \theta \rangle$

is true if, and only if, the sequent

$P \Rightarrow \langle Q'\ \theta' \rangle$

is true (where we are writing ⟨Q θ⟩ to denote *the query to which Q reduces in θ*). P is the collection of assertions in the machine. The original query Q_0 provides the initial sequent

$P \Rightarrow \langle Q_0\ \{\}\ \rangle$

which is the same as

$P \Rightarrow Q_0$

Thus the deductions considered by the logic machine are of the form:

$P \Rightarrow Q_0$
$P \Rightarrow Q_1$
⋮
$P \Rightarrow Q_n$

and they can be read either up or down. Read down, they correspond to successive reductions of the initial problem Q_0. Read up, they correspond to 'the deduction of Q_0 from P'.

PROLOG ON THE DECsystem-10

David Warren

1. INTRODUCTION

Prolog [19] [16] is a simple and powerful programming language for non-numeric applications. It was originally devised around 1972 for the purpose of implementing a natural language question-answering system [8], by a team under Alain Colmerauer at the University of Marseille. At Edinburgh, we have produced a Prolog compiler/interpreter [23] for the DECsystem-10 [13]. This implementation shows Prolog to have an efficiency comparable with (compiled) Lisp.

Prolog has been put to practical use in a number of areas outside pure research. Examples include a package for doing algebraic "symbol crunching" [3], an architectural design aid to assist in planning the layout of a building [14], a system to help predict the properties of organic compounds (needed in designing drugs) [12], and the implementation of a compiler (DEC-10 Prolog itself) [24]. Applications within Artificial Intelligence research include programs for plan generation [22], equation solving [6], natural language analysis [10], and solving mechanics problems [5]. All of the above are large and complex programs which would probably never have got written at all with the available manpower, were it not for the relative ease of writing them in Prolog.

The basic idea of Prolog is that a collection of logic statements of a restricted form – **clauses** – can be regarded as a program, and that the execution of such a program is nothing other than a suitably controlled logical deduction from the clauses forming the program.

It is, however, not necessary to know about logic to understand and use Prolog. A Prolog program can be regarded simply as a collection of statements of fact – the **declarative view.** The program can also be understood as a number of procedure definitions – the **procedural view.** The different clauses in a procedure represent alternative **cases** of the procedure. The appropriate clause (or clauses) is selected by a **pattern matching** operation **(unification** [18]), according to the form of the procedure call. Pattern matching is the **sole** data manipulation operation. Data items in Prolog are called **terms**, and may be thought of as complex record structure written in a textual, machine independent form, not involving the notion of reference or pointer.

From a practical point of view, programmers like Prolog because it enables them to write clearer, more concise programs, with less effort, and with less likelihood of error. The language could perhaps be summed up as " pointer manipulation made easy".

2. THE LANGUAGE

Procedures

A Prolog program consists of a sequence of statements called **clauses.** Here is a simple example, consisting of six clauses:

```
descendant (X, Y) :- offspring (X, Y).
descendant (X, Z) :- offspring (X, Y), descendant (Y, Z).

offspring (abraham, ishmael). offspring (abraham, isaac).
offspring (isaac, esau).      offspring (isaac, jacob).
```

Clauses can be understood in two ways. Firstly, they can be interpreted as statements of fact. For instance the first clause says that, whatever may be the values of the **variables** X and Y, "Y is a descendant of X if Y is one of the offspring of X". And the last clause says that "Jacob is one of the offspring of Isaac". Note that variables in different clauses are considered distinct, even if they have the same name.

The second way to understand clauses is as pieces of program. Each clause corresponds to a "case" of a **procedure.** Looked at in this way, the first clause can be read as "To find a Y that is a descendant of X, find a Y that is one of the offspring of X", and the last clause as "When seeking an offspring of Isaac, return the solution Jacob".

The six clauses of the example serve to define two procedures, named 'descendant' and 'offspring'. Each clause consists of a **head**, or "procedure entry point", followed by a (possibly empty) **body**. The body consists of a number of **goals**, or "procedure calls". A clause with an empty body is called a **unit clause.**

How does a Prolog program actually work? To run the program, one provides an initial goal such as:-

```
descendant (abraham, X)
```

The result of executing this goal will be to enumerate descendants of Abraham and return them, one by one, as values of the variable X.

To execute such a goal, the Prolog system **matches** it against the head of some clause and then executes the goals (if any) in the body of that clause, in left-to-right order. In seeking a match, Prolog tries the clauses of the procedure concerned in the order they appear in the program text. The matching process, known technically as **unification**, succeeds if the goal and clause head can be made identical by "filling in" suitable values for the variables. For example the goal 'offspring (X, ishmael)' matches the first clause for 'offspring' if X is given the value 'abraham'. The variable X is then said to be **instantiated** to 'abraham'. When one solution to a goal has been finished with, or when no match can be found for a goal, the Prolog system **backtracks.** That is, it goes back to the most recently executed goal, and looks for an alternative match. If backtracking generates more than one solution to a goal, the corresponding procedure is said to be **non-determinate.**

So what happens when the initial goal 'descendant (abraham, X)' is executed? Through matching the goal against the first clause for 'descendant', Prolog starts off by looking for the immediate offspring of Abraham, and returns successively X = 'ishmael' and X = 'isaac'. Then backtracking causes the second clause for 'descendant' to be used. This results in the 'descendant' procedure being called recursively for each of the offspring of Abraham, giving further descendants, Esau and Jacob.

Structures

Prolog data objects are called **terms.** So far, the only kinds we have seen have been variables, and unstructured constants (called **atoms**). Prolog also provides for structured data objects (called **complex terms**). An example is the binary tree data type. The following procedure checks whether a particular item is present in an ordered binary tree:

```
in (X, tree (T1, X, T2)).
in (X, tree (T1, Y, T2)) :- before (X, Y), in (X, T1).
in (X, tree (T1, Y, T2)) :- before (Y, X), in (X, T2).
```

Here 'tree' is a **functor** of 3 **arguments.** It can be thought of as a record type with 3 fields. The arguments stand for the left subtree, the item at the root node, and the right subtree. The first clause says that X is present in the ordered binary tree <T1, X, T2>, for any values of X, T1 and T2. The last clause says that X is present in the ordered binary tree <T1, Y, T2> if Y is before X and X is present in T2, for any values of X, Y, T1 and T2.

Another, very commonly used, data type is the **list**. These are essentially the same structures as in Lisp. For example, here is the Prolog procedure for concatenating lists:

```
concatenate ([ ], L, L).
concatenate ([X | L1], L2, [X | L3]) :- concatenate (L1, L2, L3).
```

We read these clauses as 'the empty list concatenated with L yields L' and 'a list of the form X followed by L1 concatenated with L2 yields a list of the form X followed by L3, where L1 concatenated with L2 yields L3'. Thus a Prolog list is either the atom '[ ]' (the empty list), or a structured object such as '[X | L]', where X is the first element of the list and L is a variable standing for the remainder, or "tail", of the list. In fact '[X | L]' is just an ordinary term of two arguments and a particular functor, written in a special syntax. The syntax also allows one to write '[1, 2, 3]' instead of '[1 | [2 | [3 | [ ]]]]'. Executing the procedure call:

```
concatenate ([1, 2, 3], [4, 5], L)
```

produces as value for L the list '[1, 2, 3, 4, 5]'. However the 'concatenate' procedure can be used much more flexibly than this. For example, execution of:

```
concatenate (L1, L2, [1, 2, 3])
```

will return, as successive values for L1 and L2, all pairs of lists which when concatenated give the list '[1, 2, 3]'.

As a final, more meaty, example, here is a Prolog version of Hoare's "quicksort" algorithm:

```
qsort ([ ], L, L).
qsort ([X | L], R1, R) :-
    split (L, X, L1, L2), qsort (L1, [X | R2], R), qsort (L2, R1, R2).

split ([ ], Y, [ ], [ ]).
split ([X | L], Y, [X | L1], L2) :- X ≤ Y, split (L, Y, L1, L2).
split ([X | L], Y, L1, [X | L2]) :- X > Y, split (L, Y, L1, L2).
```

'X ≤ Y' and 'X > Y' are calls to **built-in** procedures which compare numeric values. As an example of how "quick-sort" is used:

```
qsort ([1, 9, 8, 4], [], L)
```

returns '[1, 4, 8, 9]' as the value of L. The interested reader should be able to figure out how the program works from what has been said already.

3. IMPLEMENTATION

At first sight, Prolog doesn't appear to be at all a machine-oriented language. However, in terms of efficiency, it can compare very favourably with other high-level languages.

I'll now describe some of the key ideas behind Prolog implementation, with particular reference to the DEC-10 compiler/interpreter. Incidentally, interpreters compatible with the DEC-10 system have been written at Edinburgh for PDP-11 [15] and (in IMP under EMAS) for ICL-system4 [11]. Other Prolog interpreters include implementations in Fortran [2], Pascal [4] and CDL [21], and systems for IBM-370 [17] and the Motorola 6800 microprocessor [9]. Other, more experimental, systems for logic programming also exist [7].

Compilation

Although most existing Prolog systems are interpreters, it is perfectly feasible to compile Prolog into the kind of instruction set typical of present-day hardware. The only case in which a call to an out-of-line routine is essential is in clauses where a particular variable occurs more than once in the head. However. to achieve compact in-line code, many other operations will typically need to be performed out-of-line.

Each symbol (ie. functor or variable occurrence) in the head of the clause will compile into instructions responsible for matching that symbol against the corresponding term in the goal. In general a symbol will map into two pieces of code. One piece will deal with the case of decomposing an existing structure. The other will be needed in the case where a new structure has to be created. However, this duplication of information can be avoided where a procedure argument is known to be either always **input** (ie. instantiated to a non-variable in the call) or always **output** (ie. instantiated to a variable in the call). The user can notify such restrictions on procedure usage by supplying optional **mode declarations**, e.g.

```
:- mode concatenate (+, +, –).
```

This declares that 'concatenate' will always be called with the first two arguments as input and the last as output.

The system can also exploit mode declarations to generate much faster code, and to save run-time storage in "structure-sharing" implementations. ("Structure sharing" is one possible method for representing the new structures (ie. complex terms) created during a Prolog execution, and is explained in [25]).

Indexing

The number of clauses in a procedure is often quite large. This is typical of "database" applications, where a relation is represented "extensionally" as many unit clauses. See, for instance, the way 'offspring' was defined above. However, even when a procedure is made up largely of non-unit clauses, there can still be a lot of them, corresponding to a procedure with many "cases". This is typical, for instance, of compiler writing applications.

With either type of procedure, one does not want the system to have to run through all the clauses in order to find the ones which match. The DEC-10 compiler therefore **indexes** the clauses according to the atom or principal functor of the first argument in the head. (Normally a user will choose this position for the main input to a procedure). Then, provided the first argument in the call is instantiated to a non-variable (ie. the argument actually is input), the only clauses which need to be even considered for a match are those which have the same functor, or a variable, in the indexed position. Often there will be only one alternative. The list of potentially matching clauses is found by a hash-coding technique in a time that does not depend on the number of clauses in the procedure. This relatively simple indexing mechanism is quite adequate in most practical cases.

Bookkeeping – the "Tail Recursion" Optimisation

As in most high-level languages, the Prolog system maintains a stack of **frames**, one for each **active** procedure. Each frame contains bookkeeping information, together with the values of variables in the clause concerned.

Because of Prolog's non-determinacy, a procedure may remain active even though it has successfully "returned". For it may still be possible to backtrack back into the procedure. In such cases the stack frame must be retained. However when a procedure returns determinately – ie. with no choices remaining inside it – it is possible to reclaim the stack frame, exactly as in a conventional language. Stack frames are also reclaimed on backtracking, as are any new structures created by the procedure. Since backtracking will always occur eventually, a conventional garbage collector is not strictly essential with Prolog (in contrast to most languages which allow a procedure to return structures). Nevertheless, DEC-10 Prolog does include a garbage collector, because the amount of structure created may grow too large to fit in available memory before backtracking gets round to reclaiming it.

As I mentioned, each stack frame contains bookkeeping information. First, there is the **call information**, a pair consisting of a pointer into the code for a clause (indicating the arguments of the call, and the position at which to resume execution: the **return address**), together with a pointer to the stack frame associated with that clause. Secondly, there are four items needed principally for backtracking. These are:

(a) a pointer to the clause (if any) which is the next alternative in this procedure;

(b) a stack pointer indicating where to backtrack to should this procedure fail;

(c) a pointer to a push-down list of variable addresses, called the **trail**, which is used on backtracking to reset variables which have been assigned to during unification;

(d) a pointer to a frame in an auxiliary stack, which contains the structures (if any) created by this procedure.

With the current DEC-10 system, this information is created on procedure entry, and is discarded on backtracking or, if the procedure is determinate, on reaching the end of a clause. However, it is possible to adopt a more sophisticated strategy, which brings quite a profound improvement. The reclaiming of the stack frame in the determinate case does not have to wait until the end of clause. It can be accomplished immediately prior to executing the last goal in the clause (provided no choices have been taken up until that point in the procedure). This modification is analogous to what has been called a "tail recursion" optimisation in other languages [20].

I am currently working on a new DEC-10 Prolog compiler, which incorporates this and other improvements. Most of the essentials are already complete, but much detailed work remains to be done before it can be released as a usable system.

To support the tail recursion optimisation, there are some details to attend to:

(a) The values of the procedure's arguments must be copied out into registers, and later stored in the new frame as extra bookkeeping information (looking exactly like ordinary variable cells).

(b) The call information now consists just of a return address and its associated stack frame pointer. This pair is called a **continuation**. The return address can no longer point to the end of a clause. Instead the system keeps track of the actual goal to be executed next.

(c) There is a snag if one of the procedure's arguments is a pointer to an uninstantiated variable in the frame about to be discarded. In practice this occurs quite rarely, but some fix must be found.

The most obvious benefit of this optimisation is that it saves stack space. 'Quicksort' now only requires a stack of size order log N instead of order N. And 'concatenate' now never uses more than **one** stack frame! Also, a determinate, tail recursive procedure which creates no new structure can now recurse indefinitely, without being limited by the size of the stack. However, in practice, most Prolog procedures do create structure, so the effect on total working storage requirements (which is what the user is aware of) is usually less dramatic.

The less obvious, but perhaps more important, benefit of this optimisation is that is saves time. When one frame is discarded and another overwrites it, most of the bookkeeping information can be retained intact. The continuation remains the same. And it turns out that none of the other items needs to be touched, except perhaps the auxiliary stack pointer in cases where new structure has been created.

The net result is that the final call in a determinate procedure is little more than a simple **goto**. For instance, if 'concatenate' has mode '(+, +, –)', the main clause:

concatenate ([X | L1], L2, [X | L3]) :- concatenate (L1, L2, L3).

compiles essentially into the following iteration:-

```
while Arg1 is a non-empty list
do
   let List be a new record with 2 fields;
   head (List): = head (Arg1);
   field pointed to by Arg3: = the list List;
   Arg3: = address of tail (List);
   Arg1: = tail (Arg1)
repeat
```

Some systems for other languages, eg. SCHEME [20], also automatically perform a tail recursion optimisation. However, as far as I know, none of them will produce iterative code for 'concatenate' (for example), because it is only in Prolog that the recursive call to 'concatenate' is the last thing to be done in the procedure. In other languages, the last step is a call to **cons** (the built-in function which creates a new list cell). The unique feature of Prolog which is being capitalised on here is the ability to create a new structure before all the parts are known, and to leave the unknown parts as variables.

Although obviously a programmer can write an iterative version of 'concatenate' if he uses a sufficiently machine-oriented language, he will have to grapple with pointers and pointer assignments, and it is easy to make mistakes. He'll probably decide that it isn't worth the trouble, and will stick to the simple recursive version. Thus by taking over responsibility for machine-oriented matters, the Prolog compiler can actually produce better code than is likely from a programmer in a low-level language.

Performance

The performance of the code produced by the current DEC-10 Prolog compiler has been compared with that of the Stanford DEC-10 Lisp compiler, which is recognised to produce quite fast code. For simple functions over lists, Prolog is somewhat slower than Lisp (by a factor of about 0.6). For examples requiring more general structures, which have to be encoded as lists in Lisp, Prolog can be significantly faster than Lisp (by a factor of as much as 2 or more).

It is too early to say precisely how the new Prolog compiler will affect these figures. However a hand calculation indicates that 'concatenate' will be 1.8 times faster than before. Although this example is in some ways a best case, it is nevertheless probably quite representative of the innermost cycle of a typical

Prolog program.

The improved speed comes partly from the tail recursion optimisation, and partly from taking fuller advantage of mode declarations. Experiments with handcoding 'concatenate', keeping the same data representation, suggest that there is room for further improvement by only a factor of 2, and most of this improvement comes from avoiding jumps to and from out-of-line routines, which greatly increases the size of the in-line code. The compiler, on the other hand, strives to produce compact code, which is more important for most users than speed.

Interactive Environment

Performance is all very well. What the programmer really needs is a good interactive environment for developing his programs. To address this need, DEC-10 Prolog provides an interpreter in addition to the compiler.

The interpreter allows a program to be read in quickly, and to be modified on-line, by adding and deleting single clauses, or by updating whole procedures. Goals to be executed can be entered directly from the terminal. An execution can be traced, interrupted, or suspended while other actions are performed. At any time, the state of the system can be saved, and resumed later if required. The system maintains, on a disk file, a complete log of all interactions with the user's terminal. After a session, the user can examine this file, and print it out on hard copy if required.

4. CONCLUSION

Most so-called high-level languages still perpetuate low-level concepts that in reality are a hangover from machine code programming. Examples are assignment, pointers, **goto**s and iteration. These concepts presuppose a particular computer architecture, what John Backus has called "the von Neumann computer".

No such concepts exist in Prolog (as far as the user is concerned). One might say that Prolog is a truly high-level language. But, as this paper has sought to show, it is often possible to compile Prolog into code which is almost exactly equivalent to that which would have been obtained by programming in a conventional language. In some cases, as an example has shown, the Prolog code is actually likely to be better. In a sense, unification subsumes assignment and pointers, while Prolog's procedure call subsumes **goto**s and iteration. And all this can be achieved with a relatively simple compiler, without the need for preliminary program transformation.

ACKNOWLEDGEMENTS

The suggestion for putting a tail recursion optimisation into Prolog came from Keith Clark. I argued at first that the optimisation was not worthwile, because the space saving would be barely perceptible in most cases, but changed my mind when I realised the potential for improving speed as well.

My work is supported by a Science Research Council grant.

REFERENCES

[1] Backus J.
Can programming be liberated from the von Neumann style?
CACM 21 (8): 613-641, August 1978.

[2] Battani G and Meloni H.
Interpreteur du langage de programmation Prolog.
Groupe d'Intelligence Artificielle, U. E. R. de Luminy, Universite d'Aix-Marseille II, 1975.

[3] Bergman M and Kanoui H.
Sycophante: Systeme de calcul formel et d'interrogation symbolique sur l'ordinateur.
Groupe d'Intelligence Artificielle, U. E. R. de Luminy, Universite d'Aix-Marseille II, 1975.

[4] Bruynooghe M.
An interpreter for predicate logic programs: Part 1.
Applied Maths & Programming Division, Katholieke Univ Leuven, Belgium, 1976.
Report CW 10.

[5] Bundy A. *et al.*
Solving mechanics problems using meta-level inference.
(this volume)

[6] Bundy A and Welham R.
Using meta-level description for selective application of multiple rewrite rules in algebraic manipulation.
Dept of Artificial Intelligence, Univ of Edinburgh, 1979. Working Paper (forthcoming).

[7] Clark K.L. and McCabe F.G.
The control facilities of IC-PROLOG.
(this volume)

[8] Colmerauer A.
An interesting natural language subset.
Groupe d'Intelligence Artificielle, U. E. R. de Luminy, Universite d'Aix-Marseille II, 1977.
[To appear in CACM].

[9] Colmerauer A, Kanoui H and van Caneghem M.
Etude et realisation d'un systeme Prolog.
Groupe d'Intelligence Artificielle, U. E. R. de Luminy, Universite d'Aix-Marseille II, 1979.

[10] Dahl, V.
Un systeme deductif d'interrogation de banques de donnēes en Espagnol.
Groupe d'Intelligence Artificielle, U. E. R. de Luminy, Universite d'Aix-Marseille II, 1977.

[11] Damas L.
[Information about EMAS Prolog is available from its author].
Dept of Computer Science, University of Edinburgh.

[12] Darvas F, Futo I and Szeredi P.
Logic based program system for predicting drug interactions.
Int. J. of Biomedical Computing, 1977.

[13] DEC.
DECsystem-10 System Reference Manual.
Digital Equipment Corporation, Maynard, Mass, 1974.

[14] Markusz Z.
Designing variants of flats.
IFIP Conference, 1977.

[15] Mellish C.
Minimal documentation of the PDP-11 Prolog system.
Dept of Artificial Intelligence, Univ of Edinburgh, 1978.
[Informal note].

[16] Pereira L M, Pereira F and Warren D H D.
User's Guide to DECsystem-10 Prolog.
Dept of Artificial Intelligence, University of Edinburgh, 1978.

[17] Roberts G.M.
An implementation of Prolog.
Master's thesis, Dept of Computer Science, Univ of Waterloo, Canada, 1977.

[18] Robinson J A.
A machine-oriented logic based on the resolution principle.
JACM 12 (1): 227-234, December 1965.

[19] Roussel P.
Prolog: Manuel de Reference et d'Utilisation.
Groupe d'Intelligence Artificielle, U. E. R. de Luminy, Universite d'Aix-Marseille II, 1975.

[20] Steele G L.
RABBIT: A compiler for SCHEME.
Master's thesis, MIT, May, 1978.
AI-TR-474.

[21] Szeredi P.
Prolog – a very high level language based on predicate logic.
2nd Hungarian Conference on Computer Science, Budapest, June, 1977.

[22] Warren D H D.
Generating conditional plans and programs.
AISB Summer Conference, Edinburgh, July, 1976.

[23] Warren D H D.
Implementing Prolog – compiling predicate logic programs.
Dept of Artificial Intelligence, Univ of Edinburgh, 1977.
Research Reports 39 & 40.

[24] Warren D H D.
Logic programming and compiler writing.
Dept of Artificial Intelligence, Univ of Edinburgh, 1977.
Research Report 44 [To appear in Software Practice and Experience].

[25] Warren D H D, Pereira L M and Pereira F.
Prolog – the language and its implementation compared with Lisp.
ACM Symposium on AI and Programming Languages, August, 1977.

THE CONTROL FACILITIES OF IC-PROLOG

K.L. Clark and F.G. McCabe

ABSTRACT

The most significant difference between IC-PROLOG and the other PROLOG implementations is the programmer's ability to control the computation using program annotations. In this paper we exemplify the use of these annotations and give them a precise semantics. We shall see that they allow a two-pass programming methodology. In the first pass the programmer concentrates on the logic of the program, in the second pass, on the control. To make the paper self-contained, and to lay the necessary foundations for our description of the control facilities, we have included a general introduction to Horn clause logic programming.

INTRODUCTION

The paper is divided into three sections. Section 1 gives a brief history of logic programming and defines the syntax of a special class of logic programs, the Horn clause programs. We show how a given program can have several different procedural uses. In Section 2 we define an abstract interpreter for Horn clause programs. The input to the interpreter is a logic program, and a computation rule. In Section 3 we consider ways in which the computation rule can be specified. In IC-PROLOG it is partly implicitly given, by the text ordering of the program, and partly explicitly given, by clause annotations. Using them the programmer can specify a separate execution strategy for each procedural use of the program. They also enable him to indicate that certain sub-computations should be coroutined, with the resumptions and suspensions being triggered by the flow data through a shared variable.

1. SYNTAX OF HORN CLAUSE PROGRAMS

In this section we introduce the idea of sets of sentences of first order logic as programs. We consider, in particular, the special case of Horn clause logic programs.

1.1 Inference as computation: a brief history

Robinson's machine-oriented resolution inference rule for the clausal notation of predicate logic (Robinson 1965) was the first essential step along the road to viewing inference as computation. Then Green (1969) showed that a resolution theorem prover could be used to 'simulate' a computation. However it was Hayes (1973) and Kowalski (1974) who gave resolution inference an explicit procedural interpretation, Kowalski for the Horn clause subset of predicate logic and Hayes, for the most part, for logic programs comprising a set of equality statements. The final credibility was provided by the Marseilles (Roussel 1975) and Edinburgh (Warren et al. 1977) PROLOG implementations. These are essentially computationally efficient Horn clause theorem provers. The Edinburgh implementation, which borrowed and extended the implementation techniques of the Marseilles PROLOG, is particularly impressive. It pre-compiles much of the work of a unification (the basic unit of computation of a logic program) as a sequence of machine level instructions associated with the program clauses. For list manipulation programs it compares favourably with compiled pure LISP; Warren et alia (1977) has the details. PROLOG has also been implemented in Budapest (Futo et al. 1977), Leuven (Bruynooghe 1976), London (Clark and McCabe 1979) and Waterloo (Roberts 1977).

We shall follow Kowalski and use Horn clause implications as the basic programming notation. We assume some familiarity with the concepts of unification and resolution, however we shall give a brief explanation of these ideas.

1.2 Syntax of Horn clause programs

Definitions

(1) A *Horn clause implication* is a sentence of the form

$$R(t_1, \ldots, t_n) \leftarrow A_1 \,\&\, \ldots \,\&\, A_m \quad m \geqslant 0 \tag{1}$$

Each A_i, like $R(t_1, \ldots, t_n)$, is an atomic formula. When m = 0, and the antecedent of the implication is empty, we call the implication an assertion. We will generally drop the '←' when writing assertions.

(2) Something is an *atomic formula* (or *atom*) if it is of the form $R(t_1, \ldots, t_n)$ where R is an n-adic relation name (predicate) and $t_1, \ldots t_n$ are terms.

(3) A *term* is a variable, a constant, or of the form $f(t_1, \ldots, t_n)$, where f is an n-adic function name (functor) and $t_1, \ldots, t_n$ are terms.

We assume a denumerable set of names comprising finite length strings over a finite alphabet which does not include the logical symbols '←' ',' '(' ')' and '&'. Whether or not a name is a functor or a predicate can be determined by context. To distinguish variables and constants we adopt the convention that names beginning with a lower case letter are variables. All other names in the context of a variable or constant are assumed to be constants. Informally, we shall use infix notation for both terms and atoms. For example, we shall write 'u *in* u.x' instead of 'in(u, . (u,x))'. We shall assume that all infix functors associate to the right, so '2.3.NIL' is syntactic sugar for '.(2,. (3,NIL))'. We will italicise infix predicate symbols.

Declarative reading. If $x_1, \ldots, x_k$ are all the variables of implication (1) we can read it as:

For all $x_1, \ldots, x_k$, $R(t_1, \ldots, t_n)$ if A_1 and A_2 . . . and A_m.

Alternatively, if $y_1, \ldots, y_i$ are variables that only appear in the antecedent $A_1 \& \ldots \& A_m$, and $z_1, \ldots, z_j$ are all the other variables, we can read it as:

For all $z_1, \ldots, z_j$, $R(t_1, \ldots, t_n)$ if
there exists $y_1, \ldots, y_i$ such that A_1 and . . . and A_m.

The alternative reading derives from the fact that a universally quantified implication

$$(\forall x)\ [P \leftarrow Q]$$

is logically equivalent to

$$[P \leftarrow (\exists x)Q]$$

when x does not appear in P. We use '(∀x)' when we want to explicitly indicate a universal quantification of a variable x, '(∃x)' for an existential quantification.

We shall say that implication (1) is about the predicate R, because R is the predicate of the consequent atom of the implication.

Definition. A *logic program for a predicate R* comprises a set of Horn clause implications about R, together with logic programs for any other predicates that appear in the antecedents of these clauses.

As in all programming notations we shall assume that some predicates are primitive, with a fixed 'system' provided program. An example would be the product predicate. Atoms that use the predicate will usually be written as $t_3 = t_1 * t_2$, t_1, t_2 and t_3 being the terms of the atom and ' . . = . .*. . ' being the infix relation name. Conceptually, we treat the system provided implementation as equivalent to the infinite set of assertions:

$$0 = 0 * 0$$
$$0 = 1 * 0$$
$$0 = 0 * 1$$
$$1 = 1 * 1$$
$$\vdots$$
$$4 = 2 * 2$$
$$\vdots$$

Of course, in practice only a finite subset of these assertions will be accessible, that subset being represented procedurally so as to make use of the hardware operations of the machine. We shall elaborate on this procedural implementation of a set of assertions in Section 3.

1.3 Example Logic Programs

Example program - 1

append(NIL,x,x)
append(u.x,y,u.z) ← append(x,y,z) (2)

is a logic program for the predicate 'append'. As the mnemonic content of this relation name indicates, the two statements of the program can be read as statements about appending list structures. We take 'NIL' to be the name of the empty list, and '.' to be the name of a list constructor such that u.x is the list x with u 'consed' onto the front. With this interpretation the assertion of the program tells us that for all x, appending the empty list onto x leaves it unchanged. The implication tells us that for all x, y, z and u, if z is the result of appending x and y then the list u.z is the result of appending u.x and y.

Recursive data structures. A term of the form $t_1 . t_2 . . . t_n$. NIL is the name of the list $[t_1, t_2, . . t_n]$. The set of all such terms is the recursive data structure implicitly introduced by this logic program. Note that the 'cases' treated by each clause are indicated by the 'patterns' of terms in the consequent atom of the clause, the 'procedure head' as Kowalski calls it. This is a common form of logic programs for relations on recursive data structures. Since we usually give the form of both the 'input' and 'output' structures it corresponds to a slight generalisation of the case format proposed by Hoare (1973) for programs manipulating recursive data structures.

Computational use. Suppose we want to compute the concatenation of two lists, say the two unit lists [2] and [3]. We do this by asking for the (single) instance of the unary relation:

x is a concatenation of [2] and [3].

Under our assumed meaning of the 'append' predicate this relation is named by append(2.NIL,3.NIL,x), and a request for an instance of this relation is expressed by the goal clause

← append(2.NIL,3.NIL,x)

An evaluation of this clause using the program clauses is a constructive proof, using the program clauses as premises, that there is an x such that append (2.NIL,3.NIL,x). It is constructive since it will result in x being bound to '2.3.NIL'. That this term names the concatenation [2,3] of the lists [2], [3] is guaranteed by the fact that under our 'reading' of 'NIL' as the empty list and '.' as an add front element list constructor each of our logic program clauses is a true statement about the append relation for lists. Because the computation of the output binding is an inference, which preserves truth, it must denote a true instance of the relation:

x is a concatenation of [2], [3].

This truth-preserving aspect of a logic program computation is its crucial property. It enables us to understand a logic program *declaratively* or *procedurally*; to understand it as a set of statements about the relation we want to compute, or as a recipe for finding instances of the relation.

In the case of our append program its declarative reading is as a pair of universally quantified statements about the list append relation. Its procedural reading depends on its intended use. As a program for appending a pair of lists it should be read as:

to append the empty list NIL to a list y return y,
otherwise, to append a constructed list u.x to a list y first append x to y
giving z, then return u.z.

Non-deterministic use. We can use the same logic program non-deterministically to split a list into front and back sublists. To split the list [2,3] we use the goal clause

← append(x,y,2.3.NIL)

since this names the relation

{⟨x,y⟩: [2,3] is the concatenation of x,y}

As we shall see, each of the substitutions

{x/NIL,y/2.3.NIL}
{x/2.NIL,y/3.NIL}
{x/2.3.NIL,y/NIL}

is a possible answer substitution. Each correctly denotes an instance of the relation. The ability to use the same set of clauses to compute both a function and its inverse, and more generally to find an instance of any relation that can be named by a goal clause, is a particular feature of logic programs.

As a program for decomposing a list into front and back sublists, the append program has the procedural reading:

To decompose the empty list NIL, return ⟨NIL,NIL⟩,
otherwise, to decompose a constructed list u.z
either return ⟨NIL,u.z⟩
or decompose z into ⟨x,y⟩ and return ⟨u.x,y⟩.

The *either, or* indicates a non-deterministic branch.

Most general answers. The goal clause:

← append(x,y,z)

is a request for any tuple of lists in the append relation. As we might expect there are an infinite number of possible answer substitutions. However, our goal clause evaluator will return answers that denote not a single instance, but an infinite set of instances. This is because the evaluator always returns 'most general answers' whenever possible. One answer is

{x/NIL,y/y,z/y}

which denotes the infinite set of list tuples

{⟨[],1,1⟩:1 any list}

Another answer is

{x/u.NIL,y/y,z/u.y}

which gives the general form of the infinite set of append instances that have a unit list as first argument. Each answer substitution for this goal clause denotes not just a single instance of the relation named by the clause but an infinite subset of the relation.

As a program for generating the general form of an instance of the append relation our logic program has the procedural reading:

Either return the instance ⟨NIL,x,x⟩,
or find an instance ⟨t_1, t_2,t_3⟩ and return ⟨u.t_1,t_2,u.t_3⟩ where u is a variable not appearing in t_1,t_2,t_3.

Example program-2

When we describe the abstract interpreter in the next section we shall see that the generation and modification of answer substitutions is the data structure construction and manipulation of a logic program evaluation. Viewed as data structures, answer bindings that contain variables have a special role. This is because the answer binding x/t, where t contains variables, is implicitly modified to an answer binding x/t′ whenever any variables in t are bound by a subsequent evaluation step. This gives the effect of a data structure modification that would normally require an explicitly programmed assignment. The following logic program is an example of a program that can be used to manipulate most general answers in just this way. It is a program for the predicate 'front' which is intended to name the relation which holds between a number n and a pair of lists z,x when x comprises the first n elements of z. It makes use of the above program for 'append' and an auxiliary program for the list length relation.

front(n,x,z) ←length(x,n) & append(x,y,z)

length(NIL,0)
length(u.x,s(n)) ←length(x,n)

Let us note in passing that the program implicitly 'declares' two recursive data structures. The first is the set of lists generated from the empty list, named by 'NIL', using the list generator named by '.', which we have already come across. The other is the recursive data structure of the natural numbers, the set of objects generated from zero, named by '0', using the number generator, add 1, named by 's'. The term 's(0)' denotes the number 1, 's(s (0))' the number 2, and so on. We can, and we shall, use the normal decimal notation numerals as syntactic sugar for these term structure names.

Returning to our example program, relative to the intended interpretation of its predicates and function names ←front(2,A.B.C.NIL,x) names the unary relation that is true of x when it names the list [a,b] of the first two elements of the list [a,b,c]. One computational use of the program to construct the answer substitution {x/A.B.NIL} (and as we shall see in section 3 there is another quite different use) is equivalent to an evaluation of the goal clause ←length(2,x) to produce an answer substitution {x/u.v.NIL} , followed by an evaluation of the goal clause ←append(u.v.NIL,y,A.B.C.NIL) to produce the final answer substitution {x/A.B.NIL} . The first answer binding for x gives us the general form of a list of two elements, and the second answer binding is generated when the evaluation of ←append(u.v.NIL,y,A.B.C.NIL) 'fills-in' the u,v slots by generating the substitution {u/A,v/B} .

This two-pass style of data structure seems to be unique to logic programming. It provides the logic programmer with an elegant and powerful programming feature. (Warren et alia (1977) elaborate on this point.) It is, incidentally, an unavoidable consequence of using a resolution theorem prover as the program executor.

Example program-3

The two sets of assertions:

Jack *fathered* George	Tom *married* Mary
Tom *fathered* Bill	Bill *married* Jane
⋮	⋮
Bob *fathered* Tom	Jack *married* Susan

(3)

are a quite different kind of logic program. They are more like a data base than a program in the conventional sense. With the English language meaning of the relation names we can read them as a description of certain family relations that prevail amongst a group of people named 'Jack', 'George', etc.

Data retrieval. We 'compute' with the data-base-style program in exactly the same way as with the 'recursive' program for append. Thus a goal clause

←Tom *fathered* x & x *married* Jane

is a request for an instance of the unary relation (presumably the only instance) that is satisfied by offsprings of Tom that are married to Jane. The evaluation of this goal clause will be a search over the '*father-of*' and '*married-to*' assertion sets. One result is the binding x/Bill.

2. PROCEDURAL SEMANTICS

The abstract interpreter we shall describe in this section is a resolution theorem prover. The unit of computation is a resolution inference of which the essential component is a unification. Unification is the process of finding a substitution that makes two atoms syntactically identical. Before describing the interpreter we shall give a brief introduction to the concepts of substitution and unification. For more detailed information the reader should consult Robinson (1965) or his more recent book (Robinson 1979).

2.1 Substitutions and substitution instances

Definitions

(1) A *substitution* is a set

$$\theta = \{ x_1/t_1, \ldots, x_k/t_k \}$$

of variable/term pairs in which the $x_1, \ldots, x_k$ are distinct variables. We say that x_i is bound to the term t_i.

(2) A *substitution instance* of a clause C is any clause that can be obtained from C by simultaneously replacing each of the variables bound by a substitution θ, at each of its occurrences in C, by the term to which it is bound. We use $C\theta$ to denote this substitution instance

(3) For a substitution

$$\theta = \{x_1/y_1, \ldots, x_k/y_k\}$$

which binds all the variables $x_1, \ldots, x_k$ of a clause C to a tuple of terms which are just k distinct variables $y_1, \ldots, y_k$, the substitution instance $C\theta$ is called a *variant* of C.

(4) The *composition* $\theta_1 * \theta_2$ of two substitutions

$$\theta_1 = \{x_1/t_1, \ldots, x_n/t_n\}, \theta_2 = \{y_1/t'_1, \ldots, y_k/t'_k\}$$

is the substitution

$$\theta'_1 \ \theta'_2$$

where

$$\theta'_1 = \{x_1/[t_1]\theta_2, \ldots, x_n/[t_n]\theta_2\}$$

and θ'_2 is θ_2 with any bindings for the variables $x_1, \ldots, x_n$ deleted.

Examples

If C is the clause

$$P(f(x,a),g(b,y)) \leftarrow Q(x,z) \ \& \ P(y,z)$$

and

$$\theta_1 = \{x/u,y/v,z/x\}$$
$$\theta_2 = \{x/h(u),y/x,z/b\}$$
$$\theta_3 = \{u/g(b),x/h(u)\}$$

then $[C]\theta_1$ is the C variant

$$P(f(u,a),g(b,v)) \leftarrow Q(u,x) \ \& \ P(v,x)$$

$[C]\theta_2$ is the substitution instance

$$P(f(h(u),a),g(b,x)) \leftarrow Q(h(u),b) \ \& \ P(x,b)$$

and $\theta_2 * \theta_3$ is the substitution

$$\{x/h(g(b)),y/h(u),z/b,u/g(b)\} .$$

A clause variant just 'says the same thing' using different variables. The definition of a substitution is a little different from the standard one. Normally identity bindings such as x/x are excluded as the addition of an identity binding does not change the effect of a substitution. We allow identity bindings in substitutions since we want to include them in answer substitutions produced by a logic program evaluation. For us two different sets of bindings θ_1 θ_2 are the *same* substitution, i.e.

$$\theta_1 = \theta_2$$

if they are identical *sets* of bindings after the deletion of any identity bindings. Thus the identity substitution, the substitution that leaves any clause unchanged, is denoted by any set of identity bindings, including the empty set. Composition of substitutions is defined so that

$$[C\theta]\theta' = [C]\theta*\theta'.$$

It also has the property that composition is associative. In consequence we shall leave out the brackets in expressions such as $\theta_1*\theta_2*\theta_3$.

Definition. A *unifier* of two atoms A_1,A_2 is a substitution θ such that $[A_1]\theta$ and $[A_2]\theta$ are syntactically identical. It is a *most general unifier* (m.g.u.) if every other unifying substitution θ' is such that $\theta' = \theta*\theta''$ for some substitution θ''.

Example. The substitution

{w/2.z,u/2,x/NIL,y/3.NIL}

is an m.g.u. for the pair of atoms

append(2.NIL,3.NIL,w) & append(u.x,y,u.z).

When applied to each atom it produces the substitution instance

append(2.NIL,3.NIL,2.z).

An algorithm which tests whether or not two atoms are unifiable, and which returns an m.g.u. if they are, is a unification algorithm. Robinson (1965) gives such an algorithm and proves it correct. For us unification does the work of data structure component selection (the bindings u/2, x/NIL in the above example), and unification and composition does the work of data structure construction (the binding w/2.z composed with some binding for z). Most of the pairs of atoms that must be unified during a logic program evaluation fall within the confines of a special case for which a much faster, modified form of Robinson's algorithm can be used.

The two atoms never have variables in common and it is nearly always the case that one of the atoms only has a single occurrence of each of its variables. For this special case, the expensive *occur check* of Robinson's algorithm is not needed. This is the check, which must normally be performed each time a variable x is matched against a non-variable t, that x does not occur in t. If it does then the attempted unification fails. However for the special case we have described an occur failure *cannot* arise. For this reason most PROLOG implementations never perform the occur check, and in IC-PROLOG in must be explicitly requested.

2.2 An abstract interpreter

Any resolution theorem prover can be used as a Horn clause program executor. However the inference system which is most obviously computational is LUSH resolution (Hill 1974). This is the inference system that Kowalski describes when he talks about the procedural interpretation of predicate logic (Kowalski 1974).

The LUSH inference rule defines a search space of alternative derivations. We prefer to think of these alternative derivations as alternative paths of a non-deterministic evaluation of a 'call' of the logic program given by some *goal clause*

$$\leftarrow B_1 \& \ldots \& B_n$$

Here, $B_1, \ldots, B_n$ are all atomic formulae, and, if $x_1, \ldots, x_k$ are the variables of the clause, it is a 'call' for the computation of a substitution

$$\theta = \{x_1/e_1, x_2/e_2, \ldots, x_k/e_k\}$$

such that

$$\langle e_1, e_2, \ldots, e_k \rangle$$

denotes an instance, or set of instances, of the relation 'named' by the conjunction $B_1 \& \ldots \& B_n$ for any 'reading' of the program as a set of true statements. If there are no variables in the goal clause it is a request for the confirmation that for any such reading $B_1 \& \ldots \& B_n$ is a true statement.

The trace of some evaluation path of the computation is given by a sequence of goal clauses

$$C_1, C_2, \ldots, C_n, \ldots$$

each one derived from the proceeding one by the following evaluation step. We shall follow Kowalski (1974) and refer to the program clauses as procedures. The consequent atoms of the clauses are then procedure heads and the antecedent atoms are procedure calls. We shall also refer to the atoms of the goal clause as procedure calls.

Evaluation step. Suppose the current goal comprises the conjunction of procedure calls

$$\leftarrow B_1 \& \ldots \& B_k$$

An evaluation step is the execution of one of these calls. Which one it should be is determined by a *computation rule*, a rule which for any conjunction of procedure calls encountered during the evaluation uniquely determines which call is to be executed first. For now we shall not concern ourselves with how the computation rule is specified or applied. We shall simply assume that there is an effective rule that will select a single call from the goal clause. Any such rule is a possible computation rule.

Assume that the selected call is B_i, and that this is the atom $R(t_1, \ldots, t_n)$. An attempt is made to execute this call using a procedure

$$R(t'_1, \ldots, t'_n) \leftarrow A_1 \& \ldots \& A_m$$

which is a variant of one of the program clauses for R that does not contain variables appearing in the goal clause. If there is more than one program clause for R the choosing of the procedure is a non-deterministic step in the evaluation, each alternative procedure giving us an alternative branching of the evaluation.

We try to unify $R(t_1, \ldots, t_n)$ with $R(t'_1, \ldots, t'_n)$.

If they do not unify this branching of the evaluation path terminates with *fail*.

If they do unify, with most general unifier θ, this branching of the evaluation path leads to a new conjunction of procedure calls, a new goal clause, which is the resolvent

$$\leftarrow [B_1 \& \ldots \& B_{i-1} \& A_1 \& \ldots \& A_m \& B_{i+1} \& \ldots \& B_k]\theta$$

Note that the substitution instance of the conjunction of procedure calls in the body of the program procedure have replaced B_i in the new goal clause. But also note that the unifying substitution is applied to all of the procedure calls of the new goal clause. This means that any output binding of the substitution, any binding of a variable x that was in the executed call B_i, is immediately communicated to any other call B_j in which x appears. As we shall see later, we can use the idea of data flow through the shared variables of procedure calls to specify and implement data flow computation rules.

Finally, if there are no program procedures for R, we consider that there is just one next step for the evaluation path that has produced the goal clause $\leftarrow B_1 \& \ldots \& B_k$ which gives an immediate *fail.*

Successful evaluation. An evaluation path terminates with *success* when the empty goal clause is generated. This happens when the last step is the execution of the single call of a goal clause ←B using an assertion procedure $B' \leftarrow$.

Computed answer substitution. Suppose $\theta_1, \ldots \theta_n$ is the sequence of unifying substitutions of a successful evaluation, θ_1 being the substitution of the first step, θ_n that of the last step. Let

$$\theta = \theta_1 * \theta_2 * \ldots * \theta_n$$

be the composition of these unifying substitions. The subset of θ that gives bindings for the variables of the initial goal clause C, augmented with the identity substitution x/x for any variable of C not bound by θ, is the answer given by that successful evaluation. If there are no variables in C, the answer is *true*.

Procedural vs. Declarative semantics. The above definition effectively provides us with a *procedural semantics* for answer substitutions. It characterises answer substitutions in terms of a mechanism for computing them. In Van Emden and Kowalski (1976) and Clark (1979) a quite different declarative semantics is given. In the declarative semantics answer substitutions are characterised in terms of models of the program clauses and the corresponding denotations of the goal clauses. In what amounts to a completeness proof for LUSH resolution, first given in Hill (1974), it can be shown that for *any* computation rule the procedural and the declarative semantics characterise essentially the same set of answer substitutions. This independence of the computation rule is a great boon. It enables the logic programmer to select a computation rule purely on the grounds of computational efficiency. We shall return to this point later.

Evaluation trees A logic program P, a goal clause C, and a computation rule R, together define an evaluation tree of all the possible evaluation paths for C. The form of the tree is as depicted in Fig. 1. Each interior node in the tree is a clause derived from its parent by an evaluation step. Each of the children of a node are the results of attempted executions of the selected procedure call of that node.

A fail node offspring records a failed unification. A success leaf node marks the end of each successful evaluation path. Some of the evaluation paths may be infinite.

Figs. 2 and 3 are evaluation trees for two of the calls to the logic programs of the preceding section. The computation rule used is 'select the leftmost call'.

The very first step of the successful evaluation path of Fig. 2 requires the unific-

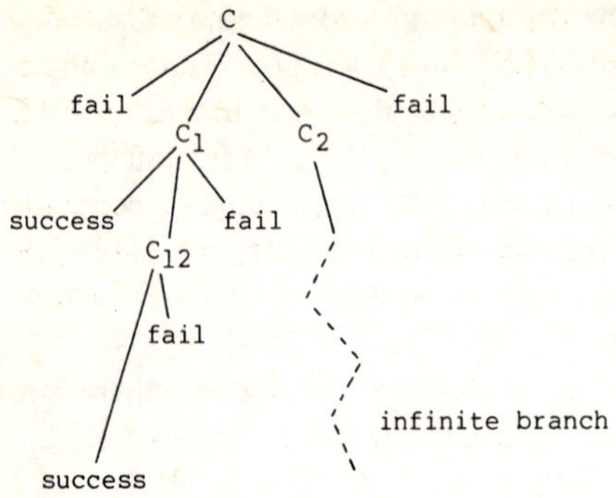

Figure 1. An evaluation tree

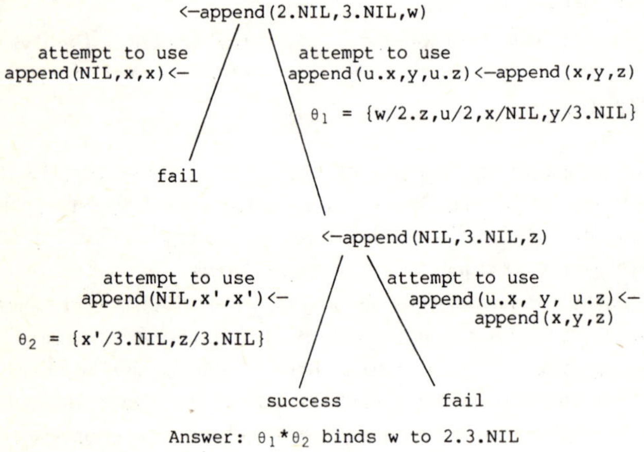

Figure 2. Evaluation of append

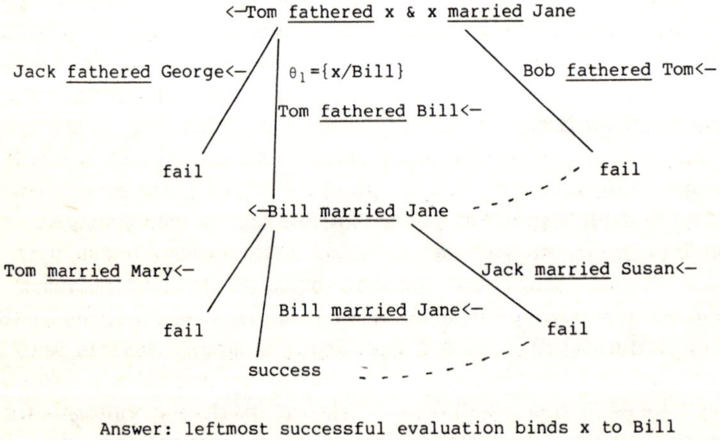

Figure 3. Evaluation of fathered

ation of append(2.NIL,3.NIL,w) and append(u.x,y,u.z). The m.g.u. binds u to 2 and x to NIL, that is it decomposes the 'input' 2.NIL into its head and tail sublists. As we mentioned above, the selection of components from data structures in accordance with a given pattern, in this case the pattern 'u.x', is one of the major roles of unification. The other major role is the production of partial approximations, templates, for the output. This is illustrated by the binding 2.z for w. This binding gives us a first approximation to the answer substitution w/2.3.NIL which is the final output of the evaluation path. It tells us that any answer for the path will bind w to 2.'something'. This first approximation is a partial result that could now be accessed by another procedure call in which w appeared. We shall return to this idea of 'data flow' activation of procedure calls in Section 3.

Both evaluation trees of Figs.2 and 3 are finite. Hence a back-tracking search, which is a walk over an evaluation tree as depicted in Fig.4, can be used to search for a successful evaluation.

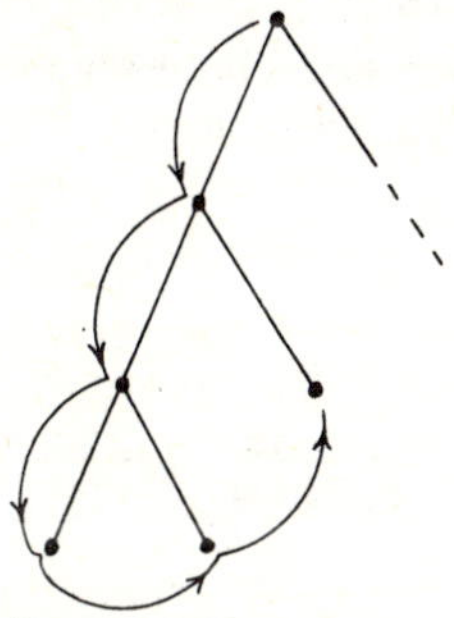

Figure 4. Backtracking

Such a walk over the evaluation tree of Fig.3 amounts to a double loop search over the '*fathered*' and '*married*' assertion sets. A similar walk over the evaluation tree of Fig.2. does not involve significant backtracking. Each failure node is an immediate offspring of the one and only successful evaluation path. Evaluation trees such as this record an essentially deterministic computation. At each step there is only one clause whose consequent will unify with the selected call of the goal clause.

A genuinely non-deterministic use of the append program is depicted in Fig.5. It is the evaluation tree for the goal clause ←append(x,y,2.3.NIL). Each of the answer substitutions gives one of the possible decompositions of the list [2,3] into front and back sublists.

A note on implementation. A partially constructed branch of the evaluation tree can be represented as a stack of activation records. Extending this branch to derive a new goal clause is then a stack push operation which adds an activation record to the stack. This contains a pointer to the program clause that was used, and a pointer to a binding environment containing the bindings for all the new variables introduced by that clause. This stack representation of the current and preceeding goal clauses, which is essentially the Boyer and Moore (1972) structure sharing representation of resolvents, corresponds to the conventional stack implementation of recursion. It also carries an added bonus. Backtracking to try an alternative clause for the previous

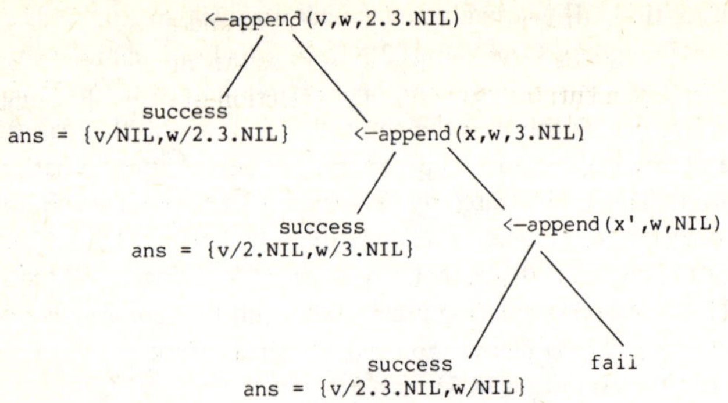

Figure 5. Non-deterministic append evaluation

evaluation step is little more than a stack pop operation. So a backtracking search for a successful evaluation is an interleaved sequence of stack pushes and stack pops. Because backtracking is so easy to implement, all the PROLOG implementations use backtracking as the search strategy. For more details on implementation the reader should consult Warren (1977).

3. CONTROLLING THE EVALUATION

The search strategy and the computation rule are the control components of a logic program. A logic programming implementation should enable the programmer to specify, at least partly, the computation rule and the search strategy.

3.1 Search Control

As we remarked above, for reasons of efficient implementation all PROLOG systems use backtracking as the search strategy. This leaves the programmer with limited search control. He can only control the order in which the program clauses are tried. He specifies this implicitly by the before-after order in which the clauses are written. Although a fixed try order is not adequate for 'problem solving' uses of the evaluator (Kowalski 1979b), which in any case would usually need some sort of breadth-first search strategy, a judicious choice of the try order is all that is required for nearly all the LISP-style, and even the data-base-style, logic programs. A programmer quickly learns how to exploit the backtracking, and to appreciate it as a powerful control primitive of logic programs.

Clause indexing. As an additional search facility we could index the clauses. The Edinburgh PROLOG automatically indexes all the program clauses on the constant or top-level functor of the first argument. This cuts out much of the shallow backtracking of the search for an applicable clause. Alternatively, one could allow the programmer to specify which clauses should be indexed, and the degree of indexing required.

IC-PROLOG gives the programmer just such indexing control. For any predicate the programmer can request indexing of all the clauses for the predicate on any or all of the argument positions. For each indexed argument the index groups together all the clauses that have the same constant, the same top-level functor, or a variable in that argument position. The indexing is particularly useful for data-base-style programs. By indexing the set of assertions that provide the extensional definition of a data base relation we can access directly the subset, even the individual assertion, that can possibly match the call. Indexing can also be useful for the LISP-style programs. It can make the try order irrelevant for most calls, the index effectively providing us with a conditional branch to the appropriate clause.

Indexing for data-base style programs. To see how indexing can affect the evaluation of a goal we look again at the example program-3 from Section 1.3. In particular, we see how indexing affects the evaluation of

← Tom *fathered* x & x *married* Jane (1)

If we just index on the first argument of the *fathered* relation, then for the call 'Tom *fathered* x' indexing 'extracts' from the *fathered* relation all those instances where 'Tom' is mentioned in the first argument. In other words, indexing on the first argument will cause only those assertions mentioning children of Tom to be considered by the interpreter. The backtrack search mechanism will then iterate through this set of assertions, trying to evaluate the second call: 't *married* Jane' for each possible 't'.

For this second call we can have three different kinds of search behaviour depending on the indexing we apply to the *married* relation (assuming we do some indexing). If we index on just the first argument, then the index access will be controlled by the result of the first call. Indexing will extract from the *married* relation those instances where t is married to someone. The interpreter will then search through these instances to see if the someone is in fact 'Jane'. If the backtrack search fails the next candidate child of Tom is used, a new access to the index is made, using the new child as the key, and so on until a solution is found. The behaviour we get by indexing on the first argument of each relation is that of the iteration:

for each child x of Tom
    for each y married to x
        if y = Jane, exit with x.

If instead, we index on the second argument of the *married* relation then access via the index will return as candidate assertions only those where 'some-one is married to Jane'. In this case the accesses to the indexes are independent (and could be done in parallel). The backtracking evaluation of the two call goal clause effectively computes the intersection of the children of Tom and spouses of Jane. The behaviour is equivalent to:

for each child x of Tom
    for each spouse y of Jane
        if x = y, exit with x.

Finally, suppose we have indexed on *both* arguments of the *married* relation. In this case index access for the second call amounts to a look-up of the married relation to confirm (or otherwise) that the child of 'Tom' returned by the first call is indeed married to Jane. The behaviour of the goal clause evaluation is that of the iteration:

for each child x of Tom
    if x is married to Jane, exit with x.

Compare these search behaviours with the case when no indexing is done. The whole of the *fathered* relation is sequentially searched until an occurrence of 'Tom *fathered* t' is found. Each time one is found the whole of the *married* relation is sequentially searched to see if 't is *married* to Jane'. The behaviour is that of:

```
for each fathered pair ⟨x,y⟩
         if x = Tom,
                  for each married pair ⟨y',z⟩
                           if z = Jane & y = y', exit with y.
```

For large relations this is an expensive method of searching, which indexing can eliminate. As we have seen, indexing can be used to get some interesting search behaviours from data-base style programs; in particular, an unacceptable sequential search can be transformed into an acceptable direct look-up.

Indexing for LISP-style programs. Consider the length program (from example program-2 in Section 1.3). If we index on both arguments, we get a case analysis on both the list structure (NIL vs. u.v) *and* the size of the length; ie. whether the length of the list is 0, or greater than 0 (0 vs. s(x)). This means that whether we use the program to find the length of a list, or to find a list of a given length, the abstract interpreter always only tries to use the correct clause. In this case, the access via the index is a conditional branch to the appropriate clause.

The notion of indexing on the top-level function names and constants, generalises to indexing on lower-level terms as well. This would allow finer discrimination, which would be useful for certain LISP-style programs, though rather less useful for common data-base style programs.

Arithmetic Data Base. We can now be more specific about the nature of the built-in arithmetic relations discussed in Section 1.2. The reader will recall that the implementation of the addition relation was stated as being equivalent to a data base of assertions, each of which described a single arithmetic sum. We will now say a little about the representation of these assertions. We have already seen how indexing can turn an apparently inefficient sequential search through a relation, into a fast look-up into the relation. The implementation of these arithmetic predicate is in fact equivalent to a fully indexed set of assertions.

This means, that when the interpreter is evaluating an addition procedure call, instead of searching through all the assertions in the addition relation trying to find the correct ones, only those portions of the relation that are directly relevant to the call are considered. For example, in evaluating the goal:

$\leftarrow x = 2 + 3$,

only the instance '5 = 2 + 3' will be looked at by the interpreter, from the whole addition relation. Normal evaluation, using this assertion, will cause the answer binding x/5 to be made. For 'normal' computation the evaluation of arithmetic expressions will be straight-forward. Each expression will be evaluated just as in any ordinary programming language, there is no searching 'for the correct next step'.

Of course we do not *actually* have this large set of assertions stored somewhere, nor do we *actually* use the indexing mechanism to sort the relation. What in fact happens is the interpreter uses the underlying hardware to do the additions etc., the 'indexing' is translated into a case analysis of the call: depending on the actual usage of the arithmetic relation, the hardware will be requested to do additions, subtractions, multiplications and so on.

We do not sacrifice any flexibility however, the 'arithmetic data base' still reflects faithfully the declarative semantics of an indexed set of assertions. For example, in the evaluation of the call ←5 = x+y the instances of the addition relation considered by the interpreter will be:

5 = 5+0 with answers for x and y: {x/5, y/0}
5 = 4+1 {x/4, y/1}
⋮ ⋮
5 = 0+5 {x/0, y/5}

The interpreter will search through this set of assertions in the normal way, finding values for x and y, and check that they satisfy the constraints of the other call(s) in the goal. Because of the indexing, no other instances from the addition relation will be considered. This is an example of a non-deterministic use of the arithmetic data-base. To our knowledge no other implemented language allows the non-deterministic use of arithmetic primitives.

We can use this flexibility in the arithmetic data base to write some very elegant programs, for some examples of this, and for a more detailed explanation of the way indexes are requested, constructed and used, the reader is referred to the IC-PROLOG reference manual (Clark and McCabe 1979).

3.2 Computation Rule Control

The computation rule is an area in which we can more usefully exploit control flexibility. In this, IC-PROLOG differs significantly from the Marseilles and Edinburgh PROLOG implementations. Both of these use a fixed, leftmost call computation rule. As with the use of a fixed search strategy, this means that programmer control is rather limited. By the left-to-right ordering of the procedure calls of each clause he does control the order which they will be selected. However this given order is then fixed for each use of the clause, and the sequence of calls are always evaluated in a strictly sequential fashion. We shall see that this fixed order, strictly sequential execution has considerable drawbacks, that it does not enable us to fully exploit the potential of logic programming. On the credit side, sequential execution, being the norm for programming languages, is a control concept that is easy to understand and use, and the leftmost call computation rule is extremely easy to implement. If we are to allow more elaborate programmer specified computation rules, which is possible in IC-PROLOG, we must make sure that they embody equally intuitive control concepts. We must also make sure that they impose the minimum run-time overhead.

Drawbacks of a fixed order strictly sequential execution. To see what sort of control facilities might prove useful let us consider the disadvantages of the leftmost call rule. There are two main disadvantages. The first is a consequence of the fact that the textual left to right order of the procedure calls of a clause defines the execution order for *every* use of the clause. This means that, despite the theoretical possibility of using a logic program to find any unspecified arguments of a relation, it is usually only computationally viable for one input-output pattern. The second disadvantage is a consequence of the depth first evaluation, the fact that each call, once selected, is completely evaluated before control moves to an adjacent call.

To illustrate these drawbacks let us consider the procedure:

R(x,z) ←P(x,y) & Q(v,z).

This tells us that x and z are in the R relation if there is some y which 'connects' x and z via the P and Q relations.

With the given ordering of the procedure calls we can expect that the use of this procedure is computationally viable for calls in which both x and z are given, or for calls in which x is given and a corresponding z is to be computed. However, for calls of the form ←R(x,t), in which a non-variable term t supplies a value for z and a corresponding x is to be found, the given order of the calls is far from suitable. It will result in the call ←P(x,y), rather than the more suitable ←Q(y,t), being used to generate the intermediary value for y. Thus, the candidate values for y will be produced by unconstrained 'guesses', while the computation of a y value that satisfies Q(y,t) might be essentially deterministic. To fully exploit the input-output flexibility of logic programs we should at least make the order of execution of the calls of a procedure dependent upon the input-output of the invoking call.

However, even for calls of the form ←R(t,z), for which the given order of the calls is satisfactory, a strictly sequential execution can be far from optimal. Let us suppose that the evaluation for the derived call ←P(t,y) is truly non-deterministic, that there are several values for y that satisfy P(t,y). Let us further suppose that each of these values is denoted by a term t′ which is approximated to by a sequence of partial results, $t_1, t_2, \ldots, t_n$ that are produced at various stages of the evaluation of P(t,y). We observed this partial result phenomena in Fig.2. We saw that even the first step in the evaluation of the call ←append(2.NIL,3. NIL,z) produces the partial result 2.x as the first approximation of the final value 2.3.NIL. In these circumstances, which are not uncommon, the best execution strategy is to co-routine between the P and Q evaluations. The Q evaluation is entered, and then re-entered, whenever a new partial result is generated, and the P evaluation is resumed whenever a new partial result is required. If at any stage the latest partial result that is communicated to Q cannot denote any value that satisfies the Q relation, we shall benefit from an early failure. The overall evaluation can then backtrack to find an alternative partial result for y, and we have saved what might have been a lengthy computation of the complete result for the abandoned ←P(t,y) evaluation.

3.3 Control Annotation

In IC–PROLOG the medium for the specification of the computation rule is program annotation. With quite simple syntactic additions to the basic Horn clause syntax the programmer can define a computation rule which changes the try order of the calls of program procedure in accordance with its input-output use, and he can specify a computation rule that will result in a co-routining interaction between certain sub-computations that is triggered by the flow of data through shared variables.

Control alternatives. In order to allow for input-output dependent use of a procedure the programmer can give for each procedure an explicit list of control alternatives. This is a list of annotated program clauses

$[C_1, C_2, \ldots, C_k]\ , k > 0,$

each of which, ignoring the annotations and the order of the antecedent atoms, is an exact copy of a single clause

$B \leftarrow A_1 \& \ldots \& A_n.$

Declaratively, the list of control alternatives is equivalent to this single implication. Procedurally, it also represents just a single alternative for the nondeterministic selection of a program clause to respond to the procedure call $\leftarrow B'$. If B' unifies with B at most one of the clauses in the list may be used for the evaluation step. Which one is used is determined by the '^', '?' annotations attached to terms in the procedure head of each copy of the clause.

These annotations specify extra constraints that must be satisfied by the unification of B' and B before that particular clause can be used. Intuitively, the annotated term 't?' tells us that t must be used as an input template. More formally it signals the requirement that each of its variables must have been matched against a non-variable, or an *input variable of the* call. If t does not contain variables, it signals the requirement that t must have been matched against an identical variable free term. We must wait until the discussion of the data flow coroutining before we can define input variable. Roughly speaking, it is a variable through which the call will eventually 'receive' data, in the form of a non-variable binding, generated by some other procedure call.

The annotation '^' signals the opposite use. A term t, annotated t^, must be used as an output template. More formally, in the unification it must have been matched against an *output variable of the* call. An output variable is any variable that is not an input variable.

Example-1. The list of control alternatives

[Grandparent (x?,z) ← Parent(x,y) & Parent(y,z),
Grandparent(x^,z?) ← Parent(y,z) & Parent(x,y)]

for the clause defining grandparent would be used to indicate that the intermediary parent y is to be found by looking up the children of the grandparent when the grandparent is given, and by looking up the parents of the grandchild when the grandchild is given and the grandparent is to be found.

Example-2. Suppose we have a data-base of assertions for two binary predicates R and Q and that we have requested indexing on the first argument of R and the second argument of Q. We should use the control list:

[P(x?,y) ← R(x,y) & Q(x,y) ,
P(x^,y?) ← Q(x,y) & R(x,y)]

as a program that computes the intersection of Q and R.

Selection rule. When a clause appears as one of a list of control alternatives then it can be selected only if all the match constraints signalled by the procedure head '?', '^' annotations are satisfied. The first clause in the list with its match constraints satisfied is the one which is used. If there are none, then the evaluation terminates with a control error.

In the above example-1 there is no clause copy for the case when both x and z are to be found. The attempt to use this set of control alternatives for this case will result in a control error. Thus the I/O annotation also gives the programmer a run-time check that no unexpected input-output use will arise.

Data flow co-routining. Having found a control alternative whose input-output conditions are satisfied control 'enters' the body of the selected procedure. In the absence of control annotations in the procedure body the sequence $A_1\& \ldots \&A_n$ of calls will be executed in a strictly left-to-right order. That is, for each i the call A_i is selected only when the evaluation of $A_1\& \ldots \&A_{i-1}$ is complete.

To relax this strict left-to-right evaluation, to enable the evaluation of the call A_i to be commenced prematurely, we can attach a '?' or '^' annotation to one of the variables of A_i. The effect of this is to make the annotated variable, v, a *data channel* for A_i. If the '?' annotation is used A_i is an *eager consumer* of the data that will be sent down the channel by the evaluation of $A_1\& \ldots \&A_{i-1}$. If the '^' annotation is used then A_i is a *lazy producer* of the data that it sends down the channel.

A_i as an eager consumer. If the channel variable v does not appear in at least one of the calls $A_1, \ldots ,A_{i-1}$ the annotation 'v?' on the occurrence of v in A_i has no effect. If it does appear, the effect is to make the evaluation of A_i a special process that can co-routine with the evaluation of $A_1\& \ldots \&A_{i-1}$.

During the evaluation of $A_1\& \ldots \&A_{i-1}$ we can expect that the final output binding for v is approximated to by a sequence

$$t_1,t_2, \ldots ,t_n$$

of non-variable terms. Here, t_1 is the first partial result. It is generated when the composition of the unifying substitutions being generated by the evaluation of $A_1\& \ldots \&A_{i-1}$ first gives a non-variable binding for v. Thereafter, t_{j+1} is the term t_j with one or more of its variables replaced by non-variables. It is generated when the composition of the unifying substitutions induces such a change in the previous binding for v.

A *data call* of A_i occurs whenever one of these partial results t_j is generated. A *data return* from A_i occurs when the computation of the A_i is completed, or, more usually, when it generates the 'need' for the next partial result t_{j+1}. A_i generates the need for t_{j+1} when the next step in its evaluation would result in one or more of the variables of t_j being bound to non-variable terms. That is, when it is about to 'guess' the next partial result. On the return from A_i the evaluation of $A_1\& \ldots \&A_{i-1}$ is resumed at the point of the last data call. Similarly the next data call of A_i, which occurs when the evaluation of $A_1\& \ldots \&A_{i-1}$ generates the required t_{j+1}, will resume the required evaluation of A_i at its last suspension point.

The effect of the sequence of data calls and returns is to co-routine the evaluation of A_i with the evaluation of $A_1\& \ldots \&A_{i-1}$. Each slice of the evaluation of $A_1\& \ldots \&A_{i-1}$ is the generation of a new partial output binding for v, and each slice of the evaluation of A_i is the consumption of this partial output. We call A_i an *eager consumer* because it 'runs' as soon as the next partial output is generated.

The co-routining interaction terminates if either the evaluation of $A_1\& \ldots \&A_{i-1}$

or that of A_i is successfully completed. If it is the former default sequential execution takes over but with the evaluation of A_i picked up at its last suspension point. If it is A_i, then, following what is the last data return from A_i, the evaluation of A_1& . . &A_{i-1} runs to completion, irrespective of whether or not it generates any more partial results for v. On completion, the default sequential execution continues with A_{i+1}.

A_i as a lazy producer. If the occurrence of the variable v in A_i is annotated v much the same co-routining interaction takes place. The significant difference is that this time it is the evaluation of A_i that generates the sequence of partial output bindings for v. Correspondingly, the call and return triggers are reversed.

This time a data call of A_i occurs when the evaluation of A_1& . . &A_{i-1} needs the next partial result, i.e. just before the evaluation step that would result in a variable of the current partial result being bound to a non-variable. A data return from A_i occurs as soon as the next partial result is generated, i.e. just after the evaluation step that so binds a variable of the current partial result. Since we return from A_i as soon as it produces this next level of approximation, we call it a lazy producer.

Nested co-routining. In the above description of the data flow co-routining we have deliberately imposed no constraint on the 'internal' evaluations of the procedure call segment ←A_1& . . &A_{i-1} and the procedure call A_j, j<i, is also data flow annotated with a '?' or a ' '. (The current IC-implementation allows only one eager consumer/lazy producer for each variable. For lazy producers this is a reasonable restriction. For eager consumers it slightly cramps one's style.) This will cause a co-routining interaction between the evaluation of ←A_1& . . &A_{j-1} and ←A_j, within the evaluation of ←A_1& . . &A_j& . . &A_{i-1} . . Other, 'internal' co-routining can take place as a result of data flow annotations in the procedure bodies of the clauses used in the evaluation of ←A_1& . . &A_{i-1} and in the evaluation of ←A_i. Each of these low-level co-routining interactions takes place in accordance with the above procedural semantics.

Lazy evaluation mode. By systematically making all the producers of intermediary results lazy producers the programmer can signal a lazy evaluation mode for his logic program, causing it to compute answer bindings in a lazy LISP fashion (Henderson & Morris 1976, Friedman & Wise 1976). Thus, where he would normally use the annotated clause

R(x?,w^) ←R(x,y) & Q(y,z) & T(z,w)

for a strictly sequential computation of the output w which corresponds to some input x, for a lazy evaluation he can use

R(x?,w^) ←T(z,w) & Q(y,z^) & R(x,y^).

Similarly, if the goal clause

←P(t,x) & R(x,w)

would be used for the sequential construction of x and w bindings, it is rewritten as

←R(x,w) & P(t,x^)

to signal the lazy construction.

Eager evaluation mode. An alternative, eager evaluation mode, can be requested by making all the consumers of the intermediary results eager consumers. For this, one would write the above program clause as

R(x?,w^) ←R(x,y) & Q(y?,z) & T(z?,w)

and the above goal clause as

←P(t,x) & R(x?,w).

In execution, the eager mode program contains much the same data transmissions and requests as the lazy mode program. It just starts by doing some work on generating the first intermediary result, whereas the lazy mode starts by doing some work generating the final result.

Mixed Mode. The fact that lazy or eager interaction is explicitly requested by an annotation means that they can be mixed. For example, one can signal a lazy construction with an eager test, by the annotated clause

P(x?,z^) ←Q(y,z) & R(x,y^) & T(z?)

This ability to mix the execution modes offers a control dimension that we have not yet fully explored. To our knowledge only Schwarz (1977), with his annotated recursion equations, offers a programming notation with the same mixed mode facility. However, that is for an essentially deterministic programming language. As we shall see in our later examples, the conjunction of data flow coroutining and back-tracking search is the really novel control mix offered by IC-PROLOG.

Input variables. We can now define input variable. To make the definition precise we need the concepts of data-transmission and data request. A *data transmission* is a call of an eager consumer or an early return from a lazy producer. A *data request* is a call of a lazy producer or an early return from an eager consumer.

Definition

Let v be a data channel for a call A_i.

Case (1) v is as yet unbound and A_i is a lazy producer of v. v is an input variable of any call selected before the first data request to A_i.

Case (2) v is currently bound to a term t which is one of the partial approximations to the final output binding and A_i is an eager consumer or lazy producer of v. Any variable in t is an input variable for any call selected after the data transmission that communicated t but before the data request for the next partial approximation.

Informally, input variables are those variables that can only be bound to a non-variable by an evaluation step involving some other call.

Delaying the data transfer as described above, a data transfer occurs immediately after the evaluation step that generates the next partial result. However, it might be that this evaluation step has made use of one of several clauses that would have matched the call, a situation which arises when the 'pattern' of terms in the procedure heads of the alternative clauses does not, on its own, determine a single clause which must be used. In this circumstance the appropriate clause is usually selected by one or more test calls that begin each procedure body. Any output that the invoking unification may have produced is really conditional upon the successful execution of the test calls. We should therefore delay any data transfer until after the evaluation of these calls.

The annotation to request such a delay is a ':' used instead of the '&' which immediately follows the test calls. Thus, if we write

P(f(u),g(v)) ←T(u) : R(u,v)

instead of

P(f(u),g(v)) ←T(u) & R(u,v)

this will delay any data transfers that would normally immediately follow the evaluation step that uses this clause until after the evaluation of the call ←T(u) is completed. We call the ':' the clause bar.

More formally, the clause bar can be inserted at any point in the sequence of procedure calls of a program clause, even after the last call. The effect of the bar in a clause

$B \leftarrow A_1\& \, . \, . \, \&A_i{:}A_{i+1}\& \, . \, . \, \&A_n$

is to delay any data transfers out of this procedure until the evaluation of the call segment $A_1\& \, . \, . \, \&A_i$ is complete. A data transfer *out of* the procedure is either a data return from a producer that is an ancestor of $A_1\& \, . \, . \, \&A_n$ (i.e. the use of the clause was an evaluation step of the producer), or it is a data call of an eager consumer that is a sibling of some ancestor of $A_1\& \, . \, . \, \&A_n$. The bar has no delaying effect on suspensions of the procedure evaluation due to data requests.

3.4 Using the Control

For further information on the syntax, and certain restrictions on the use of the producer/consumer annotations, we refer the reader to the complete IC-PROLOG reference manual. We shall content ourselves with two examples of logic programs that use the annotations, which should help to clarify the ideas.

Example-1. For our first example we shall look again at the clauses that describe the relation front(n,1,1′) which holds when 1 comprises the first n elements of the list 1. We made use of these in example program-2, in Section 1, to give an example of the use of answer substitutions that contain variables. This time we shall annotate them so that we get a co-routining construction of the list of the front n elements that simulates the counting down transfer of elements of 1 to 1′.

Leaving aside considerations of their computational use we can simply write down the implications of the program in any order, and with any ordering of the antecedent atoms. In general, this should be the first stage of writing a logic program; we should first concentrate on the logic component of the program, using and reading the clauses as first order statements about the input-output relation we want to compute. As a second stage we can concern ourselves with their computational use, with the control component. We do this by choosing a suitable ordering of the clauses and their antecedent atoms and by adding the appropriate annotation for the use we have in mind. At this stage we might conceivably revise the logic component, changing it to a more 'pragmatic' description should a viable computational use be impossible to achieve (we shall have to do this in the next example program). This two-stage program writing methodology, which is another novel feature of logic programming, is a consequence of the independence of the logic and the control.

Let us take the clauses

front(n,z,x) ←append(x,y,z) & length(x,n)

length(NIL,0)
length(u.x,s(n)) ←length(x,n)

append(NIL,x,x)
append(u.x,y,u.z) ←append(x,y,z)

as our first order description of the front relation.

We now address the computational use of these first order implications to strip off the first n elements of a list in answer to a call of the form ←front(n,1,x) in which x is the only variable. If the clauses were to be used as they stand the back-tracking search strategy will result in pairs of candidate decompositions of the in-put list 1 being generated by the non-deterministic evaluation of ←append(x,y,1). The first pair will be x = NIL, y = 1, the second x = a_1.NIL, y = 1′ where a_1 is the first element of 1 and 1′ its tail, and so on. Each of these candidate decompositions will be checked in turn by a complete evaluation of ←length(x,n). When this fails, because the length of x is not yet n, a back-track leads to a costly complete re-computation of the next candidate decomposition. This is not a viable computational use.

What we should be doing is counting down on the length parameter n as the recursive decomposition of 1 adds each new element to the partial output binding for x. When we have counted down to zero this partial output, which will be of the form $a_1.a_2 \ldots a_n.x'$, can be completed by a last step of the decomposition that binds x′ to NIL.

Exactly this behaviour will result if we use the annotated clause

front(n?,z?x^) ←append(x,y,z) & length(x?,n).

This makes the length call an eager consumer of the partial output bindings for the front sublist x, and restricts the use of this control regime to calls of the appropriate form.

The data calls of length(x?,n) actually serve two purposes. The sequence of the calls is best viewed as a sequence of pairs of calls. The first call of each pair follows each use of append(NIL,x,x)← in the non-deterministic evaluation of the append call. Following this data call the next step in the suspended length evaluation can only succeed if the length of the front sublist has reached n. This call is the ‘loop’ exit test. If this step fails only the last step in the append evaluation is undone. This is immediately followed by the use of the recursive append clause, and the second data call of length. On this second call only the recursive clause for length can be used and its use effectively decrements the length count by 1.

Example-2. Let us consider the problem of describing a solution to the eight queens chess problem using only Horn clause sentences.

First, we have to find some way of naming candidate solutions, configurations of eight queens distributed on a chess board. We can simplify our task if we only consider configurations in which each row and columns contains only one queen, a constraint that we know must be satisfied by any solution to the problem. A list of the numbers 1 to 8, in some arbitrary order, is a name for such a configuration if we take the ith number on the list as the column number of the queen in the ith row; with this naming convention, the set of permutations of the numbers 1 - 8 names the set of all the board configurations we are considering. A solution to the problem is one of these permutations that is safe, that is one which represents a configuration in which no queen is on a diagonal with any other.

The Horn clause:

Queen-sol(x) ←Perm(1.2 . . . . 8.NIL,x) & Safe(x) (1)

is the formal statement of the condition where 'Perm' names the list permutation relation and 'Safe' names the unary relation which is true of a list of numbers only if for any number on the list in position i, and any other number n on the list in position j, $j > i$, $|m - n| \neq j - i$. This ensures that the list of numbers names a queen configuration that is safe.

We now need to give the Horn clause descriptions, of the Perm and Safe relations. Trivially the empty list is a permutation of itself. A list u.x is a permutation of a list v.z if v is on the list u.x, and y is a permutation of u.x with v removed. Fig.6 illustrates this recursive definition.

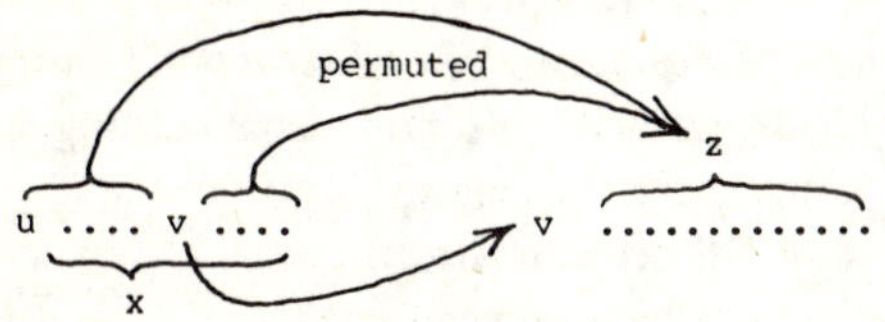

Figure 6. A permutation of lists

It is embodied in the two Horn clauses:

Perm(NIL,NIL)

Perm(u.x,v.z) ←delete(v,u.x,y) & Perm(y,z)

where 'delete' names the relation that is true when y is the list u.x with v removed. The clauses:

delete(v,v.x,x)

delete(v,u.x,v.y) ←delete(v,x,y) (2)

are a Horn clause description of the delete relation. We leave the reader to check that they provide a correct description which covers all the cases.

We now turn to the description of the Safe condition. Clearly an empty list of numbers represents a safe placing of queens on consecutive rows. A constructed list u.x will be safe if the list x of queen positions is safe and, taking into account that it is the column position for a queen one row away from the x sequence, a column u is not on a diagonal with any of the consecutive columns positions of the list x. This gives us the clausal description:

Safe(NIL)

Safe(u.x) ← no-diagonal(u,x,1) & Safe(x) (3)

Finally we need to describe the no-diagonal relation. This is a relation satisfiied by a column position, u, a list of column positions for consecutive rows, x, and a number, n, when a queen placed in column u, n rows away, cannot take any of the queens placed according to the list x. It is:

no-diagonal(u,NIL,n)

no-diagonal(u,v.x,n) ← no-take(u,v,n) & no-diagonal(u,x,s(n)) (4)

no-take(u,v,n) ← v > u & v = u + w & w ≠ n

no-take(u,v,n) ← u > v & u = v + w & w ≠ n

Here, '>', '. . = . . + . .' and '≠' are assumed as primitive arithmetic predicates.

The clauses (1), (2), (3) and (4) constitute a Horn clause axiomatisation of the concept of an eight queens problem solution. Note that they are much closer to a specification than a program. The ability to use logic programs that are more like specifications than programs is one of the bonuses of having a rich control component. Kowalski (1979a) elaborates on this point. Let us now turn our attention to their computational use.

With a mind to this computational use we have already chosen a suitable try order for the clauses of each predicate and for the procedure calls of each clause. However the computational use of the clauses as written suffers from considerable redundancy. The major problem is the generate and test method for finding a safe permutation which results from the back-tracking use of the clause:

Queen-sol(x) ← Perm(1.2 . . . . 8.NIL,x) & Safe(x)

Each time we back-track to try a new permutation the evaluator will recompute an entire permutation. At the very least, we need to set up a co-routining interaction between these two calls, by annotating the clause:

Queen-sol(x) ← Perm(1.2 . . . . . 8.NIL,x) & Safe(x?)

The procedures that will be invoked by these two calls are:

Perm(u.x,v.z) ←delete(v,u.x,w) & Perm(w,z)

Safe(u.x) ←no-diagonal(u,x,1) & Safe(x)

A data call to the Safe computation will take place as soon as the shared variable of Perm(1.2. . . . 8.NIL,x) and Safe(x?) is bound to the template 'v.z', before the v giving the first queen position has been computed by the delete(v,u.x,y) call. It is better if we delay the call until v is known. We do this by changing the '&' of the Perm procedure to a ':'.

There is another more serious redundancy which cannot be remedied using a control annotation. The problem is with the recursive description of Safe, which must be changed to a more computationally useful description. Our recursive description implicitly involves a double recursion, since the no-diagonal relation is itself recursively defined. Computationally this means that the evaluation of the no-diagonal(u,x,1) call of the Safe procedure will generate a sequence of data requests that results in the complete construction of a permutation. In other words, a complete permutation will be constructed in order to test that the first queen does not take any of the tail list of queens. Thus, when the third queen position is given on some data transfer from Perm, only the diagonal constraint with the first queen is checked. The diagonal constraint with the second queen is embedded in the recursive call of the Safe procedure, and will not be checked until all the diagonal constraints involving the first queen have been checked.

A richer control regime would enable us to 'extract' a viable computation from the program as it stands. We need to be able to signal the quasi-parallel execution of the no-diagonal(u,x,1) and Safe(x) calls of the Safe procedure. More precisely, we want the Safe(x) evaluation to be started, and then run in parallel with the evaluation of no-diagonal(u,x,1), when its argument becomes bound. The use of annotations to constrain a parallel evaluation of the procedure calls of a logic program, rather than to liberate the strictly sequential execution, has been investigated by Bruynooghe & Clark (1979). There is currently no implementation of such a control regime.

To make do with the control facilities that are available in IC-PROLOG we must revise the logic of our program. Behaviourally, we want the new description of the Safe relation to be such that each newly generated queen position is checked against all the preceeding queens rather than all the queens yet to be positioned. Intuitively it exploits the fact that a queen list is Safe iff its reverse is Safe.

To get this behaviour we must re-describe the Safe relation using an auxiliary relation, Safe-pair. Safe-pair is true of pairs of queen lists y and x iff x is a Safe list and no queen in the x sequence can take any queen in the reverse of the y sequence, when the reverse of y followed x is taken as a queen board configuration (see Fig. 7).

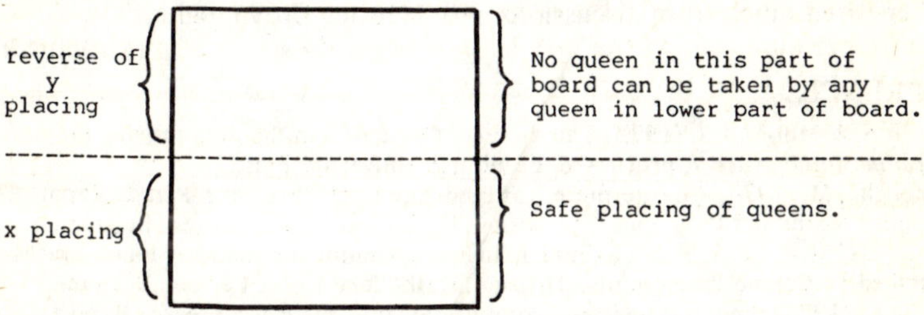

Figure 7. y and x are a safe-pair of queen placings

We leave the reader to check that, with this intended interpretation of the predicates 'Safe' and 'Safe-pair', each of the following clauses is a true statement:

Safe(x) ← Safe-pair (NIL,x)

Safe-pair(y,u.x) ← no-diagonal(u,y,1) & Safe-pair(u.y,x)
Safe-pair(y,NIL)

They embody a conceptualisation of the Safe relation as a special case of the Safe-pair relation, and a recursive description of Safe-pair.

Our final, revised and annotated program is:

Queen-sol(x) ← Perm(1.2.3.4.5.6.7.8.NIL,x) & Safe(x?)

Perm(NIL,NIL)
Perm(u.x,v.z) ← delete(v,u.x,y) : Perm(y,z)

delete(u,u.x,x)
delete(v,u.x,u.y) ← delete(v,x,y)

Safe(x) ← Safe-pair(NIL,x)

```
Safe-pair(y,NIL)
Safe-pair(y,u.x) ← no-diagonal(u,y,1) & Safe-pair(u.y,x)

no-diagonal(u,NIL,n)
no-diagonal(u,v.x,n) ← no-take(u,v,n) & no-diagonal(u,x,s(n))

no-take(u,v,n) ← v>u & v = u+w & w≠n
no-take(u,v,n) ← u>v & u = v+w & w≠n
```

The execution of the program corresponds to the simple-minded back-tracking algorithm which places the queens one at a time on successive rows. It always tries to place the next queen on the left-most free column (because of the try order for the 'delete' clauses). If it cannot place a queen on the next row in a position in which it cannot be taken by an earlier queen, it back-tracks and tries to move the previous queen to the right.

ACKNOWLEDGEMENTS

Our implementation of the control facilities in IC-PROLOG built upon the experience gained by Chris Stevens' pilot implementation (Stevens 1977). We have also benefited much from discussions with Maurice Bruynooghe.

REFERENCES

Boyer, R.S. & Moore, J.S. (1972) The sharing of structure in theorem-proving programs. *Machine Intelligence* 7, pp.101-16. Edinburgh University Press.

Bruynooghe, M. (1976) An Interpreter for Predicate Logic Programs, Part 1. Report CW 10, Applied Maths and Programming Division, Katholieke Univ., Leuven, Belgium.

Bruynooghe, M. & Clark, K.L. (1979) Parallel programming in predicate logic. Draft report, Applied Maths and Programming Division, Katholieke Univ., Leuven, Belgium.

Clark, K.L. (1979) Predicate logic as a computational formalism. Research Report (in preparation), Imperial College, London

Clark, K.L. & McCabe, F. (1979) *IC–PROLOG Reference Manual*. CCD Rep. 79/7, Imperial College, London.

Friedman, D.P. & Wise, D.S. (1976) CONS should not evaluate its arguments. *Automata, Languages and Programming*. Third International Colloquium. Edinburgh University Press.

Futo, I., Darvas, F. & Cholnoy, E. (1977) Practical application of an AI Language 2. *Proceedings of the Hungarian Conference on Computing*, Budapest, pp.385-400.

Green, C.C. (1969) Theorem-proving by resolution as a basis for question-answering systems. *Machine Intelligence 4*, pp.183-205. Edinburgh University Press.

Hayes, P.J. (1973) Computation and deduction. *Proc. 2nd MFCS Symp.*, Czechoslovak Academy of Sciences, pp.105-18.

Henderson, P. & Morris, J. (1976) A lazy evaluator. *3rd. Symp. on principles of programming languages*. Atlanta, pp.95-103.

Hill, R. (1974) LUSH Resolution and its completeness. DCL Memo No. 78, University of Edinburgh, School of Artificial Intelligence, August 1974.

Hoare, C.A.R. (1973) Recursive data structures. Computer Science Dept., Stanford University, STAN-CS-73-400.

Kowalski, R.A. (1974) Predicate logic as programming language. *Proc. IFIP 74*, pp.569-74. North Holland Publishing Co., Amsterdam.

——(1979a) Algorithm = Logic + Control. To appear in CACM.

——(1979b) Logic for Problem Solving. To be published by North Holland, N.Y.

Robinson, J.A. (1965) A machine-oriented logic based on the resolution principle. *J.A.C.M. 12* (January 1965) 23-41.

——(1979) *Logic: Form and Function*. Edinburgh University Press.

Roberts, G. (1977) An implementation of PROLOG. MSc Thesis. University of Waterloo.
Schwarz, J. (1977) Using annotations to make recursion equations behave. Research Memo, Dept. of Artificial Intelligence, University of Edinburgh.
Steven, C. (1977) The application of call-by-need to automatic theorem-proving. MSc Thesis. Department of Computing and Control, Imperial College, London.
Van Emden, M.H. & Kowalski, R.A. (1976) The semantics of predicate logic as a programming language. *J.A.C.M. 23*, no.4, 733-42.
Warren, D.H.D. (1977) Implementing PROLOG. Res. Rep. 39, 40, Dept. of A.I., Univ. of Edinburgh.
Warren, D.H.D., Pereira, L.M. & Pereira, F. (1977) PROLOG – The language and its implementation compared with LISP. Proc. Symp. on AI and Programming Languages, SIGPLAN Notices, vol.12, no.8, and SIGART Newsletters no.64, August 1977, pp.109-15.

PROBABILISTIC AND LOGICAL INDUCTION SYSTEMS

MODEL DESIGN IN THE PROSPECTOR CONSULTANT SYSTEM FOR MINERAL EXPLORATION*

Richard Duda, John Gaschnig and Peter Hart

ABSTRACT

Prospector is a computer consultant system intended to aid geologists in evaluating the favorability of an exploration site or region for occurrences of ore deposits of particular types. Knowledge about a particular type of ore deposit is encoded in a computational model representing observable geological features and the relative significance thereof. We describe the form of models in Prospector, focussing on inference networks of geological assertions and the Bayesian propagation formalism used to represent the judgmental reasoning process of the economic geologist who serves as model designer. Following the initial design of a model, simple performance evaluation techniques are used to assess the extent to which the performance of the model reflects faithfully the intent of the model designer. These results identify specific portions of the model that might benefit from "fine tuning", and establish priorities for such revisions. This description of the Prospector system and the model design process serves to illustrate the process of transferring human expertise about a subjective domain into a mechanical realization.

I. INTRODUCTION

In an increasingly complex and specialized world, human expertise about diverse subjects spanning scientific, economic, social, and political issues plays an increasingly important role in the functioning of all kinds of organizations. Although computers have become indispensable tools in many endeavors, we continue to rely heavily on the human expert's ability to identify and synthesize diverse factors, to form judgments, evaluate alternatives, and make decisions – in sum, to apply his or her years of experience to the problem at hand. This is especially valid with regard to domains that are not easily amenable to precise scientific formulations, i.e., to domains in which experience and subjective judgment plays a major role.

The precious resource of human expertise is also a fragile and transient one: the departure of a crucial expert from an organization may cause serious dislocations; senior people impart their knowledge to younger colleagues, but the demand for their talents may not leave sufficient time for such educational efforts.

---

* This work was supported in part by the Office of Resource Analysis of the U.S. Geological Survey under Contract No. 14-08-0001-15985, and in part by the Nonrenewable Resources Section of the National Science Foundation under Grant AER77-04499. Any opinions, findings, conclusions, or recommendations expressed in this publication are those of the authors, and do not necessarily reflect the views of either the U.S. Geological Survey or the National Science Foundation.

During recent years research in the field of artificial intelligence has produced effective new techniques for representing empirical judgmental knowledge and using this knowledge in performing plausible reasoning. The best known application of these techniques has been in the area of medical diagnosis, where computer programs have achieved high levels of performance (Pople et al., 1975; Shortliffe, 1976; Weiss et al., 1977; Yu, 1978; Szolovits, 1976). Other applications include planning experiments in molecular genetics (Martin 1977) and monitoring instruments in intensive care units (Fagan 1978). This paper concerns a similar computer program, called Prospector, that is being developed to help geologists in exploring for hard-rock mineral deposits. The characteristic of plausible reasoning shared by the domains of medical diagnosis and mineral exploration is common, to some degree, to many other diverse evaluation tasks as well. Hence the purpose of this paper is to illustrate, by a case study for the domain of mineral exploration, the general process of capturing and encoding human expertise into a mechanical realization.

II. OVERVIEW OF THE PROSPECTOR SYSTEM

The Prospector system is intended to emulate the reasoning process of an experienced exploration geologist in assessing a given prospect site or region for its likelihood of containing an ore deposit of the type represented by the model he or she designed. Here we use the term "model" to refer to a body of knowledge about a particular domain of expertise that is encoded into the system and on which the system can act. The empirical knowledge contained in Prospector consists of a number of such specially encoded models of certain classes of ore deposits. These models are intended to represent the most authoritative and up-to-date information available about each deposit class.

In Prospector's normal interactive consultation mode, the user is assumed to have obtained some promising field data and is assumed to desire assistance in evaluating the prospect. Thus, the user begins by providing the program with a list of rocks and minerals observed, and by inputting other observations expressed in simple English sentences. The program matches these data against its models, requests additional information of potential value for arriving at more definite conclusions, and provides a summary of the findings. The user can ask at any time for an elaboration of the intent of a question, or for the geological rationale for including a question in the model, or for an ongoing trace of the effects of his answers on Prospector's conclusions. The intent is to provide the user with many of the services that could be provided by giving him telephone access to a panel of senior economic geologists, each an authority on a particular class of ore deposits.

The performance of Prospector depends on the number of models it contains, the types of deposits modeled, and the quality and completeness of each model. Because the Prospector program is primarily a research project, its coverage is still incomplete. It currently contains five prospect-scale models, one regional-scale model, and one drilling site selection model. The prospect-scale models consist of a Kuroko-type massive sulfide model contributed by Charles F. Park, Jr., a Mississippi-Valley-type carbonate lead/zinc model contributed by Neil Campbell, a near-continental-margin porphyry copper model contributed by Marco T. Einaudi, a Komatiitic nickel sulfide model contributed by Anthony J. Naldrett, and a Western-states sandstone uranium model contributed by Ruffin I. Rackley. The regional scale model is a variation of Mr. Rackley's model. The drilling site selection model, for porphyry copper deposits, was contributed by Mr. Victor Hollister, and differs somewhat from the other models: it derives its inputs from digitized maps of geological characteristics, and produces as output a color-coded graphical display of the favorability of each cell on a grid corresponding to the input map. These models were selected for a variety of reasons, including their economic significance, the extent to which they are well understood scientifically, the availability of expert geologists who could collaborate with us in the model development, and the new research issues that their implementation would raise.

Each model is encoded as a separate data structure, independent of the Prospector system per se. Thus, the Prospector program should not be confused with its models. Rather, Prospector should be thought of as a general mechanism for delivering relevant expert information about ore deposits to a user who can supply it with data about a particular prospect or region.

This paper describes briefly the process of developing and encoding such models for Prospector. General overviews of the technical principles are given in Hart, Duda and Einaudi (1978), mathematical aspects in Duda et al. (1976, 1978a), and detailed expositions in Duda et al. (1977, 1978b) and Hart, Duda and Konolige (1978).

III. FORMALISM FOR ENCODING EXPLORATION MODELS

A. Inference Networks of Assertions

For use in Prospector an ore deposit model must be encoded as a so-called inference network, a network of connections or relations between field evidence and important geological hypotheses. Since we sometimes do not wish to distinguish between evidence and hypotheses, we shall refer to either one as an assertion. To illustrate these ideas, we shall draw upon examples taken from M.T. Einaudi's porphyry copper model, which we shall denote by PCDA. Typical assertions in PCDA are "Hornblende has been pervasively altered to biotite" and "The alteration suggests the potassic zone of a porphyry copper deposit." The former would normally be thought of as field evidence, the latter as a geological hypothesis. A small portion of the PCDA inference network is shown in Figure 1. Here the terminal or "leaf" nodes correspond to field evidence asked of the user, while the other nodes represent hypotheses. The text in the boxes in Figure 1 is concise for reasons of graphical display; the actual questions asked of the user are more definitive.

Although assertions are statement that should be either true or false, in a given situation there is usually uncertainty as to whether they are true or false. Initially, the state of each assertion is simply unknown. As evidence is gathered, some assertions may be definitely established, whereas others may become only more

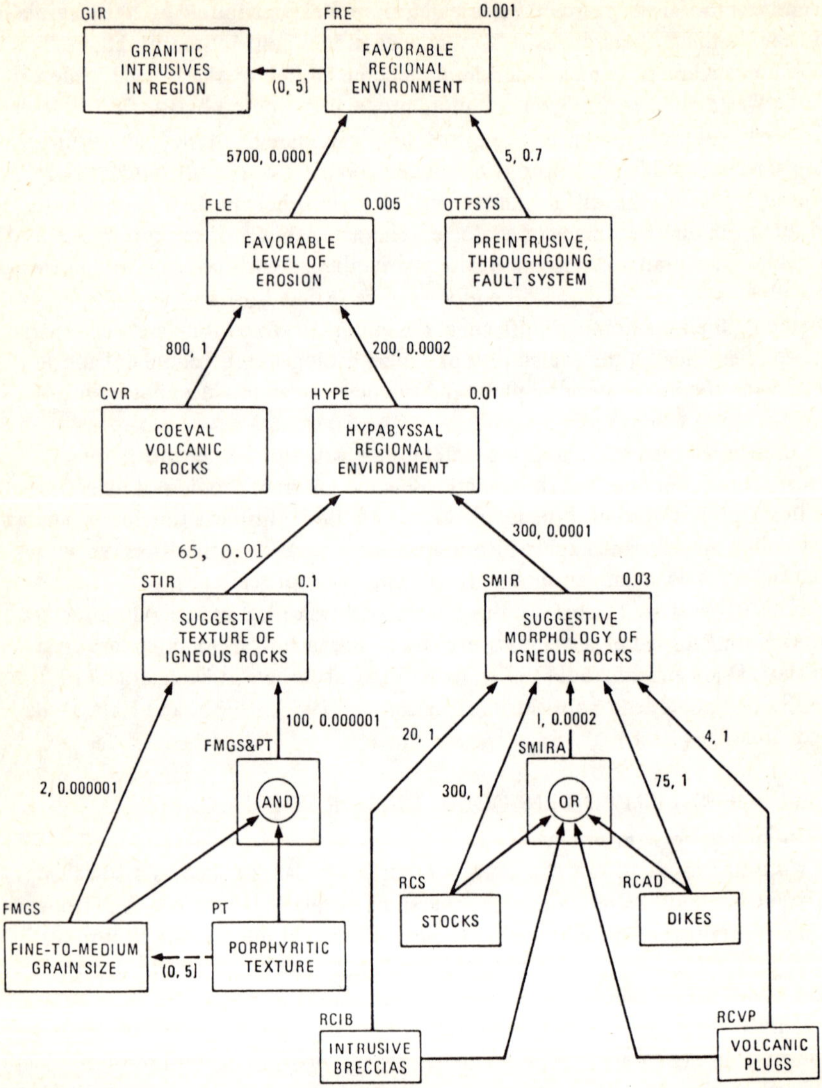

Figure 1. Portion of a Prospector model for porphyry copper deposits. See text for interpretation

or less likely. In general, we associate a probability value with every assertion. The "connections" in the inference network determine how a change in the probability of one assertion will affect those of other assertions.

The principal or top-level assertion in an inference network for a model is the assertion that the available evidence matches that particular model. To establish this assertion, it is usually necessary to establish several major factors. For example, to establish the top-level assertion in PCDA, we must establish the following hypotheses:

1. The petrotectonic setting is favorable for PCDA;
2. The regional evironment is favorable for PCDA;
3. There is an intrusive system that is favorable for PCDA.

Were any of these assertions field-observable evidence, they could be established merely by asking the user of the program whether they were true. However, since all of these factors are hypotheses, each must be further related to other factors. For example, the favorability of the petrotectonic setting can be established through the following three factors, each of which happens to be determinable (at least in principle) from observational evidence:

1. The prospect lies in a continental margin mobile belt;
2. The age of the belt is post-Paleozoic;
3. The prospect is subject to tectonic and magmatic activity related to subduction.

In general, the ore deposit models in Prospector have this type of hierarchical structure. The top-level assertion is determined by several major second-level assertions, each of which may be determined by third-level assertions, with this refinement continuing until assertions are reached that can be established directly from field evidence. This is illustrated in Figure 1, which shows graphically that portion of the PCDA model that describes the regional environment. In addition to this "top-to-bottom" development in terms of successive levels of assertions, the models also often exhibit a "left-to-right" organization in terms of spatial scale, from the petrotectonic setting on the left to the local details of mineralization and texture on the right. Exactly how these considerations interact is determined by the relations that exist among the assertions. The following section explains the nature of these relations and illustrates their occurrence in Figure 1.

B. Relations

Three basically different kinds of relations are used in Prospector to specify how a change in the probability of one assertion affects the probability of other assertions. We distinguish these as logical relations, plausible relations, and contextual relations.

1. *Logical Relations*. With logical relations, the truth (or falsity) of a hypo thesis is completely determined by the truth (or falsity) of the assertions that define it. Such relations are composed out of the primitive operations of conjunction (AND), disjunction (OR), and negation (NOT). When several assertions must all be true for a hypothesis to be true, the hypothesis is the conjunction of the assertions. When the hypothesis is true if any of the assertions is true, the hypothesis is the disjunction of the assertions. Negation merely complements an assertion, interchanging truth and falsity. As an example of a logical relation, the PCDA model says that alteration of plagioclase is indicative of the barren-core zone if

1. Plagioclase has been altered to
    a. albite
    or
    b. minor sericite (or both)

and

2. Plagioclase has not been altered to major epidote.

Other examples of logical relations are shown in Figure 1.

Of course, in general we do not know whether the assertions are true, but can only estimate a probability or degree of belief that they are true. With logical relations, to compute the probability of a hypothesis from the probability of its component assertions we employ the fuzzy-set formulas of Zadeh (1965). Using these formulas, the probability of a hypothesis that is defined as the logical conjunction (AND) of several pieces of evidence equals the minimum of the probability values corresponding to the evidence. Similarly, a hypothesis defined as the logical disjunction (OR) of its evidence spaces is assigned a probability value equal to the maximum of those values assigned to the evidence spaces. One property of this procedure is that it often gives no "partial credit." In particular, if all but one of the assertions have been established, but the user can not even guess about the last, then the probability of their conjunction often remains at the value it had when the states of none of the assertions were known. This may be the appropriate conclusion. When it is not, one has the option of using plausible relations.

2. *Plausible Relations.* With plausible relations, each assertion contributes "votes" for or against the truth of the hypothesis. This would be expressed by relating the assertions to the hypothesis through a set of plausible inference rules. Each rule has an associated rule strength that measures the degree to which a change in the probability of the evidence assertion changes the probability of the hypothesis. This change can be positive or negative, since as assertion can be either favorable or unfavorable for a hypothesis. As with all parts of a model, these rule strengths are obtained by interviewing an authority on the corresponding class of ore deposits. Initially he may express the strengths in verbal terms, such as "rather discouraging" or "very encouraging." This is ultimately translated into numerical terms (as shown in Figure 1), the changes in probability being computed in accordance with the rules of Bayesian probability theory, as outlined below and described in detail in Duda et al. (1977).

Prospector's plausible reasoning scheme is based on Bayesian decision theory (Raiffa, 1968), exploiting an elementary theorem of probability known as Bayes' rule. For our purposes, the so-called "odds-likelihood" form of the rule is most convenient. This form relates three quantities involving an evidence assertion E and a hypothesis assertion H: the prior odds O(H) on the hypothesis, the posterior odds O(H | E) on the hypothesis, given that E is observed to be present, and a measure of sufficiency LS. Then Bayes' rule can be stated as

$$O(H \mid E) = LS * O(H) \qquad (1)$$

Odds and probabilities are freely interchangeable through the simple relation $O = P / (1 - P)$, where P denotes probability, and hence $P = O / (1 + O)$. The sufficiency measure LS is a standard quantity in statistics called the likelihood ratio, and is defined by

$$LS = \frac{P(E|H)}{P(E|\sim H)} \tag{2}$$

where ~H means "not H."

Equation (1) prescribes a means for updating the probability (or odds) on H, given that the evidence E is observed to be present. An inference rule for which LS is large means that the observation of E is encouraging for H – in the extreme case of LS approaching infinity, E is sufficient to establish H in a strict logical sense. On the other hand, if LS is much less than unity, then the observation of E is discouraging for H, inasmuch as the observation of E diminishes the odds on H.

A complementary set of equations describes the case in which E is known to be absent, that is, when ~E is true. In this case, we can use Bayes' rule to write

$$O(H \mid \sim E) = LN * O(H) \tag{3}$$

where

$$LN = \frac{P(\sim E \mid H)}{P(\sim E \mid \sim H)} \tag{4}$$

The quantity LN is called the necessity measure. If LN is much less than unity, the known absence of E transforms neutral prior odds on H into very small posterior odds in favor of H. In the extreme case of LN approaching zero, E is logically necessary for H. On the other hand, if LN is large, then the absence of E is encouraging for H.

Hence to define an inference rule

IF E

THEN (to degree LS, LN) H,

the model designer must articulate E and H, and must supply numerical values for LS, LN, and O(H).

In general, the user may not be able to state that E is either definitely present or definitely absent. In this case, the updating formulas (1) and (3) cannot be applied directly, but can be extended to accommodate the uncertainty in the evidence. The extension used in Prospector involves a linear interpolation between the extremes of E's being definitely present or definitely absent. See Duda (1976, 1977) for details. The user expresses his certainty about E on an arbitrary –5 to 5 scale, where 5 denotes that the evidence is definitely present, –5 denotes that it is definitely absent, 0 indicates no information, and intermediate values denote degrees of certainty.

We illustrate this plausible inference scheme with examples taken from Figure 1. The two numbers associated with each inference rule in Figure 1 are its LS and LN values, respectively. The number appearing above each box representing a nonterminal node is the prior probability of that assertion's being true. For example, the figure indicates that the existence of stocks is a more highly sufficient indicator of "suggestive morphology of igneous rocks" (i.e., LS = 300) than is the existence of either dikes, intrusive breccias, or volcanic plugs (i.e., LS = 75, 20, and 4, respectively). Similarly, "favorable level of erosion" (FLE) is a highly sufficient and highly necessary factor for establishing "favorable regional environment" (i.e., LS = 5700 and LN = 0.0001), whereas the existence of a "preintrusive throughgoing fault system" (OTFSYS) is only mildly sufficient and mildly necessary for establishing "favorable regional environment." Hence the positive (LS) or negative (LN) votes of FLE are weighted much more heavily than those of OTFSYS.

The section of the model concerned with establishing "suggestive morphology of igneous rocks" (SMIR) illustrates how logical and plausible relations can be combined as building blocks to accomplish the intent of the economic geologist designing the model. This section of the PCDA model can be described as follows. "There are four positive indicators for establishing a suggestive morphology for igneous rocks (SMIR), namely intrusive breccias, stocks, dikes, and volcanic plugs. Each of these factors contributes independently to establishing SMIR, although to differing degrees. The absence of any one of these four factors individually is unimportant [i.e., LN = 1 for those rules]. However, if it is known that none of these factors is present [implying that the disjunction node SMIRA is false], then the probability of a suggestive morphology of igneous rocks is essentially zero [LN = 0.0002 for SMIRA]." In defining an inference network for a model, the object is to induce the model designer to articulate such statements, and then to translate the statements into network constructions.

To see how the effect of a piece of evidence propagates upward through the model, suppose that the user has indicated only that intrusive breccias are present, but this is definite. This fact multiplies the odds of SMIR by a factor of 20, hence raising its probability from 0.03 to 0.382. (The prior odds on SMIR are 0.03 / (1 – 0.03) = 0.030927, giving posterior odds on SMIR equal to 20 * 0.030927 = .61855, which corresponds to a probability of 0.61855 / (1+0.61855) = 0.382.) This in turn increase the odds on HYPE by a factor of 300 weighted by the degree to which SMIR has increased from its prior probability, i.e, by the factor 300 * (0.382–0.03) / (1–0.03) = 108.866. Hence the posterior probability of HYPE is 0.52373, which in turn increases the odds of FLE by a factor of 200 * (0.52373–0.01) / (1–0.01) = 103.78, giving a posterior probability for FLE of 0.34276. The propagation continues in this manner upward through the network.

It should be noted that Prospector expresses its conclusions to the user on the same –5 to 5 certainty scale that the user employs to express his certainty about evidence requested by the system. Prospector maps internal probability values to external certainty scores in a piecewise linear fashion, such that the posterior certainty is proportional to the difference between the posterior probability and the prior probability. For example, since the prior probability of

FLE is 0.005, a posterior probability of 0.34276 corresponds to a posterior certainty of 5 * (0.34276–0.005) / (1–0.005) = 1.697. Similarly, a posterior probability of 0.001 corresponds in this case to a posterior certainty of 5 * (0.001 – 0.005) / 0.005 = –4. See Shortliffe (1975) for a description of the subjective certainty scale used in the MYCIN medical diagnosis system.

3. *Contextual Relations.* It sometimes happens that assertions cannot be considered in an arbitrary order, but must be considered in a particular sequence. For example, one should determine that there is a relevant continental margin mobile belt before considering its age. This is more than a matter of preference, since it would be meaningless for the program to ask about the age of a non-existent belt.

To treat such situations we employ the third class of relations, contextual relations. In general, we use contexts to express a condition that must be established before an assertion can be used in the reasoning process. In the above example, the existence of a continental margin mobile belt would be specified as a context for asking about the age of the belt. Thus, before inquiring about the age, the system would employ all its resources to establish the existence of the belt, and would not ask about its age unless the probability of the belt were greater than its initial value.

Contextual relations are also used when one assertion is geologically significant only if another assertion has already been established. In such instances it would not be nonsensical to ask the former question without first establishing the latter, but it is the case that the former evidence is geologically irrelevant without the latter to establishing a match to the model. Two such instances are depicted by dashed arrows in Figure 1. In one of these instances, the entire "favorable regional environment" section of PCDA model will not be pursued unless it has first been determined that there are granitic intrusives in the region.

IV. OVERVIEW OF THE MODEL DEVELOPMENT PROCESS

Although the development and encoding of a model for Prospector is not a routine process, it does progress through several distinct phases whose general nature can be described. The four most important phases are summarized below.

A. Initial Preparation

Model development is a cooperative enterprise involving an exploration geologist, who is an authority on the type of deposit being modeled, and a computer scientist who understands the operation of the Prospector system. The first step in developing a model is one of introducing the exploration geologist (model designer) to the inference network formalism, and introducing the computer scientist (model implementor) to the general nature of the class of deposits being modeled. In particular, this includes the identification of several known deposits that should fit the model well, and several known deposits that may fit partially, but that lack certain important characteristics. These specific cases help to establish the various factors that must be taken into account.

B. Initial Design

The initial design of the inference network is the most creative phase of the process. It requires the identification of the various assertions, the organization of the assertions into a hierarchical structure (as illustrated in Figure 1), the determination of the types of relations (logical, plausible, and contextual) that exist among assertions, and the estimation of values for the parameters (the voting strengths and initial probabilities). The magnitude of this task depends upon the size and complexity of the model being developed; as a point of reference, the smallest model currently in Prospector contains 28 assertions and 20 inference rules, while the largest contains 212 assertions and 133 inference rules. The initial design is usually facilitated by considering factors in the "top-down" and "left-to-right" sequence described earlier. Delicate refinement is best avoided at this time, since subsequent revision often causes significant sections of the model to be reorganized, enlarged, or otherwise modified.

In addition to the connections between assertions exhibited directly by the inference network, there are connections that exist because of the geological meaning of the assertions. For example, the statement that there are sulfide minerals is obviously related to the statement that there is pyrite in quartz veins; assertion of the latter implies the former, and denial of the former denies the latter. Recognition of such connections within a model avoids redundant or foolish questioning; recognition of such connections between different models allows the program to consider more than one deposit class at a time. Prospector can automatically recognize many of these assertions if each assertion is properly articulated. This articulation, which is described in more detail in Duda (1978b), should also be completed during the initial design.

C. Installation and Debugging of the Model

At the end of Phase B, the model exists in a "pencil-and-paper" form. To be incorporated into the program, the encoding must be given a formal description. This is done through the use of a model description language (see Duda, 1978b). The details of this language are not particularly important here. However, the task itself is important; upon its completion the program can be run, and accidental blunders or bugs can be corrected. In addition, the program can produce a questionnaire for the model that is useful in gathering data for subsequent testing and revision.

D. Performance Evaluation and Model Revision

Given the questionnaire data for a number of actual deposits, it is possible to make a serious quantitative evaluation of how well particular deposits match the model. In our experience, this evaluation inevitably exposes various shortcomings of the model as encoded, requiring revision of the work done in Phases B and C. Some care must be exercised here to avoid "overfitting" the model to the data. In general, the goal is to produce a model that can discriminate different types of deposits without losing the ability to generalize, so as to allow for the variations one would expect in new situations. Achievement of that goal currently remains as much an art as a science. The following section describes in some detail the use of simple performance evaluation techniques as an aid to refining a model.

V. USE OF PERFORMANCE EVALUATION IN REFINING A MODEL

To demonstrate that the performance of an expert knowledge-based system is (or is not) comparable to that of the experts it emulates, it is useful to subject the system to an appropriate objective evaluation. The simple performance evaluation experiments reported in this section serve several purposes: (1) to provide an objective, detailed, quantitative measure of the current performance of a model; (2) to pinpoint those sections of the model that are not performing exactly as intended, thereby establishing priorities for future revisions; (3) to assess consistency of performance across different exploration sites.

We now evaluate a model for a class of porphyry copper deposits (PCDA) designed by Prof. Marco Einaudi of Stanford University. Input data were available for three test cases, namely, the known deposits called Yerington (Nevada), Bingham (Utah), and Kalamazoo (Arizona), each of which is considered an exemplar of the PCDA model.[2] On the –5 to 5 certainty scale described earlier, the overall certainty scores computed by Prospector are 4.769 for the Yerington deposit, 4.721 for Bingham, and 4.756 for Kalamazoo, indicating a good match of these sites to the PCDA model.

To show performance in detail, we give below the hierarchical structure of the major sections of the PCDA model. Included at the right in this enumeration is the total number of questions that may be asked by Prospector for each of the major sections of the model, thus showing the relative distribution of these questions. (The questions in the FAMR section may be asked several times during a consultation session, once for each geographically distinct zone within the prospect area. Each such zone has relatively homogeneous geological characteristics, as determined by the user.)

	Total Number of Questions Defined in PCDA Model (Version 2)
Porphyry Copper deposit, type A (PCDA)	81
Favorable petrotectonic setting (FPTS)	4
Favorable regional environment (FRE)	9
Favorable PCDA intrusive system (FPCDAIS)	68
Favorable composition in differentiated sequence (FCDS)	4
Favorable intrusive system (FIS)	9
Favorable alteration and mineralization relations (FAMR)	56

[2]The questionnaire input data used in the present tests are reported in Duda et al., 1978b, pp.185-93.

As a calibration exercise, Prof. Einaudi offered a target value for the certainty score that should be assigned to each of the three deposits for each of the major components of the model listed above, based on the values in the input data set for each prospect site. The target values are given either in the form of a single number (on a –5 to 5 scale), or as two numbers establishing an upper and lower bound on a certainty interval. The estimates are listed in Table 1 on the left for each site in turn, with the scores as determined by execution of Prospector recorded on the right. (We informed Prof. Einaudi of the values on the right only after he had given us those on the left.)

Yerington Deposit

Name of Model Node	Einaudi's Estimate	Prospector Score
PCDA	4.5 to 5.0	4.769
FPTS	4.5 to 5.0	4.528
FRE	4.5	4.540
FPCDAIS	4.5 to 5.0	4.787
FCDS	5	4.524
FIS	5	4.744
FAMR	4.5 to 5.0	4.225

Bingham Deposit

Name of Model Node	Einaudi's Estimate	Prospector Score
PCDA	4.5	4.721
FPTS	3.5 to 4.0	4.449
FRE	4.0 to 4.5	4.829
FPCDAIS	4.5 to 5.0	4.729
FCDS	5	2.407
FIS	5	4.744
FAMR	4.0	4.225

Kalamazoo Deposit

Name of Model Node	Einaudi's Estimate	Prospector Score
PCDA	4.0 to 4.5	4.756
FPTS	4.0 to 4.5	4.449
FRE	3.5	1.784
FPCDAIS	4.5 to 5.0	4.791
FCDS	5	4.722
FIS	5	4.744
FAMR	4.0	4.225

Table 1. Prospector Scores for Several Levels of the PCDA Model (Version 2)

The data in Table 1 show that Prospector scores each of these sections of the model with high certainty for each site, with the exception that model node FCDS for the Bingham deposit and model node FRE for the Kalamazoo deposit are scored somewhat lower. In most cases shown in Table 1 Prospector agrees very closely with Prof. Einaudi's estimate. These conclusions can be expressed quantitatively by first identifying the values in Table 1 with a concise notation, then defining a simple formula for the relative error of Prospector in predicting Prof. Einaudi's estimates. Thus:

Let C(X, Y, Z) = Certainty score given to model node Z by agent X for site Y,
where X denotes either Prospector or Einaudi

For example, C(Prospector, Yerington, FPCDAIS) = 4.787. When Einaudi gave an interval of certainty values instead of a single value, we use the midpoint of the interval as the value of C. Then an error measure is given by

$$E(Y, Z) = \frac{C(\text{Einaudi}, Y, Z) - C(\text{Prospector}, Y, Z)}{C(\text{Einaudi}, Y, Z)}$$

For example, E(Yerington, FPCDAIS) = (4.75 – 4.787) / 4.75 = –0.008, meaning that Prospector's prediction is accurate to within 0.8% in this case. Since Table 1 gives values for seven nodes of the model for each of three known deposits, we can compute the value of E for 21 different instances. For 5 of the 21 data points Prospector predicted Einaudi's estimate to within 1%, while 15 of the 21 data points show agreement to within 10%. The grand average over the 21 data points is 10.3%. For convenience, we list these 21 values of E in Table 2, expressed as percentages.

	Yerington	Bingham	Kalamazoo	Average of Absolute Values
PCDA	–.3 %	–4.9 %	–11.9 %	5.7 %
FPTS	4.7	–18.6	–4.7	9.3
FRE	–.9	–13.6	49.0	21.2
FPCDAIS	–.8	.4	–.9	.7
FCDS	9.5	51.9	5.6	22.3
FIS	5.1	5.1	5.1	5.1
FAMR	11.1	5.6	5.6	7.6
Average of Absolute values:	4.1	14.3	11.8	10.3

Table 2. Relative Error (E) of Prospector Scores as Predictors of Einaudi's Estimates (derived from data in Table 1)

Inspection of Table 2 indicates that efforts to revise the PCDA model should focus on the FRE and FCDS sections. When such revisions are completed, an updated version of Table 2 will indicate the extent to which the revisions achieved the objectives that motivated them.

The small number of cases tested, and the fact that all the present test cases are exemplars of the PCDA model, and the fact that the model designer himself supplied the input data concerning the test cases, are limitations; the present tests are more necessary than sufficient conditions for good performance. Despite these limitations, the preliminary results reported here have proved useful in the ongoing model refinement process. More extensive performance evaluation results are reported in Duda et al. (1978b).

VI. REMARKS

This paper has outlined the typical procedures used to develop an exploration model for the Prospector system. We have described the inference network and Bayesian propagation scheme underlying Prospector models, and we have illustrated the use of simple performance evaluation techniques in "fine-tuning" a model systematically. Our experience indicates that the model design process inherently requires feedback. Although different problem solving domains differ in many details, we believe the process of constructing Prospector-like plausible reasoning systems follows certain general patterns and stages of development such as are described here. Hence we have presented a concrete case study, in the domain of mineral exploration, that may credibly suggest what might be expected in attempts to apply a similar methodology to other domains of expertise.

Besides the running program, there appear to be several other benefits to this type of expert system approach. The model design process challenges the model designer to articulate, organize, and quantify his expertise. Without exception, the economic geologists who have designed Prospector models have reported that the experience aided and sharpened their own thinking on the subject matter of the model. In addition, most of the geologists we know who have had experience with Prospector have remarked about its potential value as an educational tool. In this regard, the models in the system contain explicit, detailed information synthesized from the literature and the experience of expert explorationists, together with explanatory text that can be obtained upon request. Furthermore, a typical consultation session with Prospector costs only about $10 at current commercial computer rates.

VII. ACKNOWLEDGEMENTS

Prospector would not exist without the talents and efforts contributed by many economic geologists and computer scientists. Among these, we are particularly indebted to the economic geologists Alan N. Campbell, Neil Campbell, Marco T. Einaudi, Victor F. Hollister, Anthony J. Naldrett, Charles F. Park, Jr., and Ruffin I.Rackley, and to the computer scientists Phyllis Barrett, Kurt Konolige, Nils J.Nilsson, Rene Reboh, Jonathan Slocum, and B.Michael Wilber.

REFERENCES

Duda, R.O., P.E. Hart and N.J. Nilsson (1976), 'Subjective Bayesian methods for rule-based inference systems,' *Proc. National Computer Conference,* (AFIPS Conference Proceedings, Vol. 45), pp. 1075-1082, 1976.

Duda, R.O., P.E. Hart, N.J. Nilsson, R. Reboh, J. Slocum and G.L. Sutherland (1977), 'Development of a computer-based consultant for mineral exploration,' Annual Report, SRI Projects 5821 and 6415, SRI International, Menlo Park, California, October 1977.

Duda, R.O., P.E. Hart, N.J. Nilsson, and G.L. Sutherland (1978a), 'Semantic network representations in rule-based inference systems,' in *Pattern Directed Inference Systems*, D.A. Waterman and F. Hayes-Roth (Eds.), pp. 203-221, Academic Press, New York, 1978.

Duda, R.O., P.E.Hart, P.Barrett, J.Gaschnig, K.Konolige, R.Reboh and J.Slocum (1978b), "Development of the Prospector system for mineral exploration," Final Report, SRI Projects 5821 and 6415, SRI International, Menlo Park, California, October 1978.

Fagan, L.M. (1978), "Ventilator Manager: A program to provide on-line consultative advice in the intensive care unit." Heuristic Programming Project Memo HPP-78-16, Dept. of Computer Science, Stanford University, September 1978.

Hart, P.E., R.O. Duda, and K. Konolige (1978), "A computer-based consultant for mineral exploration," Second Semiannual Report, SRI Project 6415, SRI International, Menlo Park, California, April 1978.

Hart, P.E., R.O. Duda, and M.T. Einaudi (1978), "A computer-based consultation system for mineral exploration," to appear in *Computer Methods for the 80's*, Society of Mining Engineers of the AIME, 1978.

Martin, N., P. Friedland, J. King, and M. Stefik (1977), "Knowledge Base Management for Experiment Planning in Molecular Genetics," *Proc. of 5th International Joint Conference on Artificial Intelligence*, pp. 882-887, Cambridge, Mass., August 1977.

Pople, H.E., Jr., J.D. Myers, and R.A. Miller (1975), "DIALOG: A model of diagnostic logic for internal medicine," *Proc. of 4th International Joint Conference on Artificial Intelligence*. pp. 848-855, Tbilisi, Georgia, USSR, 1975.

Raiffa, H. (1968), *Decision Analysis*, Addison-Wesley Publishing Co., New York, 1968.

Shortliffe, E.H. (1976), *Computer-Based Medical Consultations: MYCIN*, American Elsevier Publishing Co., New York, 1976.

Shortliffe, E.H., and B.G. Buchanan (1975), "A model of inexact reasoning in medicine," *Math. Biosci*., Vol. 23, pp. 351-379, 1975.

Szolovits, P., and S.G. Pauker (1976), "Research on a medical consultation system for taking the present illness," *Proc. of 3rd Illinois Conference on Medical Information Systems*, pp. 299-320, University of Illinois at Chicago Circle, November 1976.

Weiss, S.M., C.A. Kulikowski, and A. Safir (1977), "A model-based consultation system for the long-term management of glaucoma." *Proc. of 5th International Joint Conference on Artificial Intelligence*, pp. 826-833, MIT, Cambridge, Massachusetts, 1977.

Yu, V.L., et al. (1978), "Evaluating the performance of a computer-based consultant," Heuristic Programming Project Memo HPP-78-17, Dept. of Computer Science, Stanford University, September 1978.

Zadeh, L.A. (1965), "Fuzzy sets." *Information and Control*, Vol. 8, pp. 338-353, 1965.

DISCOVERING RULES BY INDUCTION FROM LARGE COLLECTIONS OF EXAMPLES

J.R. Quinlan

INTRODUCTION

Induction is the process by which structures underlying and explaining a chaotic agglomeration of examples are discovered through analysis of the examples themselves. As a trivial illustration, I like curried chicken, chili con carne, Szechwan pork, Mongolian lamb, sartay, pepperoni, tabasco sauce and many other things besides. If someone were to read this list and suggest that I like all hot spicy foods, he would have arrived at this conclusion by induction. The conclusion itself may or may not be correct but at least it offers a coherent explanation for an otherwise motley assortment.

The relevance of induction to expert systems lies in the way knowledge is acquired. Most expert systems use knowledge obtained more or less painfully from a co-operating expert: the knowledge engineer ' . . . works intensively with an expert to acquire domain-specific knowledge and organize it for use by a program' but on the other hand ' . . . the acquisition of domain knowledge [is] the bottleneck problem in the building of applications-oriented intelligent agents' (both quotes from Feigenbaum 1977). Part of the bottleneck is perhaps due to the fact that the expert is called upon to perform tasks that he does not ordinarily do, such as setting down a comprehensive roadmap of some subject. (How often, for instance, is a mathematician asked to write down everything he knows about integration?) The expert may be adept at identifying landmarks, key concepts and so forth, but as soon as he is required to cover an area systematically the result is likely to suffer from omissions and inconsistencies that must then be laboriously tracked down and rectified. The lure of induction techniques is the possibility of providing the expert with assistance where he needs it most. The expert will still be responsible for concepts or new ways of viewing objects in the domain and rules of thumb for navigating it. The synthesis of a complete, consistent explanation of the domain in terms of these concepts will then be handed over to an induction-based algorithm. The success of the Meta-DENDRAL project (Buchanan 1978) in which rules of mass spectrometry were discovered demonstrates that this sort of approach can be feasible.

There have been many computer implementations of induction systems, varying both in the methods they employ to build rules and the range of induction tasks to which they can be applied. While it seems that no definitive survey has yet been written, Michalski (1978) and Smith (1977) provide many useful pointers into the literature.

In a recent paper Michie and Bratko studied the chess endgame where the pieces have been reduced to the black king and knight and the white king and rook Michie 1978). Assuming correct play, certain positions will lead to a win for white while in the rest black can achieve a draw. The authors point out that the problem of deciding to which category a given position belongs is non-trivial even for masters. But consider situations in which it is black's turn to move: we can ask the simpler question, 'Is the knight's side lost two ply?' Since (careful) capture of the knight will lead to an obvious mate, we define a black-to-move situation to be lost two ply if

1. black is checkmated, or
2. black is not stalemated, and on its next move, white can either
   checkmate black, or capture the knight
   without producing stalemate, and
   without leaving the rook vulnerable (*en prise*)

Donald Michie, who suggested this problem, also stated that chess masters can solve it 'at a glance', which seems to indicate that they are using pattern-based rather than search-based methods. Now induction is a method of discovering regularities, so it seems reasonable to investigate whether an induction-based system can construct such patterns without reference to the laws of chess, but by analysing examples of situations of either type – some lost two ply, some not. The induction machinery must come up with a correct rule to distinguish one type of situation from the other, or to use familiar pattern-recognition terminology, to *classify* situations as *lost* or *safe* (with *two-ply* understood). The number of possible situations to be catered for is large; there are more than 64 × 63 × 62 × 45 or 11 million of them.

This problem was attacked by a sort of slow ascent. A very simple subcase was defined and solved. The experience gained was used to define a second, more challenging subcase and so on; in all, seven problems were studied. At various stages the techniques for one problem were found to be not powerful enough for the next, so existing mechanisms had to be adapted or new ones invented along the way. Some of these mechanisms proved to be powerful and applicable to a range of induction tasks, and so are of more general interest.

The next sections of this article contain a brief discussion of the way that situations were conceptualized and the basic induction machinery employed. These are followed by a broad-brush account of the series of experiments and the techniques developed in the course of solving the seven problems; some of these techniques and trials with them are reported in more detail elsewhere (Quinlan 1979).

POSITIONS: SPECIFICATION AND DESCRIPTION

The sequence of problems studied all involve the same four chess pieces: the black king and knight and the white king and rook, with black's turn to move. Since there is no ambiguity the colour of the knight and rook will usually be assumed when referring to the pieces. If some fixed ordering is adopted, any configuration of the pieces (called a *position*) can be uniquely specified by four coordinates, each consisting of a pair of integers in the range 1 to 8. We could attempt to classify positions in terms of these eight small integers, but the resulting rule would be very close to a case-by-case tabulation because these eight integers are not directly related to the reasons that positions belong to one class or the other. For example one question that could be asked of any position is: 'Can the black king immediately capture the rook?' The answer is clearly yes if and only if the black king is next to the rook, and the white king is not next to the rook. Suppose that we wished to deal with this question directly in terms only of the coordinates of the rook and the two kings. We might resort to a reply

yes if and only if L

where *L* is a logical disjunction containing a large number of terms like

the rook is at position (3, 3), and
the black king is at one of the positions (2, 2), (2, 3), (2, 4), (3, 2), (3, 4), (4, 2), (4, 3) or (4, 4), and
the white king is at none of these positions

It is possible to abbreviate this vast and cumbersome logical expression, but only slightly. The trouble is that specification of a position by the coordinates of the pieces does not capture explicitly the property of adjacency of pieces, and it is precisely this property of adjacency that is needed for a succinct answer to the question.

Instead of the specification of a position we use some *characterization* or *description* of it in terms of properties that appear to be relevant to the rule that we are trying to construct. These properties are often not independent and so the characterization will contain redundant information. Surprisingly, though, it will almost always result in a compression of the data base. A single position can only have one description, but this may be shared with a number of other positions. With our four pieces, for example, rotation or reversal of the chessboard has no significance so all positions related by symmetry should have the same description. A given collection of positions will thus give rise to a smaller number of distinct characterizations. But what if two positions belonging to different classes share the same description? No rule can then be constructed that separates positions on the basis of the properties used to describe them, and so this set of properties is *inadequate* for the classification task. My passport describes its bearer by three properties: height, colour of eyes and colour of hair. The number of possible different descriptions is of the order of 3,000 which is much smaller than the number of individuals who can be described this way. While they give good compression and are fine for separating Nordic giants from the rest of humanity, these properties would be inadequate for most other classification tasks.

The idea of a 'good' set of properties to characterize a position is related to the broader issue of representation (Amarel 1968). Ideally the properties should be adequate for the task, give rise to substantial compression of the data base, be readily computable, and lend themselves to the development of concise rules. We use and invent such properties all the time, but even simple ones can involve considerable abstraction. Consider the properties *black king is next to rook* and *white king is not next to rook* that we used for the rule above. If we denote the coordinates of the black king, white king and rook as ($bk1$, $bk2$), ($wk1$, $wk2$) and ($r1$, $r2$) respectively, their derivation from these raw coordinates shown in figure 1 makes use of four types of abstraction: forming linear combinations, taking absolute values, selecting maxima and comparison with key values. The space of even simple abstractions is very large indeed. In the future some system in the vein of Lenat's AM (1977) may be built to explore these spaces and discover useful characterizations, but for the moment we assume that the properties are selected by someone familiar with the task domain and are one of the givens of the induction task.

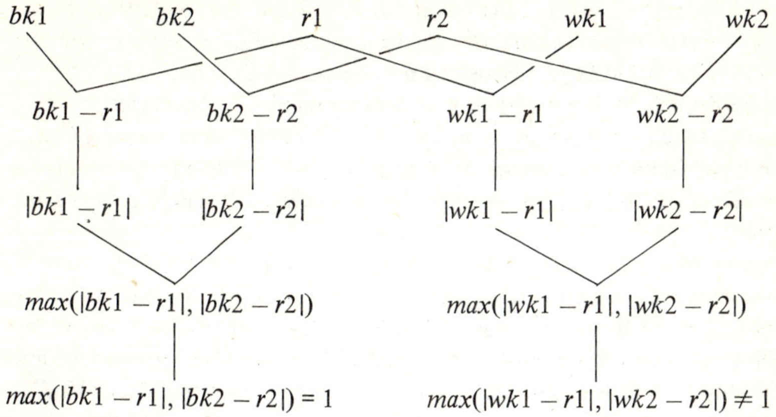

Figure 1. Derivation of two properties

THE BASIC INDUCTION ALGORITHM

The task that the induction algorithm must perform in our case can be stated as follows. The input (called a *training set*) is a collection of *instances* or characterizations of positions in terms of a predefined set of properties. The class (*lost* or *safe*) of each instance in the training set is known, and the algorithm must construct a *rule* or explanation of this class in terms of the characterization of the position. (For some applications it is sufficient if the rule explains most rather than all of the training set.) This rule is developed from the training set, but since it uses only properties which can be determined for any position it may also be relevant to instances not in the training set. Such projected relevance is the underlying assumption of pattern recognition in general: if the training set is 'typical' of the universe of instances then a rule that explains it ought to predict correctly the class of most instances outside the training set.

The induction algorithm used for this series of experiments was a relative of the Concept Learning System (CLS) developed by Hunt in the fifties and thoroughly documented in Hunt (1966). The advantages of this approach are its simplicity and proven efficacy for problems where each element of the training set can be described in the same fixed format. It should be emphasised that our version of CLS was a rather simple one, and any shortcomings it may have are not necessarily shared by the original CLS programs.

Each element of the training set is described by a fixed number of properties called *attributes*, each of which has a small number of discrete possible values. For the passport example earlier the permissible attribute values might be

height: 1.30, 1.31, ..., 2.29, 2.30
colour of hair: black, brown, red, fair, grey
colour of eyes: black, brown, green, blue, hazel

As this example illustrates, the permissible values of an attribute have no numeric significance, nor is their order important. Since each object is described by a value for each of the attributes this description can be thought of as a vector of fixed length. It is apparent that this rigidity can lead to difficulties in some applications. Michalski (1978) for instance discusses a problem in which the objects in the training set are descriptions of trains with varying numbers of carriages. While each carriage is characterized in a uniform way the number of carriages is not fixed, so it would be hard to make the description of the whole train conform to the rigid vector of CLS. For our chess problems, however, this does not present any difficulty.

Suppose then that we have a set of C of instances, each being a description of a position as above and each having a known class *lost* or *safe*. We wish to develop a rule relating these attribute values to the classes. If C is empty then we cannot say much about it, merely recording it as *null*. If C contains one or more instances and they all belong to the same class, we can associate C with this class. Otherwise C contains two or more instances, some *lost* and some *safe*. We could then choose an attribute A with permissible values $A_1, A_2, ..., A_n$ say. Each member of C will have one of these values for A, so we can sort C into subsets $C_1, C_2, ..., C_n$ where C_1 contains those instances in C with value A_1 of A, C_2 contains those with value A_2 of A, and so on. Diagrammatically we can represent this as

$$\left[\begin{array}{l}\text{attribute } A\\ A_1 \rightarrow C_1\\ A_2 \rightarrow C_2\\ \quad\vdots\\ A_n \rightarrow C_n\end{array}\right.$$

Now we have n sets of instances of the form C_i that we wish to relate to their class, so we can apply the same process to each of them. We keep going until each collection of instances is empty or all its members belong to the same class.

To clarify this process we will apply it to the simple problem from before of determining whether the black king can capture the white rook on its next move. There are two attributes,

black king is next to rook
white king is next to rook

each of which has the possible values *true* (t) and *false* (f). The two classes will be *can* and *cannot*. The training set will contain all possible instances,

{*tt:cannot, tf:can, ft:cannot, ff:cannot*}

If the first attribute is selected we will have

$$\left[\begin{array}{l}\text{black king is next to rook}\\ \quad t \rightarrow \{tt{:}cannot,\ tf{:}can\}\\ \quad f \rightarrow \{ft{:}cannot,\ ff{:}cannot\}\end{array}\right.$$

The same process is next applied to the first (sub)collection, this time selecting the second attribute.

```
┌ black king is next to rook
│
│      ┌ white king is next to rook
│ t →  │   t →  tt: cannot
│      └   f →  tf: can
│
└ f → {ft: cannot, ff: cannot}
```

All subcollections now contain instances of only a single class; we can replace the collections by the classes giving the rule

```
┌ black king is next to rook
│
│      ┌ white king is next to rook
│ t →  │   t → cannot
│      └   f → can
│
└ f → cannot
```

This rule is clearly isomorphic to the program fragment

if *black king is next to rook*
then if *white king is next to rook*
    then *cannot*
    else *can*
else *cannot*

and it is just as easy to produce one as the other. The earlier form (called a *decision tree*) will be used for the rest of this article because it is somewhat more compact and easier to follow, but this should not obscure the relationship of inductive rule discovery to automatic programming.

It is clear that any choice of attribute to test in the rule-building process above will lead eventually to a decision tree. However a series of bad choices will result in the same sort of case-by-case tabulation that classification by characterization is meant to avoid. There is no uniformly superior method of selecting an attribute; three different approaches should illustrate the range of criteria that could be used.

In the original CLS the choice was made on a cost basis. Suppose we define a set of costs $\{P_i\}$ of measuring the *i*th attribute of some instance, and $\{Q_{jk}\}$ of misclassifying it as belonging to class *j* when it really is a member of class *k*. If we arbitrarily say that all instances in *C* are members of some class even when they are not we will incur a misclassification cost which depends on the instances in *C* and the class chosen; let us denote by T_0 the minimum such cost over all classes. If we test some attribute *A* we will incur a measurement cost plus the sum of the total costs for each of the subcollections C_1, ..., resulting from testing that attribute; denote by T_1 the minimum sum over all attributes. The total cost of a rule for *C* is then the minimum of T_0 and T_1. This computation of total cost is clearly recursive and can be prohibitively expensive if there are many attributes, but it can be approximated by a fixed-depth lookahead in much the same way that the true minimax function can be approximated by a fixed-ply search. The rule that results from this approach tends to have low or even minimal cost. Such an approach would be appropriate for applications like medical diagnosis where obtaining information has significant cost, and where certain classification errors are more acceptable than others.

A second approach would be to use task-specific information to choose the attribute – that is, build an expert system to do the job. Such a system could try to make a sensible choice governed by ideas of what a correct rule ought to look like, just as Meta-DENDRAL uses a weak model of its domain to guide its search for a stronger one. The rule generated in this way should then appear plausible and understandable to human beings. This promising avenue has not yet been explored.

A third approach used in these experiments is geared to producing as simple a decision tree as possible. Simplicity has a clear relationship to generality, and it seems desirable to try to find rules that are applicable to more instances than those used to build them. By a process of trial and error a straightforward but workable complexity estimate was formulated that related the size of a rule for a collection of instances to the number of *lost* and *safe* positions in the collection. The attribute selected was one that minimized the sum of these estimates over the subcollections $\{C_i\}$ that would result from testing that attribute.

The next sections discuss the application of this basic induction machinery to the series of problems mentioned in the introduction, and the additional techniques that proved necessary for their solution.

THE FIRST PROBLEM

The series of problems was obtained from Donald Michie's *knight's side lost in two ply* question by modifications of one or both of the following types: (a) Restrictions designed to reduce the size of the underlying space of possible cases. These took the form of additional constraints on the initial configuration of the four chess pieces; (b) Simplifications of the meaning of *lost*. Both of these have the effect of making the problem easier, the first by reducing the computation required and the second by excluding some chess mechanisms and so simplifying the rule that must be found. For this first problem

> The initial configuration could not be a checkmate or stalemate position.
>
> The black knight was always *pinned* (i.e. moving the knight was illegal because it would discover check on the black king).
>
> Checkmate was ignored: the *lost* condition was satisfied only if the knight was captured without leaving the rook *en prise*.
>
> Stalemate was also ignored: the *lost* condition was satisfied even if capture of the knight would result in stalemate.

The cumulative effect of these changes is to rob the original question of almost all of its complexity.

Twelve properties were defined to characterize positions as shown in figure 2. Five of them referred to the distance in king moves between pairs of pieces. Since this distance is more important when pieces are close together, all king distances greater than two were treated as being the same value '3'. One property was concerned with the type of square occupied by the black king: in a corner, on an edge or somewhere else. The remaining six properties identified whether or not certain important conditions held in the position. The last three of them are more

Description of Property	*Values*
distance from black king to knight	1,2,3
distance from black king to rook	1,2,3
distance from black king to white king	2,3
distance from white king to knight	1,2,3
distance from white king to rook	1,2,3
type of black king's initial square	corner,edge,open
rook checks black king	t,f
rook threatens knight	t,f
knight threatens rook	t,f
black king, knight, rook in line	t,f
black king can move adjacent to knight	t,f
knight can interpose adjacent to black king	t,f

Figure 2. Properties used for the first problem

complex than the rest and may need a word of explanation. The black king, (black) knight and (white) rook are in line if they occupy a common rank or file on the board, and the white king does not appear among them. The black king can move adjacent to the knight if there is a legal move that leaves it beside the knight (and so defending it). The knight can interpose adjacent to the black king if the latter is in check and there is a knight move that interrupts the check and leaves the knight next to its king. At first glance it appears that properties such as these can only be evaluated by search but in fact they can be determined by set operations on a modest volume of tabulated information.

The induction algorithm was coded in INTERLISP (Teitelman 1978) for a DEC KA-10. A second program was written to generate at random positions conforming to the requirements of this first problem, and used to build up a collection of training sets each containing from 15 to 50 *lost* positions and the same number of *safe* ones. The induction algorithm was able to discover the correct rule shown in figure 3 from many of these training sets (in fact from all of them containing a total of 50 or more instances) in a few seconds of computer time. Notice that, of the twelve properties that could have been used in the rule, only the two that human beings would regard as crucial have been selected.

```
[black king can move adjacent to knight
[
[         [distance from white king to knight
[  t →    [    1 → lost
[         [    2 → safe
[         [    3 → safe
[
[  f → lost
```

Figure 3. Rule for the first problem (pins)

THE SECOND PROBLEM

For the first problem the configuration of pieces was restricted to pins. This condition was relaxed somewhat for the second problem in which each position was either a *pin*, *fork* or *skewer*. A fork occurs when the rook simultaneously threatens the black king and its knight; the two possible varieties which will be referred to as *linear* and *right-angle* forks are illustrated in figure 4. A skewer has the black king checked by the rook and the knight threatened when the king moves, and an example of this also appears in the figure. For this second problem, the same simplifications of *lost* were still in effect: the position was neither a stalemate nor checkmate, black could not be mated and stalemate was no defence. The same twelve attributes were also used for this problem.

Figure 4. Examples of forks and skewers

In the previous task the training set was assembled by generating random positions satisfying the constraints of the problem. This technique was not powerful enough for this more difficult problem – at least, no training set of up to 120 instances was produced that lead to a correct rule. Instead we approached the problem as one of *teaching* the rule to the induction algorithm. Starting with a random training set containing forty *lost* and forty *safe* positions, we entered a sort of tutorial mode. The induction algorithm would generate a rule from the current training set. This rule would next be checked by the human tutor, its shortcomings discovered, and a few further instances which contradicted the rule added to the training set. The augmented training set was then fed to the algorithm and the process continued. Eventually after half a dozen repetitions a training set of 105 instances was arrived at, from which the apparently correct rule shown in figure 5 was produced. This last run of the induction algorithm required about 30 seconds of KA-10 cpu time.

Two points are worth noting. The 'teaching' was a very frustrating process. Quite a lot of work was necessary to debug a partially correct rule of this complexity. It was not sufficient to say that the rule was wrong, but examples had to be found pinpointing where it went wrong. When these laboriously constructed counterexamples were added to the training set, though, the algorithm proved adept (almost perversely so) at digesting them in such a way that the new rule was concise, explained the training set perfectly, but was still in error. Secondly, there is still a lingering doubt about the final rule. It certainly seems correct, but such a rule would be difficult to prove correct. For both of these reasons the tutorial approach would probably be infeasible when the rule to be constructed was much more detailed. The family of different correct rules would expand, and it would simply be too much work for the teacher to find out whether a rule was wrong let alone thinking up counterexamples to demonstrate the errors.

```
black king can move adjacent to knight
t → distance from white king to knight
    1 → distance from black king to rook
        1 → distance from white king to rook
            1 → lost
            2 → safe
            3 → safe
        2 → knight can interpose adjacent to black king
            t → safe
            f → lost
        3 → lost
    2 → safe
    3 → safe
f → knight can interpose adjacent to black king
    t → distance from black king to knight
        1 → null
        2 → safe
        3 → distance from black king to white king
            2 → distance from white king to rook
                1 → lost
                2 → safe
                3 → safe
            3 → safe
    f → distance from black king to rook
        1 → distance from white king to rook
            1 → lost
            2 → safe
            3 → safe
        2 → lost
        3 → lost
```

Figure 5. Rule for the second problem (pins, forks and skewers)

THE THIRD PROBLEM

This represents something of a break in the sequence of problems because it was defined by another research worker, Alex Strong of Stanford University. There are no restrictions on the configuration of pieces, but the concept of *lost* has been altered considerably. Stalemate and checkmate were again excluded as were 'edge effects'; a position was not *lost* unless the same pattern of pieces on an infinite board would have the same outcome. Moreover a position was classed as *lost* only if the knight was captured as a result of a pin, linear fork or skewer. Three of Strong's examples in figure 6 illustrate the idea. The first is *lost* because, no matter where the black king moves, the knight can be taken by white on its next move. The second position, however, is *safe* since the knight can be captured only because the edge of the board forces the black king to move away. The third example is also *safe* because the loss of the knight does not result from a pin, linear fork or skewer.

Figure 6. *Lost* and *safe* positions for the third problem

The seven properties used for describing positions in this problem are given in figure 7. The first five of them were also used in the previous problems and so should be familiar. The remaining two use the concept of the rook *bearing on* another piece, meaning that they are in the same rank or file and the white king is not in the way. The rook bears on one black piece even if the other black piece lies between them, so it bears on both black pieces in every pin, fork or skewer.

Description of Property	*Values*
distance from black king to knight	1,2,3
distance from black king to rook	1,2,3
distance from white king to knight	1,2,3
distance from white king to rook	1,2,3
black king, knight, rook in line	t,f
rook bears on black king	t,f
rook bears on knight	t,f

Figure 7. Properties used for the third problem

This problem was used to explore some ideas for bypassing the demanding role of tutor. We assume that the training set available to the experimenter is substantial – it may even contain all possible instances. Such a training set will usually be too large to present to the induction algorithm, requiring either too much memory or excessive computation. The approach taken with this problem was to select a subset of it called a *window* and to modify this subset in the light of the rule discovered using it. The underlying structure is iterative, and can be sketched as:

1. Choose an initial window from the data available.
2. With this window as a training set, use the induction algorithm to find a rule satisfactory for the window.
3. Test the rule on the remainder of the data.
4. If exceptions to the rule are found, modify the window and repeat from step 2.

This is similar to the tutorial approach taken for the previous problem but replaces the checking of the rule and the construction of pertinent counterexamples by a simple test of the rule on the remainder of the instances in the original training set. Since this test will be expected to uncover many counterexamples to an incorrect rule and not just the archetypal ones, the way that the new window is formed in step 4 has to receive more attention.

Two such methods were investigated. In the first the window is allowed to grow by having exceptions added to it at each iteration. The exceptions are chosen randomly from amongst those discovered when testing the rule, but the number chosen at each iteration is strictly limited to prevent the window being swamped. The second method is rather more complicated and keeps the window size constant – this would be important for induction tasks that approach the bounds of available memory. Although the rule is known to be incorrect because exceptions to it have been found, parts of it probably are correct and we would like them to be reflected in any new rule. When a new window is formed it seems advisable to preserve as many as possible of the key instances used for the rule, because otherwise the next rule may fail to take them into account. The idea is then to try to identify in the window parcels of instances that had a similar influence in the formation of the rule. At least one representative of each parcel is carried forward into the new window and blended with a random selection of exceptions (again a limited number of them). Any space remaining is filled with other instances from the current window.

For this experiment we did in fact use a complete data base. The training set contained the description in terms of the properties mentioned of all legal configurations of the pieces – there were 647 of them – each with its known class. The properties were adequate in the sense that no two positions with the same description belonged to different classes, and they gave excellent compression since millions of positions have been reduced to a few hundred instances. The completeness of the data meant that any rule discovered to explain it was necessarily a correct one; there can be no lingering doubts that the teacher has overlooked an error.

Both methods of modifying the window were tried. For the first, the initial window was formed by selecting at random 30 instances from the data and allowing at most 10 exceptions to be added at each iteration. A correct rule for the entire 647 instances was found after 6 iterations and 211 seconds of cpu time; the window from which this correct rule was constructed contained 68 instances. Using the second method and a fixed window size of 50 instances the same correct rule was discovered in 7 iterations requiring 224 seconds. The rule itself is shown in figure 8. Notice that the second method, in finding a correct rule from a window containing only 50 instances, has thereby managed to sort out a subset of about 7% of the 647 instances that captures all the action. It has performed something akin to the role of a tutor selecting a small number of cases of special pedagogical importance from a much larger collection.

- black king, knight, rook in line
  - t → rook bears on knight
    - t → rook bears on black king
      - t → distance from black king to knight
        - 1 → distance from white king to knight
          - 1 → distance from black king to rook
            - 1 → *safe*
            - 2 → *lost*
            - 3 → *lost*
          - 2 → *safe*
          - 3 → *safe*
        - 2 → distance from white king to knight
          - 1 → distance from black king to rook
            - 1 → distance from white king to rook
              - 1 → *lost*
              - 2 → *safe*
              - 3 → *safe*
            - 2 → *lost*
            - 3 → *lost*
          - 2 → *safe*
          - 3 → *safe*
        - 3 → distance from black king to rook
          - 1 → distance from white king to rook
            - 1 → *lost*
            - 2 → *safe*
            - 3 → *safe*
          - 2 → *lost*
          - 3 → *lost*
      - f → *safe*
    - f → *safe*
  - f → *safe*

Figure 8. Rule for the third problem

THE FOURTH PROBLEM

While this problem was similar to the second one, the iterative techniques developed for the third problem were applied to it. Configurations were limited to those in which the knight's side is neither checkmated nor stalemated, and in which there was either a pin, linear fork or skewer. The main difference is that the idea of stalemate was included in the *lost* relation for the first time; as it turned out, this was responsible for a three-fold increase in the difficulty of the task. For this problem the knight is *lost* if it can be captured without either leaving the rook *en prise* or producing stalemate. As before, checkmate does not enter into the definition of *lost*.

Description of Property	*Values*
distance from black king to knight	1,2,3
distance from black king to rook	1,2,3
distance from black king to white king	2,3
distance from white king to knight	1,2,3
distance from white king to rook	1,2,3
distance from rook to knight	1,2,3
rook checks black king	t,f
rook threatens knight	t,f
black king can move adjacent to knight	t,f
black king on edge one square from corner	t,f
white king on edge two squares from corner	t,f
white king two squares diagonally from corner	t,f
knight one square diagonally from corner	t,f
white king next to rook rank or file	t,f

Figure 9. Properties used for the fourth problem

Because stalemate is now a factor, certain positions near the corner acquire special significance. These are reflected in the list of fourteen properties used to describe positions for this problem (figure 9). Three of the attributes used for problems 1 and 2 are no longer relevant ('knight threatens rook', 'king, knight, rook in line', 'knight can interpose') as a consequence of the exclusion of right-angle forks. The 'type of black king's square' has been altered to test whether the black king is in a specific relation to a corner. Three attributes have been added giving similar information for the knight and the white king, along with the remaining king distance from rook to knight and a property relating the white king and rook. All possible positions conforming to the restrictions of this problem were generated and described in terms of these properties; the attributes were found to be adequate and gave a total data base of 1,987 instances.

It was realized that the size of this problem put it beyond effective reach of the existing INTERLISP programs. Accordingly the system was rewritten in PASCAL (Jensen 1974) with considerable attention to questions of efficiency and memory requirements. When these programs were run on a DEC KL-10 a reduction in cpu time of more than two orders of magnitude was achieved. (Although INTERLISP is inherently inefficient by comparison with PASCAL, the reduction would probably not have been so marked if the initial system had been written more carefully and by someone more attuned to evaluative languages).

A large number of experiments was conducted with this data base. In short, the iterative technique coupled with either method of modifying the window typically managed to discover a rule adequate for all 1,987 instances in about four iterations requiring a total of just over three seconds of KL-10 cpu time. Even more interestingly, the time taken was slightly less than that required when all the data was fed directly to the induction algorithm; this seems to confirm the appropriateness of the iterative approach. A correct rule for this data base is too large to appear as a figure, and so is given instead in appendix A. (As this rule will not fit on one page, three of its subtrees appear before the rule itself. These subtrees were extracted from the rule by a mechanical page-balancing algorithm and have no independent significance.)

Further experiments were carried out to find small collections of instances encapsulating the 'essence' of this large data base. The idea was to commence with a window containing few instances and to add only a few instances and to add only a few exceptions at each iteration. One technique found to speed up the convergence on a correct rule (and so result in a smaller final window) was to allow the induction algorithm to search the data base at large for instances corresponding to a *null* leaf in the current rule. If any exist, the first one found was immediately co-opted into the window rather than relying on the normal random selection of exceptions. The effect was to give priority to filling holes in the current rule. (This technique could be used on induction tasks in general, but as the size of the data base grows it would probably become less and less cost-effective.) With this addition, final windows containing as few as 88 instances (i.e. 4% of the data) were found from which correct rules for all 1,987 instances were able to be generated.

THE FIFTH AND SIXTH PROBLEMS

These problems were sufficiently similar that they can be treated together. The main feature common to both was the use of the full concept of *lost* from the original question. A position could be either stalemate or checkmate; and the knight's side is *lost* if either black could be mated on white's next move, or if the knight can be captured as before. The only restrictions concerned the position of the black king. For the fifth problem the black king was always in a corner, while for the sixth it was either in a corner or on an edge and next to a corner. The other pieces were allowed to range over all legal possibilities.

The outcome of mate two ply needed for these problems is a difficult idea to capture in terms of simple properties, as the examples in figure 10 show. In the left-hand case the knight can prevent the king being mated two ply, but in the middle one it is powerless to help. The only obvious pairwise geometric difference between these cases is a slight change in the relative positions of the knight and the white king, and the relationship between these pieces seems to be quite irrelevant to what is going on. When the threat of mate and the threat of knight capture are combined truly complex situations can arise, as illustrated by the right-hand case. Thus it is understandable that these problems needed more attributes and more complex ones at that than those used previously.

Figure 10. Three positions

The fifth problem used 23 attributes, the sixth a slightly enlarged set of 26. Since both were similar to the set of properties used for the seventh problem which are described later, these properties will just be noted as falling into four categories:

(i) Distances in king moves, e.g. *distance from black king to rook*.
(ii) Threats, e.g. *rook threatens knight*.
(iii) Positional information, e.g. *white king on an edge two squares from a corner*.
(iv) Patterns specifically concerned with possible mate, e.g. *black king's only move creates a mating square*. These were typically more complex than those in the other categories.

The first three categories are familiar from earlier problems. The last uses the idea of a 'mating square' defined with reference only to the two kings and the rook: if there is a square to which the rook can move and mate (ignoring the knight) then that is a mating square. In figure 10 the example on the left has a mating square at the bottom row and fifth column, the middle case has a mating square at the fourth row and first column, but no mating square exists in the final case.

Once again complete data bases were used. For the fifth problem there turned out to be 6,194 distinct instances and for the sixth about three times as many (just under 19,000). Each problem was attempted starting with a randomly chosen window of 400 instances and allowing up to 100 exceptions to be added at each cycle. The fifth problem was solved in eight iterations requiring 46 cpu seconds, the sixth in 15 iterations and 227 seconds. The rules discovered are not given here, but they are respectively about six and eleven times as complex as the rule for the third problem which appears in figure 8.

THE SEVENTH PROBLEM

With the preceeding six problems as a leadup we were finally in a position to tackle the original question as posed in the introduction. The rule developed for this seventh problem had to be applicable to any configuration of the four pieces to determine whether the knight's side is *lost* two ply in accordance with normal chess usage, taking account of both stalemate and checkmate.

A great deal of difficulty was experienced trying to get a suitable set of properties with which to describe positions. Each time a plausible, compact set of attributes was tried they were found to be inadequate: at least one pair of positions would turn up with the same description but with one of them *lost* and the other *safe*. On the other hand when large collections of properties were used there was too little compression of the data base, and the file of instances that was generated exceeded the mass storage available to the author. The difficulty was compounded by the cost of trying out a new set of properties. After symmetric alternants have been excluded there are still about 1.8 million possible configurations; it typically took more than an hour of KL-10 cpu time to examine each of them, evaluate the properties, and check whether the description obtained matched that of some earlier configuration.

The dilemma was resolved by a suggestion from Donald Michie that an appropriate answer to the question might be a blend of a property-based rule and search. The rule produced then need not always provide an answer but might in a (very) few cases refer the query to some other mechanism. In our case this comes down to allowing the leaves of the decision tree to be labelled

lost or *safe*, meaning that the question has been answered as indicated;

null, meaning that there are no legal configurations that match the description at this leaf; or

search, in which case the question must be resolved by some other means.

The *lost* and *safe* answers must of course be absolutely correct – there is no intention to compromise the rule by allowing it to make wrong classifications. Referring back to the basic induction algorithm, if the set of attributes is inadequate there will sooner or later be a collection of instances that are not all of the same class, but which cannot be subdivided further by testing more attributes. In such a case the collection will now be related to the new pseudo-class *search*. With this modification the rule-building algorithm can function even if the properties it uses are inadequate. Minor adjustments to the iterative machinery are also necessary; instances that map to a *search* leaf of the current rule may or may not be 'exceptions' in the in the previous sense, and must be treated carefully.

A reasonable-looking set of 25 descriptors (detailed in Appendix B) was then assembled and the complete data base for the seventh problem generated as before; it contained 29,236 instances. The modified iterative technique incorporating these changes was tried on this large data base. As with the fifth and sixth problems the initial window contained 400 instances selected at random, and up to 100 exceptions could be added to this window at each iteration. The system required 20 iterations and 394 seconds to find a rule which also appears lengthily in Appendix B. The final window from which this rule was formed contained 2,160 instances or about 7% of the data base. The decision tree was built up of 393 nodes of which 11 were labelled *search*, and a total of only 75 of the 29,236 instances belonged to these nodes. Putting it another way: if this rule is used to decide whether or not a position is *lost* two ply it will give the correct answer with probability 0.9974, and with probability 0.0026 it will reply that the properties it uses are inadequate to classify the given position.

CONCLUSION

Case studies often have the failing that, by becoming enmeshed in a blow-by-blow account of what happened rather than the orderly exposition of an idea, they make it easy to lose sight of what the study was meant to achieve. It therefore seems prudent to repeat that the main point of this article is the demonstration that techniques exist for discovering complex regularities in large collections of data. The 'large' can be justified by quoting the number of instances and attributes, but the 'complex' is less easy to pin down. For this reason a lot of space has been taken up with lists of properties and rules. While these could have just been summarized as, say, 'a rule containing 393 nodes' or '14 geometric attributes', a good part of their impact would have been lost. As it is the steady growth of the level of detail of the rules is apparent, and presentation of the final rule in particular makes it clear as no summary could have that answering the original question in terms of the given 25 properties is probably beyond human abilities.

This immediately raises the question of whether these and other properties used in the study were appropriate. The answer is that they were probably not; it seems likely that a chess expert could develop more pertinent attributes in terms of which the rules and especially the final one could be couched much more compactly. As we stated before, the definition of the attributes used to describe the data is currently an expert task which our induction system takes as given. If the expert does his job well the induction problem is simplified; if a non-expert undertakes the definition of properties (as was the case here) the converse is true. But this simply states that the induction programs have solved problems that were harder than they need have been.

Preliminary information indicates that as the induction tasks get more difficult the time that the iterative techniques need to solve them increases only linearly, rather than the exponential increase that would be expected with combinatorial-type approaches, e.g. Vere (1978). For example, one reasonable estimate of the difficulty of an induction task is the product of

the number of instances to be explained
the number of attributes describing each instance
the complexity of the rule to be developed (as measured by the number of nodes in the decision tree)

On this scale the problems attempted with the PASCAL version of the system (the fourth through seventh) span two orders of magnitude in difficulty, ranging from 2.1×10^6 to 2.8×10^8. When the numbers of cpu seconds per million difficulty units required to solve these four problems are computed, the figures are 1.5, 1.8, 1.4, 1.4 respectively, which are remarkably consistent given the above range of difficulties. Consequently it would seem that no combinatorial explosion should prevent these same techniques being applied to larger problems.

This study used a series of chess problems to make its point. One advantage is that most people are familiar with this domain and long-winded explanations are unnecessary. However it has the defect that there is a well-understood mechanism by which positions can be found to be *lost* or *safe* two ply, namely the rules governing moves. This mechanism is quite opaque to the induction algorithm, which must formulate a decision tree in terms of the given properties. Because there is another way to solve them, the chess problems are atypical: the most common use of the induction approach is to discover rules in domains where the underlying mechanism is not known. Suppose there was some accumulation of 30,000 'snapshots' of business conditions, each giving the state of the economy ('boom' or 'bust') at some time together with the values some fixed time interval before of 25 expert-selected economic indicators. If we tried to discover a rule that explained the former in terms of the latter the task would be seen to be a difficult one (much more so than the last chess problem) because incomplete understanding of the underlying economic mechanism has so far prevented any human being from doing it. And yet, if the values were as coarse and a rule no more complex than those in Appendix B, the business conditions problem should prove no more difficult for the induction than the chess problem.

The areas in which expert systems are now and will increasingly be used can almost be defined as those lacking a well-understood model – in Ed Feigenbaum's terms, those without a mechanical core or whose mathematical core has already been fully exploited. The acquisition, refining and organization of knowledge for such systems has already been found to be a laborious task for the experts and others involved. Induction-based techniques provide one tool for lightening this burden.

ACKNOWLEDGEMENTS

The author is most grateful to Donald Michie of the University of Edinburgh, whose encouragement and many suggestions have been of invaluable assistance in this project. Many thanks are also due to those organizations at Stanford who generously provided computing resources.

REFERENCES

Amarel, S. (1968) On machine representations of problems of reasoning about actions, *Machine Intelligence 3* (ed. D.Michie). Edinburgh: University Press.

Buchanan, B.G. & Mitchell, T.M. (1978) Model-directed learning of production rules, in *Pattern-Directed Inference Systems* (eds. Waterman and Hayes-Roth). N.Y.: Academic Press.

Feigenbaum, E.A. (1977) The art of artificial intelligence: 1 Themes and case studies of knowledge engineering. Computer Science Department Report STAN-CS-77-621, Stanford University, Stanford, Cal.

Hunt, E.B., Marin, J. & Stone, P. (1966) *Experiments in Induction*. N.Y.: Academic Press.

Jensen, K. & Wirth, N. (1974) *PASCAL User Manual and Report*. Berlin: Springer-Verlag.

Lenat, D. (1977) Automated theory formation in mathematics. *Proc. 5th Int. Joint Conf. Artificial Intelligence,* Cambridge, Mass.

Michalski, R.S. (1978) Pattern recognition as knowledge-guided computer induction. Department of Computer Science, University of Illinois at Urbana-Champaign.

Michie, D. & Bratko, I. (1978) Advice table representations of chess endgame knowledge. *Proc. AISB/GI Conf. Artificial Intelligence.*

Quinlan, J.R. (1979) Induction over large data bases. In preparation.

Smith, R.G., Mitchell, T.M., Chestek, R.A. & Buchanan, B.G. (1977) A model for learning systems. Heuristic Programming Project Memo HPP-77-14, Stanford University, Stanford, Cal.

Teitelman, W. (1978) Interlisp Reference Manual. XEROX PARC, Palo Alto Cal.

Vere, S.A. (1978) Inductive learning of relational productions. In *Pattern-Directed Inference Systems* (eds. Waterman and Hayes-Roth). N.Y.: Academic Press

APPENDIX A: A RULE FOR THE FOURTH PROBLEM

The attribute names have been abbreviated as follows:

Abbreviation	*Attribute*
distance k-n	distance from the black king to the knight
distance k-r	ditto black king to rook
distance k-wk	ditto black king to white king
distanee n-r	ditto knight to rook
distance n-wk	ditto knight to white king
distance r-wk	ditto rook to white king
r threatens k	rook checks black king
r threatens n	rook threatens knight
k can approach	black king can move adjacent to knight
k at p2	black king is on an edge one square from a corner
wk at p3	white king is on an edge two squares from a corner
wk at p5	white king diagonally two squares from a corner
n at p4	knight is diagonally one square from a corner
wk next to r line	white king next to rook rank or file

Subtree 1

- distance k-wk
  - 2 → distance n-r
    - 1 → *lost*
    - 2 → *lost*
    - 3 → distance n-wk
      - 1 → *lost*
      - 2 → *lost*
      - 3 → distance r-wk
        - 1 → r threatens n
          - t → wk at p3
            - t → *safe*
            - f → *lost*
          - f → *lost*
        - 2 → *lost*
        - 3 → *lost*
  - 3 → *lost*

Subtree 2

```
distance k-wk
  2 → distance n-wk
        1 → lost
        2 → lost
        3 → r threatens n
              t → k at p2
                    t → wk at p3
                          t → wk next to r line
                                t → safe
                                f → lost
                          f → lost
                    f → lost
              f → lost
  3 → lost
```

Subtree 3

```
distance n-wk
  1 → distance k-r
        1 → safe
        2 → distance k-n
              1 → distance n-r
                    1 → k at p2
                          t → n at p4
                                t → safe
                                f → lost
                          f → lost
                    2 → null
                    3 → lost
              2 → lost
              3 → null
        3 → distance k-n
              1 → r threatens k
                    t → lost
                    f → n at p4
                          t → safe
                          f → lost
              2 → lost
              3 → null
  2 → safe
  3 → safe
```

Rule for Pins, Linear Forks and Skewers

k can approach
- t → *Subtree 3*
- f → distance k-r
  - 1 → distance r-wk
    - 1 → distance n-wk
      - 1 → k at p2
        - t → wk at p3
          - t → *safe*
          - f → *lost*
        - f → *lost*
      - 2 → *null*
      - 3 → r threatens n
        - t → wk at p3
          - t → *safe*
          - f → *lost*
        - f → *lost*
    - 2 → *safe*
    - 3 → *safe*
  - 2 → distance k-n
    - 1 → *lost*
    - 2 → *lost*
    - 3 → *Subtree 1*
  - 3 → distance k-n
    - 1 → *lost*
    - 2 → *lost*
    - 3 → *Subtree 2*

APPENDIX B. A RULE FOR THE ORIGINAL PROBLEM

The following properties use the idea of a square that is 'restful' for the knight, defined as a square that is threatened by neither the rook nor white king, or is threatened by one of them but is next to the black king. As with Appendix A, the attributes are referred to by an abbreviated name in the rule proper.

Abbreviation	*Attribute*	*Values*
distance k-n	distance from the black king to the knight	1,2,3
distance k-r	ditto, black king to rook	1,2,3
distance k-wk	ditto, black king to white king	2,3
distance n-r	ditto, knight to rook	1,2,3
distance n-wk	ditto, knight to white king	1,2,3
distance r-wk	ditto, rook to white king	1,2,3
distance k-ms	distance in king moves from the black king to the mating square ('x' means no mating square exists)	x,2,3
r threatens k	rook checks black king	t,f
r threatens n	rook threatens knight	t,f
k,n,r in line	the black king, knight and rook are in line with the white king not between any pair of them	t,f
n threatens r	knight can capture rook	t,f
n threatens ms	knight threatens the mating square (if there is one)	t,f
k can approach	black king can move adjacent to knight	t,f
n to rs	knight can move to a restful square so that black king is not in check	t,f
n to rs and check	knight can move to a restful square to check white king	t,f
n to rs and block	knight can move to a restful square which is either between the mating square and the black king, or from which the knight can move to a square between the mating square and the black king (if a mating square exists)	t,f
k move gives ms	the only move that the black king can make creates a mating square	t,f
k at pl	the black king is in a corner	t,f
k to pl	the black king can move to a corner	t,f
wk at p3	the white king is on an edge two squares from a corner	t,f
wk at p5	the white king is on a diagonal two squares from a corner	t,f

n at p3	the knight is on an edge two squares from a corner	t,f
n at p4	the knight is on a diagonal one square from a corner	t,f
k.n.ms	the knight is on an edge between the black king and the mating square (if there is one)	t,f
r divides k,wk	the two kings are on opposite sides of and next to a rank or file occupied by the rook	t,f

Subtree 1

```
distance k-r
  1 → null
  2 → safe
  3 → distance n-wk
        1 → distance k-ms
              x → null
              2 → safe
              3 → k at p1
                    t → n at p3
                          t → r divides k, wk
                                t → lost
                                f → safe
                          f → safe
                    f → safe
        2 → safe
        3 → null
```

Subtree 2

```
r divides k, wk
    t → lost
    f → r threatens n
            t → n at p4
                    t → k to p1
                            t → safe
                            f → lost
                    f → lost
            f → distance k-n
                    1 → safe
                    2 → wk at p5
                            t → distance n-r
                                    1 → lost
                                    2 → safe
                                    3 → distance r-wk
                                            1 → null
                                            2 → lost
                                            3 → search
                            f → safe
                    3 → null
```

Subtree 3

```
distance k-wk
    2 → distance n-r
            1 → safe
            2 → safe
            3 → r threatens k
                    t → k,n,r in line
                            t → k to p1
                                    t → wk at p5
                                            t → lost
                                            f → safe
                                    f → safe
                            f → safe
                    f → safe
    3 → safe
```

Subtree 4

- distance n-wk
  - 1 → r threatens k
    - t → k,n,r in line
      - t → distance k-r
        - 1 → *safe*
        - 2 → *lost*
        - 3 → *lost*
      - f → distance r-wk
        - 1 → r threatens n
          - t → *lost*
          - f → *safe*
        - 2 → distance k-n
          - 1 → *safe*
          - 2 → distance k-r
            - 1 → *safe*
            - 2 → *lost*
            - 3 → *safe*
          - 3 → *null*
        - 3 → *safe*
    - f → distance k-wk
      - 2 → n at p3
        - t → *lost*
        - f → *Subtree 2*
      - 3 → *lost*
  - 2 → distance k-n
    - 1 → *Subtree 3*
    - 2 → *safe*
    - 3 → *null*
  - 3 → *safe*

Subtree 5

n to rs
- t → distance k-n
  - 1 → *safe*
  - 2 → distance k-r
    - 1 → *safe*
    - 2 → *safe*
    - 3 → distance k-wk
      - 2 → distance n-wk
        - 1 → distance k-ms
          - x → *safe*
          - 2 → *lost*
          - 3 → *lost*
        - 2 → *safe*
        - 3 → *safe*
      - 3 → *safe*
  - 3 → *null*
- f → distance k-ms
  - x → *Subtree 4*
  - 2 → distance n-r
    - 1 → *lost*
    - 2 → *null*
    - 3 → *safe*
  - 3 → *safe*

Subtree 6

distance k-wk
- 2 → distance n-r
  - 1 → *lost*
  - 2 → *lost*
  - 3 → distance n-wk
    - 1 → *lost*
    - 2 → *lost*
    - 3 → distance r-wk
      - 1 → r threatens n
        - t → wk at p3
          - t → *safe*
          - f → *lost*
        - f → *lost*
      - 2 → *lost*
      - 3 → *lost*
- 3 → *lost*

Subtree 7

```
wk at p3
  t → distance r-wk
        1 → safe
        2 → safe
        3 → r threatens k
              t → safe
              f → n at p3
                    t → lost
                    f → distance n-r
                          1 → n at p4
                                t → safe
                                f → search
                          2 → search
                          3 → lost
  f → lost
```

Subtree 8

```
distance k-r
  1 → distance r-wk
        1 → r threatens n
              t → k at p1
                    t → lost
                    f → k to p1
                          t → wk at p3
                                t → safe
                                f → lost
                          f → lost
              f → lost
        2 → safe
        3 → safe
  2 → Subtree 6
  3 → distance k-wk
        2 → distance n-wk
              1 → lost
              2 → lost
              3 → r threatens n
                    t → k at p1
                          t → lost
                          f → k to p1
                                t → Subtree 7
                                f → lost
                    f → lost
        3 → lost
```

Subtree 9

```
distance k-n
   1 → lost
   2 → distance k-r
          1 → distance n-r
                 1 → k at p1
                        t → lost
                        f → k to p1
                               t → wk at p3
                                      t → safe
                                      f → lost
                               f → lost
                 2 → null
                 3 → safe
          2 → lost
          3 → lost
   3 → Subtree 8
```

Subtree 10

```
distance k-r
   1 → null
   2 → lost
   3 → distance n-r
          1 → lost
          2 → distance n-wk
                 1 → lost
                 2 → lost
                 3 → distance r-wk
                        1 → null
                        2 → k at p1
                               t → wk at p3
                                      t → search
                                      f → lost
                               f → lost
                        3 → lost
          3 → lost
```

Subtree 11

- distance k-ms
  - x → *safe*
  - 2 → r threatens n
    - t → *Subtree 10*
    - f → distance k-r
      - 1 → *null*
      - 2 → *safe*
      - 3 → distance n-wk
        - 1 → *lost*
        - 2 → *safe*
        - 3 → *safe*
  - 3 → distance r-wk
    - 1 → *null*
    - 2 → *lost*
    - 3 → r threatens n
      - t → *lost*
      - f → k at p1
        - t → wk at p3
          - t → distance n-wk
            - 1 → *lost*
            - 2 → *safe*
            - 3 → *safe*
          - f → *lost*
        - f → *safe*

Subtree 12

- distance k-wk
  - 2 → r threatens k
    - t → *safe*
    - f → distance k-n
      - 1 → *safe*
      - 2 → distance k-ms
        - x → *safe*
        - 2 → r divides k,wk
          - t → *safe*
          - f → *lost*
        - 3 → *lost*
      - 3 → wk at p5
        - t → r threatens n
          - t → distance k-ms
            - x → *safe*
            - 2 → *lost*
            - 3 → *lo*
          - f → *safe*
        - f → *Subtree 11*
  - 3 → *safe*

Subtree 13

```
k at p1
   t → lost
   f → k to p1
          t → safe
          f → wk at p3
                 t → safe
                 f → wk at p5
                        t → safe
                        f → n at p4
                               t → safe
                               f → n at p3
                                      t → search
                                      f → search
```

Subtree 14

```
k at p1
   t → lost
   f → k to p1
          t → safe
          f → n at p3
                 t → safe
                 f → n at p4
                        t → safe
                        f → wk at p3
                               t → search
                               f → wk at p5
                                      t → search
                                      f → search
```

Subtree 15

```
distance k-n
   1 → null
   2 → distance n-r
          1 → k to p1
                 t → n at p3
                        t → safe
                        f → search
                 f → lost
          2 → safe
          3 → safe
   3 → distance k-wk
          2 → distance n-r
                 1 → null
                 2 → distance r-wk
                        1 → r threatens k
                               t → safe
                               f → lost
                        2 → safe
                        3 → null
                 3 → safe
          3 → safe
```

Subtree 16

```
distance k-r
  1 → Subtree 15
  2 → distance n-r
        1 → lost
        2 → distance k-n
              1 → null
              2 → r threatens k
                    t → Subtree 13
                    f → lost
              3 → safe
        3 → distance k-n
              1 → null
              2 → safe
              3 → distance k-wk
                    2 → distance r-wk
                          1 → null
                          2 → r threatens k
                                t → Subtree 14
                                f → safe
                          3 → safe
                    3 → safe
  3 → lost
```

Subtree 17

```
distance k-ms
  x → distance n-wk
        1 → Subtree 16
        2 → distance k-n
              1 → k at p1
                    t → lost
                    f → distance k-r
                          1 → safe
                          2 → safe
                          3 → r threatens k
                                t → safe
                                f → lost
              2 → safe
              3 → safe
        3 → distance k-n
              1 → lost
              2 → safe
              3 → safe
  2 → r threatens k
        t → lost
        f → safe
  3 → r threatens k
        t → lost
        f → k at p1
              t → wk at p3
                    t → safe
                    f → lost
              f → safe
```

Subtree 18

```
n to rs
    t → Subtree 12
    f → r threatens n
            t → distance k-r
                    1 → distance r-wk
                            1 → distance n-r
                                    1 → distance k-n
                                            1 → safe
                                            2 → search
                                            3 → null
                                    2 → safe
                                    3 → lost
                            2 → safe
                            3 → safe
                    2 → lost
                    3 → lost
            f → Subtree 17
```

Subtree 19

```
k.n.ms
    t → distance k-n
            1 → r threatens n
                    t → safe
                    f → lost
            2 → safe
            3 → r threatens n
                    t → lost
                    f → safe
    f → k can approach
            t → Subtree 5
            f → k,n,r in line
                    t → distance k-ms
                            x → Subtree 9
                            2 → lost
                            3 → lost
                    f → Subtree 18
```

Subtree 20

```
k move gives ms
  t →  distance k-r
         1 → safe
         2 → safe
         3 →  n to rs
                t → safe
                f →  distance n-r
                       1 → lost
                       2 → lost
                       3 → safe
  f →  n threatens ms
         t →  r threatens n
                t →  distance k-n
                       1 →  k to p1
                              t → safe
                              f → lost
                       2 → null
                       3 → lost
                f →  distance k-n
                       1 → safe
                       2 →  distance k-r
                              1 → null
                              2 → lost
                              3 → safe
                       3 → safe
         f → Subtree 19
```

Subtree 21

```
n to rs and block
  t →  distance k-n
         1 → safe
         2 →  distance n-r
                1 →  distance n-wk
                       1 →  k can approach
                              t → safe
                              f →  r divides k, wk
                                     t → lost
                                     f → safe
                       2 → safe
                       3 → null
                2 → safe
                3 → Subtree 1
         3 → safe
  f → Subtree 20
```

Final Rule

```
n threatens r
  t → safe
  f →  n to rs and check
         t → safe
         f → Subtree 21
```

AN AIDE FOR THEORY FORMATION

I.H. Chisholm (1) & D.H. Sleeman

1.0 INTRODUCTION

The central problem addressed by this work is the acquisition of knowledge from experts, and as such it is closely related to the MYCIN [Shortliffe, 1974] and TIERESIAS [Davis, 1978] systems. In our system, the domain 'theory' is formulated as a series of production rules; the expert/user then presents the system with problems and the system will, if the rules permit, solve these problems. If desired the expert can then interrogate the system as to how the problem has been solved and can, using editing facilities analogous to MYCIN's, modify the ruleset.

In addition, we have added facilities which 'observe' certain kinds of regularities in the examples provided by the expert. That is, in Stanford's terminology [Buchanan & Mitchell, 1977], we have provided several modes which can perform model-directed inference which operate on the production rules and additional domain-knowledge provided in a semantic net. These facilities include the ability to resolve conflicts, produce analogies and carry out generalizations of features in the examples provided. We note that both the latter facilities rely on the ability to recognize the pertinent features of a problem and hence are closely related. The capabilities of these inference modes, we claim, make the current system a valuable Aide for Theory Formation, capable of active participation in checking the completeness and consistency of the domain-knowledge/theory (1). (For this reason we have named the system CONCHE, CONsistency CHEcker.)

Although CONCHE has been developed in the context of acquiring expert knowledge, we would suggest that many of these capabilities would be valuable in other contexts, for example in ICAI systems. Collins has noted that human tutors make analogies with more familiar situations when faced with new situations [Collins et al, 1975]. A teaching system incorporating some of these ideas could reason by analogy when operating with incomplete knowledge.

2.0 GENERAL OVERVIEW OF THE KNOWLEDGE ACQUISITION PROGRAM

The decision as to what information is represented as facts (in the semantic net) and what is represented as rules depends upon the degree of explanation required. For example, 'the valency of carbon is 4' could be represented as a fact in the network; however, if necessary to justify this statement then an appropriate rule must be provided (see 2.1 below) which, for example, relates valency and electron configuration. All domain-specific knowledge is repre-

(1) Such a system could be used to produce a *consistent* data base for use by a ICAI system; an example of a ICAI system which uses production rules to represent its knowledge is GUIDON [Clancey, 1979], which evolved from the MYCIN project.

sented in these formalisms so that the knowledge acquisition program is domain-independent (2).

2.1 Production Rule Sub-system

In essence the production rules are of the same general form as in MYCIN. However, by using an extended version of the FUZZY pattern matcher [Le Faivre, 1978] the user can enhance the power and scope of the rule system. The general form of a rule, as seen by the user, is:

```
IF:
    1. CONDITION 1
    2. CONDITION 2
          :
          :
  <n>. CONDITION <n>
  THEN:
<n+1>. OUTCOME (optional CERTAINTY FACTOR)
```

The CONDITIONS are implicitly ANDed together; they may be any FUZZY skeleton and therefore variables, instantiation and evaluation may be freely incorporated. The OUTCOME is a fuzzy procedure-calling-pattern, hence it may include alternatives, optional items, restrictions, etc.. The CERTAINTY FACTOR may be any expression which should yield a result in the range [–1,1] (3) and is employed as in MYCIN [Shortliffe, 1975]. (The numbering of CONDITIONs and OUTCOME is supplied by the system so that individual components may be referenced in the rule editor.)

A rule for determining valencies from electronic configurations might be:

```
IF:
    1. THE ELECT-CONFIG OF !X IS !Y
    2. !Z IS &(CALC-VALENCIES !Y)
    3. !V IS AN ELEMENT OF !Z
THEN:
    4. VALENCY OF !X IS !V
```

Here, all conditions are factual enquiries rather than conditions to be satisfied by other rules; 1) accesses an attribute value stored in the semantic net, 2) is the equivalent of an assignment statement, and 3) is similarly an assignment statement but will iterate through a list of values should backtracking occur.

2.1.1 The Deductive Mechanism. The rule system operates in a backward chaining manner; it establishes which rules are relevant by matching outcomes against the question, and for each relevant rule attempts to satisfy the conditions in order. The conditions can be satisfied either by facts or by rules, and back-

(2) LISP functions and FUZZY procedures are acceptable in certain aspects of the formalism, but should be confined to primitives used for convenience; they should never be used in any rule involved in inferences as there is no mechanism for manipulating procedural knowledge.

(3) Numeric values not in this range are converted to the nearest endpoint, NIL is converted to 0(zero) and all other non-numeric values are converted to 1.

tracking occurs if subsequent conditions are not or cannot be satisfied. Infinite deduction due to repeated subquestions is avoided (without loss of solutions) by stopping the normal deductive process when a question is repeated; the solutions already found are used to answer the reoccurence of the question. To ensure all solutions are returned, the original question is reasked until no new solutions are determined.

A trace of the deductive process can be constructed for subsequent analysis by the 'reasoning' facilities. Rules may be grouped into named subsets and conditions may specify that particular rulesets are to be employed; rulesets may also be called from the semantic net, either to determine or to validate attribute values.

2.2 Semantic Network Sub-system

The semantic network sub-system has been developed from designs proposed by Woods [1975] and more particularly Brachmann [1977]. Both these papers discuss the philosophical foundations of semantic networks, addressing the problems of earlier formulations and proposing formalisms to overcome, in particular, the difficulties caused by the inconsistent use of links. The net is constructed using a small number of primitive links to define attributes and specify concept/subconcept/instance relationships. Concepts may have any number of attributes each of which include such properties as default values and restrictions on instantiated values. Instances of a concept may have instantiated values for the attributes defined, if a value is not supplied the default applies (this may be *UNKNOWN*). A concept/subconcept network of arbitrary complexity may be constructed subject to the restriction that a concept may not be a subconcept of itself; subconcepts inherit all attribute definitions from superior concepts but these may be redefined, modified or given a specific value. In CONCHE, the rule-net interface allows the conditions of rules to access information in the net, and in addition information that can be inferred from the net's structure, e.g.

1. the value of attributes for instances/subconcepts,
2. all subconcepts of a concept,
3. common concepts of two instances.

HAS-ATTRibute, DEFault-value, SUBConcept-of, INSTantiates and ATTRIbute-VALue are some of the primitive links used by the system. (The *user* interface allows for the definition of the network in restricted natural language.) The net in Figure 1, gives a hierarchical organisation of possible features for compounds but does not contain any instances. Nets can also contain more specific information, for example, unique names [Wipke & Dyott, 1974] and the corresponding connection table of chemical structures; Figure 2 shows how this data would be encorporated.

3.0 ACQUISITION OF (CHEMICAL) EXPERTISE

We are currently developing the Aide in the context of organic reaction mechanisms; in particular the domain is that of the relative strengths of organic acids

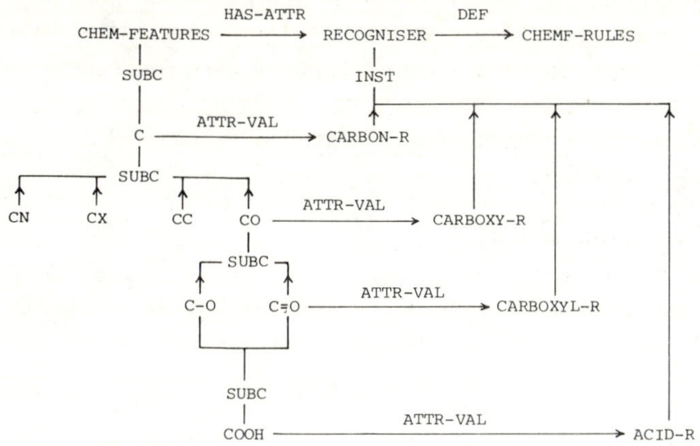

Figure 1. Partial net of chemically significant features

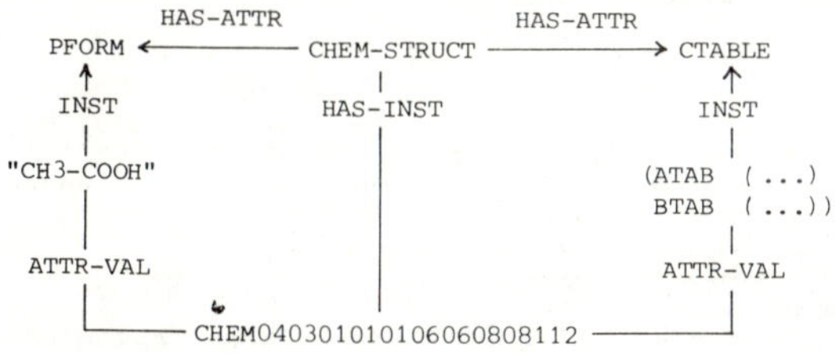

Figure 2. Partial net of basic chemical knowledge

[Sykes, 1975]. For convenience, we have chosen not to represent a sizable domain-dependent feature in the rules/facts formalism; the parser for chemical structure, which allows the user to input chemical compounds in a linear notation not dissimilar to normal chemical notation, is written in LISP.

The annotated dialogue of figure 3 demonstrates the interactive construction of a set of rules relating to the relative strengths of a selected set of organic acids. These rules are derived by the system from examples provided by the user; the user also decides if the new rule forms are acceptable or not. In this example a substantial knowledge base (KB) of chemical facts has already been established (e.g. figure 1); however, it contains no rules concerning acidity and the network lacks certain relevant concepts. In this protocol, we present only compounds consisting of carbon, hydrogen, oxygen, nitrogen and the halogen atoms. Examples are presented which allow the identification of a number of factors affecting acidity, i.e. proton donor, electron withdrawer and inductive/mesomeric effects. In particular, the system's protocol shows the effect of types of groups and the length of molecular chain.

The dialogue is slightly 'doctored' in that the current system does not print in standard chemical notation, such as Cl-CH2-COOH, but prints the unique name for that chemical, i.e. CHEM0504010101020608081511 21. (This modification will be incorporated into the system at a future date.)

```
              ;
              ; After entering the system the chemical parser and
              ; basic chemistry knowledge base are loaded.
              ; '>' should be read as "more acidic than" when it
              ; is not the CONCHE prompt character.
              ;
 1)   >IS ^F-CH2-COOH^ > ^CH3-COOH^
       ---------------------------
 2)   Question form not recognised - edit/new ? >NEW
                                                  ---
 3)   Please specify Template
 4)   >*1 IS > *2
       ----------
              ;
              ; Alternative and contradictory templates are also
              ; specified, when templates are satisfactory the
              ; program attempts to answer both forms
              ;
 5)   Don't know - What's the answer
 6)   >YES          ; i.e.  F-CH2-COOH IS > CH3-COOH
       ---
 7)   === $RULE1 ===
 8)   IF:
 9)        1. !V1 IS F-CH2-COOH
10)        2. !V2 IS CH3-COOH
11)   THEN:
12)        3. !V1 IS > !V2 (1.0)
              ;
              ; This rule is simply formed by matching the template
              ; (line 4) against the solution (comment line 4) and
              ; and generating the appropriate conditions.
              ;
13)   >IS ^CL-CH2-COOH^ > ^CH3-COOH^
       ----------------------------
14)     ! Entered LEARN-LOW
15)     ! See if missing facts - if not then analogies
16)     ! ((QUES CL-CH2-COOH IS > CH3-COOH)
17)     !  (QUES CL-CH2-COOH IS F-CH2-COOH)
18)     !  (FAND CL-CH2-COOH IS F-CH2-COOH)
19)     !  (CWNA CL-CH2-COOH IS F-CH2-COOH)
20)     !  (CNS? . $RULE1)
21)     !  (CWNA CL-CH2-COOH IS > CH3-COOH))
        ; Similarly for CH3-COOH IS > CL-CH2-COOH
22)     ! Entered COMPLETE-CHAIN?
23)     ! $RULE1 - (QUES CL-CH2-COOH IS > CH3-COOH)
24)     ! Blocked - FACT answered NO
        ; Similarly for CH3-COOH IS > CL-CH2-COOH
25)     ! Entered BEST-MATCHED-RULE
26)     ! (PRO ($RULE1 1 1 0))
27)     ! (CON ($RULE1 0 2 0))
```

Figure 3. Sample dialogue, showing how CONCHE infers that certain groups and chain-length affect relative acidities. (User input is underlined, ; precedes comment, ! precedes trace.)

4.0 EXPLANATION OF SYSTEM BEHAVIOUR

The overall behaviour of the Aide is depicted diagrammatically in figure 4; overviews of the several 'reasoning' modes are given in sections 4.1 to 4.5; a more detailed description of the analogy and generalization modes is given in section 4.6. See Chisholm (in progress) for further detail of all modes.

Having established an initial KB in terms of the semantic net and production rules the user presents problems to check the consistency and completeness of the KB. The system attempts to construct solutions for both the question and

```
28)     Yes - CL-CH2-COOH IS > CH3-COOH
29)     Is this acceptable? >YES
                                ---
30)       ! Entered GENERALIZE-RULE
31)       ! CHEM-FEATURES ((2 F (1)(1 COOH (2)))
32)       ! CHEM-FEATURES ((2 CL (1))(1 COOH (2)))
33)       ! CHEM-PAT ((2 (F CL) (1))(1 COOH (2)))
34)     Suggest condition 1 rule 1
35)     !V1 ISA (CHEM-MATCH ((1 COOH (2))(2 $C0001 (2))))
36)     Where $C0001 has instances F CL
37)     Or is concept HALIDE
38)     Do you wish to name this concept? >HALIDE
                                           ------
39)     === $RULE1 ===
40)     IF:
41)          1. !V1 ISA (CHEM-MATCH ((1 COOH (2))(2 HALIDE (1))))
42)          2. !V2 IS CH3-COOH
43)     THEN:
44)          3. !V1 IS > !V2 (1.0)
            ;
45)     >IS ^BR-CH2-COOH^ > ^H-CH2-COOH^
         --------------------------------
46)     Yes - (BR-CH2-COOH IS > CH3-COOH)
47)     Is this OK? > E
                      -
48)     Ques - (BR-CH2-COOH IS > CH3-COOH)
49)        $RULE1 MATCHED
50)           Cond 1 - (BR-CH2-COOH ISA ...)
51)              This is a FACT
            ;
            ; Remainder of the trace is similarly explained,
            ; allowing the user to check the reasoning involved.
            ;
            ; Further examples lead to greater generalization and
            ; expansion of this rule, new concepts are also added
            ; to the net as the session procedes as shown below.
            ;
53)     >IS CL-CH2-CH2-COOH > CH3-COOH
            ; ((1 HALIDE (2))(2 C-CHAIN (1 3))(3 ACID (2))
54)     >IS NO2-CH2-COOH > CH3-COOH
            ; Adds new concept, ELECT-WITHDRAWER, to the net
            ; ((1 ELECT-WITHDRAWER (2)) ... )
55)     >IS F-CH2-OH > CH3-COOH
            ; Adds concept PROTON-DONOR
            ; ((1 ELECT-WITHDRAWER (2)) ... (3 PROTON-DONOR (2)))
56)     >IS F-CH2-COOH > CL-CH2-CH2-OH
            ; Condition 2 is generalized, need further
            ; descrimination since both match condition 1,
            ; therefore proposes three new rules desciminating
            ; on electron withdrawer, length of C-CHAIN and
            ; proton donator.
```

its contradiction. For example, if the question asked is:

IS ^C1-CH2-COOH^ MORE ACIDIC THAN ^CH3-COOH^

then the system will also have to ask the reverse question (contradiction):

IS ^CH3-COOH^ MORE ACIDIC THAN ^C1-CH2-COOH^

To enable the questions to be transformed the user is asked to supply templates when new question forms are encountered, e.g. line 4. (The use of templates is a short-term expedient.) As shown in figure 4, the number and nature of the solutions found determines which reasoning modes are subsequently entered.

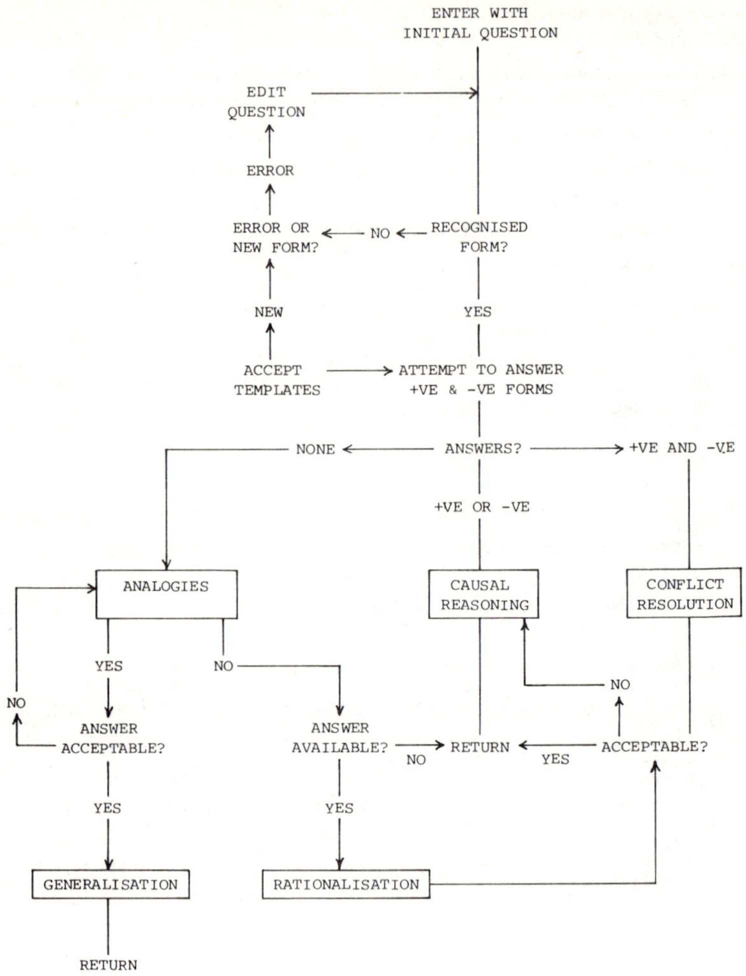

Figure 4. Flow diagram of Aide's behaviour

4.1 Causal Reasoning

Causal reasoning is the ability of the system to explain its derivation of a solution in terms of rule chaining, facts accessed and unsatisfied/unsatisfiable conditions. If the system produces the correct solution the facility may be used to check that it was for the right reason, however, this facility is of most use when an incorrect solution is produced.

The simplest form of using this facility is to ask the system to E(xplain) (line 47) its deduction, this produces a readable trace (lines 48-51). When the errors have been located the expert can either amend the facts, define new rules, or edit a particular rule via an interface accepting simple natural language commands.

4.2 Rationalization

We have defined rationalization as the ability to complete previously blocked reasoning chains when told by the expert what the correct solution should be. Knowing the correct solution the system can infer that the conditions of certain rules are satisfied, and that certain other conditions are not satisfied. The implications drawn depend upon the previous reason for failure and the particular form of the condition involved. Reasons for failure which occur in the protocol, include:

FFFA (Facts Fail to Find an Answer) – an enquiry to the semantic net yields *UNKNOWN*.

FANO (Facts Answer NO) – the condition, encountered in the course of answering the original question is unsatisfiable, i.e. contradicts the known facts.

4.3 Conflict Resolution

Conflict resolution is used when solutions are found for *both* the question and its contradiction. When told by the expert what the correct solution should be the causal reasoning chains are examined to determine if facts/rules can be amended so that the erroneous solution is not produced.

4.4 Analogy

When the system fails to produce a solution an attempt is made to find a solution by analogy prior to asking for the solution. One of two forms of analogy is employed dependent upon whether rules have matched the original question or not, in both cases successful analogy is a precursor to rule generalization.

Firstly, when no rules are fully matched the outcomes of rules may be compared with the question to determine the partial match that proposes the most acceptable solution. Analogies of this form use the question templates to determine correspondences which are then compared using information stored in the semantic net. (This form of generalization will never be applicable if all rules are learnt from examples because the system always generates rules with the most general form of outcome, i.e. variables in the question template correspond to variables in the outcome (lines 4 & 12).)

The analogy facility which is applicable when rules have matched is described in section 4.6.

4.5 Generalization

Generalization modifies the conditions or outcome of a rule so that it now applies in a larger number of instances, utilizing information about common attributes or superior concepts discovered during analogy formation. Problems arise in attempting to control the degree of generalization and the closest existing concept, the user deciding which is adopted. For example (lines 36-38), a generalization involving CHLORINE and FLUORINE proposes a new concept having only chlorine and fluorine as instances and also proposes the concept HALOGEN.

It would be possible to relieve the user of the decision between the minimal generalization and the closest existing concept provided he answered questions from the system concerning other subconcepts/instances of the closest existing concept. Further, it may also be possible to provide additional controls to prevent over-generalization by adapting the concept of 'Version Spaces' [Mitchell, 1977].

4.6 Detailed Examples of Analogy and Generalization

Lines 13-44 of the dialogue (figure 3) show a trace of a problem involving analogy and generalization when some rules have matched the top-level question but have failed to produce a solution. In this situation the system examines the trace of the deductive process (16-21) to see if the reason for failure is FFFA (fact failed to find answer); if this were the case then the system would ask for the missing information and see if it were possible to proceed. However, this is not so (22-24), the only rule that matched ($RULE 1 – lines 7-12) failed because FANO (fact answered no – line 18); $RULE 1 is similarly blocked attempting to answer the contradiction.

Entering analogy proper, CONCHE determines the most nearly successful rule (25-27), here it is $RULE 1 attempting to answer the original question because it has one condition satisfied and one condition not satisfied, whereas $RULE 1 attempting to answer the contradiction has no conditions satisfied and two conditions not satisfied. Based on this observation the system proposes a solution and asks if this is acceptable; on acceptance, the system attempts to generalize the appropriate rule (28-29).

Generalization is then entered, knowing that condition 1 of rule 1 needs to be modified and determine from the form of the condition that this must involve F-CH2-COOH and CL-CH2-COOH. These are both CHEM-STRUCTs (figure 2) and as such can be described in terms of CHEM-FEATURES (FEATURES is an attribute to ALL-CONCEPTS, the value of this attribute for CHEM-STRUCT is CHEM-FEATURES). The ruleset CHEM-FEATURES analyses the connection table representation of each molecule using the network shown in figure 1. For each carbon atom in the table the most specific featural description is determined, e.g. having determined that the carbonyl group is present an attempt is made to identify subconcepts of C=O and if an acid group is found then COOH is returned as the feature rather than C=O.

The new instance is matched against the existing pattern; this matching produces the correspondence in line 33 because F and CL are more closely related in the network than are either F & COOH or CL & COOH. A generalized form of the condition is proposed (35) using this pattern in the condition form 'VAL ISA (RULESET ARG)', which is satisfied if RULESET run on the problem VAL IS A ARG finds a solution. If the modified condition is acceptable the rule is modified (40-44).

5.0 POSSIBLE EXTENSIONS TO THE INFERENCE MECHANISMS

The facilities provided by the current inference modes, as shown in figure 4, demonstrate these abilities for the present domain. Different inference modes, or combinations of inference modes, may be required for other domains. Indeed, some additional facilities could be helpful in this present domain. For example, when the wrong solution is deduced the system could ask the expert for the correct solution, rationalization could produce the required reasoning chain and then conflict resolution could be applied to block the wrong solution.

The adaption of 'Version Spaces' would lead to rules being represented in both most specific and most general forms. This could provide a short-cut on the analogy procedure that would work as follows: in attempting to answer questions the most specific rule forms would be used, if no solutions were found the system would attempt to answer using the most general forms. If acceptable solutions were formed CONCHE would generalize the most specific form of the successful rule; if a general form produced an unacceptable solution it would be specialized.

Finally, further consideration has to be given to the question of when to apply inferencing. At present, the inferencing modes are used only when CONCHE has completed the attempt to answer the original question; they could be applied to every lower level question generated by the conditions of rules. "What other strategies are there?" And "When should they be used?" are questions deserving thorough investigation.

6.0 FURTHER WORK & CONCLUSIONS

The Aide has been developed in a specific situation and some possible future developments applicable to this context were proposed in section 5. Although in principle domain-independent, the program will require further development for other domains and an extension of the question template mechanism. The examples presented to the system so far have been carefully chosen to enable the correct inferences to be made knowing the final rule form desired. On the other hand it would be very instructive to allow the system access to a data base of known acidities, allowing it to select examples to discriminate between minimal generalization and the closest existing concept (cf section 4.5). There are many problems we have yet to address but our experience with the present system leads us to believe it is worthwhile to continue development.

7.0 ACKNOWLEDGEMENTS

We gratefully acknowledge the use of the Department's DEC System-10 and of the LISP and FUZZY systems implemented by Rick Le Faivre (Rutgers). We would also like to thank a number of chemists at the Universities of Leeds, York and Durham for their helpful comments, suggestions and continued interest.

IHC wishes to acknowledge the financial support provided by an SRC Studentship.

9.0 REFERENCES

BRACHMANN, R.J. (1977): "What's in a concept: structural foundations for semantic networks". *Int. J. Man-Machine Studies*, 9, pp127-152.

BUCHANAN, B.G. & T.M. MITCHELL (1977): *Model-directed learning of production rules*. CS Report 597, Stanford University.

CHISHOLM, I.H. (in progress): *CONCHE: an intelligent aide for scientific theory formation.* Doctoral Dissertation, Leeds, University.

CLANCEY, W.J. (1979): "Tutoring rules for guiding a case method dialogue". *Int. J. Man-Machine Studies,* 11, pp25-49.

COLLINS, A.M., E.H. WARNOCK, N. AIELLO & M.L. MILLER (1975): "Reasoning from incomplete knowledge". In *Representation and Understanding: Studies in Cognitive Science*, D.G. Bobrow & A.M. Collins (eds.), Academic Press, New York, pp383-415.

DAVIS, R. (1978): "Knowledge acquisition in Rule-Based systems – Knowledge about representations as a basis for systems construction and maintenance" in *Pattern-Directed Inference Systems*, edited by D.A. Waterman and F. Hayes-Roth, Academic Press, pp99-1354.

LE FAIVRE, R. (1978): *FUZZY reference manual.* Comp. Sci. Dept., Rutgers University.

MITCHELL, T.M. (1977): *Version spaces: an aproach to rule revision during rule induction.* Dept. Comp. Sci., Stanford University.

SHORTLIFFE, E.H. (1974): *MYCIN: a rule-based computer program for advising physicians regarding antimicrobial therapy selection.* Doctoral Dissertation: Stanford University.

SHORTLIFFE, E.H. (1975): "A model of inexact reasoning in medicine". *Mathematical Biosciences*, 23, pp351-379.

SYKES, P. (1975): *A guidebook to mechanism in organic chemistry*, 4th edition. Longman Group Limited, London, pp52-76,

WIPKE, W.T. & T.M. DYOTT (1974): "Stereochemically unique naming algorithm". *J. Am. Chemical Society*, 96, pp4834-42.

WOODS, W.A. (1975): "What's in a link: foundations for semantic networks". In *Representation and Understanding: Studies in Cognitive Science*, D.G. Bobrow & A.M. Collins (eds.), Academic Press, New York, pp35-82.

EXPERT SYSTEMS FOR TEACHING

LEARNING THROUGH MODEL BUILDING

J.A.M. Howe

INTRODUCTION

Twenty years ago, educationists had such an impoverished understanding of human learning processes that they expected to replace teachers with machines within a decade. Today, we are more aware of the deep pedagogical problems that would have to be solved before this task could be accomplished. For example, when a pupil flounders around unable to start on a new problem, what should the machine do? It wouldn't want to give the game away, so it would wish to hint rather than direct. But how are these hints generated and evaluated? Again, if a pupil gets stuck in the middle of a problem, the system would need to interpret what he had done and provide assistance in tune with the pupil's thinking. If his difficulty is due to an early error, ought the system to have allowed him to carry on regardless, or ought it to have interrupted his work when the error was made? Indeed, if the error was hidden because the relevant working was not shown to the system, how would the system figure out sensible questions which might reveal basic misconceptions? Given these kinds of pedagogical problems, *and* financial considerations *and* the teacher's traditional dislike of machines in the classroom, we can confidently anticipate that expert systems in the shape of computerised tutors will play a minor role in education for many years to come. So instead of talking about expert systems, we want to talk about systems which experts, i.e. teachers, can use as a resource to help them achieve their objectives, e.g. teach maths, physics, literary style and so on. The notion, which will become clearer in due course, is to use the computer to simulate a modelling system which a learner can use to carry out model-building experiments.

BUILDING PHYSICAL MODELS

When the average person hears the word "model", he probably thinks of the kits of parts from which children assemble miniature plastic replicas of aeroplanes, space ships, buildings and a host of other familiar objects. For the moment, we will take advantage of this association to begin our discussion of model building.

Since a toy model captures the essential form of an object, it is a pleasing representation of its *structure*. But a child can also buy the finished product, so why does he bother with a kit of parts? Almost certainly the answer is that he enjoys the activity of assembling the model. Indeed, a child is often more interested in grappling with the problems of assembling the object from its parts than he is in playing with the final product. What he is engaged in is learning the process of model assembly which involves such skills as identifying parts and their relationships, and ordering the assembly sequence.

But besides learning to assemble models which represent familiar structures, the child can also learn to assemble models which represent mechanisms. Here we refer to models which simulate mechanisms such as the steering system in a car or the actuating system for flaps and rudder in an aeroplane. The advantages of working with these representations of real world mechanisms are two-fold. First of all, working models are more compelling as simulations of reality and secondly the child might come to understand the general principles underlying the mechanisms. Of course, the latter cannot be assumed since a child might simply follow assembly instructions in an unthinking way.

To promote real understanding of mechanisms, there is a need for a modelling system which allows a child to be creative. It should provide him with an opportunity to alter pre-determined models, and even to create his very own models. What we are talking about now is a very different kind of kit of parts: instead of a set of particular components needed to assemble a particular object, we need a set of general purpose components in terms of which a child can conceive a design and execute it. An example of such a kit of parts would be a collection of electronic components. These could be assembled into working circuits to a child's own design, given enough knowledge of electronic circuit principles and access to facilities to test the characteristics of the circuits at various intermediate points since all but their final behaviour is hidden from view.

Another example which may be more comfortable for many of you is a mechanical construction set, called Meccano. It comprises a collection of perforated metal strips, plates, brackets, wheels, axles and gearwheels, and so on, which can be bolted together to form models. To the uninitiated, a box of Meccano parts is a bewildering collection of pieces of metal. Give such a box to a novice without instructions and he can make little sense of the parts: the models which he builds are unstable and the working mechanisms usually stop working as soon as they are run. The point is that learning to use Meccano creatively and successfully involves a long period of apprenticeship. The size of the task becomes clearer when we identify what a child has to know.

1. He has to become completely familiar with the full range of components, e.g. strips, plates, tubes, axles, gearwheels, brackets.
2. He has to learn the basic operations for assembling components to form models, e.g. making measurements, establishing correct relationships between the parts, and so on.
3. He has to understand the structure and the mechanism used in the machine he wants to model so that he can represent their essential features, e.g. the structure of a mechanical grab and its winding gear.
4. To represent these structures and mechanisms successfully in Meccano, he has to learn to apply important general knowledge about mechanical construction, e.g. the importance of triangular bracing, the use of plates to provide stiffening, the need for standardisation of parts for interchangeability, the need for alignment between parts (tolerance), the need to minimise friction, and so on.
5. He also has to learn how to plan an assembly sequence, involving breaking down the object into a set of sub-parts, e.g. chassis, suspension, steering

gear, final transmission, gearbox, engine, body, etc. which can be separately assembled but which are subject to mutual constraints when brought together.

6. Finally, he has to learn to cope with any mismatches which occur between the plan and its execution in terms of the available components, making modifications to overcome problems not anticipated in the design.

So learning to use Meccano creatively is a formidable undertaking, requiring a great deal of time and a great deal of help and guidance. But the manufacturers realised this situation; they organised the teaching most carefully. First of all, they designed a series of Meccano models of objects such as cars, cranes, bridges, and so on, which ranged from very simple models made from a few components which were but sketchy representations of the real objects to highly elaborate models, made out of many hundreds of components, which could simulate a working system. Next, they graded these projects into 10 levels of difficulty and made up 10 standard sets of components which could be used to assemble all the objects encompassed by a particular level of difficulty provided the detailed assembly instructions were followed. The manufacturer also provided conversion kits, containing the components necessary to increment from one level to the next one up. We can see that their teaching strategy was to match the projects to a child's level of expertise in assembly, beginning with a small set of components and a few simple tasks and gradually widening the scope. Such an approach provides the kind of close guidance which a novice needs on being introduced to new skills, new concepts and new ideas. Yet it does allow him to experiment and to be creative.

We can contrast the simplicity of the novice's model with the complexity of the expert's model by comparing Figure 1 and Figure 2, both of which depict a Lifting Shovel. The details of the mechanism that simulates the real object's function is shown in Figure 3.

BUILDING COMPUTER MODELS

Can we create modelling systems for other non-engineering domains which will provide similar opportunities to experiment and to be creative? Perhaps the most versatile modelling system is the digital computer. Using the computer as a modelling tool is similar to using a kit of components as a modelling tool because the computing activity centres on using a programming language to describe how some structure or mechanism is made.

The designers of the Meccano system had to decide what components should be provided, and how they would be combined to form meaningful structures and mechanisms. The designer of a computer-based modelling system has to face up to exactly the same problem. He has to decide which instructions should be included in the modelling language, and how they would be combined to form models. What we are referring to here is designing an appropriate representational system for a particular class of task, e.g. composing tunes, generating poetry, making drawings. In practice, this is a very difficult problem, and one which is shared by research workers in Artificial Intelligence who are trying to create and experiment with computer-based models of complex cognitive

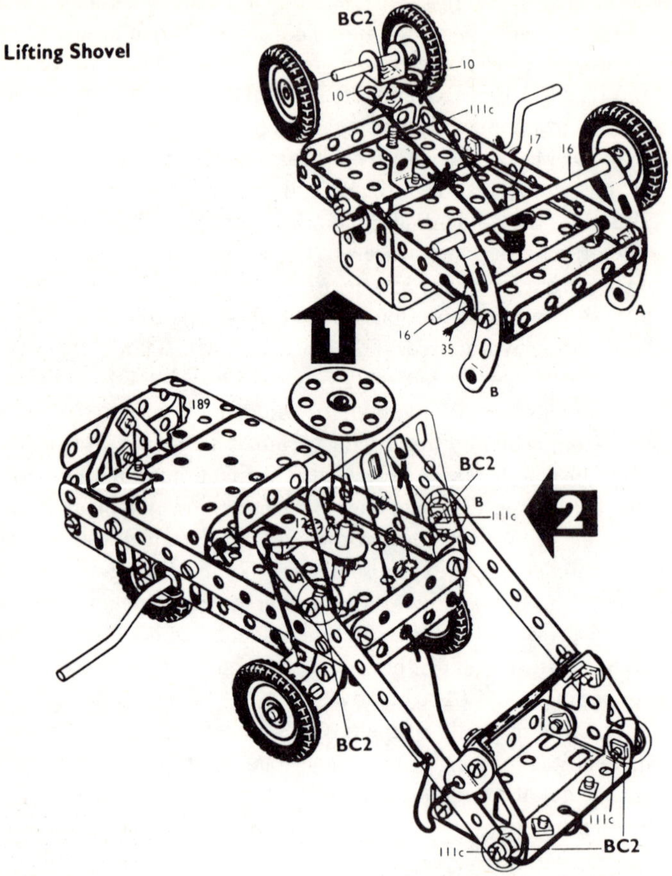

Figure 1

processes like seeing the objects in this room, making sense of the words I am using and understanding the issues I am raising.

Once such a system has been designed, it can be implemented on a general purpose computing machine, converting that machine into a domain specific representational system. This involves writing the domain-specific modelling language which is used to describe the structures and mechanisms, i.e. processes, in that domain. Notice that instead of starting from scratch, the modelling language can be written in one of the existing high-level structured programming languages, such as POP-2 (Burstall *et al.*, 1971); LOGO (Feurzeig *et al.*, 1977) or Smalltalk (Ingalls, 1978). This saves time and eases the process of altering or extending the modelling language in response to modelling needs, but suffers from the disadvantage that the modelling language inherits the host language's weaknesses and limitations.

Since this explanation is quite difficult to grasp, let me illustrate it with a

Figure 2

Figure 3

simple example of a representational system for drawing pictures. Suppose the modelling language provides commands which can control the movement of a mechanised pen around a drawing surface, for example FORWARD ⟨a distance⟩ BACK ⟨a distance⟩, LEFT ⟨a rotation⟩, RIGHT ⟨a rotation⟩. These commands can be used to make a program which describes the process of drawing some object, for example an equilateral triangle. The description might look like this:

```
DEFINE "TRIANGLE   [its name]
        FORWARD 500
        RIGHT 120
        FORWARD 500
        RIGHT 120
        FORWARD 500
        RIGHT 120
        END
```

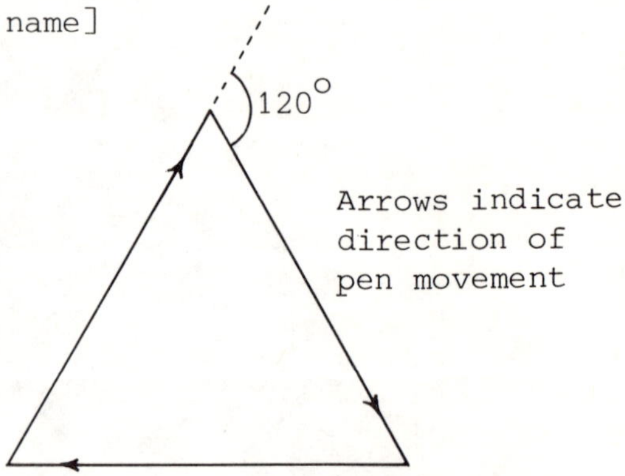

When this description of the process of drawing a triangle is typed in, the computer becomes a mechanism for drawing a triangle. Operating the mechanism, i.e. running the program, produces the drawing of the triangle. Notice that the program can be stored in the computer's memory, and can be re-used by calling it by name. Suppose the child wants to draw a house: all he needs to do is break down the house into two components, namely square and triangle. Having worked out how to draw a square in terms of basic pen movements, and having defined and stored the corresponding program, he can define a new object called house which is described in terms of a call to the object named square and a call to the object named triangle.

Notice that by defining and storing descriptions, the representational power of the drawing system is being made more readily available. This is like building up standard sub-units from Meccano parts, e.g. a gearbox, which is used subsequently in a variety of different vehicle types. In fact, instead of expecting children to assemble everything from the basic components, modern Meccano systems contain sub-units like cabs for lorrys. In similar fashion, a drawing system might contain instructions which would invoke pre-defined programs for drawing unit forms such as the house described above, and that drawing system might become a sub-part of another representational system. For example, du Boulay (1978) uses the change in size of a simple house outline as an iconic representation of fraction operations in mathematics. The following picture illustrates multiplication of $^{3}/_{4}$ by $^{2}/_{1}$

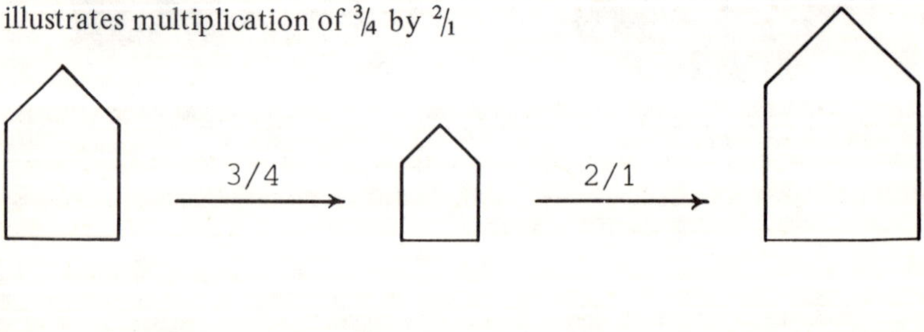

and the next illustrates $^2/_3$ divided by $^1/_4$,

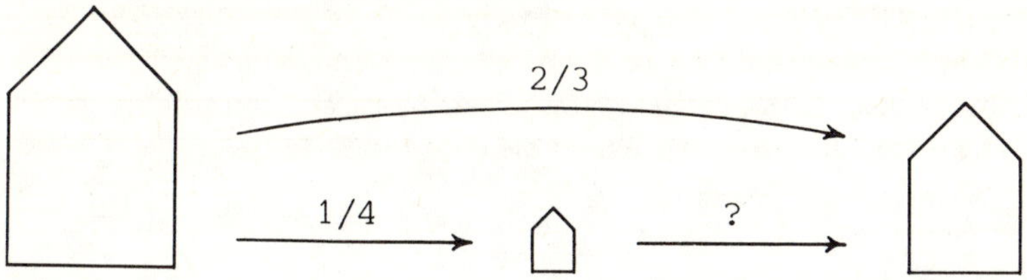

presented as an inverse process to turn it into the form "what multiplied by $^1/_4$ would produce $^2/_3$?".

The drawing system described earlier was devised by Papert (1972) to enable children to learn about geometry. Since it is a relative geometry, couched in terms of changes in the heading of the pen, it is easy to use it to describe regular figures. Movements of the pen correspond roughly to a child's own movements through space, so he can try to "act out" the role of the pen to help him work out how to construct a particular shape, or how to correct a drawing that has gone wrong.

Just as using Meccano creatively involves a long period of apprenticeship, the same applies to learning to use the drawing system creatively to find out about geometry. For example,

1. He has to become completely familiar with the basic maths concepts, e.g. straight line, arc of circle, angle as rotation.
2. He has to learn how to assemble components to form descriptions, e.g. build procedures; use inputs, counters, conditionals.
3. He has to learn how to plan drawings, e.g. breaking down a complex drawing into a set of more familiar sub-parts which can be separately constructed but which are subject to mutual constraints when brought together.
4. He has to learn to cope with mismatches between the planned behaviour and the actual behaviour of the program, making modifications to solve problems. This is known as "debugging activity".

To these activities which are primarily concerned with learning the characteristics of the drawing system, and learning to use it to build descriptions of geometrical forms can be added a third activity, namely using the programs as structured apparatus which can be explored by a pupil in a consistent way to yield new insights concerning the domain being represented. For example, in the geometry application a child will write a series of programs to describe a range of different shapes. After a while, he is likely to notice that some of the descriptions are quite similar. This finding is likely to prompt him to construct a generalized programe which can produce a class of shapes, and to understand the relationships between families of apparently different shapes by experimenting with the generalised program.

As clarification, consider Figure 4, which lists programs for drawing a variety of shapes. Having learned how to write a program to draw an equilateral triangle (shown on top left), he is introduced to the notion of a sub-program and the use of the REPEAT instruction. This makes him aware of the repetition of side and angle, i.e. FORWARD and LEFT, in his original program, and he defines a new program called TRIBIT which when executed draws one side and changes the heading. Now an equilateral triangle is drawn by a new program which runs TRIBIT three times. Notice how easy it is to generalize, and construct programs to draw squares and hexagons (shown on the right hand side).

```
DEFINE "TRIANGLE              DEFINE "SQBIT
 10 FORWARD 200                10 FORWARD 200
 20 LEFT 120                   20 LEFT 90
 30 FORWARD 200               END
 40 LEFT 120
 50 FORWARD 200               DEFINE "SQUARE
 60 LEFT 120                   10 REPEAT 4 SQBIT
END                           END

DEFINE "TRIBIT                DEFINE "HEXBIT
 10 FORWARD 200                10 FORWARD 200
 20 LEFT 120                   20 LEFT 60
END                           END

DEFINE "TRIANGLE              DEFINE "HEXAGON
 10 REPEAT 3 TRIBIT            10 REPEAT 6 HEXBIT
END                           END
```

Figure 4

In due course, when introduced to the notion of an input, greater generality can be achieved since the child can define now a program for drawing a range of regular figures. Called POLYGON, this is shown in Figure 5. It uses a general sub-program called POLYBIT, which is run the number of times specified by the value assigned to POLYGON's input. The value of POLYBIT's input is determined by dividing 360° by the number of sides bounding the shape, e.g. POLYGON 3 specifies a triangle, POLYGON 4 a square and so on.

Of course, it would be difficult to use a relative geometry to construct irregular plane shapes. For this, quite a different kind of representational system would be required, namely a system based on the use of co-ordinates and vectors. Working with these would impose quite different demands on a child's understanding of mathematical concepts, and would extend it in very different ways. Besides geometry, representational systems have been developed for a variety of school maths topics (du Boulay, 1978; Howe *et al.*, 1979); composing tunes (Bamberger, 1972); orbital mechanics (diSessa, 1975); simple electrical circuits (Borning, 1979).

RELEVANCE TO EDUCATION

In the introduction, we suggested that the child enjoyed the activity of model building more than playing with the final product. This accords with Papert's view (Papert, 1972) that the programming approach should emphasize problem-solving skills in the expectation that when a child has worked in several different domains he will recognize the similarities between the methods used to make plans and to debug them. In this way, he will build up genuinely domain-independent study skills. While not wishing to deny the importance of such skills, others would take the view that these skills can only be appreciated when a

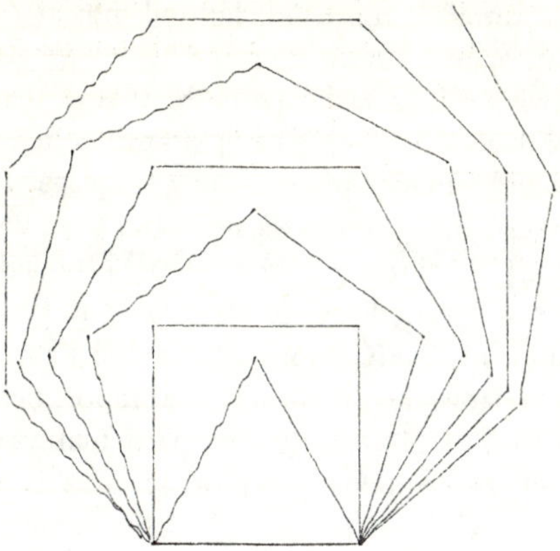

```
DEFINE "POLYBIT "ANGLE
 10 FORWARD 200
 20 LEFT VALUE "ANGLE
END

DEFINE "POLYGON "NUMBER
 10 REPEAT VALUE "NUMBER POLYBIT (DIVIDE 360 VALUE "NUMBER)
END


POLYGON 3
POLYGON 4
POLYGON 5
POLYGON 6
POLYGON 7
CENTRE
POLYGON 8
POLYGON 9


LOGO CANNOT FULLY EXECUTE THIS COMMAND:-
     10 FORWARD 200
IN PROCEDURE POLYBIT, BECAUSE
THE TURTLE WILL GO OFF THE EDGE OF THE PAPER
```

Figure 5

person has extensive domain-specific knowledge, suggesting that in the early stages of learning emphasis should be placed on content learning.

The point is that the preferred emphasis affects the choice of objective with consequent effects on the way teaching is organized. For example, a highly structured approach has to be adopted if the objective is to teach domain-specific knowledge. In common with Goldberg and Kay (1977), the structure which we favour involves getting a child to learn by providing him with a model in program form which he types in and runs. This is followed by exercises which involve modifying the specimen procedure in minor ways, and finally adapting it to some other problem area. This approach is followed whether the objective is to teach computational ideas as an aid to building programs (du Boulay and O'Shea, 1976) or to teach mathematics (Howe *et al.*, 1979). In contrast to this emphasis on content, other investigators such as Papert (1972) and Dwyer and Critchfield (1978) focus on teaching problem-solving skills. New ideas are learned as and when necessary in the course of solving a selection of problems drawn from different domains.

Given these differences in emphasis, what evidence is there that children learn by building models in program form? It must be admitted that at the present time the evidence of benefit is scanty, irrespective of whether we are talking about content or problem-solving skills. Dealing with the first of these first, in one of the earliest studies Feurzeig *et al.* (1969) taught arithmetic and algebra to 13-year-old children, using the LOGO programming language. But the participants' scores on a standardised ability test were no better than those of a control group. In contrast, Milner (1973) reported that LOGO programming increased children's scores on an unstandardised test of variables, and Bjork *et al.* (1975) describe how programming in BASIC improved numerical ability, especially among the less able children. Howe and O'Shea (1978) report marked gains in the mathematical self-confidence of 11-year old boys participating in a mathematics course based on LOGO programming, and more recently Howe *et al.* (1979) report that both these boys' understanding of mathematics as measured by a standardised test and their ability to do school mathematics as measured by a series of unstandardised school maths tests improved relative to the performances of a more able control group. Finally, in a case study of trainee teachers who investigated topics in primary school mathematics through LOGO programming, du Boulay (1978) suggests that not only did they begin to understand the meaning of many basic mathematical rules, but they also found that they could make enjoyable personal mathematical discoveries by exploring the mathematical representations which du Boulay provided.

Turning now to problem-solving skills, there is less evidence of benefit. Statz (1973) records little improvement in children's ability to cope with problem-solving tasks after a year's programming activity. This problem of estimating improvement in problem-solving skill through programming is reminiscent of the problem faced by psychologists like E.L. Thorndike who tried unsuccessfully to collect evidence to support the strongly held belief that learning Latin helps a child to learn to reason. Like learning Latin, the belief that learning to program involves problem-solving must remain an act of faith until evidence appears. But in the meantime it would be wrong to conclude that the shortage of evidence supporting the programming approach indicates that it lacks educational value. After all, most educational schemes rest on the teachers' faith in their usefulness, and not on the results of a formal educational evaluation. Indeed one might be tempted to question the need to produce such evidence to support the programming approach when everyday teaching procedures lack such substantiation.

Perhaps the most telling criticism is that most of the evidence available has been gathered in studies by committed investigators. The need now is to try out the modelling approach in educational institutions under the control of the institution's teachers, in conjunction with an on-going programme of teaching. Survival under these circumstances is probably the best testimonial of educational worth. Given increased access to computers, we can expect relevant evidence to emerge from studies of the modelling approach in a classroom context during the next decade.

ACKNOWLEDGEMENTS

I would like to express my gratitude to the Social Science Research Council for its sponsorship of the research on which this paper is based. I am also grateful to my colleague Dr. B. du Boulay for constructive comments.

REFERENCES

Bjork, L-E., Loftrup, B. and Nilsson, R. (1975) An Introductory Computer-Programming Course and Some of its Effects on the Teaching of Mathematics. In *Computer in Education* (Eds Lecarme & Lewis) Amsterdam: North Holland.

Borning, A.H. (1979) ThingLab – A Constraint-Oriented Simulation Laboratory. Ph.D. Dissertation, Department oF Computer Science, Stanford University.

Bamberger, J. (1972) Developing a Musical Ear: A New Experiment. *A.I. Memo 264* (LOGO Memo No. 6), Artificial Intelligence Laboratory, M.I.T.

Burstall, R.M. Collins, J.S. and Popplestone, R.J. (1971) *Programming in POP-2*. Edinburgh: Edinburgh University Press.

diSessa, A.A. (1975) ORBIT: A Mini-environment for Exploring Orbital Mechanisms. In *Computers in Education* (Eds Lecarme & Lewis) Amsterdam: North Holland.

du Boulay, J.B.H. (1978) Learning Primary Mathematics Through Computer Programming. Ph.D. Dissertation, Department of Artificial Intelligence, University of Edinburgh.

du Boulay, B. and O'Shea, T. (1976) How to Work the LOGO Machine: A Primer for LOGO. *Occasional Paper No. 4,* Department of Artificial Intelligence, University of Edinburgh.

Dwyer, T.A. and Critchfield, M. (1978) *Basic and the Personal Computer.* Addison-Wesley.

Feurzeig, W., Papert, S., Bloom, M., Grant, R. and Solomon, C. (1969) Programming Languages as a Conceptual Framework for Teaching Mathematics. *BBN Report No. 1889,* Bolton Beranek & Newman, Cambridge, Mass.

Feurzeig, W., Lukas, G. and Lukas, J.D. (1977) *The LOGO Language: Learning Mathematics Through Programming*. Portsmouth, U.S.A.: Entelek.

Goldberg, A. and Kay, A. (1977) Methods for Teaching the Programming Language Smalltalk. *Technical Report SSL-77-2*, Xerox Palo Alto Research Center, California.

Howe, J.A.M. and O'Shea, T. (1978) Computational Metaphors for Children. In *Human and Artificial Intelligence* (Ed. Klix). Berlin: Deutscher Verlag.

Howe, J.A.M., O'Shea, T. and Plane, F. (1979) Teaching Mathematics Through LOGO Programming: An Evaluation Study. In *Proceedings of IFIP Working Conference on C.A.L.,* London.

Ingalls, D.H.H. (1978) The Smalltalk-78 Programming System: Design and Implementation. In *Conference Record of the Fifth Annual ACM Symposium on Principles of Programming Languages,* Tucson, Arizona.

Milner, S. (1973) The Effects of Computer Programming on Performance in Mathematics. Paper presented at American Educational Research Association. ERIC Reports ED 076 391.

Papert, S. (1972) Teaching Children Thinking. *Programmed Learning and Educational Technology, 9*, 245-255.

Statz, J. (1973) Problem Solving and LOGO. In *Final Report* of Syracuse University LOGO Project, Syracuse University, New York.

RULE-BASED COMPUTER TUTORS

Tim O'Shea

Two important components of any computer tutor are the tutorial strategy and the student model. Production Rules (PRs) can usefully be employed in the design and implementation of both these components. The use of PRs forces careful analysis of the taxonomic aspects of computer tutor design. PRs are modular, explicit, amenable to automatic manipulation and hence applicable to the construction of adaptive tutors. Their use provides a valuable link to work on the analysis of human information processing strategies.

TUTORIAL STRATEGIES (TSs)

In most computer tutors these are partially ordered sequences of teaching actions, a small number of such actions being associated with any tutorial situation. From this 'programmed text' view of teaching the design of a TS rests on establishing the possible branches between the various teaching actions. In contrast a good human tutor adapts to the needs of his student by continually monitoring and acting on many different aspects of a tutorial situation including: what the student has been taught, what he might have learned, his motivation, etc. In the case of the 'branching' approach the primary concern will be with *control* decisions whereas in the latter case the design should centre on developing a detailed *taxonomy* of tutorial situations. For this last approach PR programming is an appropriate methodology. The natural style of PR analysis is to identify explicitly the various classes of condition that may obtain in the task concerned. PRs are therefore a suitable language in which to implement adaptive TSs (i.e. TSs which adapt to the individual student during the course of a lesson). These can then be employed as a model of the adaptive TS. In turn, provided some way of evaluating teaching performance is viable, it becomes possible to experiment with the way the TS adapts to the student. So the TS itself can then be modified on the basis of cummulative teaching experience. One method of implementing this is to express a list of changes in TSs and associated possible effects on teaching performance as a set of unordered data-driven PRs. A scheme of this type proved workable in a self-modifying computer tutor for quadratic equations (O'Shea, 1979).

An Example

The type of production systems employed here are based directly on Waterman's work, and a comprehensive discussion of them can be found in his thesis (1968). Other types of production system are reviewed by Davis and King (1975), Rychener (1976) and Waterman (1977). In the production rule systems employed here the mechanism used for conflict resolution (that is, which rule gets fired if more than one is potentially applicable) is rule order.

The use of production rules in a CAI context will first be illustrated by their application in a simple hypothetical CAI teaching situation. Consider three teaching operations T(i) (i = 1, 2 or 3), the execution of which results in the student acquiring an associated concept C(i) (with probability <1) and the testing of the student's new knowledge state. Let the acquisition of C(3) be the objective of the teaching task, and let the acquisition of C(1) or C(2) be usually, but not always, a prerequisite for acquiring C(3). Assume there is no forgetting. Suppose that with each student is associated a relevant score PS on some pre-test ($0 \leqslant PS \leqslant 10$). Further suppose it is known that, for students with high PS scores, they are slightly more likely to acquire C(1) via T(1) than C(2) via T(2). However, students with low PS scores are much more likely to acquire C(2) via T(2) than C(1) via T(1). Further, suppose that there is for some practical reason a limit of ten teaching operations per student.

Our systems of production rules comprise a state-vector, a set of partitions, and an *ordered* set of condition-action rules. For the above example a suitable state-vector would be (LASTOP, STATE, SCORE, NUMOP) where LASTOP is the last teaching operation which has been executed, STATE is the current state of student knowledge (i.e., the concepts he has acquired), SCORE is PS, the pre-test score, and NUMOP is the total number of teaching operations performed.

A suitable set of partitions might be:

LASTOP→LASTOP1 if LASTOP = T(1)
→LASTOP2 if LASTOP = T(2)
STATE →STATE1 if STATE = C(1) or STATE = C(2)
→STATE2 if STATE = C(3)
SCORE →SCORE1 if SCORE ⩽ 5
→SCORE2 if SCORE > 5
NUMOP →NUMOP1 if NUMOP > 4
→NUMOP2 if NUMOP > 7 NUMOP < 10
→NUMOP3 if NUMOP = 10

The partitions are employed as follows. If the values of the variables in the state-vector are (T(2), C(1), 6, 8) this is parsed with the partitions to yield the symbolic state-vector (LASTOP2, STATE1, SCORE2, (NUMOP1, NUMOP2)).

An appropriate set of condition-action rules might be:

1 (*, STATE2, *, *)→STOP
2 (*, *, *, NUMOP3)→STOP
3 (*, STATE1, *, *)→T(3)
4 (LASTOP1, *, SCORE1, NUMOP1)→T(2)
5 (LASTOP2, *, SCORE2, NUMOP2)→T(1)
6 (*, *, SCORE1, *)→T(1)
7 (*, *, SCORE2, *)→T(2)

The symbolic state-vector is compared to each of the left-hand sides in turn until the first match is found – a match occurring when all the symbols in the condition part of the rule, excepting '*'s, are present in the symbolic state-vector. In the example given, (LASTOP2, STATE1, SCORE2, (NUMOP1, NUMOP2)) matches the third rule (it would match the fifth if the third were omitted), and the right-hand side, namely T(3), is executed and the state-vector updated accordingly.

The above example illustrates the power of this form of representation. Expressed in words, the tutorial strategy embodied in the above seven condition-action rules is as follows: "Continue teaching until ten teaching operations have been executed unless the student reaches knowledge state C(3) first in which case stop at once. As soon as a student acquires either state (C1) or C(2) start teaching operation T(3). For a student with a low pre-test score, make up to five attempts to impart C(1) via T(1) and then switch to execution of T(2). For a student with a high pre-test score, make up to eight attempts to impart C(2) via T(2) and then switch to T(1)".

Note that each tutorial decision is clear, explicit, and quite separate from any book-keeping information associated with teaching performance on which tutorial decisions are not dependent.

EXPRESSING TASK ANALYSES

The example given above is essentially a simple tutorial strategy, with a task analysis implicit in the tutorial situations in which the various teaching operations are applied. The partitions on LASTOP, STATE and SCORE illustrate how classes of tutorial situation are distinguished. The partitions on NUMOP are examples of thresholds.

Where CAI programs have a non-trivial task analysis, such analyses typically take one of two forms: a task difficulty model or an ordering of concepts or teaching subgoals.

Task difficulty models can be expressed as a system of production rules where the elements of the state-vector are dependent on possible student states of knowledge and measures of difficulty on the teaching material. In this case the actions correspond to potential features of components of teaching material. Such a system would be closely analogous to the set of productions involving classes and thresholds illustrated in the above example.

On the other hand, an ordering of teaching subgoals can be expressed as a branching network of the type used by Smallwood (1962). Such networks can be translated into a system of production rules by introducing an element (the goal-element) of the state-vector in which the current tutorials subgoal is stored. Partitions can then be defined to detect the currently active teaching subgoals. This scheme does, however, necessitate the introduction of a class of dummy teaching actions. These dummy actions set up the currently active teaching subgoals. The execution of such an action will not directly result in any teaching occurring and its occurrence in a condition-action rule can be regarded as a 'comment' or 'annotation' on the likely intention involved in executing the other actions on the right-hand side of the rule. The use of such devices to impose a higher level of control on the execution of a set of production rules has been criticised by Davis and King (1975) as "not in the spirit" of production rule programming. However, such devices are of great utility if there are different levels of organisation inherent in the task being executed by a set of productions, and similar devices have been strongly advocated by various workers who have used rule-based systems for scientific discovery (see, for example, Lenat and Harris, 1977). This deviation from the standard simple form of control can be mitigated by clearly marking those actions which affect the flow of control. The values of the goal-element will correspond to the node set of the network.

STUDENT MODELS (SMs)

An important class of tutorial actions are those which invoke a SM to test some hypothesis about the students' current state of knowledge. Now Self (1974) has argued convincingly that SMs should be expressed as collections of procedures whose behaviour can be directly compared with that of the student. But if the SM is a component of an adaptive computer tutor then the SM will be updated during the course of the teaching. This will necessitate adding, deleting or changing the procedures which make up the SM. Now systems of PRs are amenable to such operations and have been successfully employed by O'Shea (1979) for the expression of normative SMs. Further, there already exists in AI a tradition of work which employs PRs for modelling the performance of information processing tasks. For example, O'Shea and Young (1978) have produced a series of PR system models for the various strategies which are employed in subtractions. From this a SM for a subtraction tutor could be developed. Using such a SM, student behaviour could be analysed by comparing it with that produced by running subsets of PRs. Accordingly, PRs are a suitable vehicle for expressing SMs and such SMs could be experimented on during instruction using the approach outlined above for TSs. The use of production rules as a tool for the construction of computer tutors could thus make a useful contribution to the development of a qualitatively rigorous educational psychology.

Two Student Model Examples

Consider two simple student models to predict whether a student has grasped the concept 'prime number'. First suppose a student has been asked whether he knows what a prime number is and this is followed by asking him whether a number 'N' is prime. Using the state-vector (FAMILIAR, ANSWER) and the partitions

FAMILIAR→A1 if FAMILIAR = YES
→A2 if FAMILIAR = NO
ANSWER →B1 if ANSWER = CORRECT
→B2 if ANSWER = WRONG

then a student model could be given by the condition-action rules:

(A1, B1)→1
(A2, B1)→f (N)
(*, B2) →0

where f(N) = 1 – (P(N)/N) if N is prime and f(N) = P(N)/N if N is not prime, and P(N) = number of primes $<$ N. The action is a measure of certainty that the student has acquired the concept. Such a measure of certainty could be used as an element of a state-vector and could be employed to help determine an appropriate teaching operation or elicit further information about the student's state of knowledge (this would involve changing the definition of f(N) above).

An alternative approach would be to simulate the various ways in which the student is performing a task. For example, suppose in the prime number example it is hypothesised that students either (a) guess, (b) believe that all odd numbers are prime, or (c) determine whether a number N is prime by successively dividing it by all numbers M where $1 < M < N$. Taking as state-vector (LASTDIVISOR, REMAINDER) and partitions:

LASTDIVISOR→A1 LASTDIVISOR = 2
→A2 LASTDIVISOR = N – 1
REMAINDER →B1 REMAINDER ≠ 0
→B2 REMAINDER = 0

then three alternative sets of condition-action rules to model the three classes of student could be as follows (with LASTDIVISOR = 1 initially):

a) (*, *) →RANDOM GUESS
b) (A1, B1) →SAY 'PRIME'
(A1, B2) →SAY 'NOT PRIME'
(*, *) →DIVIDE N BY 2
c) (A2, B1) →SAY 'PRIME'
(A2, B2) →SAY 'NOT PRIME'
(*, *) →DIVIDE N BY LASTDIVISOR + 1

Such a set of alternative student models could be used in conjunction with a tutorial strategy by 'running' each model on the material presented to the student and comparing the performance of each student model with actual student performance

EXPRESSION OF COMPLEX TUTORIAL STRATEGIES WITH PRODUCTION RULES

We may classify (Waterman, 1973) the ways of organising systems of production rules as follows:

(a) Single or multiple action – whether the right-hand side of the production rule is restricted to a single action or not.

(b) Single or multiple hit – whether a single condition evaluating true is sufficient for a rule to fire, or whether all the conditions have to evaluate true.

(c) Ordered or unordered – whether the mechanism employed to resolve conflicts when one or more rules fires is ordering of the rules.

(d) Single or multiple cycles – whether each right-hand side executed results in some change in the external environment as opposed to all the actions on a right-hand side resulting in internal changes (for example, setting flags or declaring goals.)

(e) Flat or nested – whether after execution of a right-hand side control always returns to the set of productions currently being executed as opposed to allowing actions themselves to either constitute or invoke other sets of productions.

The simple example expressing a tutorial strategy given above was single action, multiple hit, ordered, single cycle and flat. To express an entire complex tutorial strategy in this form would result in a very large state-vector, lots or parsing, and large numbers of cumbersome condition-action rules with much redundancy. This results in inefficiency, both in terms of processing time and storage space. The following design choices can be employed to gain efficiency and simpler, more transparent structures:

(a) The use of multiple actions where executing one action automatically entails the execution of another.

(b) The use of single hits as a way of expressing a logical 'or'. In a context with few actions and a large number of sparse condition-action rules, a marker can be used to denote 'or' (i.e., any single hit constitutes a match). This reduces the number of rules required.

(c) Careful choice of order of rules can reduce the number of condition-action rules needed (cf. branching network example).

(d) Single cycle operation can reduce the amount of processing required and is possible if multiple actions are employed because 'internal actions' (e.g. declaring goals) can then be associated with (i.e. used on the same right-hand side as) the appropriate external actions.

(e) Nesting can be used to implement hierarchical strategies.

Consider a set of condition-action rules representing a set of means-end guidance rules. The actions could result in the execution of a set of production expressing a student model or task analysis; that is, production rules can be used as a switch between subsets of the entire set of productions. Each subset may be regarded as a production rule 'subroutine'.

A SELF-IMPROVING COMPUTER TUTOR

All the above techniques were applied in the implementation discussed in O'Shea (1979). This is a self-improving teaching system comprising two principal components. One component is an adaptive teaching program where the teaching strategy is expressed as a set of production rules. The second component performs the self-improving function of the system by making experimental changes to the set of production rules. This component employs a deduction procedure which operates on a theory of instruction expressed as a set of modally qualified assertions. These assertions relate educational objectives to modifications which can be made to the teaching strategy. The cycle of operations proposed for the system is as follows – select an educational objective, make an experimental change in teaching strategy, statistically evaluate the resulting performance, and update both the set of production rules and set of assertions. It was used for the teaching of quadratic equations by the discovery method. The system taught fifty-one students, and executed five experimental changes on its teaching strategy. This trial demonstrated that it was capable of improving its performance as a result of experimentation. Its limitations include a vulnerability to problems of local optima during 'hill-climbing' and to a variant of the frame problem.

Self-improving computer tutors becomes much more practical if we assume that in practice they would be used as tools by teachers and experimental psychologists to develop and test teaching strategies and theories of instruction. In that circumstance if the teaching performance of the system greatly deteriorated the human experimenter could intervene and change any suspect production rules. Similarly if an interesting experiment or class of experiment became apparent the educationalist could add appropriate particular or general assertions. In this way a self-improving teaching system could be developed and extended in a similar synergistic mode to that successfully applied in MYCIN (Shortliffe et al., 1975). For the theory of instruction can be regarded as an action-driven production system (see Waterman, 1977) where the question to be answered by deductive inference on the assertions is "what change in teaching strategy would improve teaching performance with respect to educational objective x?"

Another approach using production rules is to take advantage of the knowledge base of a system like MYCIN and augment it with tutoring rules for explaining the domain rules. A system called GUIDON has been implemented on these principles by Clancey (1979).

REFERENCES

Clancey, W.J.L. 1979. Tutoring rules for guiding a case method dialogue. *Int. J. Man-Machine Studies, 11,* 1.

Davis, R. and King, J. 1975. An Overview of Production Systems. *Stanford Artificial Intelligence Laboratory Memo AIM-271; Computer Science Department Report No. STAN-CS-75-524.* Stanford University, October.

Lenat, D.B. and Harris, G. 1977. Designing a rule system that searches for scientific discoveries. *Technical Report,* Department of Computer Science, Carnegie-Mellon University, Pittsburgh, PA., April.

O'Shea, T. 1979. *Self-Improving Teaching Systems.* Birkhauser Verlag.

O'Shea, T. and Young, R. 1978. A production rule account of children's errors in subtraction. Proceedings of third AISB conference.

Rychener, M.D. 1976. Production systems as a programming language for artificial intelligence applications. *Department of Computer Science Report,* Carnegie-Mellon University, Pittsburgh, PA.

Self, J. 1974. Student Models in CAI. *International Journal of Man-Machine Studies, 6, 2.*

Shortliffe, E.H., Davis, R., Buchanan, B., Axline, B., Green, C. and Cohen, S. 1975. Computer-based consultations in clinical therapeutics: exploration and rule acquisition capabilities of the MYCIN system. Computers and Biomedical Research, 8, 303-320.

Smallwood, R. 1962. *A Decision Structure for Teaching Machines.* MIT Press.

Waterman, D.A. 1968. Machine learning of heuristics. Ph.D. Thesis Computer Science Department, Stanford University.

Waterman, D.A. 1973. Private communication.

Waterman, D.A. 1977. An introduction to production systems. *AISB European Newsletter, 25,* 7-10, January.

EPISTEMOLOGICAL PROBLEMS OF ARTIFICIAL INTELLIGENCE

EPISTEMOLOGY AND ARTIFICIAL INTELLIGENCE

Aaron Sloman

[Opening remarks from the Chair at the start of the session.]

INTRODUCTION

For readers unfamiliar with epistemology a very brief overview of the subject may be useful prior to reading the papers by Hayes and McCarthy, linking epistemology and Artificial Intelligence.

Epistemology is the study of knowledge. There are many different ways the subject can be approached, including the following:

1. A study of the knowledge, beliefs and concepts of different societies, or different epochs. (Sociology, Anthropology, History of Ideas.)

2. A study of the cognitive development of human individuals. Piaget calls his work in this field 'Genetic Epistemology'.

3. A study of the evolution of different kinds of knowledge and the mechanisms for using them. I call this bio-epistemology. The subject is in its infancy and will remain so until biologists accept that not only animal behaviour but also the underlying mental structures and mechanisms are worthy of scientific study.

4. Philosophical studies of knowledge. These are often not so much concerned with finding out *facts* as with establishing *norms* or *standards*. So philosophers try to find criteria for deciding whether certain beliefs are *rational*, or whether inferences from evidence to conclusions are *valid*. A closely related topic is the study of the systems of concepts required for formulating beliefs of different kinds, for instance concepts of space, time, matter, cause, and mind. As we shall see, philosophical studies of concepts and knowledge are closely related to work in Artificial Intelligence.

5. Work in Artificial Intelligence, whether aimed at modelling human minds or designing smart machines, necessarily includes a study of knowledge. Knowledge about particular domains is the basis of the expertise of all the expert systems described in this volume. General knowledge about how knowledge is acquired, represented and used, has to be embodied in flexible systems which can be extended, or which can explain their actions. A machine which communicates effectively with a variety of humans will have to use information about what people can be expected to know in various circumstances. This is especially true of a teaching machine.

PROBLEMS ABOUT KNOWLEDGE

The study of knowledge in all the aforementioned fields can be shallow or deep. A shallow study is concerned simply with what is known by some system – a person, community, or machine capable of performing certain tasks. Deeper investigations are concerned with the *basis* of such knowledge. We can identify a series of questions of increasing depth and difficulty, about some knowledgeable system X, actual or hypothesised.

1. What are the things which X knows, or believes? What does X need to know in order to perform some task?

2. What system of *concepts* is used in such knowledge? (The system of concepts will usually define a more general class of possible facts, rules, etc, than that actually grasped by X. See Sloman, 1978, chapter 2.

3. What formalism, or set of formalisms is used for expressing such concepts and combining them into beliefs, rules, intentions, etc.? What inference rules does the formalism use? (In general a formalism e.g. Predicate calculus, or the notation of maps, or a programming language, will support a more general class of concepts than those actually used by X).

4. What are the mechanisms by which the formalism is implemented and used? (The underlying mechanism may be capable of supporting a wider range of formalisms – symbolisms, notations – than those actually used by X.)

For each of these questions there is an additional dimension in which new questions of increased depth and difficulty can be asked. We can ask about a class of beliefs, or concepts, or notations, or mechanisms, what the alternatives are, and how one can choose rationally between alternatives. E.g. why is it better to use this information than that? Why are these concepts more useful than some others? Why is this a good formalism to use? This subsumes much philosophical discussion of questions like "It is rational to believe there is an external world?" "Is it rational to accept predictions based on extrapolation from past experience?" "Is it rational to use concepts not definable in terms of the contents of experiences?"

These questions are all clearly relevant to the design of working expert systems, but the depth of study is related to the ambitions of such a design. For instance if a system is merely intended to be a data-base of information on some topic, able to answer questions about what has been stored explicitly, then question (1) is all that need be considered, and the question "Why store these facts rather than some others?" need not arise. The set of items to be stored defines the task, unlike cases where the task is defined by some other goal, such as accurate diagnosis of a range of diseases.

If the system is to be able to check for consistency, or to make inferences to conclusions not explicitly stored, then the designers will have to go into questions about how the concepts used are related, what general patterns of inference are valid, methods for weighting uncertain evidence or merely probable conclusions, etc.

If the system is to be able to store many different kinds of knowledge, and to exercise some independence in choosing which subset is relevant to a given problem, then issues about generality of the formalisms, trade-offs between different sorts of formalisms and underlying mechanisms, etc., become paramount.

Finally, if the system is to be able to explain its decisions to people, then the form in which facts and inference rules are stored must relate closely to what people can understand. This may not always be what is computationally most economical.

We can illustrate the importance of question 3 above, not only for philosophical and AI studies of knowledge, but for all science, by noting that until recently there were few good ways of expressing theories about complex processes. The formalisms available were mainly derived from the concepts of physics, and were therefore mostly concerned with changes in scalar (discrete or continuous) variables. But although many social scientists and psychologists continue to use such descriptive methods, it is now clear that they are grossly inadequate for the description and analysis of processes involving the manipulation of complex symbolic structures. No computer scientist would dream of trying to describe the behaviour of a compiler or operating system in terms of a few equations relating a handful of measureable quantities. More complex ideas, such as are embodied in programming languages (concepts like conditional instructions, recursion, data-structures, networks, etc.) are required for adequate descriptions. And yet many scientists studying human beings and social systems continue to try to force their theories into the quantitative framework derived from physics.

A favourite area of disagreement among AI researchers concerns the selection of a formalism for specifying computational mechanisms. Many of the papers in this book report systems based on the idea of a set of production-rules, namely rules with a condition and an action. The underlying mechanism is, in the simplest cases, a machine which repeatedly looks for a rule whose *condition* matches some data-base, and then obeys the *action*. By contrast the papers by McCarthy and Hayes tend to favour explicit use of predicate calculus as a formalism for expressing knowledge, where the contents of rules will normally be expressed in some universally quantified assertion. Detailed comparative studies of such alternative formalism and mechanisms are still awaited, though the papers by Warren and Young begin to compare predicate calculus and production systems (respectively) with conventional programming languages. The criteria to be used in such comparisons may well be radically revised as we acquire a deeper understanding of distributed computing systems, in which many processors collaborate, working in parallel. (For more on this question of alternative representations, see Hayes 1974, Bobrow 1975, Sloman 1978, chapter 7.)

DIFFERENT KINDS OF EXPERTS

Most of the expert systems described in this volume embody highly specialised concepts and knowledge, of medicine, chemistry, geology or some other topic which is not widely understood. By contrast, the papers by McCarthy and Hayes are concerned with concepts and knowledge possessed by all ordinary people. We all know that people can know things, can believe things, can think about things. We all know a great deal about physical objects, events and processes that can occur in our environment.

Machines which are able to think about people and take decisions about them (or give advice about them) will need to use mentalistic concepts of the sorts discussed by McCarthy, especially if they are to be able to explain their reasoning. In theory, they might function, up to a point, by simulating physical and chemical processes in human brains – but such a system would be as hard to understand as a human brain. When people think about, and reason about, other people (which we all do in our every day lives) it seems unlikely that we unconsciously simulate the brain processes of other people. Rather, we function with abstract descriptions of their mental states.

Similarly, in thinking and taking decisions about objects in our environment, for instance in deciding how to hold a teapot whilst pouring tea into a cup, it seems certain that we do not similate the underlying atomic or sub-atomic events. Rather we perceive the world, think about the world, and act on the world using macroscopic concepts like *spout, rim, falling, tilting, spill, splash, nearly full*, and so on. Intelligent machines capable or explaining their actions to people, and capable of receiving instructions from people, will have to use similar concepts for representing physical states and processes. Such concepts are not required for machines which plan and monitor trajectories of space probes and moon shorts, since the normal idealisations of physics suffice for that sort of job. Paradoxically, designing a domestic robot, able to clear up the dishes after dinner and wash them in the sink, is much harder.

The analysis of such everyday concepts, described by Hayes, like McCarthy's analysis of mental concepts, is very close to the kind of "conceptual analysis" practised by philosophers. (See Sloman, 1978, chapter 4). However, the motivation is different, since philosphers are often concerned merely to refute scepticism about the physical world, or simply to understand the conceptual frameworks used by people. It is at first sight curious that the philosophical activity of trying to understand aspects of human thought and language should have so much in common with the activity of designing intelligent machines. But there may be unique solutions to some complex design problems.

One issue that arises in the design of intelligent machines is how knowledge should be represented so as to be efficiently and effectively useable. (McCarthy and Hayes 1969 called this the problem of heuristic adequacy.) This issue does not arise when philosophers analyse concepts. They merely wish to record results in a form useful for communication with other philosophers. In addition they may wish to prove theorems *about* certain bodies of knowledge, or systems of concepts. A mode of representing knowledge that is useful for such philosophical and mathematical enquires may be very different from what is practical for a machine which has to *use* the knowledge. The requirements of such a machine may also be closer to the requirements of ordinary people in their ordinary thinking and acting – as opposed to the explicit theorising of philosophers and AI researchers.

Such practical uses may require elaborate indexing, explicit storage of much redundant information, "procedural embedding" of knowledge in strategies or programs for performing actions, and explicit storage of cues and procedures for controlling the selection of knowledge relevant to current problems. When Hayes and McCarthy recommend the use of predicate calculus as a formalism it is not clear whether they are talking about the needs of human theorists, or the needs of a working system. It is hard to believe that ordinary people and other intelligent animals use predicate calculus. We currently know very little about what sorts of formalisms and mechanisms are possible.

It is perhaps worth noting that not all forms of human expertise are readily articulated and formalised. Facts and theories explicitly studied by experts can often be expressed in English after a certain amount of reflection. Not so our knowledge of how to understand English, our knowledge of how to see, our knowledge of how to acquire new skills and concepts. This knowledge, if it can be called such, is very widely shared, and frequently used in everyday life, yet it is extremely difficult to explain how we understand speech, see objects or learn concepts. Paradoxically the types of expertise which are hardest for ordinary people to *acquire* (e.g. knowledge of science, mathematics, chess, and medicine) are easiest to *articulate* for the benefit of designers of expert systems. Visual expertise, shared between humans and many other animals, is particularly difficult to account for.

TOOLS vs THEORIES

Richard Young's paper stresses the contrast between the goal of producing a useful machine and the goal of modelling and explaining human abilities. There is an enormous amount of overlap between the two sorts of research. In part this is because both require detailed analysis of *task* requirements.

For instance designing a speech-understanding machine and designing a model of human speech processing both require a study of the significant structures and relations in speech sounds, and an analysis of the syntax and semantics of natural languages. Just as ordinary people don't need to simulate details of each other's brain processes, so also can scientists studying some aspect of the human mind represent their theories at a level which ignores details of the working of the brain. For this reason, computational theories cannot be criticised simply because computers are very different from brains, any more than a meteorologist can be criticised for not trying to represent the movements of individual sub-atomic particles in a weather-map.

Where there are alternative means of achieving the same task, the question arises: which of them best explains human abilities? Experimental studies of the externally observable behaviour of the system may be very indecisive. For instance very many different algorithms can all give the same input output relations. The methodological issues are discussed at length by Pylyshyn (1978) and the commentators in the same journal. My view is that at the present time existing theories are much too simple to be taken seriously as explanations or human abilities. We don't yet know how to build sufficiently complex theories.

In particular human abilities involve a degree of generality, flexibility and extendability not matched by any present-day expert system. The ability to "degrade gracefully" in the face of increasing difficulties, which humans often display, will be especially important when expert systems are put to real use in the field. Sudden and inexplicable failures of complex systems arising out of a combination of circumstances not anticipated by the designers could be very annoying, if not disastrous. Similarly a consultant program unable to answer a question should be able to notice partial analogies with problems it can solve, and give hints or suggest relevant lines of exploration, instead of simply saying "I don't know". More generally, programs designed with a natural-language interface should be able to cope with mispellings, metaphors, bad grammar, false starts, elliptical sentences and other vagaries of human linguistic production. Notice how the task of explaining human abilities merges with the task of designing cleverer machines than we already have.

These requirements impose constraints on the way knowledge is represented and organised, and the amount of meta-knowledge (knowledge a system has about its own knowledge) needed by an expert system. This aspect of heuristic adequacy is a new field of epistemology whose study is still in its infancy. Examples of the issues involved include: the need for such systems to include mechanisms by which "demons" or "monitors" can be set up to watch out for special circumstances and take appropriate action, the need for methods of describing and drawing conclusions from similarities and differences between complex descriptions which are partly but not completely alike, the need for ways of extracting useful information from unsuccessful attempts at solving a problem, the need to be able to describe classes of problems or situations at a suitable level of generality, and so on.

My own impression is that production systems, predicate calculus and other existing formalisms are at best only relatively low-level "machine-languages" out of which far more powerful descriptive formalisms and inference systems will need to be constructed. Alternatively they may turn out to be limiting special cases. For instance both use matchers – but not network matchers, only tree-matchers.

CONCLUSION

This paper has attempted to supplement the detailed studies of expertise in the other conference papers with some general remarks about epistemological issues arising out of Artificial Intelligence. It should be clear that these issues are not unique to the design of clever artefacts. They are central to the study of the human mind. For this reason AI can have a powerful impact on philosophy, psychology, biology and perhaps even social studies of knowledge, combating their theoretical poverty, which arises out of a lack of good concepts and formalisms for representing complex processes.

But as the ideas diffuse throughout culture they may also begin to revolutionise much less specialised modes of thought. Weizenbaum (1976) has argued that this could be very harmful. Boden (1977) and Sloman (1978) argue that on the contrary computationally informed thinking will enrich our understanding of ourselves and other people. Perhaps only time will tell who is right, since the science of social forecasting is still waiting to be born.

BIBLIOGRAPHY

Bobrow, D.G. 'Dimensions of Representations' in D.G. Bobrow and A Collins (Eds.) *Representation and Understanding* Academic Press 1975.

Boden, M.A. *Artificial Intelligence and Natural Man* Harvester Press and Basic Books 1977.

Hayes, P.J. 'Some Problems and non-problems in representation theory' in proceedings AISB Summer Conference 1974.

McCarthy, J. & Hayes, P.J. 'Some Philosophical Problems from the standpoint of Artificial Intelligence', in B Meltzer and D. Michie (Eds.) *Machine Intelligence 4*, Edinburgh University Press, 1969.

Pylyshyn, Zenon 'Computational models and empirical constraints', in *The Behavioural and Brain Sciences*, Vol 1, No 1, 1978.

Sloman, Aaron *The Computer Revolution in Philosophy* Harvester Press and Humanities Press, 1978.

Weizenbaum, Joseph *Computer Power and Human Reason* W.H. Freeman & Co. 1976.

THE NAIVE PHYSICS MANIFESTO

Patrick J. Hayes

The garden still offered its corners of weed, blackened cabbages, its stones and flowerstalks. And the house its areas of hot and cold, dark holes and talking boards, its districts of terror and blessed sanctuary; together with an infinite range of objects and ornaments that folded, fastened, creaked and sighed, opened and shut.

from 'Cider with Rosie'
by Laurie Lee

0. INTRODUCTION

Artificial Intelligence is full of 'toy problems': small, artificial axiomatisations or puzzles designed to exercise the talents of various problem-solving programs or representational languages or systems. The subject badly needs some non-toy worlds to experiment with. In this document I propose the construction of a formalisation of a sizable portion of common-sense knowledge about the everyday physical world: about objects, shape, space, movement, substances (solids and liquids), time, etc.

In what follows I will outline the proposal and distinguish it from some others, superficially similar; discuss some of the general issues which arise; argue that it *needs* to be done; that it *can* be done; and outline a way of *getting* it done. Along the way I will outline the theory of meaning which this proposal assumes, and criticize some others.

1. THE PROPOSAL : SUMMARY

The proposal is to construct a formalisation of a large part of ordinary everyday knowledge of the physical world. Such a formalisation could, for example, be a collection of assertions in a first-order logical formalism, or a collection of KRL 'units', or a microplanner program, or one of a number of other things. The proposal is *not* to develop a new formalism to express this knowledge in. Although we recognise that formalism-hacking may become necessary in due course, we believe that existing, well-understood formalisms have many, as yet unexplored, possibilities. The proposal is *not* to write a program which can solve problems, or plan actions, or whatever, in the formalism. Although it is important to bear control and search issues – in short, *computational issues* – in mind, we propose to deliberately postpone detailed consideration of implementation. All too often, serious work on representational issues in AI has been diverted or totally thwarted by premature concern for computational issues.

The formalism we propose should have the following characteristics (we elaborate on these later):

(i) *Thoroughness*. It should cover the whole range of everyday physical phenomena: not just the blocks world, for example. Since in some important sense the world (even the everyday world) is infinitely rich in possible phenomena, this thoroughness will never be perfect. Nevertheless, we should *try* to fill in all the major holes, or at least identify them.

(ii) *Fidelity*. It should be reasonably detailed. For example, such aspects of a block in a block-world as shape, material, weight, rigidity and surface texture should be available as concepts in a blocks-world description, as well as *support* relationships. Again, since the world is infinitely detailed, perfect fidelity is impossible: but we should try to do better than the very low fidelity of the common 'toy problem' axiomatisations, in which, for example, the relationship of one block being 'above' another is merely a partial ordering, so that the integers are a possible model of the axioms.

(iii) *Density*. The ratio of facts to concepts needs to be fairly high. Put another way: the units have to have *lots* of slots. Low-density formalisations are in some sense trivial: they fail to say enough about the concepts they contain to pin down the meaning at all precisely. Sometimes, for special purposes, as for example in foundational studies, this can be an advantage: but not for us.

(iv) *Uniformity*. There should be a common formal framework (language, system, etc.) for the whole formalisation, so that the inferential connections between the different parts (axioms, frames, . . .) can be clearly seen, and divisions into subformalisations are not prejudged by deciding to use one formalism for one area and a different one for a different area.

(As I shall emphasize later, I also think it is methodologically important to allow the use of a variety of formalisms: often a particular subarea can be neatly expressed in some idiosyncratic way. But there is no contradiction: for we will also insist that such idiosyncratic formalisms are systematically reducible to the basic formalism: they will be regarded as 'semantic sugar'. This is important: for although *computational* properties of a representation may depend crucially upon the use of such idiosyncratic formalisms, there must be a common *representational* framework within which the meaning-content of any piece of representation can be related to that of any other.)

I believe that a formalisation of naive physics with these properties can be constructed within a reasonable time-scale. The reasons for such optimism are explained later. It is important however to clearly distinguish this proposal from some others with which it may be confused, because some of these seem to be far less tractable.

2. WHAT THE PROPOSAL ISN'T

(a) It is *not* proposed to make a computer program which can 'use' the formalism in some sense. For example, a problem-solving program, or a natural language comprehension system with the representation as target. It is tempting to make such demonstrations from time to time. (They impress people; and it is satisfying to have actually *made* something which works, like building model railways; and one's students can get PhD's that way.) But they divert attention from the main goal. In fact, I believe they have several more dangerous effects.

It is perilously easy to conclude that, because one has a program which *works* (in some sense), its representation of its knowledge must be more or less *correct* (in some sense). Regrettably, the little compromises and simplifications needed in order to get the program to work in a reasonable space or in a reasonable time, can often make the representation even less satisfactory than it might have been.

This is not to say that computational questions should be *ignored* in constructing the proposed formalisation. For example, the question of the *length of derivations* of ordinary common-sense inferences is important, and our notion of 'density' has direct computational consequences, for example for storage and retrieval strategies. But the construction of 'demonstration' programs seems to serve no really useful purpose (McDermott 1977 argues similarly).

I emphasize this point because there is a prevailing attitude in AI that research which does not result fairly quickly in a working program of some kind is somehow useless, or at least, highly suspicious. This may be partly to blame for the dearth of really serious efforts in the representational direction, and the proliferation of programs and techniques which work well (or sometimes badly) in trivially small domains, but which are wholly limited by scale factors, and which therefore tell us nothing about thinking about realistically complicated worlds. (Backtracking search and the STRIPS representation of actions by add and delete lists are two good examples. I suspect that production systems are another).

Ideally, one should in principle be able to get a working program from the formalisation by assuming a particular inference mechanism and adding *further* information at the meta-level, which 'controls' the inferences this mechanism performs (Hayes 1973, Kowalski 1977, Pratt 1977, Bundy 1978). Looked at this way, a formalisation can be thought of as a 'core' of inferential abilities, whose appropriate deployment at any moment for a particular task has to be further specified. (However, this pleasant picture has no doubt to be modified to account for idiosyncratic representations which have especially desirable computational properties.)

The decision to postpone details of implementation can be seen as an implicit claim that the representational content of a large formalisation can be separated fairly clearly from the implementational decisions: this is by no means absolutely obvious, although I believe it to be substantially true.

(b) It is *not* proposed to develop a new formalism or language to write down all this knowledge in. In fact, I propose (as my friends will have already guessed) that first-order logic is a suitable basic vehicle for representation. However, let me at once qualify this.

I have no particular brief for the usual *syntax* of first-order logic. Personally I find it agreeable: but if someone likes to write it all out in KRL, or semantic networks, or 'fancy' semantic networks of one sort or another, or what have you; well, that's fine. The important point is that one *knows what it means*: that the formalism has a clear *interpretation* (I avoid the word 's*m*nt*cs' deliberately). At the level of interpretation, there is little to choose between any of these, and most are strictly weaker than predicate calculus, which also has the advantage of a clear, explicit model theory, and a well-understood proof theory (Hayes 1977, 1978a).

Secondly, let me emphasize again that idiosyncratic notations may sometimes be useful for idiosyncratic subtheories. For example, in sketching an axiomatic theory of fluids (Hayes 1978b), I found it useful to think of the possible physical states of fluids as being essentially states of a finite-state machine. This summarizes a whole lot of lengthy, and rather clumsy first-order axioms into one neat diagram. Still, it *means* the same as the axioms: first-order logic is still, as it were, the reference language. Other examples are the 'evaluable' predicates and functions sometimes included in theorem-proving preograms, where for example the term '(plus 2 3)' is *evaluated* to the constant '5', no axioms being provided for arithmetic expressions. But this can always * be regarded as a computationally efficient way of representing the same *meaning* as would be represented by the (infinite) collection of axioms '(plus 2 3) = 5', '(plus 2 2) = 4', etc.

Thirdly, first-order logic as it stands is almost certainly not rich enough and will need to be extended. I have already found two extensions which I think are necessary: quotation, so that the formalism can describe its own formulae; and a sort of non-unique Skolem function, similar to Hilbert's ϵ-symbol. The notion of the default may be another (although I have not felt any particular need for this concept so far). I expect that such extensions will arise naturally through difficulties in using the formalism; and as I think it is dangerous to try to predict such difficulties ahead of time, I will not try.

3. THE AXIOM-CONCEPT GRAPH: CLUSTERS AND DENSITY

Let us imagine that a naive physics formalisation exists (I tend to believe that it does, in fact, inside my head), and try to analyse its structure. It consists, fundamentally, of a large number of assertions, involving a large number of (nonlogical) symbols: relation symbols, function and constant symbols (*or*: frame headers, slot names, etc; *or*: node and arc labels, etc. In future I will not bother to re-emphasize these obvious parallels, but will assume the reader is aware of them.) For a neutral word, let us call these symbols *tokens*.

The *meaning* of the tokens is defined by the structure of the formalisation, by the pattern of inferential connections between the assertions. This structure can be very complex, but we can make some fundamental points by treating it in an essentially qualitative way.

Let us say that a formalisation is *dense* if, for each token, there are many axioms involving it. A dense formalisation has many links between the separate concepts expressed by tokens in the formalisation. Density is clearly a matter of degree. Formalisations which are not dense in this way (*sparse* formalisations) are unsatisfactory, since they do not pin down exactly enough the meanings of the tokens they contain. If all a formalisation says about the relation *above* (in the blocks world) is that it is the transitive closure of *on*; and all it says about *on* is that if nothing is *on* a block then you can pick it up; and all it

*This remark slurs over a minefield of technical difficulties. It is not appropriate to go into these here, however.

says about *picking* up is that after *picking*, the block is *held*, etc. (in the familiar way); if this is *all* that it says with these tokens, then one can hardly say that the concepts of *on, above*, etc. are represented in the formalisation at all. For, these concepts have connections to many other concepts as well, in our heads. If one thing is above another, there are all sorts of consequences. Maybe the first will fall on the second, if its supports fail: there are consequences for the relative appearance of the two objects: the top one might provide a shelter for the bottom one: if the bottom one supports the top one, then the bottom one will be under some strain due to the weight of the top one: and so on. We need to try to capture this *richness* of conceptual linking.

(It is worth emphasizing that the view of meaning espoused here differs profoundly from the view which holds that tokens in a formalisation are essentially words in a natural language (Wilks 1977). According to this latter view, the tokens *do* represent the concept intended, by *fiat*: they are 'semantic primitives', out of which all other meanings are composed. I will return to this idea shortly.)

Any formalisation which hopes to approach the richness of our own conceptual apparatus must be dense. Of course, density is not a *sufficient* condition for success: it is not difficult to invent wholly useless axiomatisations of arbitrarily high density.

It is useful to consider a simplified model of a formalisation. Imagine a graph whose nodes are tokens of the formalisation, and whose arcs correspond to axioms: an arc links two nodes if the corresponding axiom contains those two tokens. (Strictly speaking, this has to be a polygraph (Landin 1970), since axioms may well contain more than two tokens. However, we will be making only heuristic use of the idea, in any case, so technicalities are inappropriate.) We will call this the axiom-concept (a-c) graph. The formalisation is dense if the a-c graph is highly connected, sparse if the graph is sparse. However, we cannot expect density to be uniform: there will be more dense clusters of concepts with many relationships between them, less tightly linked to the rest of the formalisation.

Identifying these clusters is both one of the most important and one of the most difficult methodological tasks in developing a naive physics. I think that several serious mistakes have been made in the past: here, for example, causality is, I now tend to think, *not* a cluster: there is no useful, more-or-less self-contained theory of causality. 'Causality' is a word for what happens when other things happen, and what happens, depends on circumstances. If there is liquid around, for example, things will often happen very differently from when everything is nice and dry. What happens with liquids, however, is part of the *liquids* cluster, not part of some theory of 'what-happens-when'. Mistakes like this are hard to overcome, since a large conceptual structure *can* be entered anywhere. The symptom of having got it wrong is that it seems hard to say anything very useful about the concepts one has proposed (because one has entered the graph at a locally sparse place, rather than somewhere in a cluster). But this can also be because of having chosen one's concepts badly, lack of imagination, or any of several other reasons. It is easier, fortunately, to recognise when one is in a cluster: assertions suggest themselves faster than one can write them down.

There is also a useful notion of a super-cluster: a cluster which is related to a large number of other clusters. I think that the collection of concepts to do with three-dimensional shape and orientation are a super-cluster in our own mental conceptual structures: concepts such as above, below, tall, fat, wide, behind, touching, resting on, angle of slope, edge (of a surface), surface (of a volume), side, vertical, top, bottom, . . . These obviously have many internal relationships: they form a cluster. They also must appear significantly in whatever conceptual frameworks underlie visual perception and locomotion in space; they are crucial in describing assemblies; in the theory of liquids (Hayes 1978b); also, I believe, in the descriptions of physical actions and events (Hayes 1978c); and so on.

Superclusters can be recognised by the fact that they crop up, in this way, in a variety of other clusters. Other plausible candidates for superclusters include a theory of measuring scales (which should provide such notions as accuracy, vagueness, utility for various kinds of tasks), a theory of time-measurement, and the collection of notions concerned with *inside, outside, containment* and *ways through* from one place to another.

This suggestive terminology of clustering should not be taken literally: I do not mean to suggest that there are many sharply isolated parts of our conceptual structure which can be developed in total isolation from all others. And the 'a-c graph' model of an axiom system is itself over-simplified in several gross respects, in any case. Nevertheless, I think the basic idea, that there are collections of concepts which have close connections between one another, is substantially correct and quite important.

4. THE A/C RATIO AND REDUCTIONIST FORMALISATIONS

Let me turn now to an even cruder model of a formalisation: the *ratio* of axioms to concepts (the a/c ratio). For a dense axiomatisation, a/c will be large. Any interesting axiomatisation will have a/c greater than one; but there *are* interesting axiomatisations in which a/c will be very close to unity.

Consider an axiomatic set theory. The idea, for foundational research, is to have a *small* axiomatic theory (e.g. Zermelo-Fraenkel set theory which has $c = 2$, viz. 'ϵ' and '*set*', and $a = 8$, so $a/c = 4$) which enables one to *define* a large number of mathematical concepts (e.g. the integers can be defined as sets of any one of several special kinds; the rationals are sets of pairs of integers; the reals are sets of infinite sets of rationals . . .) in such a way that the desired properties of these concepts (e.g. the principle of induction for integers: the continuity of the real line) *follow from* the structure of these definitions, and the axioms of the basic theory. It is important to realise that these properties of the defined concepts are *theorems* of the axiomatisation which consists of set theory together with the definitions of the concepts. They are not axiomatic assumptions themselves, needed to pin down the meaning of the introduced concepts: the definitions pin down the concept as completely as it can be: all else then follows. Mathematics is reduced to a series of *lemmas* to set theory: or at least, that is the idea. (When one thinks of it this way, it seems almost incredible that such an audacious programme should have so nearly succeeded.)

I want to emphasize how different this approach to capturing meaning in a formalism is, from the axiomatic approach to naive physics which I am proposing. Set theory is reductionist in the extreme: I am urging a richly connected formalisation, with many interactions between assumptions. The reductionist approach leads, indeed, to axiomatic theories, but they are extraordinarily *sparse*.

Consider the effect of adding a definition of a new concept *to a formalisation*. This increases both a and c by one. If a/c is large, this will decrease it appreciably. (Indeed, one will have to add approximately (a/c) many axioms to bring the ratio back to what it was.

This emphasizes what is intuitively clear, that definitions which do not pay their keep by introducing concepts which are going to be of some general use, are probably a mistake: they dilute the formalisation.) Suppose however that a and c are both small, say $a = 8$, $c = 2$. Then adding one definition reduces a/c from 4 to 3. Adding another reduces it to 2.5: adding 1000 definitions reduces a/c to 1.059. Clearly, as the number of definitions in the formalisation increases, a/c tends asymptotically to unity. The *a-c* graph of such a formalisation has one very small cluster at the centre, surrounded by a cloud of nodes each linked radially to a few nodes closer to the centre. It is almost as sparse a connected graph as one could have, containing the concept tokens that it does. It has quite a different 'shape' from the connected, clustered graph of a dense axiomatic theory.

The existence of such a reductionist theory for mathematics is a remarkable fact, and it would indeed be astonishing if one could find an analogous reductionist theory for common sense reasoning: a small-ish collection of concepts, and axioms connecting them, such that all other concepts (e.g. all those expressed by English words) could be defined in terms of these few. In fact, this would be *so* astonishing that I feel confident in asserting that no such small theory exists. And yet, many approaches to the formal representation of meaning, in the AI literature, make such an assumption. These are the 'semantic primitive' approaches, exemplified by the work of Wilks (1975, for example) and Schank (1975, for example). Here, members of a smallish collection of tokens (Wilks 90 or so, Schank $14+n$ for some n, as yet unknown) are taken as *primitive*. The *meaning* of an English word is then some formal expression built out of these primitive tokens, using some formal apparatus (which in Schank's case is usually presented graphically, although this is not essential). In our terms, the formalisation consists mostly of definitions: its a/c ratio tends to unity, just like axiomatic set theory. In the work of Schank and his students one can clearly see that the axiomatic structure of the 'core' theory – cf. Rieger's 'inference molecules' associated with the 14 primitive action-tokens – is intended to serve the same sort of central organising role that the set axioms play in the development of set theory. That is, desired properties of non-primitive concepts (such as *buying* or *giving*) follow from their definitions, and the meaning given to the primitives by the core theory. In Wilks' work, there does not seem to *be* any core formalisation at all: we are merely present (cf Wilks 1977) with a list of tokens and a brief description of the concept they are supposed to mean. To think that a *formal* symbol has any meaning other than that specified by the structure of the formalisation in which it occurs, that it has any *intrinsic* meaning, is to make a particularly unfortunate mistake. Wilks, however, takes the view that his semantic primitives are, in fact, *words*, like English words, not mere formal tokens, thus neatly escaping this objection, and explaining why it is not necessary to give any formalisation in which they occur. I confess to still being puzzled as to how it is that his *program* knows what they mean.

This reductionist, semantic-primitives approach to meaning is essentially bound to low-fidelity, low-density representations. Such representations have their uses – they may be adequate for information-retrieval or machine translation applications, for example – and when they *do* work, have some very useful computational properties. But at some point we will have to face up to the problem of representing *detailed* knowledge of the world. This will require the abandoning of the 'definition' view of meaning of tokens. As Wilks says, 'No representation in primitives could be expected to distinguish by its structure the senses of *hammer, mallet* and *axe* . . .'. Perhaps not: but naive physics should be able to.

5. MEANINGS, MODEL THEORY AND FIDELITY

It might be asked: if the meanings of tokens are not specified by definitions, how *are* they specified? In one sense there is no answer to such a question. One cannot point to a particular structure and say, *that* is the meaning of a token. One can only say that a token *means* a concept to the extent that *the formalisation taken as a whole* enables a sufficient number of inferences to be made whose conclusions contain the token, i.e. which mention the concept. This operational definition of meaning can, if the formalisation has an adequate model theory, be recast in an extensional way: a token means a concept if, in every possible model of *the formalisation taken as a whole*, that token denotes an entity which one would agree was a satisfactory instantiation of the concept in the possible state of affairs represented by the model.

Now, to do this requires that it be possible to think of a model as a 'state of affairs'. And since we want to formalise the common-sense world of physical reality, this means, for us, that a model of the formalisation must be recognisable as a facsimile of physical reality: one in which the concept we are interested in can be recognised.

A model for a first-order axiomatisation is a set – the set of entities which exist in the 'state of affairs' represented by the model – and a particular mapping from the tokens of the axiomatisation into this set and the sets of relations and functions, of appropriate arity, over it. This is usually presented, in textbooks of elementary logic, in a rather formal, mathematical way: and this fact may have given rise to the curious but widespread delusion that a first-order model is merely another formal description of the world, just like the axiomatisation of which it is a model; and that the Tarskian truth-recursion is a kind of translation from the latter to the former: a translation from one formal system to another (e.g. Wilks, 1977). This is quite wrong. For a start, the relationship between an axiomatisation and its models (or, dually, between a model and the set of axiomatisations which are true of it) is quite different from a translation. It is many-many rather than one-one, for example. Moreover, it has the algebraic character called a Galois connection, which is to say, roughly, that as the axiomatisation is increased in size (as axioms are added), the collection of models – possible states of affairs – *decreases* in size. It is quite possible for a large, complex axiomatisation to have small, simple models, and vice versa. In particular, a model can always be gratuitously complex (e.g. contain entities which aren't mentioned at all in the axiomatisation). But the deeper mistake in this way of thinking is to confuse a *formal description* of a model – found in the textbooks which are developing a mathematical approach to the metatheory of logic – with *the actual model*. This is like confusing a mathematical description of Sydney Harbour Bridge in a textbook of structural engineering with the actual bridge. A Tarskian model can actually *be* a piece of reality. If I have a blocks-world axiomatisation which refers to three blocks, called 'A', 'B', and 'C' (i.e. these are the tokens used in the axiomatisation to mention the blocks), and if I have a (real, physical) table in front of me, with three (real, physical) wooden blocks on it, then the set of those three blocks can *be* the set of entities of a model of the axiomatisation (provided, that is, that I can go on to interpret the relations and functions of the axiomatisation as physical operations on the wooden blocks, or whathever, in such a way that the assertions made by the axiomatisation about the wooden blocks, when so interpreted, are *in fact* true). There is nothing in the Tarskian model theory of first-order logic which *a priori* prevents the real world being a model of an axiom system.

On the other hand, it is also true that many axiomatisations have models which do not contain solid physical objects, but in which tokens denote, say, integers or other symbols. In fact, any first-order axiomatisation which has any model at all (i.e. which is consistent) also has a model in which only symbols exist – this is the 'Herbrand interpretation' in which we let tokens denote themselves. Thus, Tarskian model theory does not guarantee that axiomatisations are 'about' any particular world. It is always possible to consistently believe that the only things which exist are the symbols of the formalisation itself.* This might be called the 'solipsist' interpretation: denying the existence of the external world, while at the same time having an elaborate theory of it.

Given then, that any axiomatisation will have several (usually infinitely many) models, we cannot justify an axiomatisation as an adequate description by merely exhibiting a model of it which is somehow similar to reality. For it may have a very much simpler model than that, and if it has such a simpler

*Although in the usual formalisation of first-order logic, this belief cannot be expressed: and in at least one extension in which it *can* be expressed, its negation – that some things exist which are not symbols – can also be expressed.

model, then the tokens occurring in it mean no more than they mean in that simpler model. This is exactly what I mean by 'fidelity'. A low-fidelity formalisation of, say, the blocks world will admit models which are very much simpler than the intended one: a model, for example, in which the 'blocks' are integers and *above* means greater than, etc.; or perhaps, a model in which 'blocks' are points in a discrete 2-dimensional space, or whatever. An adequate formalisation of a blocks world – a high-fidelity formalisation – will be such that any model of it must have an essentially three-dimensional structure. Thus, SHRDLU's blocks-world axiomatisation (Winograd 1972) uses three-dimensional Cartesian coordinates. (It would be interesting to find a useful but less quantitative way of describing three-dimensional structure: for example, that a rigid attachment needs *three* points of contact: two-legged stools fall over.)

A good guide to the fidelity of a formalisation is how closely its *simplest* model resembles the *intended* model. This is, I think, an excellent argument for a representational language's having a model theory: it gives us a way of testing the fidelity of a representation. It is perilously easy to *think* that one's formalisation has captured a concept (because one has used a convincing-sounding token to stand for it, for example), when in fact, for all the formalisation knows, the token might denote something altogether more elementary, in a very simple model.

(This criterion suggests that we should pay attention to features of representational languages which can be used in a formalisation to insist upon the complexity of the simplest model. In the case of first-order logic, these include functions (the use of which claims that there is a value of the function, applied to any suitable argument), explicit existential assertions (especially 'comprehension axioms' of various kinds – more on this below), the use of equality, and the use of a highly sorted logic (or, in terms more familiar to AI, the presence of an *isa* hierarchy related to the quantifiers: although it can be much more complex than a simple hierarchy, cf. the sorted logic used in Hayes 1971. We might expect, therefore, that these features will be heavily used in developing a naive physics.)

On this account of the meaning of a token, it depends upon the *entire* formalisation of which the token is part. Thus, an alteration to any part of the formalisation can, in principle, change the meaning of every other part of it. And, I think, this is essentially correct: what it means, in introspective terms, is that learning a new fact or acquiring a new concept, is liable to have far-reaching consequences for the ways in which one understands the meanings of other concepts. It also means that people with different formalisations in their heads may understand the same token in different ways. What I mean by 'water' may not be exactly what you mean by 'water': it may be possible to find a substance and a set of circumstances such that I would call it water and you would not (for example, if you had never seen opaque water, you might deny that this opaque liquid which I have in a glass on my desk, was water). And yet, *we might both be right*, since our theories of 'water' may not be identical. And this may even be possible when our beliefs about water (in the direct sense of:

all the assertions which actually contain the token 'water') are identical. Each of us might agree to everything the other said about water, and yet our concepts might be subtly different. The difference may lie in some related concept (such as viscosity, or drinkability) which we understand differently. It may not even be possible to say exactly which tokens we differ on: just that we have somewhat different theories of them. It follows from this that there is no *single* 'meaning' of a token: or at least, that to assume that there is, is to assume that people's cognitive formalisations are identical in structure. Much confusion follows if this is not borne clearly in mind. For example, Wilks has argued (Anderson et al. 1972) that since there are people who have never seen ice, the fact that water freezes *cannot* be part of the meaning of 'water': for if it were, one would have to say that those people did not understand the meaning of 'water': and that is ridiculous. One can cut through this tortuous piece of reasoning by observing that the word evidently means more to some people than to others: and to those who *do* know about ice, the fact that ice is frozen water can well be part of the meaning of 'water'.

However, in order that communication be possible at all, it should obviously be that people's cognitive structures are *similar*: and, as a working hypothesis, we will make such an assumption in developing naive physics. One of the good reasons for choosing naive *physics* to tackle first is that there seems to be a greater measure of interpersonal agreement here than in many fields.

There seems to be a notion of 'distance' in a formalisation, such that the effect of an alteration on the meaning of a token is less, the further away the token is from the alteration. It is not clear to me whether or how this suggestive intuition can be made to stand up. It is tempting to identify this distance with shortest-path distance in the axiom-concept graph, and although this is not really adequate since it ignores the structure of the axioms, it is the best I can do at present.

Thanks to this distance-dilution effect, it seems a reasonable strategy to work on clusters more or less independently at first: the meaning of the tokens in a cluster is more tightly constrained by the structure of a cluster than by the links to other clusters. It seems reasonable therefore to introduce concepts, which occur definitively in some other cluster, fairly freely, assuming that their meaning is, or will be, reasonably tightly specified by that other cluster. For example, in considering liquids, I needed to be able to talk about volumetric shape: assuming – and, I now claim, reasonably – that a shape cluster would specify these for me. Of course, their occurrence in the liquids cluster *does* alter their meaning: our concept of a horizontal surface would hardly be complete if we had never seen a large, still body of water – but the assumption of a *fairly autonomous* theory of shape still seems reasonable.

What I am claiming here is, at bottom, that although the 'definitions' view of meaning is wrong, we can – indeed, must – act *as though* it were correct, in order to make progress. It is good methodological scaffolding.

One last point on the model-theoretic view of meaning. As I have said, any consistent first-order axiomatisation has a model in which there are only symbols. For all that the simplest such model may be very complex, one might feel that if all it contains are *symbols*, it hardly can be said to be like the real physical world, even if it is in some sense similar in 'abstract' structure.

To answer this objection, we have to talk about the body and sensory input. Imagine the naive-physics formalisation has a (physical) body with sense-organs. The way in which a formalisation can be attached to the physical world is by taking a 'realist' view of the data supplied to it by its perception. Thus, part of naive physics should be a theory of *appearance*: such a theory is now being developed by work in visual perception (especially the work of Marr and Horn, which consciously attempts to relate appearance to physical structure). While it may be that a detailed, hi-fi theory of wooden blocks could all be a dream: block-tokens might denote (say) integers in some models, for example: this would not be true if the theory also specified that if (to oversimplify) one directed one's gaze at a block with *such* a kind of surface, and *such* an orientation and in *such* a kind of lighting conditions, then one would see *such* a kind of image. For, an integer, or a symbol, is not the sort of thing one can direct one's gaze towards. (And, even if it were, in some outré sense, it certainly wouldn't look like a brick.) It might be objected: but you are *assuming* that the tokens for 'directing one's gaze' must denote the physical action of so doing, which begs the question: for there may be an interpretation of these tokens in a model of the integers, say, which also satisfies the axiomatisation. And yes, I am exactly begging the question: I assume that 'motor tokens' – symbols which describe bodily movements – are *directly* related to the body. They constitute a *body image** which has a very special relationship to the (actual) body (I imagine it to be similar to that between a graphic data structure and the physical picture on the screen).

What this assumption means, then, is that a naive physics can be 'connected' to the real physical world because it has a physical body, equipped with sense organs: the notion of *directing* one's gaze (or of *feeling*, or *pushing*, etc.) is *essentially* physical, and has this character because it has a fixed interpretation in the body's sensori-motor system. It is this fixed, physical interpretation of some of the tokens in an axiomatisation which attaches the axiomatisation as a whole must contain real, physical entities and relationships. In some sense, therefore, one would expect that most of the naive physics was 'close' to the visual-appearance (or touching-and-feeling or smelling or hearing) cluster(s) of concepts: that no part of naive physics is *very* remote from sensory evidence. And indeed, when elaborate theories are evolved in real physics, containing concepts which *are* inferentially remote from the evidence, there is usually a general feeling of mild disquiet. One hears talk of *theoretical entities*, for example, (electrons are a good example) in the philosophy-of-science literature. What these discussions seem to me often to lack is a strong enough sense of the way in which even everyday, mundane ideas such as a *piece of wood* or *being wet* are constructs just as theoretical, albeit in a different and more naive theory of the world.

A moral of this for naive physics is that we should be always ready to seize

*I am indebted to Sylvia Weir for introducing me to this notion.

on a chance to relate concepts to sensory or sensori-motor concepts. In working with liquids, for example, I found a notion of movement-in-space very useful: and it has obvious utility in other areas as well. This can be related directly to a visual-perception theory. If you look at a space in which there is movement, then the movement can be *seen*. Ullman (1977) explains in delightful detail how to see it. Again, much of the richness of texture of our introspective common-sense world comes, I think, from our knowledge of *what it feels like when we do things* like pushing, pulling, lifting: from, ultimately, the proprioceptive sensors in our body joints and muscles. I am *not* optimistic that we can capture this richness in a formalisation in the foreseeable future. (It requires the construction of a suitable physical body, equipped with the necessary senses.) But I think we *can* annotate the formalisation by noting the concepts which would be 'attached' to bodily-movement-concepts – and that this would be a useful and interesting exercise.

This whole area of psychosomatic relationships is one which deserves deeper study, and which I believe AI concepts can do much to clarify.

6. THOROUGHNESS AND CLOSURE

One way to have a high *a/c* ratio, it might seem, would be to keep *c* small, and to say a lot about a few concepts. And if this could be done, it would indeed be very useful and encouraging: if we could find some small, self-contained groups of concepts which could be formalised in total isolation to a reasonable degree of fidelity.

But there don't seem to be many of these. (Geometrical shape may be one.) The typical situation one finds is that, having chosen one's concepts to start on, one quickly needs to introduce tokens for others one had not contemplated: and in order to pin down *their* meanings, yet more concepts need to be introduced, and the proliferation of tokens seems to be getting out of hand. If one thinks of this as exploring the a-c graph of our conceptual structures, this phenomenon is of course, hardly surprising (especially if we assume, as we must, that the graph is very dense). One needs a sense of direction, to stay within the current cluster while recognising paths into others. But even with such a sense (which will only be developed with experience), the proliferation of necessary concepts seems almost frightening at first.

But this proliferation *must* slow down eventually: for the formalisation is finite. The point of the 'thoroughness' requirement is to *go on until it does slow down*: until one finds that the collection of concepts has closed upon itself. so that all the things one wants to say in the formalisation can be said using the tokens which have already been introduced. In the graphical analogy, until we have *spanned* the entire graph, and need only to add new arcs, filling out the graph until its density is sufficient to capture the meanings of its tokens.

This idea of closure is familiar to anyone who has built toy-world axiomatisations. One finds, suddenly, that there are enough concepts around so that one can say 'enough' about them all: enough, that is to enable the inferences that one had had in mind all along to be made. Closure can be achieved in very small formalisations: but if a formalisation is closed *and* has high fidelity (so, high density), then it must, I believe, also be thorough: its scope must cover *all* the major concepts of common-sense reasoning. This amounts to claiming that the a-c graph is fairly strongly connected: there are no really isolated subgraphs.

This correlation between thoroughness and fidelity is a matter of degree. To achieve greater fidelity, one will need greater thoroughness. To *really* capture the notion of 'above', it is probably not enough to stay even within naive physics: one would have to go into the various analogies to do with interpersonal status, for example. (Judge's seats are raised: Heaven is high, Hell is low: to express submission, lower yourself, etc.) Only a very *broad* theory can muster the power (*via* the Galois connection of model theory) to so constrain the meaning of the token 'above' that it fits to our concept *this* exactly. (Imagine a world in which the 'status' analogy was reversed, so that to be *below* someone was to be dominant and/or superior to them. That would be a possible model of naive physics, but not of the larger theory of common sense: and it would be a very different world from ours.) A formalisation cannot be deep without being broad, and must be deep to be dense: so a dense formalisation must be deep and broad.

Clusters are exactly partial closures in this sense. A cluster contains a group of concepts which close in on one another to *some* extent: one does need other concepts, but within the cluster there are a long of things to be said about the cluster's own concepts. Clustering is also, therefore, a matter of degree, and depends upon the fidelity, the level of detail.

The whole programme of tackling naive physics in isolation from other parts of common-sense is based on the view that there is a level of detail at which naive physics forms a reasonably close cluster in the larger conceptual structure, and that this is a rich but tractable level of detail: it represents, I believe, an order of magnitude more thoroughness than has yet been achieved; but not, say, ten orders of magnitude.

7. SOME LIKELY CLUSTERS AND THEIR CONCEPTS

In this section I sketch some concrete ideas for concept-clusters. These are only sketches, and vague ones at that: fuller accounts will appear elsewhere, eventually. I do not want to suggest that this is in any way an exhaustive list.

It is quite likely that many of these are not clusters in any real sense. They may, for example, split into pieces on closer investigation; or, new links may be revealed which blur the edges of the clusters. Nevertheless, they seem to me to be quite good places to start exploring.

7.1 Measuring Scales

We need to be able to express *quantities* such as size, extent, amount (of a liquid or powder), weight, viscosity, etc. These seem to be properties of things. But we can measure weight, for example, in pounds or in kilograms, so we have to introduce the notion of various measuring scales which measure the same physical quantity. We could have various functions from objects to (say) the rationals, called weight-in-lbs and weight-in-kilos, etc.: but this is awkward, unnatural and does not support a very dense collection of axioms. I think we should introduce a notion of an 'abstract space' of *weights (sizes, amounts),* so that *weight* is a function from objects to weights, and *lbs* (etc.) are functions from rationals to weights, and we can write:

weight (Fred) = pounds (150.32) = kilos (68.25)

These *measure spaces* of weights, sizes, etc. have, I think, a theory of their own. They probably have the structure of a tolerance space (Zeeman 1962), i.e. they have a finite 'grain'. They are notions of approximation, nearness, 'typical' measures of various kinds (normal-sized for an elephant), of inequalities, and of other related matters: and I guess much of this is independent of the particular quantity being measured.

One remark which may be apposite here is this. It is often argued that 'common sense' requires a different, fuzzy logic. The examples which are cited to support this view invariably involve fuzzy measuring scales or measure spaces. This, I believe, is where fuzziness may have a place: but that is *no* argument for fuzzy truth-values.

7.2 Shape, Orientation and Dimension

Physical 3-dimensional shape. This cluster is not much investigated, it seems to me, in spite of the considerable work in robot manipulator languages (cf. Bolles 1976). It is also related to topics in visual perception, and as there is more work here, this may be a good way into it. I wish there were more I could say about shape, but I can make only a few loose remarks.

For naive physics, vertical gravity is a constant fact of life, so vertical dimensions should be treated differently from horizontal dimensions: 'tall' and 'long' are different concepts. An object's shape is also often described differently when it is against a rigid surface (such as a wall) than when it is free-standing (width and length; or depth – from the wall – and width *or* length along the wall: width if one thinks of the object as being *put against* the wall, length if one thinks of it as *running along* the wall). I suspect – the details have not been worked out – that these differing collections of concepts arise from the reconciliation of various coordinate systems. A wall, for example, defines a natural coordinate system with a semi-axis along its normal.

An important aspect of shape is the relationship of surfaces to solids and edges to surfaces. The different names available for special cases indicates the richness of this cluster: top, bottom, side, rim, edge, lip, front, back, outline, end. Roget's thesaurus (class two, section two) supplies hundreds more. Again, these are *not* invariant under change of orientation, especially with respect to the gravity vertical. Such boundary concepts are also crucial in describing the shape of space, and are the basis of homology theory and differential geometry.

7.3 Inside and Outside

Consider the following collection of concepts: (inside), (outside), (door, portal, window, gate, way in, way out), (wall, boundary, container), (obstacle, barrier), (way past, way through).

I think these words hint at a cluster of related concepts which are of fundamental importance to naive physics. This cluster concerns the dividing up of 3-space into *pieces* which have physical boundaries, and the ways in which these pieces of space can be connected to one another; and how objects, people and liquids can get from one such *place* to another.

There are several reasons why I think this cluster is important. One is merely that it seems so, introspectively. Another is that these ideas, especially the idea of a *way through* and the things that can go wrong with it, seem widespread themes in folklore and legend, and support many common analogies. Another is that these ideas have cropped up fairly frequently in looking at other clusters, especially liquids and histories (see below). Another is that they are at the root of some important mathematics, viz. homotopy theory. But the main reason is that *containment limits causality*. One of the main reasons for being in a room is to isolate oneself from causal influences which are operating outside, or to prevent those inside the room from leaking out (respectively: to get out of the rain, to discuss a conspiracy). A good grasp of what kind of barriers are effective against what kinds of influence seem to be a centrally useful talent needed to be able to solve the 'frame problem'.

It is interesting to contrast these ideas with ideas of shape. Here, we are concerned with space as a place to be in: *room to move*, as it were; whereas in describing shape, space is *space occupied* by a substance. There are many concepts useful in both areas, however.

7.4 Histories: Describing Happenings

The now-classical approach to describing actions and change, pioneered by John McCarthy, is to use the concept of *state* or *situation*. This is thought of as a snapshot of the world at a given moment: actions and events are then functions from states to states. This framework of ideas is used even by many who deny that their formalism contains state variables, and has been consciously incorporated into several AI programming languages. I now think however, that it is a mistake or at least a gross over-simplification.

Consider the following example (which Rod Burstall showed me many years ago, but which I did not appreciate at the time). Two people in New York agree to meet a week later in London. Then they go their separate ways: one to Edinburgh, one to San Francisco. Each of them leads an eventful week, independently of the other, and they duly meet as arranged. In order to describe this using situations, we have to say what happens to each of them after every event that happens to the other: for each situation, being conceptually a state of the whole world, encompasses them both.

What we need is a notion of à state of an event which has a restricted spatial extent. By a *history* I mean such an object, viz. a connected piece of space-time, typically bounded on all four dimensions, in which 'something happens' (where I intend this to include the special case of nothing happening).

A three-dimensional spatial cross-section of a history is a place at a certain moment, i.e. a state of that place. Places can be larger or smaller, and can be nested inside one another: a room, a hotel, a street (understood as being the space inside all the buildings which open onto the street) and a city can all be places. A typical history will be, for example, the inside of a certain room from 1.00 p.m. until 4 p.m. on a certain afternoon. Space is, conceptually, made up of places, and space-time is made up of histories, fitted together in a jigsaw pattern. One can also think of a history as *the extension of* (an occurrence of) a process.

Any well-defined object or piece of space can be trivially extended into a history by multiplying it (in the algebraic direct-product sense) by a time-interval, but there are also somewhat less simple histories, such as trajectories, which 'slope' in space-time.

It is very useful to be able to refer to the *shape* of a history as well as of an object or piece of space. For example, a column of falling water (pouring from a jug, for example) defines a history, the shape of which is a vertical cylinder. The top and bottom of this cylinder are of some importance in relating this history to others in which liquid is moving.

Histories can be related to one another in various ways. There are *adjacency* relationships, both spatial (e.g. vertically-above and touching, as in a column of water falling onto a table-top) and temporal (e.g. immediately-following, as in touching a switch, thus starting a motor), and hybrid (as in a collision between aircraft, which is the intersection of two trajectories). There are shape properties and relative-position relationships between places and hence between histories. There are the spatial containment relationships similarly inherited from places and objects, and also temporal containment relationships ('while'). And there are relationships between histories and various global coordinate systems, both of space and of time: what we might call the *address* of a history. There are many possible addressing systems, not all being metric coordinate frames, e.g. room-numbering systems within a building. All of these define what might be called a naive geometry of space-time.

Not every patch of space counts as a well-defined place, and not every patch of space-time as a history. There have to be 'natural' boundaries defining the edges. What counts as a natural boundary is (deliberately) open-ended, but physical barriers are obvious examples, such as the walls of a room.

Since places can be nested (indeed, perhaps every place is *inside* some other place), every event is contained in many (perhaps infinitely many) histories. But for each type of event, there is a smallest which strictly contains it, viz. the smallest one which is spatially bounded by barriers which are opaque to the causal consequences of that sort of event. (*Roughly*, this place is the natural answer to the question 'where did (the event) happen?' (possible answers – in front of the desk; in the living room; in that house: in London)). The importance of this idea has already been mentioned: such barriers limit the extent to which causal consequences of events have to be pursued, and hence make prediction easier. One can predict, from a *static* description of the barrier-geometry, that various kinds of event can affect only a few histories. For example, only a restricted class of very unusual events taking place in a closed room (large explosions, flooding, large fires), can directly affect histories outside the room.

There are several other important increases in expressive and predictive power which histories give us, compared to the classical situations/actions ontology, but it would take too long to go into more detail here. A fuller account is in preparation.

7.5 Energy and Effort

In making predictions, there is a distinction which seems crucial between events which can 'just happen' (such as fallings) and events which require some effort or expenditure of energy (such as rocks flying through the air). The point being, of course, that if there is no effort being made in a given history, then the latter kind of event is ruled out.

Such a distinction runs counter to the law of conservation of energy, and I think quite correctly so for naive physics (or we could say merely that the intuitive concept of 'effort' does not exactly correspond to the physics notion of 'work'). There are many everyday situations where energy is expended with little apparent result. (Hitting a nail into a brick, for example).

I am not sure what else can be said about the concept of effort: perhaps that sources of effort have a finite capacity (they wear out or get tired). It may be that this is not so much a cluster as a concept which loosely links together a number of other clusters.

Agents can be sources of energy, but the two concepts are distinct, since some actions require no energy (speaking, for example), and there are sources of energy which have no volition. However, it may be that the two are equivalent notions within naive *physics*, and can only be distinguished by the use of 'psychological' concepts such as volition.

7.6 Assemblies

Many solid physical objects are made from parts assembled together in some way: while others are simply a piece of (some kind of) stuff, such as a block of wood. There are a number of concepts which are connected with this idea of an assembly: notions such as being a component of, being a part of (for example, one's hand is a part of one, but not a component: one's liver is (arguably) a component: it is, as it were, detachable), attachment point, assembling and taking apart; glueing, nailing, screwing, etc. . . There are also notions to do with the ways in which assembled parts can move relative to one another (shafts, pulleys, keyways, hinges), and these connect to the spatial-geometry concepts of shape and movement. And there are concepts to do with the mechanical properties of different kinds of stuff: rigidity, hardness, flexibility, being able to cut easily, being able to be glued, etc.

7.7 Support

Objects (or liquids) fall, if left to themselves. To stop them falling they must be supported. I think we can make a short list of all the ways in which a thing can be supported, as follows.

(a) Something is underneath it, holding it up. Of course, this must be supported too, and so on: but the *ground* does not require support: *it* is the bottom of all support relationships (from which it follows that the ground is not an object).

(b) Something is above it, and it is *hanging from* that thing.

(c) Something is alongside it, and it is *attached to* that thing (cf. assemblies).

(d) It is *floating* on some contained liquid.

(e) It is *flying*, i.e. holding itself up in some way, without touching anything solid. This requires great effort on the part of the flying object, so that inanimate, 'passive' objects cannot fly (although kites may be an exception).

Of these, (a) is by far the safest: in all the others, a failure of some component (respectively: a breaking (e.g. of string), a detaching, a leak, a cessation of effort: all of these are histories of one kind or another) which can mean the ending of the support and hence the sudden beginning of a falling history, and falling histories have dangerous endings (typically). Hence, there is a mini-cluster of concepts around the idea of 'support-from-below': notions such as pile, tower, wall, etc.: stability and the ways it can fail (falling over, crumbling, coming apart, sliding, subsidence).

7.8 Substances and Physical States

There are different kinds of *stuff*: iron, water, wood, meat, stone, sand, etc. And these exist in different kinds of *physical state*: solid, liquid, powder, paste, jelly (jello for U.S. readers), slime, paper-like, etc. Each kind of stuff has a *usual* state: iron is solid, water is liquid, sand is powder, etc., but this can sometimes be changed. For example, many stuffs will melt if you make them hot enough (which for some things is *very very* hot, i.e. *in practice* they can't be melted, e.g. sand; and others will *burn* when heated, e.g. wood or flour). Any liquid will freeze if you make it cold enough. Any solid *can* be powdered if you pulverise it with enough effort and determination, etc. There is no obvious standard way of changing a powder into a solid (but wetting it to get a paste, then drying the paste carefully, sometimes works).

Sometimes we have a separate concept for the same substance in two different states. Sand and rock are a good example. This is, I think, worthwhile when it is (a) extremely difficult to convert one to another, and (b) both occur in nature. (Contrast iron filings, which satisfies (a) but not (b).)

Some substances, left to themselves, *decompose*, i.e. change slowly into some other (useless) substance; or *mature*, i.e. change slowly into some other (useful) substance. Rusting and wet rot are examples of decomposition, cheese-making an example of maturation.

Every physical object which is not an assembly must be made of some stuff, and many of the properties of the object are in fact properties of the stuff of which it is made (rigidity, colour – unless it has been painted – hardness, etc.). It is, I think, important to separate these properties of a thing from those which are are essentially connected with the shape or structure of the thing. Some objects are essentially defined by one kind of property (a lump of lead), others by other (a building block). Properties such as *weight*, which involve both size and material, have different implications depending upon the kind of object: a heavy lump of lead is a big lump of lead, whereas a heavy building brick must be made of some especially dense material. Solid objects must be made of materials whose physical state is solid, for only solids can be said to have a shape. It follows that if a solid object is heated to the melting-point of the material of which it is made, it must cease to exist as an object, since the requisite state of its substance no longer obtains. This is, I think, a very convincing account of melting.

Cookery would seem to be a good area in which to explore the possible transitions between physical states of various semisolid substances, and manufacturing processes (moulding, casting, forging) another. I think the various methods of measuring amount and quantity might also be a useful area to explore. Wood and metal, for example, are wholesaled by weight or volume (basically), but retailed in various different systems depending upon the shape of the pieces (strip-like or surface-like or solid).

7.9 Forces and Movement

Naive physics is pre-Galilean. I can still vividly remember the intellectual shock of being taught Newtonian 'laws of motion' at the age of 11: how could something be moving if there was no force acting on it? It is interesting to read Galileo's "Dialogue Concerning the Principal Systems of the World" (1632), where he argues very convincingly, from everyday experiences, that Newton's first law must hold. But it takes a great deal of careful argument, and relies on the reader having some experience of smooth, polished surfaces and near perfect spheres. Another non-Newtonian intuition which every child has is that a released slingshot travels radially outwards, rather than tangentially. Other examples can be found.

If an object is moving, there are only five possibilities. It may be *falling*; or it may be being *pulled or pushed* by something; or it may be moving *itself* along, expending effort as it does so (and therefore cannot be a passive object), or it may be *sliding* (by which I mean to include sliding on a slippery surface or down a slippery slope); or it may be *rolling*, in which case it must either be or have rollers or wheels. The last two cases can keep on going for a while after all effort has ceased. (We would call this phenomenon *coasting*: a gesture to Galileo.) This list does not include rotary or oscillatory motions: it is meant to cover all movements in the sense of *change of position*.

I believe there may be actually two distinct ways of conceptualising motion: as a displacement or as a trajectory. Displacement motion requires effort, and when the effort stops the motion stops: and it is characteristically under constant servo-control relative to position, i.e. it is conceptualised as *change of position*. Trajectory motion has inertia, keeps going unless stopped, (when there is an impact), is characterised as smooth motion *along a path*. It requires effort to start up, to stop or to alter, but less effort, or no effort, to maintain. Examples are a thrown projectile, a car, sliding on ice, jumping. Displacement motion is Greek, trajectory motion is Galilean. Concepts such as aiming, impact, velocity (as a measure space), acceleration, are connected with the latter: concepts such as going, coming, dodging, avoiding, movement towards, away, are connected with the former. Both displacements and trajectories are histories, but the former are, essentially, merely transitions from their beginnings to their ends, which are positions of an object, whereas the latter have a definite *shape*: they can be extrapolated in time, for example, whence the concept of aiming. Falling, slidings, rollings and jumpings are examples of trajectories.

Forces can be transmitted in various ways. A rigid body can transmit a push, a string can transmit a pull. Luger and Bundy (1977) consider this mini-cluster in some detail.

7.10 Liquids

Liquid substances pose special problems, since, unlike pieces of solid stuff, 'pieces' of liquid are typically individuated *not* by being a particular piece of liquid, but by being in a particular *place* (a lake), or in some special relationship to a solid object (inside a cup). In Hayes 1978b I enlarge on an approach to solving these problems.

8. SOME STRUCTURED FORMALISATION TECHNIQUES

Constructing axiomatic formalisations which are 'heuristically adequate' (McCarthy & Hayes 1969) is an art, rather as writing good programs is an art. It is not yet very well developed (and indeed, one of the main aims of tackling naive physics is to gain skill in this relatively unexplored area), but a few stylistic points seem to be emerging.

One is the importance of *taxonomies*: finite exhaustive lists of the various types or categories of a kind of thing or of the possible states of a thing. We have seen these emerging already: ways of being supported, kinds of physical states, possible states of a fluid, (there are six: contained, flowing, spreading, wetting, falling or flying). In each case we have a group of axioms with the following form:

$$\phi(x) \equiv \phi_1(x) \vee \ldots \vee \phi_n(x)$$
$$\phi_1(x) \supset T_1$$
$$\vdots$$
$$\phi_n(x) \supset T_n$$

where the T_i are theories of what these particular cases are like. Such exhaustive lists can be very useful in making inferences, by a generalisation of the graphical consistency-checking computations widely used in vision (cf. Mackworth 1977). Intuitively, the iff ($\equiv$) means that if all but one of the disjuncts can be ruled out, then the remaining one must be the case. If the collection (T_i) of sub-theories is appropriately structured, then this can be a powerful technique for obtaining short proofs. For example, in the case of *support*, we can rapidly infer that if a passive thing is held up by a string (and that's all), and the string breaks, then it must fall: for there is nothing underneath (case 1), there is no liquid for it to float on (case 3), it isn't attached to anything (case 2), and it can't fly: so it must be supported. So (by the basic *support* axiom), it must fall (i.e. this moment is the beginning of a falling history). A similar way of arguing can be used to show that water which flows to the edge of a table will fall (rather than, say, keep going horizontally, or pile up at the edge).

It may be significant that such taxonomies have the syntactic form of a definition (of ϕ in terms of the ϕ_i), but do not serve the role of definitions since the 'defined' token already occurs elsewhere in the axiomatisation.

A second stylistic point concerns existence and comprehension axioms. As we pointed out earlier, axioms which establish the existence of entities are vital in a formalisation which is to have nontrivial models. Examples we have met include the spaces (places) defined by physical boundaries (rooms, insides of cups), or by various (metric *and* non-metric) coordinate systems, and the histories which ensue when various states obtain, e.g. the falling which inevitably follows a state in which an object is unsupported. In these, and no doubt other, cases, there will be *comprehension axioms* which assert the existence of the required entity, and its relationship to the entities already established (the space *between* the walls: or *behind* the door: the falling *after* (and below) the moment (and place) where the object loses its support, and so on).

The point I want to make here, however, is that these are all *restricted* comprehension axioms. We cannot take arbitrary pieces of 3-space or 4-space-time and treat them as individuals: only ones which are related in a describable way to entities we already have confidence in, as it were. This selectiveness in ontological commitment is one of the characteristic differences, I believe, between common-sense reasoning and 'hard' scientific or philosophical reasoning. Common sense's ontology is prolix – entities of all sorts, concrete and abstract (objects, materials, colours, spaces, times, histories, events,. . .) are used with scant concern for philosophical tidiness, little appeal to an underlying ontological simplicity (compare subatomic physics, for example, or even Chemistry's periodic table): and yet it is also very controlled: contrast Goodman's (1966) nominalism, or axiomatic set theory, or the comprehension axiom scheme of the typed λ-calculus. The effect of both of these differences is to give a far more richly structured collection of entities: *fewer* than in these 'uniform' formalisations, but of far more *sorts*, and with a much richer collection of *kinds of relationship* between them.

One further point here: the use of global metric coordinate frameworks essentially restores the unrestricted comprehension by the back door. For, by using suitable coordinates, we can describe *any* piece of 3-space (air traffic corridors, for example, which have no physical boundaries at all), or *any* piece of space-time or *any* piece of fluid (e.g. the cubic centimetre whose top north-east corner was 5 cm below the surface at such-and-such a place in a certain river, at 19:30:06.8 hours on the 24 May, 1962). The resulting ontological *freedom* and uniformity is probably one reason why coordinate systems are so useful in (real) science.

9. WHY IT NEEDS TO BE DONE

I take it as obvious that the construction of a program which can be said to have common sense must involve, ultimately, the formalisation and commonsense knowledge such as naive physics in some way or other (and also, of course, naive psychology, naive epistemology, etc.). While there are those who would disagree with this – those, for example, who believe that a simple uniform learning procedure might eventually exhibit intelligence – their pre-theoretical assumptions differ so much from those made by most AI workers that it is better, I think, to regard such work as belonging to an essentially different field. I shall, in any case, not discuss this particular issue further here.

There is real room for disagreement, however, on methodology. The most dominant view within AI seems to be that it is necessary to construct a 'complete' program in order to demonstrate that one's ideas on representation are feasible. Working systems which exhibit an impressive total behaviour are taken to be the ultimate criterion of success. So strong is this requirement, indeed, that in many centres it is difficult for a student to obtain a PhD unless he has implemented an impressive working program. The naive physics proposal, as outlined here, deliberately avoids the construction of such a complete program. Our aim is to construct a formalisation which defines a *heuristically adequate* search space of possible inferences. Questions of how, exactly, to search this space; of controlling an interpreter; of information retrieval and relevancy – what might be called computational questions – as well as questions of the choice of data structures; how to implement fast searches; the choice of programming language – what might be called implementational questions – all will be deliberately ignored.

Relatively few workers in AI are adopting a similar methodological position, and yet I believe that it is vital to adopt it, in order to make substantial progress on representational issues. McCarthy (1977) makes some similar arguments.

It is not just a question of diverting resources, although this is an important issue. The more fundamental reason is, that quick success in constructing a complete working program seems necessarily to involve making simplifications and restrictions which make it impossible to tackle the essential representation problems. This happens in two ways.

Firstly, to achieve success in making an AI performance program, one must choose the domain of the program very carefully indeed. To be tractable, it must be restricted in some way, usually fairly drastically. A standard style of restriction is to limit the scope of the program: a restricted subject-matter for a reasoning program, a restricted vocabulary for a micro-world for a natural-language program, a restricted range of see-able objects for a vision system, etc. It follows, then, that the representation needed by the program is one which is not particularly *thorough*, in the sense used earlier. Moreover, the representation often can (and often does) rely on this restricted scope in using techniques which work for small 'toy' worlds, but which are simply inapplicable to more thorough uses. I have noted several examples above.

Secondly, computationally effective representations tend to be of rather low density. There is a good reason for this: a dense representation necessarily defines a large and explosively expanding search space of possible inferences. *If* the only heuristic devices available for controlling an inferential search are weak and general (numerical) heuristics, depth-first search as in MICROPLANNER local procedure invocation as in KRL-0, etc.), then effective computational behaviour cannot be achieved with such a search space. But these weak, general methods are essentially the only ones we know: hence, to be computationally effective, we must have sparse representations.

These two pressures, then, taken together, encourage the construction of sparse representations of limited scope which are tailored carefully to the particular desired behavioural repertoire of the task domain chosen for the performance of the program. But, as I have argued, thoroughness and density are essential properties of a representation which can be said to capture the meaning of common-sense knowledge adequately.

This is a methodological point, but there is a closely related point concerned with adequacy. A popular view in AI is that only the adequate performance of a program can be a criterion of success of an AI theory. (Indeed, I suggest elsewhere (Hayes 1978d) that this criterion is exactly what distinguishes AI from 'information processing psychology'). Accepting this, it is only a small step to accepting a sort of behaviourist criterion of adequacy for a representation: viz, that it support an adequate behaviour in some performance program. This criterion would accept a sparse, limited representation over a dense, thorough one, given the present state of the implementer's art. If the program *works*, so the argument would go, then its representation must adequately capture the intended meanings: for that is what we *mean* by 'adequate'.

The problem with this position, at least in its simpler versions, is that it takes no account of scale effects. One cannot make a program which behaves adequately in a large 'world' by any simple process of adding together programs which perform adequately in a number of smaller sub-worlds of that world. At least, this is so far the everyday world of common-sense. The world just doesn't split up that neatly: one needs the interaction between the parts as well. Thus, a representation of, say, the blocks world which is adequate for reasoning merely about blocks, on this criterion, will be less adequate for reasoning about blocks in the context of liquids, strings, rods, friction, pulleys, etc. And the pressures just noted, towards tailoring representations of limited scope, militate against what might be called upward compatibility of formalisations. Thus, even accepting the criterion as an ultimate test of an AI theory, which I do, I would still argue that applying it too rigorously too soon (typically, after 3 years work) is self-defeating. *We are never going to get an adequate formalisation of common-sense by making short forays into small areas, no matter how many of them we make.*

It might be objected that if all this is true, then a dense, thorough formalisation *cannot* be part of an effective AI program. But this is false. I have argued that weak, general methods of control are unable to handle dense, thorough formalisations: clearly, we need more powerful control methods. There is one idea which I introduced in Hayes (1973) – see also Kowalski (1977), Pratt (1977), McDermott (1976), Davis (1976) – which suggests how to achieve the kind of power needed: to regard control not as a problem of defining a mechanism, but as itself a representational problem. We need to formalise the knowledge of *how* to make inferences, as well as the knowledge of the world which makes inferences possible. This meta-information can itself take part in the reasoning process, but also has a different and special relationship to the deductive interpreter: it describes its activity, rather than merely being grist for its mill. The development of formalisms, and associated interpreters, for expressing such meta-knowledge seems to me to be one of the most important tasks facing AI. But – and this is the crucial point for the present argument – the structures of both the formalisms and the meta-formalisations expressed in it, depend upon those of the world-knowledge formalism and the formalisations expressed in it. We cannot develop meta-formalisations in a vacuum (unless they be merely formalisations of the weak, general heuristics we already have); we must first have some realistically complex examples of common-sense formalisations, whose deductive properties will be described in the meta-formalisation.

10. WHY IT CAN BE DONE

A different objection to the naive physics proposal is that it is impossibly ambitious: that we don't know enough about formalisations to embark on such a large representational task; that it would take centuries, etc. Ultimately the only answer to such objections is to make the attempt and succeed, so all I can do here is to convey my reasons for feeling optimistic. There are four.

The first is based on my recent experiences in tackling the 'liquids' problem, which I have long believed was one of the most difficult problems in 'representation theory' (Hayes 1975). The idea of quantifying over pieces of space (defined by physical boundaries) rather than pieces of liquid, enables the major problems to be solved quite quickly, to my surprise. The key point here was finding the correct procedure for *individuating* a liquid object: the criterion by which one could refer to such a thing. I believe a similar concern for individuating criteria may well lead to progress in other clusters as well. McCarthy (private communication 1977) has, for example, begun a new approach to epistemic formalisations based on the individuation of 'concepts', i.e. thoughts in people's heads.

The second reason for optimism is the idea of histories outlined earlier. I believe that formalisations of the physical world have been hampered for years by an inadequate ontology for change and action, and that histories will provide a way round this major obstacle. The third reason is based on the no-programming methodology already discussed. To put it bluntly: hardly anybody has *tried* to build a large, heuristically adequate formalisation. We may find that, when we are freed from the necessity to implement performance programs, it is easier than we think.

The fourth reason is that there is an obvious methodology for getting it done, and this methodology has, in recent years, proved very successful in a number of areas.

11. HOW TO GET IT DONE

There is a tried and true way of getting knowledge out of people's heads and into a formalisation. Within AI, it has been called 'knowledge engineering' by Feigenbaum (1977); but essentially the same technique is used by linguists. It works as follows. In consultation with an 'expert' (i.e. a human being whose head contains knowledge: one knows it does because he is able to do the task one is interested in), one builds a preliminary formalisation, based upon his introspective account of what the knowledge in his head is. This formalisation then *performs* in a particular way, and its performance is compared with that of the expert. Typically it performs rather badly. The expert, observing this performance of the formalisation in detail, is often able to pinpoint more exactly the inadequacies in his first introspective account, and can offer a more detailed and corrected version. This is formalised, criticised and corrected: and so on. Typically, the expert, continually confronted with the formal consequencies of his introspections, becomes better at detailed introspection, as time goes by.

In 'knowledge engineering', the expert is a specialist of some kind, and the formalisation is, typically, a collection of condition-action rules which can be run on a suitable interpreter: a very modular program, in a sense. In linguistics, the formalisation is a grammar of some sort which assigns syntactic structures to sentences, and the expert is a native speaker: indeed, the expert is usually the linguist himself. In both areas, the technique has proven extremely successful.

I believe this process of formalisation, confrontation against intuition, and correction, can also be used to develop naive physics. Here is a domain in which we are all experts, in the required sense. The *performance* of a formalisation is, here, the pattern of inferences which it supports. Performance is adequate when the 'experts' agree that all and only the immediate, plausible consequences follow from the axioms of the formalisation. (In fact, this is a weak notion of adequacy: the stronger notion would be that the *derivations* of the plausible consequences were also plausible. Attempting to use this stronger notion gives rise to severe methodological problems, since it requires one to have '2nd order' introspections. Linguistics has an exactly analogous notion of strong adequacy for a grammatical theory, and suffers exactly similar methodological difficulties.) It seems to be sound to have several 'experts' involved, as it is easy to miss some obvious distinctions when working alone.

The ideal way to make progress is to have a committee. Each member is assigned what seems to be a cluster, and has to try to formalise it. They tell one another what they require from the other clusters: thus the 'histories' cluster will need some 'shape' concepts, and the 'assemblies' cluster will need some 'histories' concepts, and so on. Fairly frequently, the fragmentary formalisations are put together at a group meeting, criticised by other members (in their common-sense 'expert' role), and tested for adequacy. I will anticipate that some clusters will dissolve, and new ones will emerge, during these assembly meetings.

Initially, the formalisations need be little more than carefully-worded English sentences. One can make considerable progress on ontological issues, for example, without actually *formalising* anything. Fairly soon, however, it will be necessary to express the intuitions formally. Here, I think one should be liberal in allowing a free choice of formal language. Many people find frame-like notations agreeable: others like semantic networks, etc. There is no reason why such superficial variants of first-order logic, or even more exotic formalisms, should be banned: the only important requirement is that the inferential relationships between the various formalisms should be made explicit. In practice, this means that they should all be translatable into predicate calculus: but this is no problem, since they all are. A more serious point is that particular clusters may suggest special ad-hoc representations. Shapes may be represented diagrammatically, for example. One can imagine a cluster, represented in some idiosyncratic way, whose internal inferential relationships were inaccessible from outside, but which was interfaced to the rest of the formalisation by a defined translation of part of itself into the reference formalisation (first-order logic): say statements of relative position and orientation. It will be difficult to prevent such things happening, and maybe one should not try. But there are grave dangers, since this way of proceeding prejudges the possible interactions in the formalisation as a whole, and this may encapsulate a serious mistake in a way which will be hard to detect and even harder to rectify.

There are several other ways to find concept-clusters. For example: looking in a thesaurus; choosing a particular domain (cookery, volumetric measurements of various substances) and attempting to describe it; analysing some everyday act in detail (e.g. spreading a sheet over a bed by holding two corners and flicking: why does that work?). I expect these, and others, will be useful starting-points.

12. IS THIS SCIENCE?

It will be objected that to attempt to formalise knowledge in the abstract, i.e. divorced from particular sensory modality or task domain, is unscientific because there are no clear criteria of success or failure. What would it be like to fail? If this question cannot be answered, then naive physics is mere literary criticism.

I think this objection is well taken and needs a more adequate reply than I am currently able to give. The point is, that one can always get *somewhere* with a formalisation: who is to say that where one has got to is not far enough? One can only say, I think, that people's common intuition is the guide. If there are some 'obvious' physical facts which cannot be made to follow 'easily' or 'naturally' from the axioms, then more work has to be done. One can apply the usual scientific judgements of 'elegance', 'economy', etc. to compare rival formalisations. (All the quoted words cry out for further discussion, which I will not attempt here.) It is worth remarking that linguistics is in *exactly* the same position, and regularly squirms on the methodological hook: judgements of physical plausibility and elementary causality are certainly as reliable as judgements of grammaticality by native speakers; and indeed are largely independent of cultural and linguistic boundaries, so are probably rather more reliable as source data. (Which may suggest that we should borrow the competence/performance distinction to protect ourselves from behavioural refutation: but there are deep problems indeed about trying *that* trick.)

It would be nice if naive physics could be linked more closely with the mass of data now available in Piagetian psychology on the development of physical concepts during childhood (although none of this is uncontroversial, it seems). Certainly, *compatibility* with this data should be a constraint on naive-physics formalisation. It is however a very weak constraint, since the data is compatible with many different developmental theories, and is not usually sufficiently detailed to distinguish one from another (see Prazdny 1978 for some comments in this direction). I would hope that the construction of a naive physics might show up some new mechanism of developmental change in conceptual frameworks. To some extent this is happening already, since building a formalisation is often a matter of *developing* (in exactly the right sense) the partial formalisations one already has.

ACKNOWLEDGEMENTS

This paper was written during a sabbatical visit to the Institut pour les etudes sémantiques et cognitives, Geneva. I am grateful to the Directrice, Mme M. King, for inviting me there; and to all members of the Thursday seminar, especially Maghi King, Giussepe Trautteur and Henri Wermus. Conversations with Mimi Sinclair on Piagetian research were also of great help. My wife, Jackie, typed several drafts of the manuscript and was an unfailing source of reliable, sound, common-sense intuitions.

REFERENCES

ANDERSON et al., 1972. Beyond Leibnitz. *Memo AIM*, Stanford Artificial Intelligence Project.

BINFORD et al., 1976. Computer Integrated Assembly Systems. *MEMO AIM-285,* Stanford Artificial Intelligence Project.

BOLLES, 1976. Verification Vision within a Programmable Assembly System. Stanford AI Memo No. 295, 1976.

BUNDY, 1978. Exploiting the Properties of Functions to Control Search. (To appear.)

DAVIS, 1976. Applications of Meta-level Knowledge to the Construction, Maintenance and Use of large Knowledge Bases. *HPP MEMO 76-7*, Stanford University.

FEIGENBAUM, 1977. Themes and Case Studies of Knowledge Engineering. *Proc. 5th IJCAI Conference*, M.I.T.

GOODMAN, 1966. The Structure of Appearance. New York, Bobs-Merrill Co.

HAYES, 1971. A Logic of Actions. *Machine Intelligence 6*, Edinburgh University Press.

HAYES, 1973. Computation and Deducation. *Proc. 2nd MFCS Sympsoium, Czechoslovakian* Academy of Sciences.

HAYES, 1975. Problems and Non-problems in Representation Theory. *Proc. 1st AISB Conference*, Sussex University.

HAYES, 1977. In Defense of Logic. *Proc. 5th IJCAI Conference*, M.I.T.

HAYES, 1978a. The Logic of Frames. *The Frame Reader.* (To be published by De Gruyter, Berlin.)

HAYES, 1978b. Naive Physics: Ontology of Liquids. *Working Paper 35*, Institute for Semantic and Cognitive Studies, Geneva.
HAYES, 1978c. Naive Physics II: Histories. (In preparation.)
HAYES, 1978d. On the Difference between Psychology and Artificial Intelligence. *AISB Bulletin*. To appear.
KOWALSKI, 1977. Algorithm = Logic + Control. Memorandum, Imperial College, London.
LANDIN, 1970. A Program-Machine Symmetric Automata Theory. *Machine Intelligence 5*, Edinburgh University press.
LUGER & BUNDY, 1977. Representing Semantic Information in Pulley Problems, *Proc. 5th IJCAI Conference*, M.I.T.
MACKWORTH, 1977. Consistency in Networks of Relations. *Artificial Intelligence, 8.*
McCARTHY & HAYES, 1969. Some Philosophical Problems from the Standpoint of Artificial Intelligence. *Machine Intelligence 4*, Edinburgh University Press.
McCARTHY, 1977. Epistemological Problems of Artificial Intelligence. *Proc. 5th IJCAI Conference*, M.I.T.
McDERMOTT, 1976. Flexibility and Efficiency in a Computer Program for Designing Circuits. *PhD thesis*, MIT Artificial Intelligence Lab.
McDERMOTT, 1977. Artificial Intelligence and Natural Stupidity. *SIGART Newsletter*.
PRATT, 1977. The Competence-Performance Distinction in Programming. *Proc. 4th ACM Symposium on Principles of Programming Languages*, Los Angeles.
PRAZDNY, 1978. Stage two ofthe Object Concept Development: a Computational Study. *Memorandum*, Essex University.
SCHANK, 1975. Conceptual Information Processing. North-Holland.
ULLMAN, 1977. The Interpretation of Visual Motion. *PhD thesis*, M.I.T.
WILKS, 1975. A Preferential, Pattern-Matching Semantics for Natural Language Understanding. *Artificial Intelligence, 6.*
WILKS, 1977. Good and Bad Arguments about Semantic Primitives. *Memo 42*, Artificial Intelligence Dept., Edinburgh University.
WINOGRAD, 1972. Understanding Natural Language. Edinburgh University Press.
ZEEMAN, 1962. The Topology of the Brain and Visual Perception. *Topology of 3-Manifolds* (ed. K. Fort), Prentice-Hall.

FIRST-ORDER THEORIES OF INDIVIDUAL CONCEPTS AND PROPOSITIONS

J. McCarthy

ABSTRACT

We discuss first-order theories in which *individual concepts* are admitted as mathematical objects along with the things that *reify* them. This allows very straightforward formalizations of knowledge, belief, wanting, and necessity in ordinary first-order logic without modal operators. Applications are given in philosophy and in artificial intelligence. We do not treat general concepts, and we do not present any full axiomatizations but rather show how various facts can be expressed.

INTRODUCTION

'. . . it seems that hardly anybody proposes to use different variables for propositions and for truth-values, or different variables for individuals and individual concepts' (Carnap 1956, p.113).

Admitting individual concepts as objects – with concept-valued constants, variables, functions and expressions – allows ordinary first order theories of necessity, knowledge, belief and wanting without modal operators or quotation marks and without the restrictions on substituting equals for equals that either device makes necessary.

In this paper we will show how various individual concepts and propositions can be expressed. We are not yet ready to present a full collection of axioms. Moreover, our purpose is not to explicate what concepts are, in a philosophical sense, but rather to develop a language of concepts for representing facts about knowledge, belief, etc. in the memory of a computer.

Frege (1892) discussed the need to distinguish direct and indirect use of words. According to one interpretation of Frege's ideas, the meaning of the phrase "*Mike's telephone number*" in the sentence "*Pat knows Mike's telephone number*" is the concept of Mike's telephone number, whereas its meaning in the sentence "*Pat dialled Mike's telephone number*" is the number itself. Thus if we also have "*Mary's telephone number = Mike's telephone number*", then "*Pat dialled Mary's telephone number*" follows, but "*Pat knows Mary's telephone number*" does not.

It was further proposed that a phrase has a *sense* which is a *concept* and is its *meaning* in *oblique contexts* like knowing and wanting, and a *denotation* which is its *meaning* in *direct contexts* like dialling. *Denotations* are the basis of the semantics of first-order logic and model theory and are well understood, but *sense* has given more trouble, and the modal treatment of oblique contexts avoids the idea. On the other hand, logicians such as Carnap (1947 and 1956), Church (1951) and Montague (1974) see a need for *concepts* and have proposed formalizations. All these formalizations involve modifying the logic used; ours doesn't modify the logic and is more powerful, because it includes mappings from objects to concepts. Robert Moore's forthcoming dissertation also uses concepts in first-order logic.

The problem identified by Frege – of suitably limiting the application of the substitutivity of equals for equals – arises in artificial intelligence as well as in philosophy and linguistics for any system that must represent information about beliefs, knowledge, desires, or logical necessity – regardless of whether the representation is declarative or procedural (as in PLANNER and other AI formalisms).

Our approach involves treating concepts as one kind of object in an ordinary first order theory. We shall have one term that denotes Mike's telephone number and a different term denoting the concept of Mike's telephone number instead of having a single term whose denotation is the number and whose sense is a concept of it. The relations among concepts and between concepts and other entities are expressed by formulas of first-order logic. Ordinary model theory can then be used to study what spaces of concepts satisfy various sets of axioms.

We treat primarily what Carnap calls *individual concepts* like *Mike's telephone number* or *Pegasus* and not general concepts like *telephone* or *unicorn*. Extension to general concepts seems feasible, but individual concepts provide enough food for thought for the present.

This is a preliminary paper in that we don't give a comprehensive set of axioms for concepts. Instead we merely translate some English sentences into our formalism to give an idea of the possibilities.

KNOWING WHAT AND KNOWING THAT

To assert that Pat knows Mike's telephone number we write

true Know(Pat, Telephone Mike) (1)

with the following conventions:

1. Parentheses are often omitted for one-argument functions and predicates. This purely syntactic convention is not important. Another convention is to capitalize the first letter of a constant, variable, or function name when its value is a concept. (We considered also capitalizing the last letter when the arguments are concepts, but it made the formulas ugly.)
2. *Mike* is the concept of Mike; that is, it is the *sense* of the expression "*Mike*". *mike* is Mike himself.
3. *Telephone* is a function that takes a concept of a person into a concept of his telephone number. We will also use *telephone* which takes the person himself into the telephone number itself. We do not propose to identify the function *Telephone* with the general concept of a person's telephone number.
4. If *P* is a person concept and *X* is another concept, then *Know(P, X)* is an assertion concept or *proposition* meaning that *P knows* the value of *X*. Thus in (1) *Know(Pat, Telephone Mike)* is a proposition and not a truth value. Note that we are formalizing *knowing what* rather than *knowing that* or *knowing how*. For AI and for other practical purposes,

knowing what seems to be the most useful notion of the three. In English, *knowing what* is written *knowing whether* when the "knowand" is a proposition.

5. It is often convenient to write *know(pat, Telephone Mike)* instead of *true Know(Pat, Telephone Mike)* when we don't intend to iterate knowledge further. *know* is a predicate in the logic, so we cannot apply any knowledge operators to it. We will have

   know(pat, Telephone Mike) ≡ *true Know(Pat, Telephone Mike)*. (2)

6. We expect that the proposition *Know(Pat, Telephone Mike)* will be useful accompanied by axioms that allow inferring that Pat will use this knowledge under appropriate circumstances, that is, he will dial it or retell it when appropriate. There will also be axioms asserting that he will know it after being told it or looking it up in the telephone book.
7. While the sentence "*Pat knows Mike*" is in common use, it is harder to see how *Know(Pat, Mike)* is to be used and axiomatized. I suspect that new methods will be required to treat knowing a person.
8. *true Q* is the truth value, *t* or *f*, of the proposition *Q*, and we must write *true Q* in order to assert *Q*. Later we will consider formalisms in which *true* has another argument – a *situation*, a *story*, a *possible world*, or even a *partial possible world* (a notion we suspect will eventually be found necessary).
9. The formulas are in a sorted first-order logic with functions and equality. Knowledge, necessity, etc. will be discussed without extending the logic in any way – solely by the introduction of predicate and function symbols subject to suitable axioms. In the present informal treatment, we will not be explicit about sorts, but we will use different letters for variables of different sorts.

The reader may be nervous about what is meant by *concept*. He will have to remain nervous; no final commitment will be made in this paper. The formalism is compatible with many possibilities, and these can be compared by using the models of their first-order theories. Actually, this paper isn't much motivated by the philosophical question of what concepts really are. The goal is more to make a formal structure that can be used to represent facts about knowledge and belief so that a computer program can reason about who has what knowledge in order to solve problems. From either the philosophical or the AI point of view, however, if (1) is to be reasonable, it must not follow from (1) and the fact that Mary's telephone number is the same as Mike's, that Pat knows Mary's telephone number.

The proposition that Joe knows *whether* Pat knows Mike's telephone number, is written

Know(Joe, Know(Pat, Telephone Mike)), (3)

and asserting it requires writing

true Know(Joe, Know(Pat, Telephone Mike)), (4)

while the proposition that Joe knows *that* Pat knows Mike's telephone number is written

$K(Joe, Know(Pat, Telephone\ Mike)),$ (5)

where $K(P, Q)$ is the proposition that P knows *that* Q. English does not treat knowing a proposition and knowing an individual concept uniformly: knowing an individual concept means knowing its value, while knowing a proposition means knowing that it has a particular value, namely t. There is no reason to impose this infirmity on robots.

We first consider systems in which corresponding to each concept X, there is a thing x of which X is a concept. Then there is a function *denot* such that

$$x = denot\ X. \tag{6}$$

Functions like *Telephone* are then related to *denot* by equations like

$$\forall P1\ P2.(denot\ P1 = denot\ P2 \supset denot\ Telephone\ P1 = denot\ Telephone\ P2). \tag{7}$$

We call *denot X* the *denotation* of the concept X, and (7) asserts that the denotation of the concept of P's telephone number depends only on the denotation of the concept P. The variables in (7) range over concepts of persons, and we regard (7) as asserting that *Telephone* is *extensional* with respect to *denot*. Note that our *denot* operates on concepts rather than on expressions; a theory of expressions will also need a denotation function. From (7) and suitable logical axioms follows the existence of a function *telephone* satisfying

$$\forall P.(denot\ Telephone\ P = telephone\ denot\ P). \tag{8}$$

Know is extensional with respect to *denot* in its first argument, and this is expressed by

$$\forall P1\ P2\ X.(denot\ P1 = denot\ P2 \supset denot\ Know(P1, X) = denot\ Know(P2, X)), \tag{9}$$

but it is not extensional in its second argument. We can therefore define a predicate $know(p, X)$ satisfying

$$\forall P\ X.(true\ Know(P, X) \equiv know(denot\ P, X)). \tag{10}$$

(Note that all these predicates and functions are entirely extensional in the underlying logic, and the notion of extensionality presented here is relative to *denot*.)

The predicate *true* and the function *denot* are related by

$$\forall Q.(true\ Q \equiv (denot\ Q = t)) \tag{11}$$

provided that truth values are in the range of *denot*, and *denot* could also be provided with a (*partial*) *possible world* argument.

When we don't assume that all concepts have denotations, we use a predicate $denotes(X, x)$ instead of a function. The extensionality of *Telephone* would then be written

$$\forall P1\ P2\ x\ u.(denotes(P1, x) \wedge denotes(P2, x) \wedge denotes(Telephone\ P1, u) \supset denotes(Telephone\ P2, u)) \tag{12}$$

We now introduce the function *Exists* satisfying

$$\forall X.(true\ Exists\ X \equiv \exists x.denotes(X, x)). \tag{13}$$

Suppose we want to assert that Pegasus is a horse without asserting that Pegasus exists. We can do this by introducing the predicate *Ishorse* and writing

$$true\ Ishorse\ Pegasus \tag{14}$$

which is related to the predicate *ishorse* by

$$\forall X\, x.(denotes(X, x) \supset (ishorse\ x \equiv true\ Ishorse\ X)). \tag{15}$$

In this way, we assert extensionality without assuming that all concepts have denotations. *Exists* is extensional in this sense, but the corresponding predicate *exists* is identically true and therefore dispensable.

To combine concepts propositionally, we need analogs of the propositional operators such as *And*, which we shall write as an infix and axiomatize by

$$\forall Q1\ Q2.(true(Q1\ And\ Q2) \equiv true\ Q1 \wedge true\ Q2). \tag{16}$$

The corresponding formulas for *Or, Not, Implies,* and *Equiv* are

$$\forall Q1\ Q2.(true(Q1\ Or\ Q2) \equiv true\ Q1 \vee true\ Q2), \tag{17}$$

$$\forall Q.(true(Not\ Q) \equiv \neg\, true\ Q), \tag{18}$$

$$\forall Q1\ Q2.(true(Q1\ Implies\ Q2) \equiv true\ Q1 \supset true\ Q2), \tag{19}$$

and

$$\forall Q1\ Q2.(true(Q1\ Equiv\ Q2) \equiv (true\ Q1 \equiv true\ Q2)). \tag{20}$$

The equality symbol "=" is part of the logic so that $X = Y$ asserts that X and Y are the same concept. To write propositions expressing equality, we introduce *Equal*(X, Y) which is a proposition that X and Y denote the same thing if anything. We shall want axioms

$$\forall X.true\ Equal(X, X), \tag{21}$$

$$\forall X\ Y.(true\ Equal(X, Y) \equiv true\ Equal(Y, X)), \tag{22}$$

and

$$\forall X\ Y\ Z.(true\ Equal(X, Y) \wedge true\ Equal(Y, Z) \supset true\ Equal(X, Z) \tag{23}$$

making *true Equal*(X, Y) an equivalence relation, and

$$\forall X\ Y\ x.(true\ Equal(X, Y) \wedge denotes(X, x) \supset denotes(Y, x)) \tag{24}$$

which relates it to equality in the logic. We can make the concept of equality *essentially* symmetric by replacing (22) by

$$\forall X\ Y.Equal(X, Y) = Equal(Y, X), \tag{25}$$

that is, making the two expressions denote the *same concept*.

The statement that Mary has the same telephone number as Mike is asserted by

$$true\ Equal(Telephone\ Mary, Telephone\ Mike), \tag{26}$$

and it obviously doesn't follow from this and (1) that

$$true\ Know(Pat, Telephone\ Mary). \tag{27}$$

To draw this conclusion we need something like

$$true\ K(Pat, Equal(Telephone\ Mary, Telephone\ Mike)) \tag{28}$$

and suitable axioms about knowledge.

If we were to adopt the convention that a proposition appearing at the outer level of a sentence is asserted and were to regard the denotation-valued function as standing for the sense-valued function when it appears as the second argument of *Know*, we would have a notation that resembles ordinary language in handling obliquity entirely by context. There is no guarantee that general statements could be expressed unambiguously without circumlocution; the fact that the principles of intensional reasoning haven't yet been stated is evidence against the suitability of ordinary language for stating them.

FUNCTIONS FROM THINGS TO CONCEPTS OF THEM

While the relation *denotes*(*X, x*) between concepts and things is many-one, functions going from things to certain concepts of them seem useful. Some things such as numbers can be regarded as having *standard* concepts. Suppose that *Concept*1 *n* gives a standard concept of the number *n*, so that

$$\forall n.(denot\ Concept1\ n = n). \tag{29}$$

We can then have simultaneously

true Not Knew(*Kepler, Composite Number Planets*) (30)

and

true Knew(*Kepler, Composite Concept*1 *denot Number Planets*). (31)

(We have used *Knew* instead of *Know*, because we are not now concerned with formalizing tense.)

(31) can be condensed using *Composite*1 which takes a number into the proposition that it is composite, that is,

*Composite*1 *n* = *Composite Concept*1 *n* (32)

getting

true Knew(*Kepler, Composite*1 *denot Number Planets*). (33)

A further condensation can be achieved by using *Composite*2 defined by

*Composite*2 *N* = *Composite Concept*1 *denot N*, (34)

letting us write

true Knew(*Kepler, Composite*2 *Number Planets*), (35)

which is true even though

true Knew(*Kepler, Composite Number Planets*) (36)

is false. (36) is our formal expression of "*Kepler knew that the number of planets is composite*", while (31), (33), and (35) each expresses a proposition that can only be stated awkwardly in English, for example, as "*Kepler knew that a certain number is composite, where this number (perhaps unbeknownst to Kepler) is the number of planets*".

We may also want a map from things to concepts of them in order to formalize a sentence like, "*Lassie knows the location of all her puppies*". We write this

$\forall x.(ispuppy(x, lassie) \supset$
$\quad true\ Knowd(Lassie, Locationed\ Conceptd\ x)).$ (37)

Here *Conceptd* takes a puppy into a dog's concept of it, and *Locationd* takes a dog's concept of a puppy into a dog's concept of its location. The axioms satisfied by *Knowd, Locationd* and *Conceptd* can be tailored to our ideas of what dogs know.

A suitable collection of functions from things to concepts might permit a language that omitted some individual concepts like *Mike* (replacing it with *Conceptx mike*) and wrote many sentences with quantifiers over things rather than over concepts. However, it is still premature to apply Occam's razor. It may be possible to avoid concepts as objects in expressing particular facts but impossible to avoid them in stating general principles.

RELATIONS BETWEEN KNOWING WHAT AND KNOWING THAT

As mentioned before, "*Pat knows Mike's telephone number*" is written

$$true\ Know(Pat,\ Telephone\ Mike). \qquad (38)$$

We can write "*Pat knows Mike's telephone number is* 333-3333"

$$true\ K(Pat,\ Equal(Telephone\ Mike,\ Concept1\ \text{"333-3333"})) \qquad (39)$$

where $K(P, Q)$ is the proposition that $denot(P)$ knows the proposition Q and $Concept1$("333-3333") is some standard concept of that telephone number.

The two ways of expressing knowledge are somewhat interdefinable, since we can write

$$K(P, Q) = (Q\ And\ Know(P, Q)), \qquad (40)$$

and

$$true\ Know(P, X) \equiv \exists A.(constant\ A \wedge true\ K(P, Equal(X, A))). \qquad (41)$$

Here *constant* A asserts that A is a constant, that is, a concept such that we are willing to say that P knows X if he knows it equals A. This is clear enough for some domains like integers, but it is not obvious how to treat knowing a person.

Using the *standard concept* function $Concept1$, we might replace (41) by

$$true\ Know(P, X) \equiv \exists a.true\ K(P, Equal(X, Concept1\ a)) \qquad (42)$$

with similar meaning.

(41) and (42) express a *denotational* definition of *Know* in terms of K. A *conceptual* definition seems to require something like

$$\forall P\ X.(Know(P, X) =$$
$$Exists\ X\ And\ K(P, Equal(X, Concept2\ denot\ X))), \qquad (43)$$

where $Concept2$ is a suitable function from things to concepts and may not be available for all sorts of objects.

REPLACING MODAL OPERATORS BY MODAL FUNCTIONS

Using concepts we can translate the content of modal logic into ordinary logic. We need only replace the modal operators by *modal functions*. The axioms of modal logic then translate into ordinary first order axioms. In this section we will treat only *unquantified modal logic*. The arguments of the modal functions will not involve quantification, although quantification occurs in the outer logic.

Nec Q is the proposition that the proposition Q is necessary, and *Poss* Q is the proposition that it is possible. To assert necessity or possibility we must write *true Nec* Q or *true Poss* Q. This can be abbreviated by defining *nec* $Q \equiv$ *true Nec* Q and *poss* Q correspondingly. However, since *nec* is a predicate in the logic with t and f as values, *nec* Q cannot be an argument of *nec* or *Nec*.

Before we even get to modal logic proper we have a decision to make – shall *Not Not* Q be considered the same proposition as Q, or is it merely extensionally equivalent? The first is written

$$\forall Q.Not\ Not\ Q = Q. \qquad (44)$$

and the second

$$\forall Q.true\ Not\ Not\ Q \equiv true\ Q. \qquad (45)$$

The second follows from the first by substitution of equals for equals.

In *Meaning and Necessity*, Carnap takes what amounts to the first alternative, regarding concepts as L-equivalence classes of expressions. This works nicely for discussing necessity, but when he wants to discuss knowledge without assuming that everyone knows Fermat's last theorem if it is true, he introduces the notion of *intensional isomorphism* and has knowledge operate on the equivalence classes of this relation.

If we choose the first alternative, then we may go on to identify any two propositions that can be transformed into each other by Boolean identities. This can be assured by a small collection of propositional identities like (44) including associative and distributive laws for conjunction and disjunction, De Morgan's law, and the laws governing the propositions T and F. In the second alternative we will want the extensional forms of the same laws. When we get to quantification a similar choice will arise, but if we choose the first alternative, it will be undecidable whether two expressions denote the same concept. I doubt that considerations of linguistic usage or usefulness in AI will unequivocally recommend one alternative, so both will have to be studied.

Actually there are more than two alternatives. Let M be the free algebra built up from the "atomic" concepts by the concept-forming function symbols. If $\equiv\equiv$ is an equivalence relation on M such that

$$\forall X1\ X2 \in M.((X1 \equiv\equiv X2) \supset (true\ X1 \equiv true\ X2)), \tag{46}$$

then the set of equivalence classes under $\equiv\equiv$ may be taken as the set of concepts.

Similar possibilities arise in modal logic. We can choose between the *conceptual identity*

$$\forall Q.(Poss\ Q = Not\ Nec\ Not\ Q), \tag{47}$$

and the weaker extensional axiom

$$\forall Q.(true\ Poss\ Q \equiv true\ Not\ Nec\ Not\ Q). \tag{48}$$

We will write the rest of our modal axioms in extensional form.

We have

$$\forall Q.(true\ Nec\ Q \supset true\ Q) \tag{49}$$

and

$$\forall Q1\ Q2. \quad (true\ Nec\ Q1 \wedge true\ Nec(Q1\ Implies\ Q2) \supset true\ Nec\ Q2). \tag{50}$$

yielding a system equivalent to von Wright's T.

S4 is given by

$$\forall Q.(true\ Nec\ Q \equiv true\ Nec\ Nec\ Q), \tag{51}$$

and S5 by

$$\forall Q.(true\ Poss\ Q \equiv true\ Nec\ Poss\ Q). \tag{52}$$

Actually, there may be no need to commit ourselves to a particular modal system. We can simultaneously have the functions *NecT*, *Nec*4 and *Nec*5, related by axioms such as

$$\forall Q.(true\ Nec4\ Q \supset true\ Nec5\ Q) \tag{53}$$

which would seem plausible if we regard S4 as corresponding to provability in some system and S5 as truth in the intended model of the system.

Presumably we shall want to relate necessity and equality by the axiom

$$\forall X. true\ Nec\ Equal(X, X). \tag{54}$$

Certain of Carnap's proposals translate to the stronger relation

$\forall X\, Y.(X = Y \equiv true\ Nec\ Equal(X, Y))$ (55)

which asserts that two concepts are the same if and only if the equality of what they may denote is necessary.

MORE PHILOSOPHICAL EXAMPLES – MOSTLY WELL KNOWN

Some sentences that recur as examples in the philosophical literature will be expressed in our notation, so the treatments can be compared.

First we have "*The number of planets* = 9" and "*Necessarily* 9 = 9" from which one doesn't want to deduce "*Necessarily the number of planets* = 9". This example is discussed by Quine (1961) and Kaplan (1969). Consider the sentences

$\neg\, nec\ Equal(Number\ Planets, Concept1\ 9)$ (56)

and

$nec\ Equal(Concept1\ number\ planets, Concept1\ 9).$ (57)

Both are true. (56) asserts that it is not necessary that the number of planets be 9, and (57) asserts that the number of planets, once determined, is the number that is necessarily equal to 9. It is a major virtue of our formalism that both meanings can be expressed and are readily distinguished. Substitutivity of equals holds in the logic but causes no trouble, because "*The number of planets* = 9" may be written

$number(planets) = 9$ (58)

or, using concepts as

$true\ Equal(Number\ Planets, Concepts1\ 9),$ (59)

and "*Necessarily* 9 = 9" is written

$nec\ Equal(Concept\ 1\ 9, Concept1\ 9),$ (60)

and these don't yield the unwanted conclusion.

Ryle used the sentences "*Baldwin is a statesman*" and "*Pickwick is a fiction*" to illustrate that parallel sentence construction does not always give parallel sense. The first can be rendered in four ways, namely *true Statesman Baldwin* or *statesman denot Baldwin* or *statesman baldwin* or *statesman*1 *Baldwin* where the last asserts that the concept of Baldwin is one of a statesman. The second can be rendered only as *true Fiction Pickwick* or *fiction*1 *Pickwick*.

Quine (1961) considers illegitimate the sentence

$(\exists x)(Philip\ is\ unaware\ that\ x\ denounced\ Catiline)$ (61)

obtained from "*Philip is unaware that Tully denounced Catiline*" by existential generalization. In the example, we are also supposing the truth of *Philip is aware that Cicero denounced Cataline*". These sentences are related to (perhaps even explicated by) several sentences in our system. *Tully* and *Cicero* are taken as distinct concepts. The person is called *tully* or *cicero* in our language, and we have

$tully = cicero,$ (62)

$denot\ Tully = cicero$ (63)

and

$denot\ Cicero = cicero.$ (64)

We can discuss Philip's concept of the person Tully by introducing a function $Concept2(p1, p2)$ giving for some persons $p1$ and $p2$, $p1$'s concept of $p2$. Such a function need not be unique or always defined, but in the present case, some of our information may be conveniently expressed by

$$Concept2(philip, tully) = Cicero, \tag{65}$$

asserting that Philip's concept of the person Cicero is *Cicero*. The basic assumptions of Quine's example also include

$$true\ K(Philip, Denounced(Cicero, Catiline)) \tag{66}$$

and

$$\neg\ true\ K(Philip, Denounced(Tully, Catiline)). \tag{67}$$

From (63), . . . (67) we can deduce

$$\exists P.true\ Denounced(P, Catiline)\ And\ Not\ K(Philip, Denounced(P, Catiline)), \tag{68}$$

from (67) and others, and

$$\neg \exists p.(denounced(p, catiline) \wedge \neg\ true\ K(Philip, Denounced(Concept2(philip, p), Catiline))) \tag{69}$$

using the additional hypotheses

$$\forall p.(denounced(p, catiline) \supset p = cicero), \tag{70}$$

$$denot\ Catiline = catiline, \tag{71}$$

and

$$\forall P1\ P2.(denot\ Denounced(P1, P2) \equiv denounced(denot\ P1, denot\ P2)). \tag{72}$$

Presumably (68) is always true, because we can always construct a concept whose denotation is Cicero unbeknownst to Philip. The truth of (69) depends on Philip's knowing that someone denounced Catiline, and on the map $Concept2(p1, p2)$ that gives one person's concept of another. If we refrain from using a silly map that gives something like *Denouncer*(*Catiline*) as its value, we can get results that correspond to intuition.

The following sentence attributed to Russell is discussed by Kaplan: "*I thought that your yacht was longer than it is*". We can write it

$$true\ Believed(I, Greater(Length\ Youryacht, Concept1\ denot\ Length\ Youryacht)) \tag{73}$$

where we are not analysing the pronouns or the tense, but are using *denot* to get the actual length of the yacht and *Concept*1 to get back a concept of this true length so as to end up with a proposition that the length of the yacht is greater than that number. This looks problematical, but if it is consistent, it is probably useful.

To express "*Your yacht is longer than Peter thinks it is* " we need the expression *Denot*(*Peter, X*) giving a concept of what Peter thinks the value of *X* is. We now write

$$longer(youryacht, denot\ Denot(Peter, Length\ Youryacht)), \tag{74}$$

but I am not certain this is a correct translation.

Quine (1956) discusses an example in which Ralph sees Bernard J. Ortcutt skulking about and concludes that he is a spy, and also sees him on the beach, but doesn't recognize him as the same person. The facts can be expressed in our formalism by equations *true Believe(Ralph, Isspy P*1) (75)

and

*true Believe(Ralph, Not Isspy P*2) (76)

where *P*1 and *P*2 are concepts satisfying *denot P*1 = *ortcutt* and *denot P*2 = *ortcutt*. *P*1 and *P*2 are further described by sentences relating them to the circumstances under which Ralph formed them.

We can still consider a simple sentence involving the persons as things – write it *believespy(ralph, ortcutt)*, where we define

$\forall p1\ p2.(believespy(p1, p2) \equiv$

$true\ Believe(Concept1\ p1, Isspy\ Concept7\ p2)$ (77)

using suitable mappings *Concept*1 and *Concept*7 from persons to concepts of persons. We might also choose to define *believespy* in such a way that it requires *true Believe(Concept*1 *p*1, *Isspy P*) for several concepts *P* of *p*2, for example, the concepts arising from all *p*1's encounters with *p*2 or his name. In this case *believespy(ralph, ortcutt)* will be false and so would a corresponding *notbelievespy(ralph, ortcutt)*. However, the simple-minded predicate *believespy*, suitably defined, may be quite useful for expressing the facts necessary to predict someone's behaviour in simpler circumstances.

Regarded as an attempt to explicate the sentence "*Ralph believes Ortcutt is a spy*", the above may be considered rather tenuous. However, we are proposing it as a notation for expressing Ralph's beliefs about Ortcutt so that correct conclusions may be drawn about Ralph's future actions. For this it seems to be adequate.

PROPOSITIONS EXPRESSING QUANTIFICATION

As the examples of the previous sections have shown, admitting concepts as objects and introducing standard concept functions makes "quantifying in" rather easy. However, forming propositions and individual concepts by quantification requires new ideas and additional formalism. We are not very confident of the approach presented here.

We want to continue describing concepts within first-order logic with no logical extentions. Therefore, in order to form new concepts by quantification and description, we introduce functions *All, Exist,* and *The* such that *All(V, P)* is (approximately) the proposition that *for all values of V P is true, Exist(V, P)* is the corresponding existential proposition, and *The(V, P)* is the concept of *the V such that P.*

Since *All* is to be a function, *V* and *P* must be objects in the logic. However, *V* is semantically a variable in the formation of *All(V, P), etc.,* and we will call such objects *inner variables* so as to distinguish them from variables in the logic. We will use *V*, sometimes with subscripts, for a logical variable ranging over inner variables. We also need some constant symbols for inner variables (got that?), and we will use doubled letters, sometimes with subscripts, for these. *XX* will be used for individual concepts, *PP* for persons, and *QQ* for propositions.

The second argument of *All* and friends is a "proposition with variables in it", but remember that these variables are inner variables which are constants in the logic. Got that? We won't introduce a special term for them, but will generally allow concepts to include inner variables. Thus concepts now include inner variables like *XX* and *PP*, and concept-forming functions like *Telephone* and *Know* take the generalized concepts as arguments.

Thus

Child(Mike, PP) Implies Equal(Telephone PP, Telephone Mike) (78)

is a proposition with the inner variable *PP* in it to the effect that if *PP* is a child of Mike, then his telephone number is the same as Mike's, and

All(PP, Child(Mike, PP)
Implies Equal(Telephone PP, Telephone Mike)) (79)

is the proposition that all Mike's children have the same telephone number as Mike. Existential propositions are formed similarly to universal ones, but the function *Exist* introduced here should not be confused with the function *Exists* applied to individual concepts introduced earlier.

In forming individual concepts by the description function *The,* it doesn't matter whether the object described exists. Thus

The(PP, Child(Mike, PP)) (80)

is the concept of Mike's only child. *Exists The(PP, Child(Mike, PP))* is the proposition that the described child exists. We have

true Exists The(PP, Child(Mike, PP)) ≡
true(Exist(PP, Child(Mike, PP)
*And All(PP*1, *Child(Mike, PP*1) *Implies Equal(PP, PP*1)))), (81)

but we may want the equality of the two propositions, that is,

Exists The(PP, Child(Mike, PP)) =
Exist(PP, Child(Mike, PP)
*And All(PP*1, *Child(Mike, PP*1) *Implies Equal(PP, PP*1))). (82)

This is part of a general problem, when two logically equivalent concepts are to be regarded as the same.

In order to discuss the truth of propositions and the denotation of descriptions, we introduce *possible worlds* reluctantly and with an important difference from the usual treatment. We need them to give values to the inner variables, and we can also use them for axiomatizing the modal operators, knowledge, belief and tense. However, for axiomatizing quantification, we also need a function α such that

$$\pi' = \alpha(V, x, \pi) \quad (83)$$

is the possible world that is the same as the world π except that the inner variable V has the value x instead of the value it has in π. In this respect our possible worlds resemble the *state vectors* or *environments* of computer science more than the possible worlds of the Kripke treatment of modal logic. This Cartesian product structure on the space of possible worlds can also be used to treat conterfactual conditional sentences.

Let $\pi 0$ be the actual world. Let $true(P, \pi)$ mean that the proposition P is true in the possible world π. Then

$$\forall P.(true\ P \equiv true(P, \pi 0)). \quad (84)$$

Let $denotes(X, x, \pi)$ mean that X denotes x in π, and let $denot(X, \pi)$ mean the denotation of X in π when that is defined.

The truth condition for $All(V, P)$ is then given by

$$\forall \pi\ V P.(true(All(V, P), \pi) \equiv \forall x.true(P, a(V, x, \pi)). \tag{85}$$

Here V ranges over inner variables, P ranges over propositions, and x ranges over things. There seems to be no harm in making the domain of x depend on π. Similarly

$$\forall \pi\ V P.(true(Exist(V, P), \pi) \equiv \exists x.true(P, a(V, x, \pi)). \tag{86}$$

The meaning of $The(V, P)$ is given by

$$\forall \pi\ V P\,x.(true(P, a(V, x, \pi)) \wedge \forall y.(true(P, a(V, y, \pi)) \supset y = x) \supset denotes(The(V, P), x, \pi)) \tag{87}$$

and

$$\forall \pi\ V P.(\neg \exists x.true(P, a(V, x, \pi)) \supset \neg\, true\ Exists\ The(V, P)). \tag{88}$$

We also have the following "syntactic" rules governing propositions involving quantification:

$$\forall \pi\ Q1\ Q2\ V.(absent(V, Q1) \wedge true(All(V, Q1\ Implies\ Q2), \pi) \supset true(Q1\ Implies\ All(V, Q2), \pi)) \tag{89}$$

and

$$\forall \pi\ V Q\ X.(true(All(V, Q), \pi) \supset true(Subst(X, V, Q), \pi)). \tag{90}$$

where $absent(V, X)$ means that the variable V is not present in the concept X, and $Subst(X, V, Y)$ is the concept that results from substituting the concept X for the variable V in the concept Y. *absent* and *Subst* are characterized by the following axioms:

$$\forall V1\ V2.(absent(V1, V2) \equiv V1 \neq V2), \tag{91}$$

$$\forall V P\ X.(absent(V, Know(P, X)) \equiv absent(V, P) \wedge absent(V, X)), \tag{92}$$

axioms similar to (92) for other conceptual functions,

$$\forall V\ Q.absent(V, All(V, Q)), \tag{93}$$

$$\forall V\ Q.absent(V, Exist(V, Q)), \tag{94}$$

$$\forall V\ Q.absent(V, The(V, Q)), \tag{95}$$

$$\forall V\ X.Subst(V, V, X) = X, \tag{96}$$

$$\forall X\ V.Subst(X, V, V) = X, \tag{97}$$

$$\forall X\ V P\ Y.(Subst(X, V, Know(P, Y)) = Know(Subst(X, V, P), Subst(X, V, Y))), \tag{98}$$

axioms similar to (98) for other functions,

$$\forall X\ V Q.(absent(V, Y) \supset Subst(X, V, Y) = Y), \tag{99}$$

$$\forall X\ V1\ V2\ Q.(V1 \neq V2 \wedge absent(V2, X) \supset Subst(X, V1, All(V2, Q)) = All(V2, Subst(X, V1, Q))), \tag{100}$$

and corresponding axioms to (100) for *Exist* and *The*.

Along with these comes the axiom that binding kills variables, that is,

$$\forall V1\ V2\ Q.(All(V1, Q) = All(V2, Subst(V2, V1, Q))). \tag{101}$$

The functions *absent* and *Subst* play a "syntactic" role in describing the rules of reasoning and don't appear in the concepts themselves. It seems likely that this is harmless until we want to form concepts of the laws of reasoning.

We used the Greek letter π for possible worlds, because we did not want to consider a possible world as a thing and introduce concepts of possible worlds.

Reasoning about reasoning may require such concepts or else a formulation that doesn't use possible worlds.

Martin Davis (in conversation) pointed out the advantages of an alternative treatment avoiding possible worlds in case there is a single domain of individuals each of which has a standard concept. Then we can write

$$\forall V\, Q.(true\ All(V, Q) \equiv \forall x.true\ Subst(Concept1\ x, V, Q)). \qquad (102)$$

POSSIBLE APPLICATIONS TO ARTIFICIAL INTELLIGENCE

The foregoing discussion of concepts has been mainly concerned with how to translate into a suitable formal language certain sentences of ordinary language. The success of the formalization is measured by the extent to which the logical consequences of these sentences in the formal system agree with our intuitions of what these consequences should be. Another goal of the formalization is to develop an idea of what concepts really are, but the possible formalizations have not been explored enough to draw even tentative conclusions about that.

For artificial intelligence, the study of concepts has yet a different motivation. Our success in making computer programs with *general intelligence* has been extremely limited, and one source of the limitation is our inability to formalize what the world is like in general. We can try to separate the problem of describing the general aspects of the world from the problem of using such a description and the facts of a situation to discover a strategy for achieving a goal. This is called separating the *epistemological* and the *heuristic* parts of the artificial intelligence problem and is discussed in McCarthy and Hayes (1969).

We see the following potential uses for facts about knowledge:

1. A computer program that wants to telephone someone must reason about who knows the number. More generally, it must reason about what actions will obtain needed knowledge. Knowledge in books and computer files must be treated in a parallel way to knowledge held by persons.
2. A program must often determine that it does not know something or that someone else doesn't. This has been neglected in the usual formalizations of knowledge, and methods of proving possibility have been neglected in modal logic. Christopher Goad (to be published) has shown how to prove ignorance by proving the existence of possible worlds in which the sentence to be proved unknown is false. Presumably proving one's own ignorance is a stimulus to looking outside for the information. In competitive situations, it may be important to show that a certain course of action will leave competitors ignorant.
3. Prediction of the behaviour of others depends on determining what they believe and what they want.

It seems to me that AI applications will especially benefit from first-order formalisms of the kind described above. First, many of the present problem solvers are based on first-order logic. Morgan (1976) in discussing theorem proving in modal logic also translates modal logic into first-order logic. Second, our formalisms leaves the syntax and semantics of statements not involving concepts entirely unchanged, so that if knowledge or wanting is only a small part of a problem, its presence doesn't affect the formalization of the other parts.

ABSTRACT LANGUAGES

The way we have treated concepts in this paper, especially when we put variables in them, suggests trying to identify them with terms in some language. It seems to me that this can be done provided that we use a suitable notion of *abstract language.*

Ordinarily a language is identified with a set of strings of symbols taken from some alphabet. McCarthy (1963) introduces the idea of *abstract syntax*, the idea being that it doesn't matter whether sums are represented $a + b$ or $+ab$ or $ab+$ or by the integer 2^a3^b or by the LISP S-expression (PLUS A B), so long as there are predicates for deciding whether an expression is a sum and functions for forming sums from summands and functions for extracting the summands from the sum. In particular, abstract syntax facilitates defining the semantics of programming languages, and proving the properties of interpreters and compilers. From that point of view, one can refrain from specifying any concrete representation of the "expressions" of the language and consider it merely a collection of abstract synthetic and analytic functions and predicates for forming, discriminating and taking apart *abstract expressions*. However, the languages considered at that time always admitted representations as strings of symbols.

If we consider concepts as a free algebra on basic concepts, then we can regard them as strings of symbols on some alphabet if we want to, assuming that we don't object to a non-denumerable alphabet or infinitely long expressions if we want standard concepts for all the real numbers. However, if we want to regard *Equal*(X, Y) and *Equal*(Y, X) as the same concept, and hence as the same "expression" in our language, and we want to regard expressions related by renaming bound variables as denoting the same concept, then the algebra is no longer free, and regarding concepts as strings of symbols becomes awkward even if possible.

It seems better to accept the notion of *abstract language* defined by the collection of functions and predicates that form, discriminate, and extract the parts of its "expressions". In that case it would seem that concepts can be identified with expressions in an abstract language.

ACKOWLEDGEMENTS AND BIBLIOGRAPHY

The treatment given here should be compared with that in Church (1951b) and in Morgan (1976). Church introduces what might be called a two-dimensional type structure. One dimension permits higher-order functions and predicates as in the usual higher-order logics. The second dimension permits concepts of concepts, etc. No examples of applications are given. It seems to me that concepts of concepts will be eventually required, but this can still be done within first-order logic.

Morgan's motivation is to use first-order logic theorem-proving programs to treat modal logic. He gives two approaches. The syntactic approach – which he applies only to systems without quantifiers – uses operations like our *And* to form compound propositions from elementary ones. Provability is then axiomatized in the outer logic. His semantic approach uses axiomatizations of the Kripke accessibility relation between possible worlds. It seems to me that our treatment can be used to combine both of Morgan's methods, and has two further advantages. First, concepts and individuals can be separately quantified. Second, functions from things to concepts of them permit relations between concepts of things that could not otherwise be expressed.

Although the formalism leads in almost the opposite direction, the present paper is much in the spirit of Carnap (1956). We appeal to his ontological tolerance in introducing concepts as objects, and his section on intentions for robots expresses just the attitude required for artificial intelligence applications.

We have not yet investigated the matter, but plausible axioms for necessity or knowledge expressed in terms of concepts may lead to the paradoxes discussed in Kaplan and Montague (1960) and Montague (1963). Our intention is that the paradoxes can be avoided by restricting the axioms concerning knowledge, and necessity of statements about necessity. The restrictions will be somewhat unintuitive as are the restrictions necessary to avoid the paradoxes of naive set theory.

Chee K. Yap (1977) proposes *Virtual Semantics* for intensional logics as a generalization of Carnap's individual concepts. Apart from the fact that Yap does not stay within conventional first-order logic, we don't know the relation between his work and that described here.

I am indebted to Lewis Creary, Patrick Hayes, Donald Michie, Barbara Partee and Peter Suzman for discussion of a draft of this paper. Creary in particular has shown the inadequacy of the formalism for expressing all readings of the ambiguous sentence "*Pat knows that Mike knows what Joan last asserted*". There has not been time to modify the formalism to fix this inadequacy, but it seems likely that concepts of concepts are required for an adequate treatment.

This paper also appears, in essentially its present form, in *Machine Intelligence 9* (1979) Ellis Horwood Ltd.

REFERENCES

Carnap, R. (1956) *Meaning and Necessity*. Chicago: University of Chicago Press.

Church, A. (1951a) The need for abstract entities in semantic analysis, in "Contributions to the Analysis and Synthesis of Knowledge". *Proceedings of the American Academy of Arts and Sciences 80*, no. 1, 100-12. Reprinted in *The Structure of Language* (eds. Fodor, A. and Katz, J.) Prentice-Hall, 1964.

Church, A. (1951b) A formulation of the logic of sense and denotation, in *Essays in honour of Henry Sheffer* (ed. Henle, P.), pp. 3-24. New York.

Frege, G. (1892) Uber Sinn und Bedeutung. *Zeitschrift fur Philosophie und Philosphische Kritik 100*, 25-50. Translated by H. Feigl under the title "On Sense and Nominatum" in *Readings in Philosophical Analysis* (eds. Feigal, H. and Sellars, W.). New York 1949. Translated by M. Black under the title "On Sense and Reference" in P. Geach and M. Black, *Translations from the Philosophical Writings of Gottlob Frege*. Oxford: 1952.

Kaplan, D. (1969) Quantifying in, from *Words and Objections: Essays on the Works of W. V.O. Quine* (eds. Davidson, D. and Hintikka, J.), pp. 178-214. Dordrecht-Holland: D. Reidel Publishing Co. Reprinted in Linsky (1971).

Kaplan, D. and Montague, R. (1960) A paradox regained, *Notre Dame Journal of Formal Logic 1,* 79-90. Reprinted in Montague (1974).

Linsky, L. (ed.) (1971) *Reference and Modality,* Oxford Readings in Philosophy. Oxford: Oxford University Press.

McCarthy, J. (1963) Towards a mathematical science of computation, in *Proceedings of IFIP Congress* 1962. Amsterdam: North-Holland Publishing Co.

McCarthy, J. and Hayes, P.J. (1969) Some philosophical problems from the standpoint of artificial intelligence. *Machine Intelligence 4,* pp. 463-502 (eds. Meltzer, B. Michie, D.). Edinburgh: Edinburgh University Press.

Montague, R. (1963) Syntactical treatments of modality, with corollaries on reflexion principles and finite axiomatizability, *Acta Philosophica Fennica 16,* 153-67. Reprinted in Montague (1974).

Montague, R. (1974) *Formal Philosophy.* New Haven: Yale University Press.

Morgan, C.G. (1976) Methods for automated theorem proving in nonclassical logics, *IEEE Transactions on Computers C-25,* no. 8.

Quine, W.V.O. (1956) Quantifiers and propositional attitudes, *Journal of Philosophy 53.* Reprinted in Linsky (1971).

Quine, W.V.O. (1963) *From a Logical Point of View.* New York: Harper and Row. First published Harvard University Press (1953).

Yap, Chee K. (1977) A Semantical Analysis of Intensional Logics, Research Report *RC*6893 (29538). Yorktown Heights, New York: IBM, Thomas J. Watson Research Center.